PARALLAX RE-VISIONS OF CULTURE
AND SOCIETY

Stephen G. Nichols, Gerald Prince, and Wendy Steiner,
SERIES EDITORS

Pour Daniel,
avec mes pensés
les plus amicales

Elene

Voltaire, Couronné par les Comédiens François, le 30 Mars 1778.
Il est beau de la recevoir
Quand c'est Arlequin qui la donne.
Se trouve à Paris, chez les Marchands d'Estampes.

Styles of Enlightenment

Taste, Politics, and Authorship in Eighteenth-Century France

Elena Russo

The Johns Hopkins University Press
Baltimore

The Johns Hopkins University Press
2715 North Charles Street
Baltimore, Maryland 21218-4363
www.press.jhu.edu

Library of Congress Cataloging-in-Publication Data

Russo, Elena.
    Styles of Enlightenment : taste, politics, and authorship in
eighteenth-century France / Elena Russo.
       p.   cm. — (Parallax, re-visions of culture and society
    Includes bibliographical references and index.
    ISBN 0-8018-8476-4 (hardcover : alk. paper)
    1. French literature—18th century—History and criticism.
2. Enlightenment—France. 3. France—Intellectual life—18th
century. I. Title. II. Series: Parallax (Baltimore, Md.)
    PQ261.R87   2006
    040.9'384—dc22   2006009621

A catalog record for this book is available from the
British Library.

Frontispiece: This engraving is a provocative variation on the better-known *Homage to Voltaire,* by Moreau le Jeune, which commemorates the apotheosis of Voltaire after the sixth performance by the Comédie-Française of *Irène* on 30 March 1778, when Voltaire, who had just returned to Paris from his exile, was hailed by the audience as a hero, and his bust crowned on stage by the actors. The difference here is that Voltaire is being crowned by the lowly masks of the Comédie-Italienne, which he despised and which had produced so many parodies of his works. Arlequin lays the crown on the bust while executing a dance step; Momus, the embodiment of satire, is seated on the right, jingling his bells; and Pedrolino (or Polichinelle), on the left, kneels in submission to the great man. Is satire paying its respects to Voltaire's genius? Or is it deflecting his apotheosis in the direction of parody, as the Italians had done so many times before? Courtesy of Bibliothèque nationale de France, Paris (Estampes, Collection Hennin 9644).

To Paolo

Well now, I'm afraid that's not a view I can share, M. de Norpois said (and when I realized that the thing I set far above myself, the one thing I saw as the highest in the world, was the least of his admirations, the doubts this planted in my mind about my own intelligence were much more crippling than those which usually assailed me). Bergotte is what I call a flute-player. It must of course be admitted that he tootles on his flute quite mellifluously, albeit with more than a modicum of mincing mannerism and affectation. But when all's said and done, tootling is what it is, and tootling does not amount to a great deal. His words are so flaccid that one can never locate in them anything one could call a framework. There's never any action in 'em, well, hardly any, and especially no scope. It's their base which is their weak point—or rather, they have no base. In this day and age, when the increasing complexity of modern life leaves one barely any time for reading, when the map of Europe has undergone a profound recasting, and may well be on the point of undergoing another which may prove to be even more profound, when so many new and threatening problems are cropping up on all sides, you will allow that one may fairly claim the right to expect that a writer might aspire to be something higher than a glib wit [*bel esprit*], whose futile hair-splittings on the relative merits of merely formal matters distract us from the fact that we may be overrun at any moment by a double wave of barbarians, those from within and those from without! . . . In our day and age there are more urgent tasks than stringing jingles of words together. I must admit that Bergotte's jingles can at times be quite pretty, but all in all they add up to something which is pretty jejune, pretty precious—and pretty unmasculine, if you ask me!

—Proust, *À l'ombre des jeunes filles en fleur (In the Shadow of Young Girls in Flower),* translated by James Grieve

Contents

Acknowledgments

This book owes many debts of gratitude. I want to thank David A. Bell, Christian Delacampagne, and Marie-Hélène Huet for reading the manuscript and offering precious suggestions and encouragement. My conversations with Mary Salzman have been invaluable in helping me shape my ideas. I have also profited from the high standards and good counsel of Jean-Marie Apostolidès, Thomas Kavanagh, Rochelle Tobias, and Anne Vila. My debt to Josué Harari is greater than I am able to acknowledge. Sarah Benharrech, Gregory S. Brown, Daniel Edelstein, and Isabelle Monette in various ways offered valuable help. Elisabeth Ladenson showed me, perhaps without realizing it, how one can loosen one's style. A Mellon Fellowship from Stanford University in 1999–2000 and several leaves of absence from the Johns Hopkins University enabled me to work on the manuscript as obsessively as I wished. Special thanks go to Stephen G. Nichols for his generous support throughout. Finally, Michael Lonegro, of the Johns Hopkins University Press, has been helpful yet discreet, while Joanne Allen's stylistic discernment much improved my prose.

A part of chapter 6 was published in "The Youth of Moral Life: The Virtue of the Ancients from Montesquieu to Nietzsche," in *Montesquieu and the Spirit of Modernity,* ed. David Carrithers, Studies on Voltaire and the Eighteenth Century, 9 (Oxford: Voltaire Foundation, 2002).

I lovingly dedicate this book to Paolo Mancosu, who has been helping all along, even while pretending he was not.

Styles of Enlightenment

Introduction

There is among us much instruction and little education. We train scientists and artists of all kinds; every aspect of letters, arts, and sciences is cultivated with success. . . . But no one has thought of training men . . . in such a way that they would be accustomed to looking for their personal interest within the grand scheme of the general good and that, regardless of their profession, they would be, above all, patriots.

—Duclos

He'll stuff the bawdyhouse and the boudoir in every context.

—Diderot

In the debates that accompanied the spread of the Enlightenment the enemies of the philosophes were not limited to the champions of tradition, religious orthodoxy, and their institutional strongholds—the church, the university, the court, the parlements, the Jesuits.[1] Those enemies could be confronted head-on with honor. It was a heroic struggle that could only bring credit to the philosophes, who liked to portray themselves as so many Davids battling against Goliath, armed with nothing but their beliefs and their eloquence. But the philosophes also had to confront another kind of enemy, one that was more insidious, more difficult to pin down, and no less formidable for being less heavily armed. That enemy emerged from within the world of letters; it undermined, rather than validated, the identity of the patriotic philosophe because the philosophe constantly ran the risk of being mistaken for him. That vexing double of the philosophe was the *bel esprit*.

The *bel esprit* did not have the seriousness, the commitment, or the patriotism of the philosophe. He was, to borrow M. de Norpois's expression, a "flute-player," dedicated to ephemeral pleasures and to wordplay; he was frivolous, superficial, affected, and vain.[2] He lacked hardness and definition, powerful ideas, and, above all, virility. "I would like to call all those artists who are after miniatures *female authors*," wrote Louis-Sébastien Mercier; "all they care for is brilliance and sparkle; while they believe they are writing with *esprit*, all they do is pencil in words that are elegantly carved but mean nothing. Adornment for those authors has the same function as for some women: it makes up for the features they don't have, and it camouflages their bony chest."[3] The epitome of the *bel esprit* was Marivaux, whom d'Alembert described as a "miniaturist," one of those "calligraphers who took pride in being read only with a magnifying glass," not a forceful history painter but a painter of *bambochades*, of genre scenes focusing on low life and trivial subjects.[4] More dazzling than enlightening, *beaux esprits* made a parade of their verbal brilliance, hiding their lack of virile attributes with empty virtuosity, much as emaciated women padded their bosoms with lacy frills.

Beaux esprits embodied and disseminated *le goût moderne* (modern taste, to its detractors *le petit goût*), a kind of aesthetics that the philosophes hoped to marginalize and eventually to suppress. In the philosophes' eyes, trivial taste—*le petit goût*—threatened the revival of the *grand goût*, also referred to as *goût sévère* or *goût à l'antique,* which they supported and which was more in tune with their values.[5] *Beaux esprits* were everywhere, sowing their idle and amateurish productions in a society that they had made in their image and that had conspired to produce them. From the erotic paintings of Boucher, the official court painter and protégé of Mme de Pompadour, to Marivaux's *comédies métaphysiques,*[6] to the novels of Crébillon, to the scientific popularizations of Fontenelle, to the theatrical productions of the fairgrounds, the *goût moderne* was successful among the worldly, the powerful, and the wealthy. It was commercial and ubiquitous.[7]

If the Enlightenment could be said to be a project, that project did not consist only in remapping the world of knowledge through an encyclopedic reordering of the sciences; it also meant conquering the domain of taste and the arts. From genre and history painting to the theater, the novel, and eulogistic productions, the philosophes promoted their own ideas about the social function of the arts. They set out to reform the manner in which the work of art was conceptualized and received by the public; they aspired to redefine the identities of the artist and the audience. Such an endeavor was weighty and

momentous. In *ancien régime* France, where political argument was severely
curtailed, aesthetic debates were loaded with political implications.

Art was the mirror in which the dominant classes (the court aristocracy
and the cultivated, wealthy bourgeoisie) constructed the representation they
wished to project of themselves.[8] Criticizing a particular genre and manner
meant, therefore, rejecting the values of that part of the population that allegedly sponsored and appreciated it. Apart from early attempts such as the abbé
Du Bos's *Essai critique sur la poésie et sur la peinture* (1719), French thinkers of
the eighteenth century, unlike their British and Scottish counterparts, seemed
less interested in laying out the philosophical foundations for a comprehensive
theory of taste and aesthetic experience than in policing the world of the arts.
They often limited themselves to a critique of bad taste, which they saw as a
vehicle for bad values, and to writing poetics aimed at educating the public
and other artists. In other words, they were more concerned with berating
bad taste and prescribing various remedies for it than with approaching the
aesthetic domain as a field of study, an approach they suspected of being irrelevant, pedantic, and smacking of despotism. In a short parable by Voltaire
a French philosopher went to the theater in England and did not like what he
saw: "Uh-oh! said the philosopher, *to kalon* is not the same for the English as
for the French. After much thought, he came to the conclusion that beauty is
often a relative thing, . . . and he saved himself the trouble of writing a long
treatise on it."[9] Yet, eighteenth-century France produced vast amounts of criticism on literature, language, and the arts; in Voltaire's *oeuvre* there is perhaps
more literary criticism than other genres of writing. Taste was consubstantial
with national culture and with the degree of civilization in a given nation.
Discussions of good or bad taste thus always implied a cultural, moral, and
political debate.

From Voltaire to Diderot to Rousseau, the arts in general, but in particular
painting, architecture, and the theater, were seen as tainted by their association
with rich and tasteless patrons. In *Le temple du goût* (first published in 1733)
Voltaire ridiculed the nouveau riche. The preening financier was a stock figure
of satire and an easy target for the writer who was reluctant to offend the elites
upfront. In reality, no aristocratic family (including members of the court)
could claim to be uncontaminated by alliance with the financial class, and it
is doubtful that someone like the immensely influential and learned financier
and art collector Pierre Crozat—the patron of Roger de Piles and Watteau,
presiding over a shadow academy sustained by his own generosity (subsisting
alongside the far less well funded royal one)—would have recognized himself

in that sketch, or that anyone would have, for that matter.[10] Social mobility was universally seen as vulgar, especially by the socially mobile. Writers who were members of the bourgeoisie dressed their objections in terms of moral values; only Marivaux dared to go against the grain by portraying a financier who, in his jovial impropriety, was irresistibly seductive.[11] As Charles Pinot Duclos put it, "Rivers that surge suddenly are always a little muddy."[12] The new incarnation of the *bourgeois gentilhomme* bankrolled artists and architects to build himself a tacky palace, as in these lines from Voltaire's *Le temple du goût*:

> With happy countenance Pride rested,
> And flourished on his large face,
> And my Cresus roared:
> I have much gold and I am clever;
> I have good taste for everything;
> I have learned nothing but I know all things;
>
> Therefore I want a beautiful mansion
> Built on the spot for myself alone,
> Where all the arts will be amassed and piled up,
> Where every day I expect to be admired:
> Money is ready. Wretches, obey!
> Immediately, the rabble around him
> Zealously sets out to work.[13]

Against such ostentatiously bad taste, Voltaire evoked with fondness the golden age of royal patronage sponsored by Louis XIV and Colbert, who rebuilt the Temple of Taste from its Greek and Roman ruins and "attracted to this sanctuary the immortal cohort of the Fine Arts," turning France into an artistic and cultural pole of attraction for Europe.[14] An agenda similar to Voltaire's was espoused in 1747 by La Font de Saint-Yenne, the author of the first art criticism of a Salon, one of the skirmishes in the war against the *goût moderne*. Since 1737 the Salon exhibit had given to ordinary people of all ranks a chance to exercise the kind of artistic appreciation that until then had been restricted to a few privileged patrons; La Font claimed to speak in the name of the public and for "the glory of our nation." In order to counteract the decadence of contemporary art, he invited the king to turn the Louvre gallery into a museum filled with the best artworks from his collection. They would be exhibited for the public to admire and for artists to emulate; the former would be educated, and the latter would be held in check by this high tribunal of good taste. Against the fickleness of the "petty judges of a subaltern kind, prodigal benefactors of a weekly immortality to our printmakers . . . , fops and dandies of both sexes, but especially of the fair sex, which nowadays lords over all works of art," La Font opposed the "judgment of judicious experts, enlightened by firm principles and even more by that natural light that we call taste [*sentiment*]," a judgment that unfortunately was not equally distributed among the public but restricted to the happy few.[15]

A decade later, Diderot held a similar position in his own Salon writings, which, through their publication in the *Correspondance littéraire,* were destined to shape the taste of a handful of European potentates. While Diderot by no means shared Rousseau's prejudice against the art and the economy of the modern age, he nonetheless was very critical of what he saw as the collusion between the marketplace, a taste for luxury, and the arts. Like Voltaire, he saw corruption and decadence in a private patronage overrun by the "verminous epidemics" of the "amateurs," and he saw salvation in state intervention.[16] Left to themselves, without the guidance of an enlightened monarch (such as Frederick the Great or Catherine of Russia, both subscribers to the *Correspondance littéraire*)—or, more precisely, without the providential intervention of an enlightened community of philosophes who would undertake the task of edifying the monarch—both the artists and the public (led by the band of powerful *surintendants des arts, directeurs des bâtiments,* the undying avatars of the stock figure of the wicked courtier) made bad choices. "There is good reason for all great artists to despair over the public's judgment, to have the most perfect contempt for it," wrote Diderot.[17] In its desire to show off its ill-begotten wealth and its vanity, in its courtly turn of mind, the public sponsored venal and immoral artists—the calamitous cohort of genre painters, Watteau, Boucher, Lagrenée, Fragonard, Baudouin, and all the decorators of "overdoors,"[18] who degraded the arts and who could not rise to the true greatness of history painting:

> The talented man of whom a rich one requests a work he can leave to his son or heir as a precious inheritance will no longer be subjected to my judgment, or yours, or consideration of self-esteem, or fear of losing his reputation: it is no longer for the nation but for a private individual that he will produce, and a mediocre work of no value will be obtained from him in this way. . . . Ah! my friend, the cursed race which is that of amateurs! . . . It is these people who determine, erroneously and capriciously, an artist's reputation; . . . The tenacity of the amateurs occasionally goes so far as to obtain for mediocre artists the profit and honor of public commissions.[19]

In a nation abandoned to the "fantasy" and the "capriciousness" of private sponsors and powerbrokers genuine talent would yield to greed and lustful-ness. Unchecked by the critical eye of the philosophes and sheltered from the nation's scrutiny, the artist would surrender to his own (and his patron's) worst instincts; artistic productions would decay along with the public's taste.[20] Thus, at the time that Habermas has heralded as the birth of an independent, disinterested, commercial, and bourgeois public many of those who are credited with a role in the birth of such a public in reality demonstrated little faith in its judgment. Instead, they took refuge in the traditional schemes of state patronage, which represented a refuge from an unruly, irrational, and unregulated marketplace.[21] Voltaire cautioned the man of letters against dependence on the market, the viciousness of critics, and the vagaries of the public. It was much better not to publish at all; in other words, it was better to have one's work circulated clandestinely, preserving the right to deny one's paternity.[22] Moreover, the "nation" for whom the philosophes claimed to speak was a political fiction abstracted from the heterogeneous, bourgeois public that attended the Salon exhibits.[23] In Diderot's view, the public's increased access to artworks necessitated a stricter regulation of the material exhibited and a rigorous education of the public's taste. In Marmontel's view, literary reputations must trickle down from the opinion of *gens de lettres* to the public at large; those that originate in "frivolous circles" and then spread to the public might be compared to "an artificial pond laboriously constructed, whose waters would soon dry up."[24] And in d'Alembert's view, *gens de lettres* ought to "legislate for the rest of the nation in matters of taste and philosophy."[25]

If wealthy amateurs were responsible for sinking the arts into insignificance, *beaux esprits* were guilty of the same in the world of letters. In *Considérations sur les moeurs de ce siècle* (1751) Duclos dedicated a long chapter to the allegedly widespread obsession with *bel esprit*, separate from his chapter on professional *gens de lettres*. He described *beaux esprits* as fashionable amateurs who were culturally immature and whose taste was poor but who wanted to usurp the rewards that should have devolved on the true *gens de lettres*. "When that part of literature that goes under the name of *bel esprit* becomes a fashion, a kind of public obsession, men of letters do not profit from it, and other professions lose too. That horde of suitors to *bel esprit* is the reason why it is more difficult to distinguish those who have a right to it from those who are mere pretenders. . . . They usurp in public opinion a kind of superiority over talent."[26] It is not clear exactly whom Duclos had in mind. Was it the public of influential amateurs of letters and the arts who frequented the Salon exhibits, displayed their expertise in writing, sponsored and brokered careers—people like Louis-Petit de Bachaumont and the comte de Caylus, both proponents of neoclassicism?[27]

Was it those successful writers who hobnobbed with the elites in the salons and the court? Someone like Fontenelle, mathematician and *secrétaire perpétuel* of the Academy of Sciences, whom La Bruyère had once called "an insignificant blabberer," a "*bel esprit,*" a "mixture of the pedant and the *précieux*"?[28] Or someone like Claude-Henri Watelet, painter, playwright, landscape architect, and art theoretician, a collaborator on the *Encyclopédie,* a regular guest of Mme Geoffrin, and a member of the Academy? Or Duclos himself, who straddled all kinds of cultural venues, both high and low? Duclos was *secrétaire perpétuel* of the French Academy, the king's official historiographer, an advocate of philosophy, a protégé of Mme de Pompadour, a habitué of the Café Procope and the satirical Société du Caveau, and a friend of Rousseau. He was the author of novels exploring moral and sentimental education among the worldly (e.g., *Les Confessions du Comte de* ***, 1741) but also of such trifles as *Acajou et Zirphile,* an Oriental tale that, under the pretext of satire, illustrated the eroticism that the *nouvelle vague* of the ancients reproved in the *goût moderne* (the tale had been inspired by a set of prints made by Boucher and was quickly turned by Favart into a fairgrounds vaudeville).[29] Where exactly could one draw the boundary separating the worldly activities of the dilettantes from those of the professional writers?

The reality was that no matter how uncompromisingly the philosophes tried to categorize and hierarchize "high," professional and contestatory cultural practices, as distinct from "low" and conventionally subservient ones, their definitions always remained vague and tentative, exposing the fact that cultural life was much more integrated than they were willing to acknowledge and that practices of dissent were continuous with practices of social conformity and assimilation. As Gregory S. Brown has shown, the rhetoric of service to the *patrie,* a corollary of the classical theme of literature's usefulness in the public arena, was for the writers a self-legitimizing strategy aimed at stressing their intellectual independence, their authenticity, and the relevance of their work to contemporary issues, but it did not prevent them from also enjoying the benefits of elite-oriented networks of sociability and patronage.[30] By appealing directly to the nation and the public at large, the patriotic writer was able to position himself as an outsider to courtly patronage, as someone independent of the networks of sociability. Many writers, Louis-Sebastien Mercier being prominent among them, resorted, with varying degrees of sincerity, to such a risky strategy of self-presentation. Many others, however, such as Léonard-Antoine Thomas (a five-time winner of the French Academy's prize of eloquence, the secretary of the duke of Choiseul, a regular guest at all the major salons, and the beneficiary of a pension from Mme Geoffrin), played on both the level of patronage and that of independent patriotism. Hence, an ever-present desire to discriminate and classify, to rank writers not according to classes and alliances, which were impossibly blurred, but according to moral posture and self-fashioning rhetoric.

The perception, however, was that professional writers and artists went unrewarded, and talent unrecognized; that remained the unwavering belief of the philosophes long after the public had embraced them and the court and the academies had opened their doors to them. In their eyes, however, the danger continued to appear so pressing that in the *Discours préliminaire* to the *Encyclopédie* Jean Le Rond d'Alembert warned against the onslaught of a new, modern form of barbarity that resulted from the corruption of taste foisted by *bel esprit.*[31] It was the product of the extreme refinement brought by the closing of a cycle in a civilization that had peaked in Louis XIV's *Grand Siècle* and had been declining ever since. In other words, modernity was barbaric. In their attempt to save civilization from its looming decay the philosophes appointed themselves the reformers of the world of letters and the arts. Regenerating the nation required purging the public's taste; that was both the precondition and the goal of their endeavor.

This book is an attempt to provide a more accurate description of the true character of *le goût moderne,* which the Enlightenment and the Revolution wanted to consign to oblivion and which a literary history shaped by the classicist viewpoint has for a long time misrepresented as a culture of the *joli* and the frivolous, as "vaporous fantasy and sexual escapism."[32] But how could it have been otherwise? Since such an aesthetics had been closely identified by its opponents with the class of citizens that the Revolution was to eliminate, the *goût moderne*—renamed *rococo* by David—had by necessity to bow to the judgment of history and own up to its insignificance. Hence the image of a "deliciously decadent,"[33] trifling, selfish, pleasure-oriented, feminine, and courtly ethos cut short by the executioner's blade (which its own excesses had helped sharpen), an ethos that Baudelaire's ironic paean *À Mme du Barry,* to Mme du Barry, the *ancien régime*'s most despised mistress, illustrates quite well:

> Vous étiez du *bon temps* des robes à paniers,
> Des bichons, des manchons, des abbés, des rocailles,
> Des filles, des marquis, des soupers, des ripailles.
>
> Moutons poudrés à blanc, poètes familiers,
> Vieux sèvres et biscuits, charmantes antiquailles,

Amours dodus, pompons et rubans printaniers,
Meubles en bois de rose et caprices d'écailles.

Le peuple a tout brisé, dans sa juste fureur. . . .[34]

But in the same way that Baudelaire's modernist aesthetics was inspired by the early eighteenth century's ironic deconstruction of the classicist tenets of mimesis, the philosophes themselves in their finest moments could not avoid engaging in the very practices they professed to repudiate. The war the late Enlightenment launched against the *goût moderne* was in reality a war against itself, that is to say, against the culture of criticism and self-reflexive experimentation with language and form that had produced the Enlightenment. That is ultimately the point that I wish to make. The *goût moderne,* as I see it, illustrates a number of traits that are constitutive of the "post-absolutist thinking" analyzed by Jay Caplan: it emerges from a semiotic crisis (itself the manifestation of the crisis of authority that took place during the Regency) in which "the production and coding of signs" and the "making and interrelation between form and content" became problematic because semiotic systems were no longer grounded in a reality guaranteed by royal and divine authority.[35] Hence its rejection of the absolutist and classicist grand narrative in favor of dissonant, paratactic storytelling; its ironic use of preexisting forms; its deconstruction of classicism and its fragmentation of narrative; its use of contrarieties and contrasts; its recurring theatricality and self-referentiality; its blurring between reality and the space of representation; its use of a thematic that embraces the grotesque, the burlesque, and the bizarre; its mixture of genres and styles *(bigarrure);* and its confusion of hierarchies, be they ethical, representational, or gendered.

In her revealing study on the culture wars of the late seventeenth century (otherwise known as the quarrel between the ancients and the moderns) Joan DeJean gives us some tools for understanding what was happening in the following *fin de siècle.* DeJean has modified the Habermasian version of the emergence of a public sphere of critical reason.[36] She shows that it was in the late seventeenth century that the "intellectual upheaval that began the revolutionary shift in mentalité upon which the Enlightenment was founded" took place. "Literature became a radically more public phenomenon, the center of a cultural sphere in which a variety of previously silent groups began to engage in active participation."[37] It was through its engagement with literary debates about who was entitled to exercise aesthetic judgment that a new public was born. In the pages of the *Mercure galant,* France's first and most widely circulated journal, Donneau de Visé, its longtime editor (1672–1710), turned literary criticism, until then the province of professional (male) writers, into a public and feminine affair. Female readers were invited to write letters and express their opinion. Women were recognized as vital members of the readership and as the critical audience for literary productions. The old guardians of the republic of letters, such as Nicolas Boileau, fought vehemently against this perceived feminization of French culture. As Charles Perrault pointed out, to be truly a modern it was necessary to reason as a woman.[38]

By the eighteenth century the feminization of the public had become something of a commonplace; it was being felt in the scientific popularizations of Fontenelle, which dramatized a feminine audience; in such texts as Diderot's *Le rêve de d'Alembert* (1769), which featured a prominent salonniere, Julie de Lespinasse, and his *Entretien d'un philosophe avec la Maréchale* (1774); and in Marivaux's journals, to name just a few. In 1719 the abbé Du Bos had praised the sureness of the public's taste *(sentiment)* in judging the quality of works of art, opposing it to the cabals and the interests of the professional critics.[39] At the same time, however, that phenomenon was challenged by the renewal of neoclassicism. As the imagined site of the public broadened from the salon to the nation, the attitude of intimacy and equality that writers had previously entertained with their elite audiences was transformed. At the same time, the writers of the Enlightenment reclaimed the world of letters for the male professionals. While they claimed to speak on behalf of the public, the philosophes did not engage with it on equal terms. They no longer addressed its female component to the same extent as before: as worldliness and the feminine were being identified with each other, both were becoming obsolete; no longer figures of a reconciled public, women now stood for cultural impotence and bastardization. In his *Lettre à d'Alembert sur les spectacles* Rousseau made it clear that while taste and *esprit* were feminine, genius was an entirely masculine affair.[40] In his *Encyclopédie* article "Génie" Diderot reduced the province of taste to that of a marginal, subordinate region of the cultural realm.[41] It was confined to those who could neither produce nor understand and appreciate a work of genius: to worldly amateurs, to women and their effete doubles, the *beaux esprits*. Among the vast crowd of the credulous and the vulgar, those who were easily seduced by the decadent Boucher, Diderot counted "fops [*petits-maîtres*], scatterbrained women [*petites femmes*], young men and the worldly."[42] Thinkers of the late Enlightenment thus rejected the gender *métissage* that, as DeJean argues, had been the achievement of the seventeenth-century culture wars.[43]

In their desire to save French civilization from decadence and anomie and to take back the cultural domain the representatives of the late Enlightenment belittled some of the practices that Habermas described as constitutive of the public sphere, in particular the performance of sociability, which gave women a large role. The irony, of course, was that the philosophes were dependent on the patronage of wealthy aristocratic and bourgeois women, such as Mme Necker and Mme Geoffrin, who facilitated the philosophical exchange of ideas and the relations between writers and patrons (both private and state sponsored).[44] Essays such as d'Alembert's *Essai sur la société des gens de lettres et des grands,* Duclos's *Considérations sur les moeurs,* countless academic eulogies (a genre theorized by Antoine-Léonard Thomas's *Essai sur les éloges*) and inaugural speeches, memoirs (e.g., Marmontel's), and works of grammarians and critics, not forgetting, of course, Rousseau's works, most notably the influential *Lettre à d'Alembert sur les spectacles* and *La nouvelle Héloïse*), all questioned worldly sociability as a cultural practice, a code of manners, and a language. While on the one hand they exalted social sentiment and benevolence as abstract, universal virtues, on the other the philosophes were critical of the ways sociability was embodied and expressed. They did not take pains to discriminate between the various kinds of sociable spaces and the various classes of people who occupied them. They lumped together the court, the spaces of *la ville,* the circles and *bureaux d'esprit,* the *cafés* and theatrical culture.

With their critique of the institutions of sociability, the thinkers of the late Enlightenment rejected not only a certain conception of gender but also the language that conveyed it. In their effort to define the relationship between the philosophical project and the wider public—notwithstanding their constant appeal to the authority of public opinion—the philosophes by and large repudiated the kind of discourse that sociability had fostered (which they nonetheless continued to practice among themselves), namely, conversational reciprocity, the careful negotiation of compromise in critical thinking, a search for complicity between the speaker and the recipient, and the ironic and playful exploration of the polysemic dimension of language. "Irony becomes the poet's favorite figure, because it is that favored by the worldly," wrote Mercier, who apparently had forgotten how brilliantly Voltaire had wielded irony as a tool of philosophy), "and worldly circles are made up of three or four hundred fops who do not know what to make of themselves. . . . Hence those subtle, jerky, enigmatic ideas, those sparkles that brighten and dim, those lively, ingenious and carefully crafted expressions, those combed and ornate vices, shimmering with a thousand colors."[45] The new modes of philosophical discourse rejected such "feminized" idioms; the philosophes took inspiration from archaic and religious models that emphasized the distance between the speaker and the audience. The author and the public no longer stood on equal footing. The *homme de lettres* delivered his message to an audience that was meant to be edified, transformed, pierced through the heart by the power of his eloquence. There could be no reciprocity between them, especially because the philosophe's ideal public was not contemporary society but posterity, the new society created by Philosophy. Emotion became a weapon in the philosophical struggle, applied in order to control and unify an audience that until then had been insubordinate, scattered, and unresponsive to truth.

One did not address the nation in the same way as one addressed one's friends in the "fireside tone of conversation," in the intimacy of the conversational circle.[46] Because they wanted their words to exert as great a power and to reach as wide an audience as possible, the philosophes opted for the ancient drag, donning over their silk breeches the mantle of the classical orator (Demosthenes haranguing his fellow citizens), of the preacher invested with a sacred message. They favored the charismatic vehicle of melodrama (Richardson, Diderot, Rousseau, Mercier). They abandoned the forms that drew attention to the medium and not to the message. In particular they wished to reject the theatricality and the self-referentiality that had characterized the writings of the baroque and the *goût moderne* (as well as the vast theatrical culture of the unofficial theaters). To that purpose, language had to be purged of the scoria of mannerism. Throughout his career, Voltaire devoted countless pages to tracking down what he saw as bad taste and rhetorical impropriety, from antiquity to his days; with unflinching severity he obsessively edited, commented and often reworded all the plays of Corneille, turning his nose up at the faintest whiff of *préciosité*.[47] Anticipating Diderot's dramatic experiments, Voltaire sought to reinvent the language of the theater; he yearned to find the mythical simplicity and straightforwardness to which the ancients had had the key but which kept eluding the moderns. In the wake of the revival of Pseudo-Longinus's *Peri Hupsous,* which had been translated by Boileau at the onset of the culture wars of the seventeenth century, the philosophes aspired to free themselves of the constraints of the literary language of their time,[48] of the received molds. They wanted to recover the sacred in a language that had been despoiled. They aimed to reach that threshold of pure expressiveness, of a sublime passion that transcended the linguistic medium. But, prisoners of a reverence for antiquity that they had absorbed in the *collèges* and of too exalted an opinion of their own task, they sometimes flew too high, only to land on the soft and clammy bed of bombast, melodrama, and kitsch.

Wishing to reinvent the ideal of the writer and the artist, which demanded that they demarcate themselves from the *goût moderne* and the *bel esprit,* the philosophers of the Enlightenment defined a domain of high art as separate from merely pleasurable art *(génie* versus *goût).*[49] They labored within a cultural field that discriminated more severely than the previous century between high and low, comic and serious, between good and bad taste, between permissible and disreputable genres and venues. Sublime art tended toward the exceptional and the eternal, hence towards the normative, while pleasurable art was content with satisfying ephemeral passions (or *goûts,* as the libertine would say) and with depicting the vulgar and trivial reality of the here and now.

In *Naissance du Panthéon* Jean-Claude Bonnet has pointed out the existence of a double identity in the French Enlightenment, which he identifies with the opposite rhetorical modes of the satire and the eulogy. There was in the Enlightenment a dissociation between the language of critique and the language of belief, between the desire to debunk and undermine the reigning idols and the need to provide a foundation for new, community-enhancing values.[50] Each language involved a distinct conception of the relationship between the writer and his public and of the ethical and political role that letters were to play in society. The uneasy coexistence of those two currents fueled a debate that could not find a resolution until revolutionary Jacobinism coopted the writer into the vast project of nation building and made him the object of a national cult.[51] As Thomas Kavanagh has argued, in a book that highlights the specificity of the spirit of the early Enlightenment, the Revolution's "virulently catechistical orthodoxy" replaced an earlier cultural narrative that had relied upon "interrogations, ambiguities and subversions concomitant with the Enlightenment's dismantling of any *civitas dei*" with one in which the newly defined *civitas terrena* "coalesced into a unified and coercive ideology of progress" that "deprived [its] Enlightenment sources of the iconoclastic, corrosive and subversive role they had so consistently played within the context of the ancien regime."[52] In fact, the new, sacralized conception of the patriotic philosophe, which in the second half of the century replaced a caricaturized figure of the *bel esprit,* paved the way for the Jacobinic narrative of cultural fall and redemption.

It is not my intent in this book to tell a simple story of linear transformation in which the battle lines would be clearly drawn and writers would be drafted into one camp or the other. Even though there is much evidence that an epistemic and aesthetic change did occur at about midcentury, around the time of the publication and the suppression of the *Encyclopédie* and the controversies that ensued, much of the debate I describe cannot be narrowed to a particular timespan but was carried on, with varying intensity, throughout the century. Most important, much of the debate took place within the work of the philosophes themselves. Voltaire, Montesquieu, and Diderot all labored on the uncertain frontier between the conversational and the sublime, the satire and the eulogy, the linear unfolding of narrative and digressive slippage, good and bad taste, and theatrical and antitheatrical ethos. The "real" Diderot may be found swaying on the threshold that separates, in *Rameau's Nephew,* the bourgeois respectability of *Moi* from the grotesque, satirical, *modern* genius of *Lui;* on the line that divides the unctuous eroticism of his tributes to Greuze's pubescent girls from the elaborate trompe l'oeil of his fascinating writings on Vernet. In reality, although Diderot and Voltaire tried to harden themselves against it, both were drawn to the siren song of "bad" taste; under the pretext of satire, both practiced the very kind of aesthetics that they loudly claimed to reject.[53] Throughout his career Montesquieu remained more a *bel esprit* than a serious philosopher and historian, or so at least thought Voltaire. Voltaire, in his turn, was reprimanded by many critics, most conspicuously by the young Rousseau, for being too worldly and vain, for being too modern. Indeed, being a *bel esprit* was generally seen as a convenient charge to level against one's opponents in the republic of letters: *beaux esprits* did not have a republican spirit, and they did not belong. The ancients of the *nouvelle vague* struggled to demarcate themselves from the *beaux esprits* and the lightweights. They tried to exercise some control over the image they intended to bequeath to posterity.

But the *bel esprit* was more than simply a reflection of the contest to re-define the *homme de lettres* socially and politically. *Bel esprit* was above all the embodiment of a style that, as Proust would say, was a kind of vision and a mode of apprehending the world. Where its detractors saw theatricality and vanity (the author constantly mirroring himself in his language), we can see an attitude of self-reflexivity toward mimesis and an ironic questioning of the foundations of representation and authority, be they divine, political, or narrative.

The following chapters focus on a wide range of interrelated aspects in the confrontation between the *grand goût* and the *goût moderne* and on a cluster of representative figures: Fénelon (though not a philosophe, he exercised a great deal of influence on them), Voltaire, Marivaux, Montesquieu, Diderot, Mercier. The proponents of the *grand goût* rejected all reflexivity in the work of art (the audience's critical awareness of the art medium as such). Self-reflexivity and a ludic approach to artistic forms (which were, I argue, traits inherited from the seventeenth-century aesthetics of *galanterie*) were marginalized and confined to minor genres and subordinate artistic venues. High art sought instead a relationship with the audience that was less intimate than the one established by the *goût moderne*. Audiences were to be drawn to the artwork (visual, theatrical, or narrative), absorbed and enthralled by an illusion achieved by means of a powerful and sacred emotion. A sublime conception of mimesis demanded that language aim toward its disappearance, toward the abolition of all perception of the materiality of the artwork.[54] By the same token, narrative unity in painting and in prose had to be immediately and instantaneously apprehended, a condition that necessarily excluded the narrative fragmentation and discontinuity *(saillie, papillotage)* of the *goût moderne*, its systematic use of contrarieties and contrast, and its scarce sympathy for closure. I argue, however, that antitheatrical discourse, no matter how vehement, never entirely displaced more participatory modes of reception but, on the contrary, was always balanced by an equally powerful urge toward theatricality. Diderot, for one, embodied both aesthetics, and his statements against theatricality in the visual and dramatic arts are often contradicted by his rhetorical standing in the texts; they should also be read against the backdrop of his dialogues and his novels. It would seem, therefore, that the eighteenth century never really lost theatricality (the distinctive character of the *goût moderne*). And we, as critics, need to recover it as a tool for understanding the culture and the arts of that time.

▌ Prologue:
Boudoir and Tribune

Always little pictures, little ideas, frivolous compositions, appropriate for the boudoir of a libertine [petite-maîtresse], *for the love nest* [petite maison] *of a petit-maître; just the things for little abbés, little attorneys, big financiers, and other immoral persons with a taste for the trivial* [d'un petit goût].

—Diderot

The perfection of talent consists in the ability to paint on a grand scale, not in wasting one's efforts to polish words, to turn an idea into an epigram, to illuminate a thought.

—Mercier

The Sage par excellence, *the Word Incarnate, never laughed. In the eyes of One who has all knowledge and all power, the comic does not exist.*

—Baudelaire

The disjunction between a language of critique, irony, and satire and a language of belief involves a difference in the responses elicited from the public. An attitude of ironic distancing resulting from an effect of dissonance that splits the audience's response is offset by an attitude of abandonment to the emotions created by a discourse that presents itself as the unmediated and transparent expression of an impassioned individual. Both positions postulate a distinct relationship between the writer and the public and a distinct fictional space. While the first calls for the intimate space of conversation in the boudoir, the cabinet, the salon, or the garden, the second requires that the philosophe address his captive and enthralled audience from the height of a secular pulpit—a tribune—and, from that distance, sweep it off its feet by the force of his eloquence. The first position invites reciprocity and exchange between equals; the second presupposes distance and awe.

Under monarchical rule, before the advent of the revolutionary tribune and scaffold, such a pulpit was, of course, more often imaginary than real. While the eloquence of the magistrates was perhaps the only eloquence that had a chance of reaching an audience in real time (e.g., in the parlement's opening session), a writer usually had to content himself with a textual reconstruction of the staging of such oratorical flights. The "Prosopopée de Fabricius" in Rousseau's *First Discourse* comes to mind. The passage tries to recapture the imaginary emotion sparked in a late Roman audience by Fabricius, one of the republic's founding fathers. The resurrected orator has reached across the ages in order to confront his decadent fellow citizens. In Rousseau, such an attempt, twice removed from reality and historical time, may seem to be permeated with an underlying melancholy: such spectacles may only happen in the textual memory and in the imaginary reconstruction of a mythical past. But in his inaugural speech to the French Academy President Lamoignon de Malesherbes declared, with unabashed confidence, that "a tribunal independent of all powers, which all powers respect, has been established; it appreciates all talents and decrees on all kinds of merit. At a time when any citizen may speak to the entire nation by way of print, those who have the talent to instruct and inspire men—in one word, men of letters—play, in the midst of a dispersed people, the same function as the orators of Rome and Athens in the midst of the people assembled."[1] More fortunate even than Malesherbes, Voltaire went so far as to embody Cicero himself, not, alas, on a national tribune, but on the private stage of Sceaux, at the duchesse du Maine's, during the performance of his own play *Rome sauvée.* "I do not believe that it is possible to hear anybody who would be more truthful, more full of pathos and enthusiasm than M. de Voltaire in that role," wrote the actor Lekain, a protégé of Voltaire's; "it truly was Cicero himself thundering from the tribune and haranguing the people against some enemy of the *patrie,* laws, customs, or religion."[2]

Of course there was nothing radically new in this confrontation between two rhetorics and two ethical approaches to discourse: the distinction between a *sermo facetus* (or *conversation enjouée,* informal, affable conversation) and a *contentio orationis* (public eloquence) was classic, and it had been clearly formulated by Cicero.[3] If anything was new in this confrontation, it was its renewed urgency, and the sense that the two rhetorics were incompatible, that a choice had to be made and boundaries drawn. Beginning in approximately the mid-eighteenth century the philosophes felt that they had to take up new forms of eloquence and a new identity. This led them to summon a new covenant with their audience and to wish to reject the old ways. The classical distinction between the *sermo facetus* and public eloquence was therefore invested with new meanings and new political implications. As with much that was heralded as new, the philosophes found inspiration in antiquity: the professional and courtly *écrivain* (the *bel esprit*) was replaced with the *orateur,* not the self-interested professional but the disinterested and inspired guide to the civic community.

The two rhetorics had not always been seen as mutually exclusive, and the writer had not always been torn between them. In Cicero's *De officiis* the orator could choose between a *sermo* that was associated with conversation in private life—with the *affabilitas* and the *comitas* of *vita contemplativa* or *otium,* which expressed itself in a simple, familiar style—and the *contentio,* which belonged to *vita activa,* to the *negotia* of political and juridical activities, and found its expression in the pathos and the noble style of public speech.[4] Both rhetorics were valid within their own separate spheres of action, and both had a role to play in the life of an individual who, like Cicero, was active in his dual function as private citizen and political player. Jean-Louis Guez de Balzac, one of the early theoreticians of *honnêteté* and a classicist, explored the dual face of the rhetoric of the ancients in a text composed in 1638 and addressed to Mme de Rambouillet, who was then at the height of her influence as the sovereign of conviviality and the hostess of the most prestigious salon of the capital. Guez de Balzac, who had once aspired to put his talents at the state's disposal, had been confined, following a faux pas, to the mandatory pleasures of a *vita contemplativa* in Limousin by the ires of Cardinal Richelieu, and therefore he could not attend her gatherings. He nonetheless entitled his text *Suite d'un entretien de vive voix, ou De la conversation des romains* and lent it the illusion of conversation, as if consigning to memory a fugitive moment that perhaps had never taken place.[5] In this founding fable of French *urbanitas* Guez de Balzac invents an Aristotelian genealogy for the moderate virtues that rule civil life and make society pleasurable: moderation *(douceur),* openness *(franchise),* and joyfulness or playfulness *(enjouement),* what we would call a sense of humor.[6] While *urbanitas* is not on a par with the civic virtue of the ancient republics, it is a virtue nonetheless: "not as resplendent nor as high-minded as wisdom and magnanimity; but still a virtue acknowledged by philosophy."[7] The social virtues that characterize modern, urban life are given an illustrious genealogy in the ancient and revered world of the Romans: modernity is presented as a rediscovery of the past, since antiquity, when it is not held up as a mirror to the decadence of the present, serves to ground and legitimize it. In these early stages of the confrontation between the ancients and the moderns the hostilities are not yet fully declared between republican liberty and monarchical yoke: the time is for syncretism and self-celebration, and the world of ancient Rome and Athens naturally flows into that of modern France, its legitimate heir. Guez de Balzac may well share some of the melancholy of Montaigne when he declares that "it does not agree with us to play Camillus or Cato: we do not have the strength of those people," but the time has not yet come when Montesquieu or Rousseau will starkly oppose the communal virtue of the ancient republics to the moral corruption of modern monarchies.

Rambouillet, born Catherine de Vivonne-Savelli, from a Roman family, is presented by Guez de Balzac as the heir to Roman *urbanitas,* now reborn in her Parisian salon. Guez de Balzac would have us believe that the *bonne humeur* of the polite gatherings in which women preside is of the same nature as that of Cato and Numa; that the aggressive, masculine virtues of the warring noblemen (Roman or French) may blend easily with the politeness of the *honnête homme;* that one can pass casually from the salon to the battlefield. But then, everything seemed possible to an aristocratic audience who had not yet experienced the disappointment of an aborted revolt and the strictures of Versailles.[8] Indeed, Guez de Balzac comes perilously close to a crime of *lèse-antiquité* and to painting "Caton galant et Brutus dameret."[9] As a matter of fact, Guez de Balzac, far less struck with the celebrities of antiquity than Boileau, does not hesitate to mock the sublimity of republican eloquence and to question its sincerity:

> We cannot doubt that, when among themselves, they were capable of negligent graces and artless ornament, which our doctors do not know and which rise above rules and precepts. I don't doubt that, after having seen them thunder and overturn heaven and earth on the tribune, it was quite a relief to consider them under a more human aspect. Once they had removed their enthymemes and their rhetorical figures, their feigned exclamations and their artificial ires, they appeared in what we may assume was their true self. It was then, Madame, that Cicero was no longer a sophist nor a rhetorician; neither extolling this, nor furious against that; neither of one party nor of the other. He was then the true Cicero, and he mocked in private what he had adored on the public forum.[10]

There is, for Guez de Balzac, more than a touch of pedantry to the sublime eloquence that Cicero indicates as appropriate to matters concerning the state and the courts. No longer a pathos that, like a torrent, carries the audience away, but feigned anger whipped out of a bag of rhetorical tricks, the kind of eloquence that is the business of clerks, antiquarians, lawyers, and college pupils. The true spirit of antiquity, Guez de Balzac argues, lies not in its boastful moments, in its rhetorical ballooning *(enflure),* but in the "negligent graces," in the intimate moments when the orator abandons his contrived posture and reveals, among friends, his real (even if duplicitous) nature and the expression of a self-deprecating humor. Guez de Balzac entirely depoliticizes the eloquence of public life, devaluing it in favor of the grace of conversation in the private sphere. In Guez de Balzac's time, in the wake of Castiglione's analysis of courtly *sprezzatura,* affectation and pomp were the most infamous pitfalls for a writer, while negligence and *naturel,* the appearance of artlessness, were his most valued achievement.[11]

By the time Voltaire composed his article "Éloquence" for the *Encyclopédie,* though the elements were still the same, their value had shifted. Drawing on the same sources as Guez de Balzac—that is, on Cicero and Aristotle—Voltaire showed no inclination to depoliticize and deflate the ancient heroes. Rather, he appropriated the model for himself: trying to emancipate eloquence from the rhetoric taught in the colleges, he stressed the relationship between eloquence and the orator's conviction. Stripped of figures and forms, eloquence appears as the disembodied spirit that emanates from the pure flame of the speaker's passion:

> Eloquence was born before the rules of rhetoric, as languages are born before grammar. Nature makes men eloquent when great interests or great passions arise. Whoever is violently moved sees things differently from other men. Everything becomes to him the object of rapid comparison and metaphor: without even realizing it, he animates everything, and he communicates to the audience part of his enthusiasm.

Eloquence transcends rhetoric; it comes alive when its forgets itself. Sticking to the traditional distinction between simple, middle, and sublime style, Voltaire harbors no skepticism toward the oratorical sublime. Following Boileau's (and Longinus's) contention that liberty and sublime eloquence are one and the same, Voltaire sees the sublime as essentially political: "True eloquence appeared in Rome at the time of the Gracchis and was perfected with Cicero. . . . Like that of Athens, it perished with the Republic. Sublime eloquence belongs to freedom alone because it delivers harsh truths, strong reasoning, and powerful images. Often a master does not like truth; he fears reason and prefers a delicate compliment to strong words."[12] Sublime eloquence is the highest expression of liberty; it is the language of the ancient republics, not that of monarchical servility, which expresses itself in "delicacy" and refinement. Implicit in his words is the belief that the task of philosophy is to resuscitate it, or at the very least to bring it back to memory. Anything short of that is viewed with suspicion because it amounts to a moral and political surrender. Besides the obvious influence of the rediscovery of the pseudo-Longinus's treatise on the sublime (which Boileau had translated in 1674), nostalgia for the eloquence of the ancients also revived the Ciceronian distinction between, on the one hand, *conciliare* and *delectare,* which belong to the domain of ethics, and, on the other, *movere,* which, transcending all considerations of aesthetic judgment, focuses exclusively on the means employed to carry the audience beyond itself, with no concern for the boundaries of reason. While the former are compatible with conviviality and *enjouement,* and with the affability of everyday life, the latter is an extreme and violent measure suited for extraordinary situations of crisis:

> There are, for instance, two topics which, if well handled by the orator, arouse admiration for his eloquence. One, which the Greeks call *ethos* or "expressive of character," is related to men's nature and character, their habits and all the intercourse of life; the other, which they call *pathos,* or "relating to the emotions," arouses and excites the emotions: in this part alone, oratory reigns supreme. The former is courteous and agreeable, adapted to win benevolence; the latter is violent, hot and impassioned, and, by this, cases are wrested from our opponents; when it rushes along in full career, it is quite irresistible.[13]

Because they could not conceive a reconciliation between those two styles and those two world-views, the philosophes became somewhat schizophrenic in their perception of themselves and of their function as writers. Conscious of the magisterial responsibility they assumed toward the nation, from approximately the 1750s on (i.e., when they came into the public eye and under the fire of their opponents), the philosophes, with varied degrees of emphasis, professed to oppose those habits of irony and satire that they nonetheless were practicing in their writings. The emblematic figure they chose was Heraclitus, the sensitive philosopher who shed tears for the weaknesses of human nature, rather than Democritus, who laughed them off.[14]

Nobody lived that conflict more intensely than Diderot. Haunted by the sublime vision of Socrates' and Seneca's philosophical deaths, mindful perhaps of Bossuet's maxim that "the Sage laughs not save in fear and trembling,"[15] Diderot, who very much wanted to be a sage, wrote in his dialogue *Cinqmars et Derville* that "people who are accustomed to reflection must laugh less than others. . . . A philosopher, a judge, a magistrate, seldom laughs . . . his [the philosopher's] status shows him the constant spectacle of human misery. . . . He perceives all at once a great number of grave consequences emerging from things that seem quite insignificant to ordinary people."[16] In the same spirit, Rétif de la Bretonne dreamed that in a society more equitable and consonant with philosophy "we shall no longer laugh, but we shall be content."[17] In a letter of 1748 written in reference to the recent publication of his libertine and philosophical novel *The Indiscreet Jewels* and to his own subsequent incarceration, Diderot declared: "I want the scandal to stop, and without wasting any time in apologies, I am quitting the fool's baubles and bells for ever, and I will go back to Socrates."[18] Yet, as we know, Diderot did not stick to those sage resolutions. Certainly the impish Monsieur Hardouin—the hero of Diderot's *théâtre de société* play *Est-il bon, est-il méchant?* and a portrait of the author as a patron and a con artist—was as much a benefactor to his friends as a mischief-maker and a devilish trickster, as he acknowledged himself with more than a tinge of (self-mocking) guilt: "Ah! had I wanted, I would have been, I believe, a dangerous scoundrel. . . . I was born in essence hard, mean, perverse. . . . Hardouin, you make fun of everything; nothing is sacred to you; you are a downright monster . . . this is bad, very bad . . . you must give up this evil turn of mind."[19] But it was Dorval, Diderot's brooding and melancholic dramatist, who was the official, public face of the philosopher-playwright; he would put Hardouin to shame with his stern morality and austere taste: "A distinguished taste [*grand goût*] necessitates a great deal of reason, a long experience, a lofty spirit, a melancholic temperament and refined organs."[20]

Diderot was wary of the cult of great men of letters, which filled the halls of the academies with emphatic eulogies and resuscitated, within the confines of the republic of letters and for the likes of Thomas, La Harpe, d'Alembert, and Mercier, the grand emotions of the golden age of republican eloquence, when orators could make their audiences swoon and quiver with enthusiasm. But despite Rameau's nephew's contempt for that ethos,[21] Diderot felt that he was part of a community of great men stretching across the ages. He staked his reputation on the homage of posterity and basked in the anticipation of his posthumous eulogies: "Only a limitless crowd of adoring admirers may satiate a spirit driven towards the infinite. . . . The eulogy legitimately expected [from posterity] and guaranteed by the unanimous support of one's contemporaries, is a real pleasure for the living."[22] In his *Eloge de Richardson* Diderot devoted a private cult to a writer whose prose exerted the universal appeal of the sacred word: "The works of Richardson will be appreciated more or less by everybody at all times and places; but the number of readers who will feel the full extent of their merit will never be large: they require too severe a taste."[23] If the reader is morally transformed—"Richardson plants in the heart seeds of virtue. . . : they remain hidden until the right moment comes that shakes them up and brings them to fruition"[24]—that is because he has allowed himself to be drawn into a fictional universe that is more vivid and lifelike than his own reality: "Oh Richardson! We take, despite ourselves, a role in your works; we get involved in the conversation, we approve, we blame, we admire, we are irritated, we are incensed. How many times have I caught myself crying: 'Do not believe him, he is lying to you. . . . If you go there, you will be in trouble.' My soul was in constant turmoil."[25] The power of illusion is so strong that the reader is entirely absorbed into the fiction, as a child is drawn to a spectacle that he cannot separate from reality. The writer in Diderot is overcome by the reader in him, so that he becomes oblivious to the skill and the technique that have produced such a world: "The interest and the charm of the work conceal Richardson's craft even to those who are most able to appreciate it."[26] Having become a character among others, the reader feels lonely and bereft once he has turned the last page.[27] Diderot the reader is as open to empathy as Diderot the writer. Over and over again he evokes a scene in which someone intrudes upon him while he is in the grips of a hallucinatory enthusiasm: "I could no longer read, and I surrendered to my distress; I would address the brother, the sister, the father, the mother, the uncles, I would talk loudly, to the great astonishment of Damilaville."[28] Perhaps because the fictional world exerted such a strong pull on him, Diderot entertained a very ambivalent attitude toward illusion and trompe-l'oeil effects in the novel, on the stage, and in the visual arts. Indeed, his entire work is split between the surrender to the lure of the fictional world and the drive to uncover its workings, to expose its facticity, to brand it as deceptive. A striking example of that duality, *La religieuse,* is divided between the self-absorbed, passionate, and seductive discourse of the heroine and the ironic unveiling of the illusion in the *préface-annexe,* which offers us a glimpse of what goes on backstage. When read as a pair, the two parts produce a jarring dissonance. In contrast, *Jacques le fataliste* conflates narrative enchantment and critical deflation in such a way that neither disrupts the other.

These issues are relevant to the status of eloquence in the writings of the philosophes because eloquence draws its power more from the passions raised by such fictional worlds than from the persuasion of reason. That much was suggested in the article "Illusion" in the *Encyclopédie:* "Is there enthusiasm without illusion? . . . Bring my illusion to its apex and you will produce in me admiration, elation, enthusiasm, frenzy, and fanaticism. An orator leads through persuasion; illusion advances by the poet's side. Orators and poets are both great magicians."[29] Enthusiasm, admiration, frenzy, fanaticism—all the passions that are raised by the sublime manipulation of discourse and that are so crucial to the philosophes—depend upon the poet's (as well as the orator's) ability to induce some kind of belief in his audience. Belief, enchantment, and illusion weave their deceptions around an audience enthralled by the speaker's words. Diderot's work, however, does not fit squarely within that model, but wavers between belief and disbelief, between an ironic conception of the writer as a self-conscious spinner of lies and a sacralized conception of the writer as celebrant in a secular cult, the virtuous carrier of a truth that transcends all human practice.

The sacralized, magisterial posture of the sublime had always been wedded to the aesthetics of the ancients and to classicism. David A. Bell has shown that the cult of great Frenchmen and great men of letters that became predominant in the second half of the eighteenth century was an offshoot of the seventeenth-century quarrel between the ancients and the moderns and an important stage in the prolonged attempt to promote a national literature and to advocate the preeminence of the French idiom over other European languages, such as Spanish and Italian.[30] The celebration of great men, which marked them out as sacred, rested upon the practices and the imagery of Catholicism, with its emphasis on sacrifice and selflessness.[31] More important, that cult helped to popularize classical republican ideals (focused mostly on the bellicose Rome and Sparta) that were inherited from the Italian Renaissance. Republican ideals inhabited the imagination of the aristocracy and the judicial courts, particularly the barristers and the parliamentary magistrates, who had passionately identified with a heroic ethos and who tended to see their struggles with monarchical power through the mirror of the Roman senatorial class sacrificed to the Augustan reason of state.[32] The members of the beleaguered parlements (mostly, but not exclusively, the Parlement of Paris) were the first constituency to resort to public opinion through countless pamphlets and *mémoires judiciaires,* taking their cause to the "tribunal of the nation" rather than to the king. Their rhetoric of self-presentation paved the way for the Enlightenment philosophes, who, from Voltaire to Rousseau, borrowed the language of the barristers in claiming moral authority as representatives of the nation, guardians of legality and the public interest.

On several occasions throughout the century the parlements came to oppose the policies of the crown and the clergy by going on strike and publicly resorting to the language of republican virtue, most notably in the series of crises triggered by the papal bull *Unigenitus:* first in 1713, when it was requested by Louis XIV in order to eradicate Jansenism, and in 1730–32, when *Unigenitus* became the law of the state; then in 1752–53 with the affair of the *billets de confession* (an unpopular measure involving refusal of sacraments to the dying); and again in the fiscal crisis of 1763, before Maupeou's sweeping reform of the judiciary system in 1771. Those showdowns were well publicized by the lawyers and the magistrates, who presented themselves as the "senate of the nation" to the people of Paris, who hailed them as "true Romans and the fathers of the *patrie.*"[33] Already in his address to Parisian barristers in 1698, the future chancellor Henri-François d'Aguesseau had invoked a kind of "depoliticized republicanism" in which members of a profession for whom "virtue is the source of all nobility" were devoted to the pursuit of glory through selfless service to the public and to the *patrie.*[34] In the 1760s barristers and philosophes began collaborating on *causes célèbres;* the cooperation between Voltaire and Elie de Beaumont for the redaction of a widely circulated *mémoire judiciaire* in favor of Jean Calas's rehabilitation is a famous example.[35] In the last decades of the eighteenth century the influence between barristers and philosophes was mutual, as both claimed the title of *hommes de lettres,* invoked similar concepts of genius and sentiment, and followed similar publication strategies. Both the barristers and the philosophes saw themselves as members of a republic of virtue that stood firm against the generalized moral decay of modernity.

From the theatrical works of Corneille to the writings of Montesquieu, Rousseau, and Mably, "to the neoclassical paintings of David, to the court speeches and printed briefs of barristers denouncing the corruption and injustice, reverent images of the ancient republics proliferated at the end of the old regime, along with praise for political systems in which free, independent, and equal citizens, effortlessly resistant to the blandishments of luxury and *amour-propre,* joined together in governing and in defense of the commonwealth. In strictly political terms, however, this republicanism remained for the most part an abstraction with no direct relation to the realities of French government."[36] But the language of republicanism, with its longing for antiquity, its hostility toward mannerist painting, the royal courts, and the culture of sensuality and luxury that it portrayed as a vehicle for decadence, shaped a new sensitivity that contributed significantly to the neoclassical revival of the *grand goût* (which had always been popular among the middle bourgeoisie of merchants and artisans, even during the heyday of the rococo). Thomas Crow has analyzed the important role played by the amateur Louis Petit de Bachaumont (1690–1771) and the parlement-leaning salon of his companion Marie-Anne Doublet in fostering the classicist renewal and the critique of rococo art at the Academy in the 1740s and 1750s.[37] An important vehicle was a clandestine newsletter, the *Mémoires secrets pour servir à l'histoire de la république des lettres en France,* sponsored by the Doublet salon, which circulated news, prohibited literature, irreverent gossip, and *esprit frondeur.*[38] Among the guests of the salon figured the antiquarian comte de Caylus and La Font de Saint-Yenne. In 1754, in the wake of the parlement's struggle with the monarchy in the matter of the *billets de confession,* La Font proposed that subjects taken from Roman history could contribute to the revival of the French school of painting; moreover, he expressed the wish that the portraits of magistrates, who best embodied, among all citizens, Roman virtue, would figure more prominently at the Salon exhibit for the edification of the public: "What images could be more dear to all good subjects than those of these men made invincible by their fidelity to the laws and to their oaths? Generous to the point of sacrificing, to no personal profit, the sweet leisure of a tranquil and materially abundant life to duties which are burdensome and almost always thankless!"[39] That wish would soon be echoed by Diderot: "Wouldn't busts of those who have served their country well, whether on the battlefield, in the halls of justice, in the sovereign's council chamber, or in the course of literary or artistic careers, be more properly instructive [than Baudouin's licentious paintings]?"[40]

Le Goût Moderne

The republican ideal was conceived as a language of dissent against the existing state of affairs rather than as a viable alternative to monarchical and commercial society.[41] In spite of its nostalgic, poetic character, or rather because of it, its imagery was ubiquitous. Toward the middle of the eighteenth century we witness a return to the *grand goût,* or *goût à l'antique,* to the stylistic "simplicity" and immediacy with which the literature of the ancients had been credited and which nourished the ideals of classicism in the writings of Boileau, La Bruyère, Fénelon, and Voltaire. In the name of those values, the philosophes rejected the features that had distinguished the literature and the arts of 1715–40, which they branded as embodiments of the *petit goût,* or, more unbiased, of the *goût moderne,* as that culture had once named itself. The *goût moderne* corresponded, by and large, to the aesthetics that the generation of David was to label the rococo, or *goût rocaille.* The neoclassical critique of the rococo was omnipresent and often contradictory; it mixed indiscriminately moral and economic arguments against the luxury, speculation, corruption, lack of taste, and ignorance of the class of financiers and parvenus who were alleged to be the primary sponsors and consumers of that culture with charges that were more specifically related to aesthetic theory and to academic criteria.[42]

Among the distinctive features that came under criticism was the irreverent, demystifying, and antiheroic mode that emerged from the spate of mock-heroic poems *(poèmes héroï-comiques)* published in the mid-seventeenth century, the most famous being Paul Scarron's *Virgile travesti* (1648).[43] The neoclassical spirit rejected both the burlesque rewritings of epic subjects and the mock-heroic mode, which insolently elevated lowly subjects by treating them in a grand manner. Those travesties transgressed the strict hierarchy of styles that was officially espoused by Voltaire and by the *Encyclopédie;* they mixed high and low, serious and comic, familiar and sublime; they favored *bigarrure* (hybridization of styles and subject matter) and dissonance. They preferred digression over linear development and experimented with idiolects and genres. In his inaugural speech to the Academy in 1746, Voltaire deplored "the medley of styles" that threatened the purity of the French language and the impending "depravity of taste" imputable to those who "pretend to enliven serious and instructive works with the informal expressions of conversation. Often Marot's style intrudes into the most noble subjects: it is as if a prince were dressed with the attire of a fool." He recommended the reading of Cicero as an antidote.[44]

But it was not only in the burlesque genre that writers practiced stylistic *bigarrure.* In their attempt to open up scientific knowledge to a wider public the philosophers of the early Enlightenment had fashioned their own hybridization; heirs of Descartes' user-friendly *Discours de la méthode,* they had found a middle ground between the language of science and that of worldliness, between philosophical difficulty and *enjouement.* "I wanted to talk about philosophy in a way that would not be philosophically heavy-handed. I have tried to make it neither too dry for a polite audience, nor too facetious for the learned," Bernard Le Bovier de Fontenelle noted.[45] Later in the century, a new generation of philosophes found that such attempts had gone too far. Fontenelle's effort to ground the discourse of philosophy and science within the legitimizing sphere of politeness was now seen as shameless pandering to the ignorant and the philistine. Thus, Jean Le Rond d'Alembert was critical of Fontenelle for having "a kind of affectation for representing great subjects in a miniaturized manner."[46] Indeed, Fontenelle had dedicated his *Nouveaux dialogues des morts* (1683) to the Greek satirist Lucian; following in the footsteps of Anacreontis, Marot, and Scarron, he had treated the great men of antiquity, such as Cato and Socrates, with an indecorous humor. The notoriously satirical Jean-Baptiste Rousseau had written that Fontenelle "liked to treat grand subjects gallantly in an effeminate and worldly way [*en style de ruelle*]."[47] Voltaire, for his part, accused Fontenelle of having abused the language of conversation in his scientific treatises and of having degraded the dignity of mathematics with an affected and effeminate style that was more suited to sentimental novels than to the sciences: "He talked about science in the same way as Voiture talked of *galanterie* to Mlle Paulet."[48] In d'Alembert's *Discours préliminaire* to the *Encyclopédie,* Fontenelle received measly praise and some reproval for having dared to lend philosophy "the ornaments that seemed less fitting to it, and that most resolutely ought to have been forbidden to it," an unfortunate attempt indeed, happily counteracted by Georges-Louis Leclerc de Buffon's *Histoire naturelle,* which had been written, according to d'Alembert, with "that nobility and that elevated style which so befit philosophical subject matters and which in the writings of a wise man must portray his soul."[49] A similar critique was applied to *belles-lettres.* Among the many evils that the infamous concept of marivaudage stigmatized was a disregard for stylistic propriety, a tendency to mix high and low, serious and comic: "Marivaux crafted a style so peculiar that he had the honor of giving it his own name," wrote the critic Jean-François La Harpe. "It is the most bizarre medley of laborious gibberish [*métaphysique*], trivial expressions, convoluted sentiments and plebeian turns of phrase."[50]

The comic approach practiced in the preclassical seventeenth century was far from being outmoded one hundred years later; it reappeared throughout the eighteenth century in a variety of venues, most notably in the theater. It also reappeared in the works of Dufresny, Fontenelle, Le Sage, Marivaux, Montesquieu, and Crébillon. Marivaux in particular was still writing burlesque adaptations of heroic poems in the manner of Scarron in 1712–13, with his much reviled *Homère travesti* and *Télémaque travesti,* whose authorship he later repudiated. Even staunch critics practiced that manner, such as Diderot in *The Indiscreet Jewels* and Voltaire in *La Pucelle.* The connection between those writings and the aesthetics of the first generation of burlesque practitioners, namely, the writers of the 1650s, was still obvious in the mind of the public as late as 1780, when the architect Le Camus de Mezières wrote a scathing attack against the rococo in the decorative arts:

> Every form was allowed, provided that it sparkled and shimmered [*papilloter*]; no harmony, no agreement, no symmetry. . . . The more an ornament seemed to break with its natural form, the more precious it appeared; such have been the aberrations incurred by Vatteau [*sic*], Callot, and in literature the burlesque genre that was launched by Scarron and his epigones.[51]

In the eyes of the detractors of the *goût moderne* there was no categorical distinction between excess in literature and in the visual arts. A single line connected the works of the painter of *fêtes galantes* to the early originators of the literary burlesque: both had a weakness for the "unnatural" combination of dissimilar elements, for an economy of fantasy that undermined the boundaries between animal and mineral, animate and inanimate, the speech of a prince and that of a servant; both mediums favored the ironic and playful quotation of preexisting forms and discourses that were subverted from their original intent. To their critics, the *modernes* seemed to betray an overactive imagination gone astray and unmoored from any reference to reality. In overstepping hierarchies and boundaries, the *modernes* favored a wide range of tones that comprised wit, *galanterie*, badinage, raillery, whimsicality, parody, burlesque, and farce. By blurring styles and genres, they not only discredited the literary models transmitted from antiquity, such as tragedy and epics, but also challenged the morality of virtue and heroism that was associated with them. Finally, and most importantly, they disputed the conception of mimesis that had been the basis of the cult of the ancients in seventeenth-century classicism and eighteenth-century neoclassicism.

In their effort to forge a philosophical style capable of regenerating the nation and in their attempt to recapture the energy and the enthusiasm of the ancients, Voltaire, d'Alembert, Diderot, Grimm, Rousseau, Thomas, Marmontel, and Mercier distanced themselves from the spirit of modernity that had radiated in the early Enlightenment; they went so far as to define their identity as writers and philosophes in opposition to it. They criticized the moderns for lacking the seriousness, the moral stature, and the creative drive necessary to enlighten the audience. Suddenly, the moderns became minor authors; their success was discounted, and they were declared forgettable in the eyes of posterity. More scintillating than enlightening, more seductive than pedagogical, the moderns favored form over content, the brilliance of surface over the depth of engagement. They were decadent. "Seneca and Fontenelle, both idiosyncratic authors [*originaux*], situated among the first in letters and the sciences, have nonetheless contributed, by their brilliance, to spoil the taste of their age. They have spread upon everything a light that is more dazzling than enlightening [*un jour plus éclatant que lumineux*]."[52]

In so doing, the neoclassicists dragged into the same net a whole slice of the cultural life of their time that existed side by side with the philosophical project but which the philosophes disdained. To be sure, it was a genre that never counted on the reverence of posterity but saw itself as an ephemeral art tied to current events and the vagaries of literary fashion. I am talking about the vast productions of the unofficial theater, of the fairgrounds and the boulevard theater, the vaudevilles of the *opéra-comique,* and the parodistic productions of the Comédie-Italienne. Authors such as Fuzelier, Le Sage, d'Orneval, Allard, Pannard, Piron, and Favart created multimedia spectacles that combined singing, ballet, pantomime, and puppets. Though frowned upon, those theatrical spectacles were tremendously successful. "They attract huge crowds," wrote Mercier, who recognized the appeal of an entertainment that "draws throngs to theaters that everybody claims to despise but everybody visits."[53] Like the burlesque literature of preclassical times, those productions attracted a socially diverse public and often indulged in biting vulgarity, satirical reference to current events, and literary lampooning. It was, however, far more than disreputable entertainment for the wretched rabble. It was a learned and sophisticated art that presupposed an audience with knowledge of the texts and the discourses that served as its models, as well as an ear sharply attuned to registers of language: its comic effect emerged from the oscillation between stylistic obedience to and debunking of its models.[54] As César Chesneau Dumarsais noted in his definition of parody, that type of writing was always intertextual and relied upon dissonance and surprise: "One must preserve as many words as possible of the original one borrows from in order to bring its memory to mind. The idea of the original and its handling in a less serious subject form a contrast that surprises the imagination, and therein lies the pleasure of parody."[55] Most of the authors of the fairgrounds had benefited from a classical education. A play like Piron's *Arlequin Deucalion* (see chapter 8) was filled with references to classical mythology that only a college-educated audience could fully comprehend, though that did not prevent the play from exercising its appeal on lesser-educated audiences, granted that there existed different levels of appreciation.

My point is that there is a continuity from the early, preclassical ethos of the burlesque and mock-heroic to the conversational aesthetics of the moderns and to the lowly fairgrounds, of which contemporary audiences and critics were quite aware but which modern historians of literature have tended to overlook. What those works had in common transcended the specifics of genre (theater, novel, or poetry): they were instances of critical self-reflexivity. They took as their subject not the immediate representation of reality but the modes of mediation between raw experience and cultural forms, that is, the means of representation themselves. Most of those productions, from mock-heroic poems to comic versions of heroic novels (such as Sorel's *Le berger extravagant* and Marivaux's early novels, inspired by *Don Quixote*) to the fairgrounds theaters, were in fact rewritings of existing texts or discursive genres (mostly epics and tragedy). The intention was most often to deride the well-established and classically inspired productions of the official, "high" culture sponsored by the French Academy and by the court-supported Opéra and Théâtre-Français with plays drawn from the masks of the commedia dell'arte, such as *Arlequin Romulus* (Biancolelli, 1722), *Pierrot Romulus ou le ravisseur poli* (Lesage and d'Orneval, 1722), *Arlequin Thémistocle* (Fuzelier, 1715), or *Arlequin Endymion* (Lesage, Fuzelier, and d'Orneval, 1721). They were the products of an over-developed intertextual consciousness that undermined the belief in mimetic representation and the primacy of illusion and brought to the fore not a true-to-life experience but the mechanisms of fiction.[56] Their referent was not experience but a preexisting representation; of course, the same could be said of French tragedy, which was also a rewriting of Latin and Greek texts.[57] That, indeed, was the point: in the eyes of the parodist, as well as in those of the classically inclined playwrights (Voltaire, Diderot), the ancient dramatic language had been hijacked and perverted by the decadent mannerism of monarchical culture. But while the parodists limited themselves to satirizing the epigones, the philosophes' most ardent desire was to recapture the original language of antiquity in its pristine simplicity and power. The trouble was that in the eyes of the parodists Voltaire's attempts to renew the genre of tragedy looked very much like the efforts of yet another epigone. Hence the countless parodies to which they subjected his works.

We can now better grasp the reason for the philosophes' hostility toward this type of aesthetics, whether it came from the practitioners of the *goût moderne* or from those who wrote for the unsponsored theaters. The reforms the philosophes advocated on the stage, their ventures into the genre of tragedy, and their experiments with the *drame* were aimed at strengthening illusion and drawing the spectator into the fictional world by erasing the awareness of a discontinuity between the fictional space of the stage and that of spectatorship.

There was nothing radically new about such an enterprise, which relied upon the tenets of early classicism and the dramatic theories of the Italian Renaissance, but the issue of theatrical illusion became timely again after a period of freedom and experimentation in the 1720s and 1730s. While the moderns advocated a type of fiction that actively involved the audience in the constitution of meaning, the *nouvelle vague* of the ancients preferred to shield the audience from the perception of theatricality. The purging of spectators from the stage in 1759, a reform that had long been invoked by Voltaire, must be seen in that context.[58] It is significant that the emphasis placed on representational illusion was felt at two crucial moments in the confrontation between the public and the literary institution: in the 1640s, at the height of the monarchy's theatricalized glory (d'Aubignac's *La pratique du théâtre,* which theorized that trend, had Richelieu as its intended audience), and during the years of the philosophical struggle. In both cases it was crucial to control and educate the audience by means of emotion. The audiences of the fairs may well have sung along with the actors and talked back to the stage; the new audiences dreamed of by Voltaire, Diderot, and Mercier must be passive and mesmerized by the spectacle. The audience was reconfigured along the axis of religious and republican eloquence. Louis-Sébastien Mercier put it forcefully in an important work on theatrical reform:

> As soon as the senses and the imagination are affected, we become, luckily for us, passive beings who follow the impression imposed on us. The art of the poet consists in paying attention to that essential property of human nature, in handling it skillfully, in turning the spectator into a kind of instrument that he will play at will; once he has made himself master of the heart, mind and reason will obey too.[59]

The audience is *passive* both in the current and in the etymological meaning of the term *(patior):* it is disposed to endure passion, to receive through the senses and the imagination the powerful impressions communicated by the spectacle. The poet, ruling over the emotions of the spectators, will enjoy complete power over their reason, playing them like a docile instrument and leading them wherever he wants. Lest we be troubled by a manipulation that may evoke revolutionary terror and the sublime oratory that drives a crowd to commit violence, we should remember that for the philosophes the "poet-legislator" is "the bard of virtue, the great censor of vice, the universal man,"[60] and that the poet, like the divinely invested sovereign, is the living embodiment of the general interest. Like the king, whose authority he wishes to overtake, the poet cannot but will the good of the people, and the audience may safely surrender to his benevolent, if overpowering, sway. This attitude toward the passions raised by the stage and by fictional prose presupposed a heightened faith in the powers of representation intimately to connect with the emotions of the audience.[61]

It must also be noted that many of the plays the philosophes found objectionable often presented a satirical portrait of the philosophical movement and that there was a reactionary, antiphilosophical propaganda that used comic language to push its own agenda. The *bel esprit,* which both the philosophes and their enemies tended to identify with its offensive by-products—satire and persiflage—was seen by the latter as the quintessentially French language and the expression of a culture endangered by self-righteousness and philosophical arrogance. The first of Palissot's *Petites lettres sur de grands philosophes* (1757) chided the philosophical movement for its oracular posture: "They have announced truth, or what passed as such, with a pomp it never had. We have seen some philosophical productions heralded with a tone of authority and determination that until now was suited only to the pulpit. . . . A tone of inspiration for some, of emphasis for others, so alien to the persuasiveness of reason, has disgusted some people of good sense."[62] One of the most successful instances of such disgust was Palissot's play *Les philosophes,* which was performed not on the fairgrounds but, more scandalously, at the Comédie-Française, in 1759, the year the *Encyclopédie* was suppressed. Despite its mediocrity, the play attracted large crowds eager to see Diderot vilified as a pickpocketing rogue and Rousseau as a lunatic walking on all fours. It was certainly embittering for the philosophes to see how effectively the weapon of ridicule could be wielded to belittle their efforts and how difficult it was to educate a public that preferred entertainment to enlightenment and satire to edification. The fact that Palissot's satire got its comeuppance by becoming, in its turn, the object of several parodies must have provided little comfort: works were parodied when they flopped, but even more so when they were successful.[63]

The marginalization of comic genres was not, of course, an innovation of the philosophes. Such purism was in many ways the replay of an earlier one. Already at the time of the publication of Boileau's *Art poétique* (1672) a narrow conception of comedy had emerged that rejected the burlesque and its alliance with dance and music. The aesthetics of *galanterie*—practiced by Molière in the *comédies-ballet* for royal entertainment, such as *La princesse d'Elide, Monsieur de Pourceaugnac, Le bourgeois gentilhomme,* and *Le malade imaginaire*—soon came under attack. The mixture of genres that characterized *galanterie* and the courtly fête has been analyzed by Alain Viala and by Gérard Defaux; the latter has emphasized the demystifying character of that aesthetics, the skepticism inherent in a genre that "unveils its mechanism, undermines the dissembling powers of illusion and turns such demystification into the very heart of the spectacle."[64] André Félibien's description of the statues that occupied the southern façade of the Versailles palace reveals the alliance that once existed between Melpomène, the muse of tragedy, Thalia, the muse of comedy, and Momus, the disreputable god of satire, buffoonery, and the grotesque (whom the gods had chased from Olympus): "In the building of the middle, which represents comedy, there are four figures, which represent the muse Thalia, who oversees noble comedy; Momus, who oversees buffoonery; Terpsichoris, another muse who administers elegant dance; and the god Pan, who is the author of grotesque dance."[65] That coalition was broken by a new purism that repudiated all mixtures of styles and art media. Boileau's consecration of the *Misanthrope* over the *comédies galantes* marked all the subsequent canonical interpretations of Molière.[66]

A century or so later, in the wake of the neoclassical revival and during the rebirth of the *grand goût,* Voltaire the tragedian tried to distance his own art from that of less respectable, outrageous scribblers: "Buffoon, Buffoonery, belongs to the low comic genre, to the fairs, to Gilles [a servant in the farce], to whatever may amuse the populace. That is where, to our universal shame, tragedies started from. Thespis was already a buffoon when Sophocles was not yet a great man."[67] Even the Comédie-Italienne, which had given Marivaux his greatest triumphs, was to Voltaire "a theatre consecrated to bad taste and scandal."[68] True enough, the Italian comedians had often amused the public at Voltaire's expense with countless parodies of his tragedies. It was with bitterness that Voltaire had resigned himself to witnessing the success of the Italians. At the height of their popularity in the 1720s, stung by Fuzelier's parody of *La Henriade* (*Arlequin persée,* performed on 18 December 1722), Voltaire noted in a letter to Thieriot: "I heartily forgive the scum of authors those farces [*trivelinades*]; it is their job, and we must all stick to ours: mine is to despise them."[69]

It so happens that the critique launched against the aesthetics of the moderns by the new wave of the ancients has been handed down to us by a literary history that, from Boileau, to Batteux, to Rollin, to La Harpe, to Sainte-Beuve, to Lanson, has been preoccupied with establishing a canon of great authors that would not disparage a body of literature intended to glorify the nation. Although both the ancients and the moderns struggled to prove that they were best suited to serve what the modern, *galant* Paul Pellisson named, as early as 1655, "the glory of our nation and our time," it was the ancients who made the stronger claim.[70] In the seventeenth century the reference to antiquity served to promote the idea of a *translatio imperii* in which France triumphed over its precursors and longtime rivals, the Italians and the Spanish (who were henceforth declared the epitome of excess and bad taste); it legitimized French superiority at the same time that it concealed French culture's true debt.[71] In both centuries, reverence for antiquity served as an argument for the sacralization of the writer and his creative task. For Boileau, poetry was the product of a "divine horror" and "fury";[72] for Diderot, the inspired genius was especially attuned to the spectacle of moral beauty, and his character would share in some of its nature.[73] The image of the writer as hero and self-sacrificing celebrant of a national cult became current during the Revolution and in romanticism. By contrast, the moderns had a conception of creative activity that was more contextual and local; they embraced the contingent, and unlike the ancients, they did not propel themselves forward in time and did not turn to posterity as to their privileged audience. Their art, which was linked primarily to society and to an exploration of civility and social forms, tended to be more timely. Their work bore the marks of the particular circumstances of its production, often reflecting or alluding to current events. As Baudelaire would say, it embodied the ephemeral aspect of modern beauty.[74] That work, therefore, may be harder to appreciate when frozen in the timelessness of the canon, extracted from its surroundings and exposed on the bare walls of a museum, or in an anthology destined for the classroom.

Two Generations of Moderns

The moderns by and large were excluded from the Pantheon. When they did enter there, it was at the price of a major reconfiguration and reinterpretation; whatever did not fit into the official picture was forgotten or considered minor. That was the case of Molière, as we have seen, and of Montesquieu, whose canonization as a *philosophe à l'antique* tended to paper over his unseemly past as a *bel esprit* and a modern (illustrated by such texts as *Les lettres persanes, Le temple de Gnide,* and the *Essai sur le goût*). *Galanterie, the style régence,* and the rococo are often synonymous with frivolity, superficiality, and courtliness. What is lost in this account is the originality and the innovativeness of the aesthetics and the social thought of the moderns, which took root in the circles of the *galants* and the *précieux* that flourished between 1635 and

1670. One of the reasons why literary historians have tended to misrepresent it is that it is difficult to define. Neither the moderns of the eighteenth century nor their predecessors in the seventeenth ever formulated an explicit program; they did not see themselves as part of a school or a movement. To be sure, there were a few brief moments—such as in 1713–15, at the time of the Querelle d'Homère, which pitted the partisans of La Motte's free adaptation of the *Iliad* against those of Mme Dacier's translation—when the polarization resulting from the hostilities gave the moderns the semblance of a coherent party. But modernity was far more than a quarrel about the meaning of translation and the transmission and reception of great classics. Indeed, the literary historian is confronted with a nebula of uncertain terms, some of which, like *rococo,* are not only derogatory but foreign to the period. Thus, a movement or a tendency took form and definition mainly through the voice of its critics, who had some interest in being as heavy-handed as possible.

But even those terms that were intrinsic to the period are vague and shifty. Alain Viala has observed how important it is for the historian to be aware of the distinction between intrinsic and extrinsic classifications *(termes endogènes* and *exogènes)* that are used to frame the object of study.[75] What goes for seventeenth-century *galanterie* is equally true for the period that concerns us:

> The terms showcased in the titles of works, the theoretical texts exist, but there was no habit of creating literary movements with manifestos. *Galanterie* was a tendency rather than a movement, and literary history does not know how to deal with tendencies when they are dispersed. That aesthetics—which was both displayed (in the names it claimed for itself) and concealed (since it did not aspire to be a theory, even less a doctrine)—aimed at suggesting an "air," as Richelet would say. Now, it is difficult to theorize an *air. Galanterie* is a social phenomenon of which literature is but a part, rather than a literary theory. . . . From a linguistic viewpoint, things are not so simple. Besides the inherent ambiguity of the term *galanterie,* the galants themselves hesitated concerning the words they used to qualify themselves. . . . No French term could adequately translate that reference ideal: *urbanité* (urbanity), *mondanité* (worldliness), *atticisme* (atticism), *délicatesse* (subtlety) were rival terms; even better: *suavitas, urbanitas.* Those vacillations are inevitable when what is at stake is less a fixed model than a constantly evolving ideal.[76]

An almost unbroken line leads from the aesthetics of *galanterie* as it appears in the works of Madeleine de Scudéry, Voiture, Sarasin, Pellisson, and La Fontaine (i.e., the circle of Mme de Rambouillet and the writers of the Fouquet clan) and Molière to the aesthetics of the *goût moderne,* which flourished in the first half of the eighteenth century. Even though such continuity remains mostly unacknowledged and unformulated, most of the aesthetic and ethical criteria operative in the eighteenth century were put into place at that earlier time.

Approximately a century before Alexander Baumgarten introduced the field of *aisthetike* as the science of "sensuous imagination," the moderns were exploring the key notions of sensibility, taste, and grace, which welded literary imagination, theories of perception, and a conception of social interaction as an art form. Because they did not separate artistic self-expression from other modes of social self-presentation, the moderns were deeply embedded in the aristocratic ethos that they helped to shape. In the seventeenth century, when the literary field was not yet seen as autonomous, literature was closely dependent for its values and its modes of expression on the venues of aristocratic sociability. *Gens de lettres* from the ranks of the bourgeoisie presented themselves as worldly amateurs; many, such as Vincent Voiture and Jean-François Sarasin, did not publish their works during their lifetime, and for a time Madeleine de Scudéry published under her brother's name. Noblemen practiced literature not as a profession but as an extension of their social activities.[77] At a time when the established aristocracy was incorporating, faster than ever, new elites emerging from the royal administration, the magistracy, and the sale of venal offices, the *honnête homme* and the *homme de lettres galant* became the dominant models. Bourgeois writers, newly minted and older aristocrats, came together to produce a new ideology. Their ideals were to be appropriated later, pace Rousseau, by the Enlightenment bourgeoisie and upheld as an antidote to aristocratic manners, but by that time the aristocracy's creative role in the production of those ideals had been quite forgotten.

Galanterie is the term that best defines—rather than *preciosité*—a literary style and a style of interaction that tries to combine science with a sense of playfulness and pleasure. *Galanterie* was primarily a seductive discourse, but it was not merely a worldly game; rather, it combined a didactic purpose with a search for naturalness in an attempt to transcend the opposition between knowledge and amusement. For the *galant* writers the search for a natural style, the rejection of specialization, the cultivation of the sociable virtues and an open disposition towards others, revealed a desire to have an ethical reach, to appeal widely to all the ranks of society both through their writings and through the projection of an ideally cultivated public persona. The hope was to bring a cultural unity to the dispersed members of the body public. The writer, "spreading everywhere that good humor which is, after virtue, the greatest benefit" hoped to attract the widest possible audience: "family man, prince, magistrate, soldier, artisan." Gifted with a protean quality and capable of embodying all characters without being overpowered by any, "he was well liked by all different kinds of minds, as if all he ever wanted was to please each one of them: by the ladies, the men of letters, the courtiers, the most enlightened and the most mediocre." The appeal of the *galant* consisted in such "feminine" qualities as a desire to please, a chameleon-like capacity to adapt to all spirits, and a disposition to become the vehicle of a conviviality that would overcome the specialization of function.[78] In that sense the all-inclusive, ideal audience of *galanterie* prefigured the emergence of the unified, educated public heralded by the Enlightenment: it was in seventeenth-century *galanterie* that the conditions for such an emergence originated.

Rhetorically, the *galants* cultivated the *sermo familiaris* and the *sermo quotidianus* evoked by Cicero, Seneca, and Guez de Guez de Balzac. They privileged orality over the written word, improvisation over painstaking composition, and interaction and dialogism over solitary creation; at any rate, they sought to create the illusion of such activities in their writings. The art of dialogue, wrote Pellisson, must be "an intimate conversation, free and spontaneous, embellished with the playfulness, good humor and civility of *honnêtes gens,* so that the particular character of each would shine through and they would be known and loved."[79] Conversation was a collective creation in which the individuality of each participant was preserved, though meaning would emerge from the interplay of all the voices. With its pluralistic character, it was a polymorphous art based not on the systematic thinking and demonstrative reasoning that was taught in the schools but on digression and on the acceptance of the random nature of thought connections. It was a hybrid genre that emerged from the fragmentation and the mixture of preexisting discourses, and as such it tended, much against academic dictates, to combine styles and registers of language. Such hybridization was reflected in the protean quality of the writer and in his ambition to master all genres: "he has a mind that, acting by the general and universal principle [of reason] and mastering the notions of all genres of writing, is able to go from one to the other with perfect ease. . . . The Proteus of the fable and the chameleon of naturalists will not transform themselves more effortlessly than him."[80]

Galanterie tends to combine not only genres (prose and poetry, or, in the theater, music and dance) but also styles and tones: "He will unite subjects that are serious and subjects that are *galants;* his familiarity with the most sublime poetry will not prevent him from writing the most ordinary [*bas*] language."[81]

In conversation every topic is accepted, but "the great secret is to talk with dignity about ordinary things [*choses basses*] and with simplicity about elevated things."[82] "Great things must be expressed with simplicity: emphasis spoils them. But little things should be expressed with nobility: they need the support of expression, tone of voice, and style of delivery."[83] (This lesson of *mondanité* handed down to Proust via Sévigné will become the inalterable quality of Proust's own style, the secret spring of its underlying humor.) It must be noted that the *bas* is not necessarily the trivial or the vulgar but rather the technical, the specialized (such as legal or medical jargon), or a language that describes mundane objects too accurately; in the seventeenth century there was a tendency to call *bas* what today we would call realistic.[84]

The stylistic subversion of hierarchies was something that galanterie shared with the burlesque rewritings of the classics. Charles Perrault defined the burlesque as "a kind of ridicule which consists in the impropriety [*disconvenance*] between the representation of a thing and its true nature. . . . This impropriety may take two forms: one speaking lowly about eminent things; the other speaking portentously about lowly things."[85] There is therefore only a difference in degree between the playful mode of conversational *galanterie* and the outright effect of dissonance of the burlesque. Though the former is the art of mastering propriety *(bienséance)* and the second is an art of the ultimate impropriety, the two are connected by an uninterrupted line across varying shades of color. Those subtle analogies among comic genres and tones were fully appreciated in the early seventeenth century, at a time when the burlesque was associated not with vulgarity and excess but with the "elegant teasing of Marot *(badinage marotique)*"; not with "ease" and "license" but with the power of poetry to transcend the boundaries between genres and kinds of knowledge. Gabriel Naudé held Clément Marot responsible for having introduced in France the burlesque and "low and comic style," but he praised him for having been the first "who dared to explain serious things with comical and familiar expressions, *magna modis tenuare parvis."* The comic spirit that Naudé appreciated in Marot was not outlandish impropriety but the *enjouement* favored by the *galants,* the restrained and inward delight of *esprit:* "the style of burlesque poetry is so restrained and measured that it is content to excite a moderate laughter and an inner delight to those who read it."[86] Some twenty years later, in the *Art poétique,* Boileau will carefully separate the badinage from the burlesque,[87] an irreversible split between comic genres that the *Encyclopédie* will sanction in its final rejection of burlesque playfulness, which will then be equated with "trivial and extravagant poetry . . . superficial ease of a low style . . . ludicrous imagination, debasement and licentiousness."[88] "The burlesque genre knows no poetics and may not have any. . . . The burlesque upsets me in all circumstances," declares Dorval, Diderot's exemplary playwright—was he once more making honorable amends for his wonderfully burlesque and philosophical fantasy *Les bijoux indiscrets?*[89]

In 1721, at the height of the *goût moderne,* was published one of the greatest works of subversive, burlesque *bigarrure,* which recklessly juxtaposed theology and sex, philosophy and satire, natural law and fashion, politics and oriental romance: the *Lettres persanes.* The transgressive character of his endeavor did not prevent the author from having his characters censure (not without added irony) the very thing that he was himself doing:

> To please women, one must have a certain talent rather different from what pleases them even more. It consists of a kind of badinage, which amuses them because it seems to promise them at every instant what can be performed only very occasionally. This banter, naturally appropriate to the boudoir, gradually seems to be forming the character of the nation; they joke in the council room, they joke at the head of an army, they joke with an ambassador. Professions appear ridiculous in proportion to the seriousness of their pretentions, and a doctor would not seem as absurd if his garments were less lugubrious, and if he jested a bit while killing his patients.[90]

We have come a long way from the praise of worldly conversation to its satire: the conception of *galanterie* has been demoted to that of a badinage that barely disguises its sexual drive. Rather than bringing together a nation divided, as Pellisson had imagined, the conversation of the salons has been transported to the boudoir and is now represented as a degenerate language that degrades the character of the nation.

The *galants* practiced a form of poetry that displayed ironically a flamboyant lyricism in which figures such as hyperboles, antithesis, and oxymorons were flaunted as signs of the poet's virtuosity and his ability to draw new meaning out of preempted forms.[91] Prefiguring the productions of the fairgrounds and the vaudeville, the seventeenth-century literature of worldliness is often a self-referential activity, an irreverent reflection on traditional discourses, which it deconstructs and reconfigures. Modernity does not invent new forms; rather, it tends to accept existing frameworks, which it empties of their previous meaning, in an ironic patchwork of quotations.[92] This taste for cautious subversion may account for the universalism of the *honnête homme* and the *galant,* which has too often been seen as an effect of conformism. On the contrary, if the *galant* claims he can address any sort of public, it is because he likes to *transgress* the boundaries and the hierarchies that separate various discourses, be they scientific, religious, or worldly. The combination of high and low, serious and comic, implies the desire to appeal to as diverse an audience as possible. Those are the features of Madeleine de Scudéry's conversational ideal: "I want you to master *the art of deflecting things* so skillfully that you may venture to court the most austere woman; that you may trifle with the most stern and serious people; that you may talk science to the ignorant."[93]

The Importance of Being Earnest

Throughout the eighteenth century the identity of the writer as an *honnête homme* underwent an evolution that led to the rejection of the alliance between worldliness and literature. In fact, it may have been precisely because the integration of the intellectual into the ranks of the worldly public had been successfully carried out that writers appeared less anxious to fit in.[94] *Galanterie* and *bel esprit,* once the distinctive qualities of a selected public, broadened their appeal to include larger and more inclusive audiences. They gave rise to more universal, rallying values, such as sociability and politeness, which transcended the poetics of manners and were seen as the harbingers of a wider progress in morality, science, the arts, and the economy. In the middle of the eighteenth century d'Alembert's *Essai sur la société des gens de lettres et des grands, sur la réputation, sur les mécènes et sur les récompenses littéraires* (1753) called for the emancipation of all people of talent from their symbolic and economic allegiance to the elites; intellectuals had been freed from such dependence by membership in the state-sponsored academies. *Littérateurs* and philosophes were coming into their own, and they set out to give themselves a new mission in the public sphere. A letter written to Voltaire by the abbé de Saint-Pierre, one of the most eloquent advocates of the exalted task of the *homme de lettres* and a thinker who exercised great influence on Rousseau, testifies to a desire of transforming the identity of both the writer and his readership. Now, the *homme de lettres* can achieve the highest glory, provided he is willing to reform and educate the public and to devote himself entirely to this task:

> Devote the rest of your life no longer to amusing witty women and other such children but to instructing men, to enlightening those who instruct us and to governing those who govern us. Give us models of history. It is true that such tasks require great ambition and great patience. I do not know yet if you have enough of those, but go and try. Quit your works of vanity in order to march toward sublime glory. Heaven bless the beneficent.[95]

Voltaire is invited to reject *esprit*'s feminine world of shallow pleasure and seduction and to embrace instead the masculine world of politics and history;
he is prodded, with a severity that might have irritated a bit the author of *Le
mondain,* to pursue glory instead of vanity *(gloriole)* by becoming the peda-
gogue and the benefactor of humanity, as well as a *praeceptor regis.* The writer
is turned into the high priest of a secular cult: by becoming a sacrificial figure,
and by agreeing to be an icon for such absolute values as truth and virtue, he
becomes himself an object of public veneration. In so doing, he brings unity to
the body public. No longer limited to the narrow elite of people of good taste,
the public is invoked by the philosophes under its abstracted and universalized
form, that of the nation and of humanity.

A few years earlier, in *Le temple du goût* (1733), Voltaire had already put into
place the major critical concepts that were to lead to such a transformation.
By dint of a separation between the *bel esprit* (i.e., the modern writer) and the
genius (i.e., the new writer, the adherent to the *grand goût*) Voltaire kept out
of the temple several generations of *galants* and *modernes*—Guez de Balzac,
Pellisson, Segrais, Saint-Evremond, Voiture, Fontenelle, and Marivaux:

> Already of their thin writings, the polish is tarnished,
> They still rank among *beaux esprits*
> but are excluded from the ranks of genius.[96]

In his article "Gens de lettres," published some twenty years later in the *Encyclopédie,* Voltaire detailed the reasons for such exclusion: "A man of letters is
not what we call a *bel esprit:* the *bel esprit* requires less culture, less work, and
no philosophy; it consists only of a brilliant imagination and the graces of conversation, supported by mediocre culture."[97] (The moderns, Voltaire suggests,
have scant knowledge of the Greek and Latin classics.) Much is at stake for
Voltaire in this critique. The severity he shows toward the writers he classifies
as minor is in fact very similar to the severity he himself had to endure from
his critics. As Marivaux acutely observed, probably with Voltaire in mind: "I
know clever writers who have ten times more *esprit* than it takes to be attacked,
if the religion they profess toward the Ancients did not shield them."[98] In spite
of his success as a writer of tragedies, an academically revered genre, Voltaire's
reputation in the world of letters did not go undisputed. It was not only the
abbé de Saint-Pierre who felt entitled to chide him; his archenemy Élie-Catherine Fréron did not miss any opportunity to humiliate Voltaire by depicting
him as an effeminate and a fop. "M. de Voltaire is without any doubt one of
the most brilliant *beaux esprits* of France, and the verse polisher whose colors

are the most flamboyant," wrote Fréron. "He has all the grace and the liveliness of our fashionable women; but he is absolutely devoid of Roman beauty. . . . He will be read as a writer of great witticism [*esprit*] who lacked some essential parts."[99] And when the ambitious Rousseau launched his career in the world of letters with the loudest possible bang, he attacked Voltaire in exactly the same terms as Fréron: "Do tell us, illustrious Arouet, how many vigorous and masculine beauties you have sacrificed to our artificial politeness; how many great productions you have lost to the taste for *galanterie,* so rich in small confections."[100] Wrapped in the folds of his toga, the young author *à l'antique* berates his elder rival for not being Roman enough, or, for that matter, for not being enough of a man. Effeminate and effete, the *bel esprit* is alleged to indulge in ephemeral displays of conversational trivialities and badinage; his style is "color" without design and contour, grace and *délicatesse* without masculine energy.[101] Practitioner of a degenerate art, he lacks the virile attributes that are always associated with the virtuous and wholesome body of the ancient.

Hunting down all symptoms of effeminacy was a persistent theme in the revival of the *grand goût.* The influence of women in the cultural domain was no longer seen as reconciling and inspiring, but rather as a source of decay. Their language no longer appeared as the model that inspired male writers, modern and ancient alike, to pursue naturalness and unaffectedness—as it had at the time of Guez de Balzac and La Bruyère—but was regarded as a dangerous instrument of corruption. With the revival of republicanism, throughout the eighteenth century the public sphere tended increasingly to be conceived as a masculine world, as women were slowly but surely driven out of the public domain by an ideology imbued with misogynistic and homoerotic fantasies of ancient republics populated with austere matrons, glistening, muscular warriors, and white-bearded civic leaders. Women were accused of degrading the public spirit and threatening liberty by their irresponsible mix of sexuality and politics. They were considered the insidious instruments of a court policy that relied upon them to reduce men to passivity: sexual dependency was seen as a sure way to political slavery. In the work of Rousseau and Montesquieu monarchical rule deprives men of freedom by undermining sexual differentiation and by mixing hierarchies and categorical distinctions. "There is no longer but one sex, and we are all women in our minds," Montesquieu dourly observed.[102]

The identification between eloquence, the endorsement of a moral mission, and the writer's masculine energy is typical of the language of the philosophical culture wars in the Enlightenment. In this game of rivalry and emulation one is often hit below the belt, so to speak, as the writers are summoned to show the public that they are in fact endowed with the qualities necessary for performing their function. Invariably, the moderns are exiled to the realm of the feminine and the degenerate. The contrast between the two identities of the writer is illustrated by Diderot's comments on his portrait by Van Loo, which was exhibited in the Salon of 1767. Diderot acknowledges the resemblance and the vividness of the representation: "A fairly good likeness. . . . Very lively. It has his kindness, along with his vivacity." But he deplores the primacy given to those qualities, and the absence of grandeur from a portrait that owes too much to the dictates of the *petit goût*. That "joli philosophe," that effeminate and coquettish writer, all dressed up for display in a salon, so eager to be admired by the bystander, does not measure up to the dignity of his writings and to the seriousness of his "sad works":

> But too young, his head too small. Pretty like a woman, leering, smiling, dainty, pursing his mouth to make himself look captivating. . . . But what will my grandchildren say, when they compare my sad works to this smiling, affected, effeminate old flirt? My children, I warn you that this is not me. . . . I had a large forehead, penetrating eyes, rather large features, a head quite similar in character to that of an ancient orator, an easygoing nature that sometimes approached stupidity, the rustic simplicity of ancient times.[103]

More desirous of resembling Seneca and Socrates, at their finest and final hour, than a smiling, vivacious *bel esprit,* the author of the *Essai sur les règnes de Claude et de Néron* looks forward to the future generations to whom he has bequeathed his mostly unpublished work. He favors seriousness over *enjouement,* rustic simple-mindedness over wit and brilliance, the orator's tribune to the conversational circle and the intimacy of the boudoir.

1 ■ A Faded Coquette

Marivaux and the Philosophes

We want to replace, in our country, bel esprit *with genius and glitter with truth.*

—Robespierre

The particular characteristic of his [Gavarnis's] comic gift is a great subtlety of observation, which sometimes goes as far as tenuity. Like Marivaux, he knows the full force of understatement, which is at once a lure and a flattery for the public intelligence.

—Baudelaire

Of all the writers who cultivated a feminine *esprit* and who embodied the ethos of the moderns, Voltaire was especially irritated by Pierre Carlet de Marivaux. While Voltaire was laboriously pursuing theatrical glory by attempting to imbue the respectable but depleted genre of tragedy with a new life, Marivaux had reached celebrity in the theater with several successful comedies that explored the baffling emotions of young love and the predicaments of individuals at odds with themselves, torn between their recondite desire and the social proprieties conveyed by language. He had also gained a solid reputation as a novelist and essayist. As if that were not bad enough, Marivaux had managed to secure a place in the French Academy in 1743, three long, scandalous years before Voltaire himself was admitted among the immortals. Voltaire had a poor opinion of academicians, but he had lobbied energetically to become one of them, and he was not pleased with being passed over in favor of lightweights like Marivaux.[1] In the contentious milieu of the republic of letters, split by quarrels among factions and by mutual attacks, Voltaire—who nicely complemented his causticity toward his opponents with a dose of self-protective paranoia—suspected at some point that Marivaux was planning to write a book against him. That turned out to be untrue, but Voltaire vented his resentment in a letter to Thieriot: "Be as it may, let this wretch make money, like so many others, by abusing me. It is only fair that the author of *La voiture embourbée,* of *Télémaque travesti* and *Le paysan parvenu,* should write against the author of *La Henriade,* but it is too dishonest of him to try to rekindle the quarrel [of the *Lettres philosophiques*]."[2]

Today we may picture Voltaire rolling over in his grave at the thought that *Le paysan parvenu,* a novel he despised, is considered one of the masterpieces of French narrative, whereas Voltaire's tragedies and his epic poem *La Henriade* are tucked away in dusty in folio. Fortunately, however, Voltaire was spared any forebodings of that unpleasant reality. Marivaux's canonization only took place in the early twentieth century; during Voltaire's lifetime the reputation of his rival steadily declined.[3]

◇◇

When the young Pierre Carlet, the son of a modest *officier,* a civil servant in the town of Riom in Normandy, returned to his native Paris in 1710 with aspirations to a literary career, like most children of the administrative classes he enrolled as a law student. He also started experimenting with his identity. He added a particle to his name and timidly penned *Decarlet,* which he used with increasing assurance for the next two years. By 1713, however, he seemed uncertain about this attempt at social promotion; on the register of the Faculté de Droit his *de* looks more like an ink stain than a mark of nobility. A less than assiduous student, for a long time he let his enrollment lapse without taking any exams. Whatever hopes of improvement he had, Pierre Carlet did not pin them on the pursuit of an administrative career, on the slow and painstaking accumulation of the money necessary to buy the office that would ensure him, as it did his father, a life of struggle and humiliation in the low ranks of state service, always hanging on the threshold of privilege, never fully able to enjoy its rewards.[4] Instead, he opted for a career in letters. His first comedy, *Le père prudent et équitable,* performed in 1712, was discreetly signed M***, in keeping with the dedication to a Monsieur Rogier, *conseiller du roi* in Limoges, not exactly a resplendent patron. But in 1716, in the dedication of his mock-heroic poem *Homère travesti* to the duc of Noailles, he finally adopted the pen name Carlet de Marivaux, which marked his official admission to the ranks of men of letters and *beaux esprits.*[5] Yet the poem brought him little artistic distinction and not much social recognition. Literary lampooning and the parody of the idiom of heroism were alive and thriving in the popular theaters of the fairgrounds but had long been out of favor with the official culture sponsored by the academies. As late as 1785 d'Alembert, stiff in the starched collar of the Academy's *secrétaire perpétuel,* cast a disapproving glance at Marivaux's desecration of Homer; it was a sorry affair, one that a lifetime of honorable service in the republic of letters could barely atone for.

Self-consciousness about his social identity and the knowledge that as a comic playwright and novelist he occupied a less exalted place in the hierarchy of letters were to stay with Marivaux and feed the vein of his social satire. (As Voltaire would say in the *Encyclopédie,* novelists and playwrights were mere professional craftsmen among *gens de lettres,* unworthy of the title of philosophe.)[6] Marivaux was highly aware of the subtle nuances of status and of the many ways in which the representation of hierarchy and rank shaped people's consciousness in a society obsessed with class mobility and emulation. Unlike Voltaire, however, he never aspired to consecrate himself in the eyes of the public as a heroic writer and a poet-king invested with the authority of genius and social mission; he never wanted to play a public role and did not put his passions on display in the line of fire.[7] His public persona always remained unpretentious and modest. His *noblesse de plume* was a mask that he was quite willing to take off and show for what it was, much like those individuals he praised for carrying their mask in their hand and playing the social comedy with self-deprecating irony:

> Of those people I do not say that they are masked, because they do not wear their mask, but they carry it in their hand, and they let you know: here it is; and that is charming. I quite like this way of acting like a fool, for after all, we must all be fools, and among the many ways of being so the one that is the least to blame is, as far as I am concerned, that which does not deceive others and does not induce them into error. Vanity revolts me only when it is devious and sly.[8]

Perhaps because of his long acquaintance with the Italian comedians and the characters of the *commedia dell'arte* (who were indeed portrayed carrying a mask in their hand), Marivaux believed that masking enabled people to disclose some truth about themselves. He also thought that the only morally acceptable social comedy was one that was played with grace and self-detachment and that failed to make anyone a dupe.

What is striking in Marivaux's career is his difficulty in gaining a solid foothold in the world of letters despite the popularity of his theater,[9] his protracted isolation among his peers, and the obstacles he encountered from the early days of his involvement in the quarrel between the ancients and the moderns (he sided with La Motte against Mme Dacier), to the height of his theatrical success, to the end of his life. At the end of his career, after he had long given up, he did not benefit from his past accomplishments but saw himself outmoded and obsolete: "No one can be in as bad a mood—not even a woman who wakes up with a blemish on her nose—as an author who is in danger of outliving his reputation. Witness Marivaux and Crébillon *le fils*" wrote Diderot, who never acknowledged his debt to Marivaux.[10] While possessing many of the values of a Sarasin, a Pellisson, or a Voiture, Marivaux was no longer the *homme de lettres galant* of the 1640s, who successfully divided his allegiances between the academies, powerful patrons, service to king and state, and worldliness. Having espoused the aspirations and the doctrines of the moderns, his youthful enthusiasm for their cause and his willingness to enter the fray at their side (albeit after a year's delay) only succeeded in making him the favorite target of the sarcasm of the ancients, which lasted long after the fires of the quarrel had subsided. Marivaux was never a member of a coterie, and apart from his personal friendship with several salonnieres (notably Mme de Lambert and Mme de Tencin) and with the financier and philosophe Helvétius, he never sought to weave around himself a network of supporters in the republic of letters. Even after he was accepted into the Academy, he remained marginal among his fellow members. With his sarcasm toward the pedantic philosopher, the traditional target of *beaux esprits* of the previous generation, and in spite of his extraordinary *Indigent philosophe,* he was not a philosophe. Nothing was more alien to Marivaux's conception of the role of the writer than the preachy and proselytizing enthusiasm espoused by the philosophes. He remained impervious to the new sense of urgency emerging from the philosophical movement: in his journals the image of the philosopher is shaped by the prejudices of an earlier time against a character tainted by pedantry, affected stoicism, and fatuous dogmatism. Despite his keen powers of observation, Marivaux seems out of place in his own time: in many respects he was a precursor, in others a man faithful to an ethos that was no longer seen as relevant, but above all, he was a writer who paid a stiff price for having persevered in the singular turn of mind that he claimed for himself.

Marivaux did not preserve and edit his correspondence for the benefit of posterity, but he closely guarded his privacy and bequeathed no information about his life. He left no personal letters nor documents, only a remarkable collection of suits for all occasions. Others managed, in the void he left, to freeze him into the image of an effeminate, vacuous utterer of *phébus,* a fop, or an aging coquette: "One had to cajole and compliment him all the time, like a pretty woman," said Charles Collé.[11] "He suffered among us the destiny of a pretty woman, and of one who is nothing but that: a radiant spring, but a harsh and lonesome fall and winter. The powerful gust of philosophy has blown away, in the last fifteen years, all those reputations built on reeds," wrote Grimm in his 1763 obituary of Marivaux.[12] Throughout his life he was a target for a variety of detractors. His victories were more often than not discounted and belittled; the "defects" of his style were pointed out with uncommon persistence and gusto. One has a hard time finding anyone who did not feel entitled to patronize and upbraid Marivaux for his stylistic "sins" and to call for his linguistic reform. His detractors and satirists belonged to every walk of literary life. We find them among professional critics and grammarians, like La Harpe and the abbé Desfontaines, who filled the pages of *Le pour et contre* and his *Dictionnaire néologique* with prickly criticism of every sentence Marivaux ever wrote. We find them among the antiphilosophe crowd, which featured Palissot and Fréron; among the satirists who wrote for the fairgrounds theaters, such as Piron, Le Sage, and d'Orneval. We count them among the philosophes and their supporters, such as Voltaire, the Marquis d'Argenson, the abbé Raynal, Collé, Marmontel, and the malevolent Grimm.

While his critics tenaciously berated him, Marivaux was even worse served by his own friends, or by those who passed as such. Perhaps unique in the annals of the Academy, upon the ceremony of his reception Marivaux was treated, not to the usual compliments, but to a rambling reprimand from Langlet de Gergy, the archbishop of Sens, a pious man and author. It was not Marivaux's writings—faulted for their excessive "vivacity" and "brilliance"—but rather his good heart and exemplary conduct that had secured him a chair among the immortals, the good prelate declared.[13] As for his novels, the archbishop would not venture to read them, but he had heard, from persons he trusted, that they were scandalous and libertine. Written forty years later Jean Le Rond d'Alembert's eulogy of his fellow academician, *Eloge de Marivaux,* published posthumously in 1785, starts with an apology for its length, which surpasses that of the eulogies of other academicians "much superior to Marivaux," such as the brothers Despréaux and Massillon (one is puzzled by this comparison of a playwright and novelist with a critic and a preacher).[14] The problem, d'Alembert writes, is that both the portrait of Marivaux's character and the description of his works require painstaking meandering into "small, delicate, and fugitive details," while the portrait of a "great man" and a "great writer" may, in contrast, be brushed with "rapid and energetic strokes." D'Alembert felt the need for optical enhancement in order to appreciate Marivaux's talents: "Sentiment is depicted as a miniature," as in the works of those "masters of calligraphy who . . . pride themselves on being read with a magnifying glass."[15] Marivaux's election to the Academy was something of a scandal, according to d'Alembert, considering that he was chosen over a great man like Voltaire: "When the Academy accepted Marivaux, people were shocked . . . that the doors of that institution should open for the author of *Marianne* and *Annibal* but remain shut to the author of *La Henriade* and *Zaire*. People had good reasons to react to that outrageous preference."[16] Toward the end of the century, a time that worshipped grand spectacles, vigorously outlined plots, and the display of enthusiasm and masculine energy, Marivaux was shelved away, like Boucher, among the superfluities of the *petit genre*. In appraising his work his contemporaries did not know what to make of it and often resorted to a paradoxical mixture of admiration and dismissiveness. When they acknowledged his talent, it was to confine it to the realm of the detail, the minuscule, the ephemeral. "The works of this author are almost always witty; he has a mind for details, he treats small things with genius and sublime," wrote the Marquis d'Argenson. "He was a writer who had a lot of wit [*esprit*], and when one looks at him from a certain angle, he is not without resemblance to a man of genius," wrote Fréron, with no intent of being facetious. Lost in the intricacies of a vision that was the product of his feminine *esprit*, Marivaux was denied access to a larger perspective, to "interest" and "movement," the qualities of the energetic and creative male genius.[17]

The correlation of effeminacy and rhetorical ornament had been a commonplace in rhetorical treatises since antiquity,[18] but it was revived with particular insistence in the eighteenth century. In *Les amours déguisés*, a comedy by Le Sage and d'Orneval performed at the Foire Saint-Laurent in 1726, the dialogues were based on a parody of Marivaux's journal *Le spectateur fran-çais*, and Marivaux appeared in the guise of a *précieuse*, Mlle Raffinot.[19] In his satirical compilation *Eloge historique de Pantalon-Phoebus*, the abbé Desfontaines mocked many of the expressions used by Marivaux: since the seventeenth century *phébus* had meant a language excessively ornate or obscure and, by extension, extravagant gibberish.[20] Occasionally a lone voice was raised in praise of Marivaux: "If one were to analyze Marivaux's *Marianne* and Voltaire's *Henriade*, which of the two would get the prize, if it were awarded by a true philosophe, one who would base his decision upon the criteria of morality and sensibility?" Louis-Sébastien Mercier asked rhetorically. "Fielding and Marivaux seem to me to deserve true glory, because their philosophy is based upon image, action, and sentiment." But that meant going against the grain: "Those are indeed blasphemous words," Mercier felt compelled to add.[21]

But the most shining example of the poisonous appraisal may be found in the abbé Trublet's "portrait" of Marivaux, written in 1755 and published in Deloffre and Gilot's edition of *Journaux et oeuvres diverses,* where it is featured, quite uncritically, as a "precious document" that should enable us to set Marivaux's ideas against "his real personality."[22] Trublet's anecdotes on Marivaux, reported in his *Mémoires,* are largely responsible for spinning the image of Marivaux that persistently reappears in other allegedly firsthand testimonials, such as Marmontel's *Mémoires* and d'Alembert's own *Eloge.*[23] The abbé Nicolas-Charles-Joseph Trublet (1697–1770), another of Marivaux's detractors (or oily pseudoallies), maintained a close correspondence with Marivaux's rival in theatrical glory, Voltaire, who gave Trublet his vote when the latter was admitted to the Academy in 1761. The abbé, who had been a candidate since 1736, perhaps resented the fact that Marivaux had been sitting there for almost two decades; at any rate, the indignity he suffered merged with the resentment he felt on behalf of his patron (Trublet was in awe of Voltaire, and when the great man labeled him as mediocre, he gracefully carried the title as a badge of honor).[24] Although his admiration for La Motte and Fontenelle would classify him among the moderns, Trublet's aesthetics also belonged to the antineologist, purist movement, which counted Voltaire as a prominent member. In 1733 Trublet came up with a project for rewriting Montaigne's work in proper, modern French, purging the style of the *Essays* of its *équivoques,* "barbarisms" and "negligences" and restoring Montaigne's text to a more dignified form. Marivaux, who was convinced that thought was consubstantial with expression and who saw in Montaigne's rich linguistic peculiarities an inspiration and a model for his own style, found such an endeavor profoundly repugnant.[25]

Trublet's talent in the genre of the insidious eulogy reveals itself in his ability to turn against Marivaux the very categories of moral and psychological analysis that the latter had employed in his own work. We thus learn that Marivaux has miserably failed to carry out in his life the very ABCs of good manners, not to mention the ethics of *honnêteté,* which for more than a century had tirelessly instructed that when in the company of others one must hide as much as possible one's preference for oneself and seek instead to make others happy by being attentive, responsive, and altruistic. Alas, Marivaux, though "good and decent deep down," is affected by "an excessive love of himself which is every-where apparent; he talks about himself all the time because he cares a great deal about himself; in fact, all he cares about is himself. . . . In general, he expects much deference and consideration: one must be attentive, listen to him, and applaud him."[26] As if that were not enough, he is also extremely touchy and irritable and has the unfortunate tendency to fly into a rage (we can almost see him stomping his feet hysterically) when others do not understand him, which happens very often because his language is belabored and obscure: "Everyone knows that he is convinced that when people do not understand him, it is their fault, not his. . . . In fact, when someone more brave dares to tell him so, he gets irritated and sometimes replies with spiteful words. . . . This has often happened to me."[27] One wonders what abysses of incomprehension the good abbé might have revealed in order to drive Marivaux to such frenzied frustration. However, we know that Marivaux was the regular guest of some of the most influential and independent-minded salonnieres, such as Mme de Lambert, Mme de Tencin (he was part of her "comité des sages," a member of her inner circle),[28] Mme de Boufflers, and Mme Geoffrin, who hosted the philosophes. One has a hard time believing that someone whose company was "disagreeable because of his obscurity, tiresome, and tedious; what is more, uncomfortable, because of the constant fear of offending him,"[29] would have been invited at all. Impecunious men of letters of undistinguished social rank were welcome only on the basis of their personal charm and intellectual merits, and only when they were able to make a contribution to the general conversation.

The main reason to distrust Trublet's "portrait," however, is that not only does it look like a catalog of everything one should avoid doing if one has any hope of having a social life but it also seems to be a compilation of all that was being said against Marivaux's literary style. What is more, Trublet aptly summarizes the central themes that occupied Marivaux, from his earliest writings for the *Mercure,* to his novels, to his latest reflections presented to the Academy in the 1750s. Those themes revolve around social ethics and aesthetics. In the wake of the Augustinian moral reflection on *amour-propre,* Marivaux greatly contributed to defining a modern ideal of sociability by systematically, even obsessively, tracking down the passions that threatened to disrupt human relations from within, such as vanity, pride, the desire to humiliate others and their accompanying sequel of bad faith and self-deception. It was Marivaux's lifelong ambition to devise an increasingly subtle and flexible language capable of describing the workings of *amour-propre,* its metamorphosis and masks:

"Our weaknesses, which we fight under one form, escape us under another. We cannot hope to destroy them; we must engage in something more wearying but more heroic: tracking them down with steady persistence."[30] The rhetorical efficacy of Trublet's text lies in its familiar air, in the fact that it taps into the vast reservoir of social ridicules that Marivaux persistently satirized and turns them perversely against the author. When describing in great detail the *bel esprit*'s workings of vanity in *Le spectateur français,* Marivaux could not foresee that he had penciled the outline of himself that would pass to posterity and that he had offered his head to Trublet on a silver platter: "A *bel esprit* in such a case is so prickly, his vanity makes him so scrupulously suspicious, his sensitivity is so alert to the possibility that he might not be esteemed enough, and his suspicions are tickled by so little that it takes almost nothing to irritate his tender pride."[31]

But the stereotypes Marivaux fell victim to were not of his own making. There was at the time a well-established tradition of writings targeting the pedantic philosopher (of the scholastic type) and the *bel esprit* (the worldly author), which underlies Trublet's portrait and lends it a kind of plausibility in the eyes of the reader familiar with it. Stock characters such as Hortensius, who appears in Marivaux's *La seconde surprise de l'amour,* Charles Sorel's comic novel *Francion,* and in *Le barbon* (1648), a satirical work by Guez de Balzac, exemplify the image of the author as a pompous and pedantic babbler, ridiculously vain and unfit for social life, someone who, having forgotten his rightful place in life, has lost any status and sunk into disrepute. The pedant is condemned socially as a failed parvenu, a sorry imitator of the *honnête homme,* and a pathetic snob. In the seventeenth century's evolving contest to define the writer's identity, the pedant stood as a foil to the *homme de lettres,* who, like the *honnête homme,* had no pretensions *(ne se pique de rien),* was successfully integrated in the venues of urban, aristocratic sociability, and was able to subordinate his identity as an author to a search for communal pleasure. Such was precisely the identity that Marivaux wished to cultivate.

Excessive dependence upon worldly success, however, could also become a source of satire. An author could be ridiculed not only for abusing scholastic and technical language but also for indulging in the figurative speech that had secured the reputation of the *poètes mondains.* Gibberish *(galimatias),* the failing of the learned, was sometimes paired with *phébus,* the failing of the worldly. Charles Sorel's Hortensius, for instance, sins on both counts. He is "the king of *beaux esprits* of the University of Paris. . . ; in order to pass for a gentleman, he always wore his boots and spurs like Amadis of de Gaule, even though he never mounted a horse."[32] Although Hortensius brags that his writings are "worthy of France's best literary circles" (des plus belles ruelles de lict de France), he is told that the only *ruelle* he may aspire to is not that associated with the space of polite conversation but rather the one in which chamber pots are stored when they are full.[33] His social shortcomings are compounded by a lack of taste and judgment that renders his show of erudition pointless and absurd; alienated from the social grounding of the *sanior pars* of the public of the town and the court, which alone is entitled to validate knowledge, the *faux savant* talks himself into madness and becomes a solipsistic chatterbox.

This social and aesthetic failure is infamously crowned by a moral one. In *La recherche de la vérité* Malebranche describes the figure of the spurious scholar *(faux savant)* driven entirely by *amour-propre* and thus inclined to disrupt the balance of polite gatherings with his arrogance and his contempt for others: "Since it is vanity and the desire to appear greater than others that motivates counterfeit scholars [*faux savants*] to study, no sooner do they take part in conversation, than the passion and the desire for advancement is reawakened in them and carries them away."[34] Malebranche's satirical portrayal closely resembles that of Marivaux, courtesy of Trublet:

> They are so fearful of not being above all those who listen to them that they are angered even when followed, infuriated when someone asks them for some clarification, and even take on a proud air in the face of the slightest disagreement. In short, they say things so novel and extraordinary, but so far removed from common sense, that the wisest men have difficulty not laughing, whereas others are simply dumbfounded by them.[35]

Marivaux, who wrote extensively about "the science of the human heart" insofar as he believed it to be universal but scarcely ever wrote a line about his own personal life, is thus portrayed as a prisoner of his own discourse, refracted through the distorting mirror of his malicious readers and the prejudices of his time. His work is used to document his personality, and his personality is invoked to explain the alleged excesses of his work. D'Alembert, Trublet, and Marmontel pass for their own personal testimony what was in reality a well established commonplace of *marivaudiana,* namely, the nagging accusation that Marivaux, out of self-indulgence and a misplaced authorial vanity, courted complexity for its own sake, thus degenerating and becoming "precious and affected."[36] To the abbé Desfontaines, Marivaux appeared as "an author whose figurative and sublime language was torture for the average man, profound in the metaphysics of the heart and an expert in the art of philosophizing about phantoms."[37] To d'Alembert, Marivaux's language was a "a twisted and precious jargon foreign to nature."[38] Voltaire famously wrote that Marivaux was capable of "balancing a fly's egg in a spiderweb," a formula in which we may recognize a touch of the *préciosité* it attributes to its victim and which stuck to Marivaux (though it was not directed exclusively at him, but at the language of the moderns as a whole).[39] Unsurprisingly, the sins of the author also became those of the man. Marivaux's own conversation was reportedly convoluted and tedious for its subtlety. At Mme de Tencin's, Marmontel reminisces, where the guests arrived fully rehearsed and ready to play their role, Marivaux was the most self-conscious of the bunch:

> As his works had gained him the reputation of a subtle mind, he felt obliged to prove that he always had that turn of mind, and so he was always looking for ideas conducive to comparison and analysis in order to set them against each other and to distill their essence. He would say that such and such was true up to a point or from a certain angle, but there was always some qualification or some distinction to make that only he could understand. Such awareness was arduous for him and often painful for others, but sometimes it yielded an unexpected insight and a bright revelation. Yet, from the apprehension in his eyes, one could see that he was anxious about his success. There never was, I believe, a more sensitive and frightened *amour-propre.*[40]

The very subtlety and attention that Marivaux devoted to uncovering and denouncing the many faces of *amour-propre* became, in the eyes of the public, a clear manifestation of the *amour-propre* of the author: like a woman who puts on too much rouge and ornament, the fop fails to seduce and becomes ridiculous. Style being equated with morality, stylistic refinement is seen as a sin, a proof of moral incontinence or of an effete nature. Rather than remaining within the limits of a severe and masculine atticism, Marivaux indulges the effeminate excesses of an Asian style that delights in words detached from their referent: "The style of those effeminate philosophers is scented with amber and musk, like that of Seneca," wrote Desfontaines.[41] Marivaux is both immoral and ridiculous because he wallows in orgies of linguistic intemperance.

Thus during his whole career Marivaux had to fight against the image of himself that was cut by his critics out of the cloth of his own works. But the battle was lost in advance. The weapon he had at his disposal being his own language, he only managed to give his detractors ever-renewed fodder. The more he protested, established new distinctions, and carefully presented his innovative ideas on language and style, the more he was rebuffed for affectation and obscurity. As Marivaux was accused of being unduly concerned with his reputation as an author, any effort on his part to redress that judgment was denounced as further proof of his vanity. Indeed, it was the author's vanity that was seen as the source of the obscurity of his language. Like Boucher, Marivaux was found guilty of being enamored with his technique and of having created a purely fantastic, formally overwrought world, of being incapable of inspiring the audience with the powerful emotions elicited by a true representation of reality: "Jussum se suaque solum amare."[42] The reproach of being vain must have been particularly stinging to Marivaux, who pursued in all his works a lucid appraisal of the political, hierarchical nature of relations in the society of orders and of the wounds inflicted by a universal snobbishness. The many ways in which individuals are duped by their desire to seek self-affirmation at the expense of others was for him an endless source of fascination. Pride and shame hold a true hegemony in Marivaux's narrative production; indeed, we may say that Marivaux devoted the best of his abilities to revealing the extent to which human relations are shaped by a desire to be recognized by others, to avoid humiliation and to save face, to avoid having inflicted on one or inflicting onto others a narcissistic wound: "Am I being betrayed? I may forget it; am I being hurt? I may forgive it; but do not humiliate me," are the closing words of *L'indigent philosophe*.[43]

We may say that in that sense, and in that sense only, Marivaux, though he never wrote directly about himself, in reality wrote about nothing but himself, as an author and a social being, under the cover of many masks and borrowing many voices. From the young coquette of *Lettres contenant une aventure* to the world-weary rogue of *L'indigent philosophe,* to the many impassioned male and female figures who tell their story and plead their case eloquently in the pages of *Le cabinet du philosophe,* Marivaux could say, "C'est moi." Beyond the accidental peculiarities of individual "character" (i.e., coded types), those voices reveal a skeletal psychology reduced to its essential components: pride and humility (or shame) in their endlessly varied combinations and incarnations.[44] Most of those voices stand for the author, each illustrating one aspect of the relationship between the author and his audience: they embody the author in his vulnerability, confronting his unknown reader—perhaps a judge, perhaps a sympathetic soul mate—now seducing, now attacking, now pleading with his audience.

Well before Proust (another snob and a fellow *bel esprit* or dandy), with whom he shares the keenest ear for the accent of self-deception in the social comedy, a defiant faith in his own style and in its power to reveal, through the sinuous unfolding of complex phrases, the hidden nature of reality and the emotions, Marivaux exposed his deepest anxieties and obsessions in the belief that they were universal: "Every soul, from the weakest to the strongest, from the vilest to the noblest, every soul resembles all the others: each one of them has something of them all. We all have a glimmer of what we are lacking, thanks to which we are able to feel and understand, to a greater or lesser extent, the differences that distinguish us."[45] Writing at the dawn of the modern, psychological novel, Marivaux was able to transcend the boundaries of the individual and the personal. Much like Proust, who came at the end of that tradition, he was able to overcome the limits of the self, as well as those of language and genre. Both writers analyzed the subtle shades of the moods of the "soul" in their infinite variations and combinations; the closer they looked at the "universal fabric" from which individuals were cut, the more they were drawn to dissolve individuality in favor of a "science of the human heart" that would analyze human behavior in its essential, atomistic components. Marivaux thought that we all carry within ourselves the universal traits that may potentially expose us to the totality of human emotions. "I have known myself as much as it is possible for anyone to know oneself," wrote the *Spectateur français,* "and when I compared that man to others, or others to him, I seemed to realize that we all resemble one another."[46] It was not so much individuality as a capacity to transgress the boundaries of the personal and a disposition to borrow the emotions of others that interested him; in his eyes, it was there that one could find the source of the moral and aesthetic experience.

Afflicted by the stigma of vanity, Marivaux never gave up the attempt to show that the source of his writing lay elsewhere, in an economy of disinterestedness and uncalculated generosity, the sign of a noble heart (a *belle âme*) and an irresistible creative drive. To him, writing, like conversation, was a gift that invited reciprocity on the part of the reader. Marivaux was acutely aware of the complexities and the pitfalls of such a relationship, and he tried several ways of engaging the reader in a dynamic exchange with the text, which, particularly in his journals, deploys itself in circuitous and digressive ways, through a wealth of reflections, sentences, and anecdotes and a host of variegated characters. Although they are only detached, errant "sheets" and emphatically presented as such, when read in their totality, Marivaux's fragmented journals function as a polyphonic ensemble. They offer a pattern of echoes and repetitions through subtle displacements; each piece resonates in relation to others, contradicting or complementing them. If there is a "secret chain," as Montesquieu was fond of suggesting in reference to the *Persian Letters,* for Marivaux too the chain is concealed: no visible hierarchy or design is imposed on the text; rather the reader is encouraged to take an active role and to shape and redraw the pattern as he traces his way along the textual labyrinth.

2

Fakes, Impostors, and Beaux Esprits

Conversation's Backstage

A rascal feels remorse all the time; it troubles and torments him, but the bel esprit *has no remorse.*

—Malebranche

Nothing is capable of inspiring so much aversion to art as having a look backstage: the imagination is disenchanted.

—Mercier

The Theater of Conversation

There was in Marivaux something that deeply disturbed those of his contemporaries who yearned for the redemptive value of archaic models and that sent them scrambling for the relief of satire. While he remained faithful to the aesthetics of *bel esprit* and the comic subversion that was practiced by the first generation of the *galants* (1640–70), he fashioned it into an entirely original poetics and raised it to a pitch that had never been reached before. Ever conscious of the fact that all self-expression implies a kind of spectatorial disjunction, he tried to include in his writing a critical reflection on the act of writing. Rather than being seduced into passive acceptance, the reader was never entirely allowed to forget that he was dealing with a fictional work and that fictionality itself was the issue being explored. *Esprit* was thus the synonym of a theatrical writing, of an ironic, self-referential discourse that reflected upon the conditions of its production. Marivaux's critics, however, saw nothing but an excess of vanity in the work of an author who was constantly mirroring himself in his writing. As was typical of aesthetic debates at the time, they saw as a moral issue what was in reality a different poetics; one might say it was a new poetics were it not rooted in the seventeenth-century aesthetics of *galanterie* that the *nouvelle vague* of the ancients had repudiated.

As we have seen, the concept that most often recurs in that criticism is that of *esprit* or *bel esprit* (though the meaning of the former was much more extensive, it was often used as a synonym of the latter).[1] The examples provide an embarrassment of riches. In 1722 the critic Pierre-François Guyot Desfontaines attacked "the modern *beaux esprits* . . . the chatter of cafés . . . that subtle and precious *esprit* that many authors try to pass as legitimate," and he clamored that "the corruption of style emerges most often from an excess of *esprit.*"[2] In 1735, in Prévost's journal *Le pour et contre,* the same Desfontaines declared: "I fervently take position against the abuse of *esprit,* and I side with truth and reason against bad taste and ignorance."[3] In 1755, recalling one of the last lectures that Marivaux delivered at the Academy, the playwright and satirist Alexis Piron recounted the public humiliation endured by "the shallowest among our *beaux esprits* and certainly the least Ciceronian."[4] What, then, was a *bel esprit* in the eighteenth century?

The concept cannot be quickly defined; its career was long and eventful. The term harks back to the early seventeenth century, when it was used to denote mastery of the language of love and understanding of its subtleties.[5] The word was not used primarily as a personal epithet (as in *to be* a *bel esprit*) but merely indicated the quality of a refined and cultivated mind (one *had* a *bel esprit*), mainly of the female mind. Many a heroine of *L'Astrée* and of Maynard's poetry was reverently qualified by her lover as having a *bel esprit;* in Corneille's *La place royale* Cléante refers to Phylis's flirting as *bel esprit.*[6] That meaning, which overlapped with that of *savante* ("learned" in the ways of love and courtship) and later with that of *précieuse,* was to endure in misogynistic parlance: several generations of anxious husbands and educators, from Arnolphe to Boileau to Rousseau, were to warn their readers against the dangers of wedding a woman who was endowed with a *bel esprit* or who was one herself.[7] Soon there emerged another meaning, not unrelated to the first, which denoted an ideal of *belles-lettres:* the *bel esprit* was a skilled author, someone who had a mastery of figural language; in the *Art poétique* Boileau used it to denote the writer. Eventually it came to indicate a fashionable writer who practiced literature not as a professional but as an amateur. The *bel esprit* was now a man, but he was always marked as feminine.[8] In other words, about 1640 the *bel esprit* denoted the accomplished *homme de lettres galant,* the author who most successfully embodied the synthesis between worldliness and verbal virtuosity, between orality and the written, if not always the published, work. Like the *honnête homme,* the true *bel esprit* (for there was a *vrai bel esprit* and a ridiculous *bel esprit,* much as there was a true *précieuse* and a *précieuse ridicule,* with the *ridicule* eventually taking over and erasing all traces of a positive connotation), has no pretensions and affects no ambitions *(ne se pique de rien).*[9]

In 1751 Duclos saw the *bel esprit* as an idle and fashionable amateur characterized by vanity and an unfounded belief in his universal competence, as well as an insidious rival of the true *homme de lettres.*[10] The connotation of vanity, both in the psychological and in the religious sense, appeared very early on: *beaux esprits* were often seen as freethinkers. Père Garasse's *Doctrine curieuse des beaux esprits de ce temps* (1623) was a rambling diatribe against those writers who were atheists, those "Narcisses," who were infected with "une estrange philautie amoureuse" (an extravagant love of themselves) that led them to worship their own *esprit.*[11] In a similar manner, Pierre Nicole and Nicolas Malebranche accused worldly writers and fashionable preachers of being diabolically narcissistic. They blamed not only the writer as a social type but the very fact of cultivating language, not as a means to reach some moral truth, but for the purely sensual pleasure of its figural dimension. Led astray by an excessive imagination, the *bel esprit,* Malebranche wrote, was no longer able to perceive reality as it was but inhabited the fictional world he had been bold enough to create: "He allows himself to be seduced by his own creation: instead of considering things as they are, as their ideas represent them, he is happy to live constantly under the sway of illusion and to applaud the fictions produced by his own mind."[12] Conversely, from the pen of more secular seventeenth-century writers the *bel esprit's plaisir du texte* was derided, not because it was too worldly, but because it was not worldly enough; that is, such language was seen as affected and unnatural, tainted either with effeminate pretentiousness or with the pedantry of an ill-digested scholarly upbringing. It did not correspond to the ideal of simplicity and naturalness that distinguished true worldliness.

One is puzzled by the persistence in the eighteenth century of a term that should hold little impact and significance. Now that the figure of the writer posing as an amateur has all but vanished, we would expect the term to vanish too.[13] Indeed, while the concept of *bel esprit* has been the object of extensive study for the seventeenth century, the issue has been declared moot for the eighteenth. Scholars of the Enlightenment have widely ignored the strategic relevance of the *bel esprit.* Alain Niderst notes that "the worldly, those who are attacked and disparaged, never make an issue of the *bel esprit*. Neither Perrault nor La Motte nor Marivaux ever mentions the *bel esprit*."[14] That is not true: the *bel esprit* is very much an issue in Marivaux's work, especially in his journals. His early novel *La voiture embourbée* (1713) features a chevalier *bel esprit*, an annoying babbler who perfectly embodies all the sins habitually imputed to the worldly, including Marivaux:

> He was a man who liked to talk a great deal, who finished every sentence with a satisfied glance at himself; a man whose demeanor glowed with conceit more than with reason; who would quibble about subtleties and delve into imaginary worlds; who would lose sight of his argument and would mislay others too; and who, despite the inanity of his chatter, would keep rambling on and on.[15]

But in his late essay *Réflexions sur l'esprit humain à l'occasion de Corneille et de Racine* (1750) the paradigm has changed entirely. Marivaux now distinguishes two types of "great men" and "benefactors to humanity": the *bel esprit* and the philosopher. The first is among

> those men of genius who are at times called *beaux esprits*; . . . those sublime painters of the wonder and the misery of the human soul, who, even as they educate us through their works, persuade us, by the pleasure they give us, that they have no purpose other than pleasing us and enchanting our leisurely hours. I count Corneille and Racine among the best of them, not mentioning those of our contemporaries whom it is too early to call publicly by name but who will be rewarded by posterity for their obscurity today, though the envy of their contemporaries, by its very fierceness, already offers them a kind of homage.[16]

It could not be any clearer that, at the end of a lifetime of mortifications, Marivaux has decided to wear the infamous label like a badge of honor and has gone on to declare a national day of *bel esprit* pride. He may well be the last one in the eighteenth century to use that term positively rather than as a foil or a disclaimer. Inverting all the expected paradigms of his neoclassical age, Marivaux's *bel esprit* (in contrast to the *philosophe*) harbors no ambition other than a modest desire to persuade through pleasure, not through didactic posturing: it is pleasure and leisure, rather than doctrinal enthusiasm, that carry the moral weight. National icons such as Corneille and Racine, themselves not always exempt from the accusation of having indulged in *esprit*,[17] have been enlisted as allies in a text that confronts the literary glory of *le petit goût* in much the same manner as the eulogies of *le grand goût* that were in vogue at the time. But Marivaux is not a dupe of eulogistic pomp (though he too is counting on posterity to redress today's humiliation). Great "geniuses," he notes ironically, become the object of a national cult when they are dead; as long as they are alive, they are derided as *beaux esprits:* "Our great men receive, while they are alive, the mundane and often derisive title of *beaux esprits;* but they are ennobled, after their demise, with that of 'men of genius,' which no one dares grudge them any longer."[18]

The fact is that in the eighteenth century the *bel esprit* was still very much at the center of the debate on the identity of *gens de lettres.* The persistence of the philosophes' attacks against it is a measure of the danger that such a model of the writer still posed to them. As late as 1783, though the ancients had long gained control of the republic of letters, d'Alembert, in his underhand eulogy of Marivaux, sounded an untimely cry of alarm. The republic of letters was threatened with an infectious disease that forestalled its impending decay. Writers like Marivaux were, of course, vehicles for such decadence: "The craze for *bel esprit* has invaded, not to say infected, every rank of the republic of letters and has led people to disregard every other kind of ambition. We call our learned ancestors *scholarly pedants;* they would call us, at best, *modish scholars* [*jolis écoliers*]."[19] But *bel esprit* was no longer all the rage in d'Alembert's time. Indeed, the future secretary of the French Academy paints an anachronistic picture for the late eighteenth century, and one that was certainly not true at a time in which sociable spaces (from the salons of Mme de Lambert and Mme de Tencin to those of Mmes Geoffrin, Lespinasse, and Necker), countless private academies, clubs, circles, and *sociétés* had opened themselves up to the philosophes and to the Enlightenment. Successful *gens de lettres* straddled the spaces of the *cabinet d'études,* of the academies and those of worldliness *(mondanité):* philosophy had become fashionable. Salonnieres played the role of cultural mediators and brokers between artists and writers, on the one hand, and the public of wealthy amateurs and government officials who controlled the state-sponsored institutions of letters (academies, state-sponsored journals, pensions, charges, and sinecures), on the other.[20] The republic of letters was the diversified milieu in which all those spaces and activities intersected.

More in tune with this evolution, in his *Encyclopédie* article "Gens de lettres" Voltaire pointed out that the men of letters (i.e., the philosophes) of his time had resurrected the universalist spirit of knowledge that had flourished in antiquity, when the *grammairien* was able to master not only linguistics but also geometry, philosophy, history, natural history, poetry, and eloquence. The breadth of knowledge of the modern *homme de lettres* was actually even wider, Voltaire noted, as he was now well versed not only in the classical languages but also in the modern European ones, in Spanish, and in English. To complete this flattering portrait of the well-rounded *homme de lettres,* which was very much a self-portrait, Voltaire celebrated his full integration into elite society. However, true to the self-sacrificial vision that the philosophes held of themselves, worldly success was presented by Voltaire not as personally advantageous to the *homme de lettres* but as a vehicle for educating and enlightening the nation, destroying prejudice and spreading far and wide the benefits of a critical spirit:

> One of the great advantages of our time is this large number of learned men who pass from thorny mathematics to the flower of poetry, and who are able to judge equally well a book on metaphysics and a play. The spirit of our time has made those men as suited to the cabinet as to the convivial gathering; in that respect, they are superior to those of the previous century. They were excluded from society until the days of Balzac and Voiture; since then, they have become an essential part of it. The refined and polished reason that they have disseminated in their writings has contributed a great deal to educating and to polishing the nation.[21]

Worldliness was portrayed by Voltaire, not as a self-serving career move, but as a critical way to reach and edify a wider public. That sense of civic and intellectual responsibility was essentially what distinguished an *homme de lettres* and a philosophe from a mere novelist or dramatist. The former were distinguished by their selfless dedication to public utility, while the latter were simply self-interested professionals enjoying variable success: "Those who, having read only novels, compose novels; those who, with a limited culture, have put together a few plays or have given a few sermons, are not *gens de lettres.*"[22] Laboring as if in a time-lag, d'Alembert in his complaint about *bel esprit* thus seems to echo a distant past.

To be sure, the *bel esprit* had once been a crucial player in contention for the appropriation of prestige and influence in the world of letters, but that was long before d'Alembert's time. In the first decades of the seventeenth century that contest had pitted the *savant*—the erudite scholar and the scientist—against the *mondain* and the *galant* (or the *bel esprit*), who practiced *belles lettres,* for control of the relevant places in the academies, in the salons, and in the awarding of royal sinecures and pensions. While there had been several attempts to reconcile those two currents of the world of letters, for example, by Pellisson and Guez de Balzac, others, such as the Chevalier de Méré (the embodiment of the worldly aristocrat), would widen the gap between science and worldliness: "I told a learned man, the other day, that he talked like an author. 'So what,' he replied, 'isn't that who I am?' 'You are indeed too much of an author,' I replied laughing, 'and you would do much better to talk as a polite man [*en galant homme*]. For no matter how learned you are, you should never talk in a way that men who are intelligent and worldly cannot understand.'"[23]

The dreadful caricature of Hortensius in Sorel's *Francion* is another example of the intended marginalization of the professor of philosophy, or the *savant*, who was depicted as haunting the colleges, wearing long, dirty robes, and babbling in a scholastic jargon *(galimatias)*. Such exaggerations were to a great extent traditional stuff inherited from the Renaissance debates about humanism and scholasticism. They certainly did not describe the actual career of someone like the Jesuit abbé Dominique Bouhours (1628–1702), a linguist and a stylistician, a teacher, as well as a precursor of aesthetics, whose comments on the nature of *bel esprit* and the *je ne sais quoi* were widely circulated. The abbé, who was a conciliatory figure in the debates between the ancients and the moderns, had an exemplary career that covered a variety of social and scholarly venues, from the colleges to the court to the salons. He was able to juggle a lifelong position as a research scholar at the prestigious Collège de Clermont (later the Collège Louis Le Grand), service at court in the form of a preceptorship to Colbert's son, the Marquis de Seignelay, and assiduous attendance at the salons of Mme de Sablé, Madeleine de Scudéry, and the scholarly circle of President de Lamoignon. It is true that the abbé's career peaked around 1670–85, at a time when the *savants* and the ancients had regained their influence over the worldly. To a great extent, relations between the two factions always remained contentious. At the end of the century we can hear a note of bitterness in the words of La Bruyère, who is still pleading for the integration of the *savant* among the polite public:

> Some persons are strongly prejudiced against learned men [*savants*]; they are declared unfit for worldly politeness, tactless, wanting in human skill, unsociable, and are sent back, stripped in this way, to their cabinet and their books. . . . However, it seems to me that people ought to be more careful and take the trouble of wondering whether that same spirit which produces such great progress in the sciences, which makes people think well, judge well, speak well, and write well, might not also help them to become civil.[24]

Foreshadowing the major arguments of Dumarsais's influential essay *Le philosophe,* La Bruyère claims for the *savant* the independent space of the *cabinet d'études,* as well as the public space of worldliness. In his eyes, as in those of the later philosophes, there is a continuity between a disposition to sociability (*l'esprit de société*) and scientific *esprit*.

A wealth of connotations were clustered around the meaning of *bel esprit*. Much like other notions of seventeenth-century aesthetics, the term denoted both a form of writing—a mode of seeing and knowing, a style—and a character—that of the writer who practiced such a form. That was inevitable at a time when literary style was coextensive with manners, when the abbé Bouhours could speak of "the politeness of style" because the qualities that made a good style were of the same order as those that made an *honnête homme*. (Later in the Enlightenment the same correlation between style and character became morally and politically inflected.) The *Dictionnaire de l'Académie* (both the 1695 and the 1740 edition) defined *beaux esprits* as "those who distinguish themselves from ordinary people because of the politeness of their discourse and their works." When the equilibrium between politeness, amateurism, and the practice of *belles lettres* was upset, about 1670, the *bel esprit* became, if not an outright negative figure, like the *précieux,* at least an ambiguous one, one that needed the qualification of "true," as in *le vrai bel esprit*. It came to equate affectation in style with affectation in social interaction; thus the *bel esprit* came to suffer, in his turn, a fate similar to that previously endured by the *savant* Hortensius.

Affectation was the charge leveled at the protagonist of Montesquieu's *Histoire véritable,* a charge that the fashionable young author of the *Persian Letters* knew perhaps all too well:

> I was very popular with every circle, and I was given the task of being entertaining, which afflicted me very much. I was forbidden from saying anything stupid, even though everybody else took astonishing liberties on that count. On the other hand, there were some socialites who said that they avoided me because I was a *bel esprit*. What they meant was that I was affected and they were natural and that had they wanted it, they would have been cleverer than I was.[25]

The *bel esprit* is as much a victim of his own pretensions as of those of the public. Paraded in the salons as an amusing phenomenon, he is appointed to the role of official entertainer by hostesses, who want to get as much value out of him as they feel entitled to expect from a professional author. Forecasting Montesquieu's predicament, Molière's writer Damon, invited to dinner by a *précieuse,* is expected to defray his social obligations with some display of his trademark wit:

You know the man and his insurmountable laziness in conversation. She had invited him to supper as a *bel esprit,* and he never appeared so dull, among half a dozen people who were expecting him as a treat and who were staring at him wide-eyed as if he were of a different species from them. They all thought that he was there to defray the conversation and that every word coming out of his mouth must be a witticism or an impromptu, and that he would ask for a drink with an epigram. But he disappointed them all with his silence; and the lady was as dissatisfied with him as I was with her.[26]

Since the *bel esprit* had presented himself squarely as an amateur and a disinterested practitioner of letters, that disinterestedness was precisely what came under scrutiny when the ideal went into decline (i.e., when it became too widespread). "A *bel esprit* is a ridiculous character, indeed," says Eugène, one of the interlocutors of the abbé Bouhours's *Entretiens d'Ariste et d'Eugène* (1671).

"And I am not quite sure whether I would not prefer to pass for a simpleton rather than for what goes ordinarily under the name of *bel esprit*." "Every reasonable person thinks as you do," replied Ariste. "*Bel esprit* is now so disdained since it has been spoiled by its popularity that the most talented people hide what they do as if it were a crime. . . . There is a world of difference between *being a bel esprit by trade* and having a talent for certain things [*avoir l'esprit beau*]."[27]

In the article "Esprit," Voltaire writes in the same terms: "The bel esprit is an advertisement [*affiche*]; it is an art that requires some culture, it is a *kind of profession,* and for that reason it makes one vulnerable to envy and ridicule."[28] In a novel published in 1744 Charles Duclos aptly sums up the paradox that lurks in a term that may be used either to mock or to praise: "As for the *bel esprit,* so envied, so abused, so sought after, laying a claim to it is almost as ridiculous as truly being one is difficult."[29] The *bel esprit* is now seen as an impostor both in his function as a writer and as a member of polite society. He is an untalented writer who exploits his social relations in order to advance his career. That is the brunt of La Bruyère's ferocious satire of Fontenelle, in which the *secrétaire perpétuel* of the Academy of Sciences is portrayed under the name Cydias: "Ascanius is a sculptor, Hegio an iron-founder, Aeschines a fuller, and Cydias a *bel esprit*—that's his trade. He has a signboard, a shop, he works on command and has craftsmen working under him. . . . He is a compound of pedantry and *préciosité,* made to be admired by provincial bourgeois, in whom there is nothing great except the opinion he has of himself."[30] The mediocrity of the writer is echoed by that of the public whose approval he seeks just as in Molière's *Les femmes savantes* the preposterous Trissotin deserves the adoration of a deluded Bélise and in *Les précieuses ridicules* mainstream, Parisian world-liness is attacked under cover of attacking its bourgeois, provincial epigones. Fontenelle's successful attempt to merge academic activities with the rituals of sociability (he turned the Academy's public sessions into broadly attended, worldly events, thus giving the philosophe and the scientist further legitimacy in the public eye) played against him—a strange indictment coming from La Bruyère, who had plaintively argued against the marginalization of the *homme de lettres*.[31] Because he had hoped to straddle both worlds, the *bel esprit* ends up exiled from both. But in the eighteenth century it is the Mérés, not the Hortensiuses, who are the object of ridicule.

A common stock character of eighteenth-century satire is the *bel esprit* who fakes the rules of conversational improvisation. Patrice Leconte's film *Ridicule* (1996), which provides a rather trite portrayal of worldly manners (a must in the majority of today's depictions of eighteenth-century French society, which seem to have inherited Rousseau's prejudice against worldliness), features an odious abbé, aptly named Vilecourt. The abbé, an ambitious and scheming *bel esprit* (he will eventually be mistaken, much to his discomfiture, for an *esprit fort,* that is, a freethinker or atheist), masks his ineptitude at improvisation by having his mistress help him cheat at the game of *bouts-rimés.*[32] Punishment awaits him. Having argued, in front of Louis XVI and the court, the existence of God, the abbé promises that the next time he will argue the opposite; in-stead, he is promptly disgraced. The source of the anecdote, which is related by Diderot, is located not in the eighteenth century but in the sixteenth and features Cardinal du Perron as Vilecourt and Henri III as Louis XVI.[33] A similar character appears in the *Persian Letters.* Through the thin walls of his dingy lodgings Rica overhears a conversation between two aspiring *beaux esprits.* "I don't know why it is, but everything seems to turn against me," says the first interlocutor.

> "For at least three days I have not said one noteworthy thing. I find myself thrown pell-mell into conversation, with no one paying the least attention or speaking to me twice. I had prepared various sallies to enliven my con-versation, but no one lets me get them off. I had a fine story to tell, but whenever an opportunity approached, people evaded it as if on purpose. For four days several witticisms have been growing stale in my head without my ever using them. . . . Let me tell you, a reputation for wit [*bel esprit*] is hard to achieve, and I don't know how you managed it." "I have an idea," the other replied, "let's work together on this and form an association for the production of wit. Every day we will agree on our subject of conversation, . . . We will agree upon the places where approval should be voiced, where

to smile and where to burst into full laughter. You will see that we will give tone to every conversation, and that people will admire our lively wit and apt repartees. . . . Do what I say and I promise you a place in the Academy in less than six months."[34]

This petty conspiracy between two unimaginative parvenus of letters indicates that in the eyes of the satirist the ethos of conversation is thoroughly suspect. The pleasure that engaged the *honnête homme* and the *galant* through the communal flowering and exchange of verbal gifts was ideally conceived as a moral education and an exercise in social virtue.[35] Under ideal conditions conversation consisted in spontaneity and improvisation, in the free expenditure of evanescent orality: "Conversation must seem so free that it should give the impression that no thought is ever rejected, that we are allowed to say everything that comes to mind, with no preconceived intent to talk about one thing rather than another," said Sappho, Mlle de Scudéry's fictional alter ego.[36] In Montesquieu's personal notebooks, the reality of verbal interaction as he actually experienced it in Mme de Lambert's and Mme de Tencin's salons for once trumped the drive to satirize: "The spirit of conversation is what is generally called *esprit* among the French. It consists in a dialogue, generally good-humored, in which each person, without being too attentive to oneself, talks and is talked back to, in which everything is treated in an abrupt, quick, and lively manner."[37] (While he remarked on his intractable shyness, Montesquieu also diligently reported in his notebooks some of the witticisms and repartees that he had been fortunate enough to produce over the years.)[38] But in the *Persian Letters* such reality is approached obliquely, from the angle of satire (such debunking being proof of the weight and consequence of the ideal). Rather than seeing conversation as the privileged space for the exercise of a collective, oral kind of art that requires perfect timing, self-control, and virtues like reciprocity, complaisance, concern for others, and surrender of one's *amour-propre*, the ambitious *beaux esprits* have turned it into a forum for their social advancement and literary career. The spurious *beaux esprits* collect the stuff of extemporaneous orality. They capitalize on what should have been the expression of a wasteful (aristocratic) economy of verbal brilliance and turn it into an academic career. Conversation is like a game that has no purpose other than the fugitive pleasure it creates, but the fake *beaux esprits* rig that game so as to stake the odds in their favor.

What goes around comes around: Rica's satire of the *bel esprit* comes back to haunt its author in the *Mémoires* of Jean-François Marmontel. Like Montesquieu, Marmontel is fond of directing his barbs against the salons he frequents, particularly Tencin's and Geoffrin's. A newcomer to the Parisian literary scene in 1745, the young author (then a protégé of Voltaire's and a secretary to the financier La Popelinière) traces his first steps in the salon of Mme de Tencin, where he meets Montesquieu, Fontenelle, Mairan, Marivaux, and Helvétius and where he hopes to find ways to free himself from dependence on a private patron. However, Marmontel becomes quickly convinced that

> there was too much *esprit* for me. I realized that everybody came fully pre-
> pared to play his role and that the desire to be on stage did not allow con-
> versation to flow naturally and effortlessly. It was a race for grabbing, before
> everyone else, the chance to place one's own witticism, one's anecdote, apho-
> rism, or one-liner, and one would often grab that chance by the skin of its
> teeth. Marivaux was obviously keen to show his penetration and his sagacity.
> Montesquieu, more calm, would wait for an opportunity, but one could see
> that he was waiting for it. Mairan was on the hunt for the right moment.
> . . . Only Fontenelle would let things run their course and get his chance
> without tampering with things. He profited from the attention of others so
> sparingly that his witticisms and his tales never took more than a minute.[39]

Like Rica, the young Marmontel sees himself lifting the curtain and enter-
ing backstage in order to uncover the workings of authorial vanity. Effort,
not pleasure, and self-interest, not attention to others, regulate the exchange.
The apparent spontaneity of conversation masks the participants' anxiety to
occupy center stage and the rivalry between the guests. Everything has been
staged in advance, and each actor struggles to deliver his set piece before the
others. Fontenelle, the old player, is vindicated against La Bruyère's satire, but
Marivaux's and Montesquieu's eagerness to "place" their contribution betrays
a desire for public approval that diminishes them. Tales, anecdotes, aphorisms,
deft expressions, fine witticisms, the genres that ought to thrive in extemporaneous communality, are in reality the effect of individual work and struggle,
and as such, they are ridiculous. They constitute the loose fabric of vanity,
trifles that serve no purpose other than self-promotion.

The satirical theme of the rigged conversation appears too frequently in
the literature of the seventeenth and eighteenth centuries not to be revealing
of something important.[40] Much of that literature was in fact based on orality, both as a practice and as a fictional form featured in written works that
were presented as though they were transcriptions of actual conversations.
The culture of conversation held on to the Platonist ideal of the *furor poeti-
cus*. It pretended to devalue labor and effort, which it declared pedantic and
debased, and it saw creative grace as the effect of a noble, aristocratic disposi-

tion overflowing with an innate talent. In reality, no one was entirely the dupe of that myth. The good conversationalist was much like a jazz musician: the outpouring grace of one hour of improvisation on the stage was the product of years of labor and practice and the mastery of standards that were the starting point of infinite variations, the bedrock of tradition on which personal innovation and creativity laid their foundation. The greater the preparation and effort that took place behind the scene, the easier and more natural the performance would appear. (The same went for the "improvisation" of the *commedia dell'arte,* which was also based on the control of verbal and gestural *topoi.*) In the reality of *ancien régime* sociability, whether it was worldly or academic, there was no dichotomy between *savoir* and *bel esprit,* between rhetorical expertise and the virtuosity of worldly conversation: both talents (for men, at least) were sharpened in the *collèges.* It was the purpose of a good Jesuit education to have the students master oral as much as written composition; the rhetorical exercise of the *extemporanea oratio,* which prepared the students to react quickly and to immediately come up with the appropriate answer, relied upon memorization and *inventio,* that is, upon the creative use of a wealth of commonplaces, anecdotes, portraits, maxims, witticisms, and poems, many of which were published in countless collections of *anas.*[41]

The challenge for the conversationalist as for the writer—and it is important to remember that most *gens de lettres* were both—was to master one's craft well enough to produce the effect of spontaneity and total *à propos* (or propriety) both orally and in writing. Those who could not master that art betrayed the "professionalism" of their craft and the fundamental imposture of improvisation; they could not hide the effort that a more successful artist and conversationalist was able to keep under control. Their sincerity and disinterestedness, qualities traditionally required of the Ciceronian orator, were also at stake. Those considerations are important because conversation was not subservient to the written work: it was a form of art in its own right, one that entered in a fruitful exchange with the written work. We would be greatly mistaken if, in order to understand its relevance and significance, we were to turn to its exponents in a later age, such as Proust: Mme Verdurin and the Princesse de Guermantes can no more explain Mme de Tencin or Mme Necker than Proust himself can explain Diderot.[42] Toward the end of the eighteenth century, when worldly orality had lost favor with a literary establishment eager to reach the whole nation through the written and published work, through journals, and through the theater, even a detractor of worldly orality such as Mercier wrote enthusiastically about Diderot's excellence in this art form:

The man in Paris who talks the best about all the arts and whose inexhaustible conversation is not inferior to his style, the man who fills you with enthusiasm in his cabinet even more than in his works, that man is Diderot. I have never heard a more eloquent, more lucid, more varied speech. No one can, like him, join naturally and forcefully so many diverse expressions; no one is more capable of delivering so many ideas and so many lively and colorful turns of phrase. He is to be considered a first-rate improviser.[43]

As for the fact that the dialogism of conversation is the structuring principle of Diderot's own writings, from his philosophical dialogues (one of which features Mlle de Lespinasse, a prominent salonniere) to *Jacques le fataliste,* that is a point I need not belabor further.

The charge of "professionalism" that was thrown at the *bel esprit* must be understood not only in the sense of someone holding a profession (a *métier*) and making a profitable trade out of a noble art but also in the sense of *professing* or affirming something, of publicly declaring one's position and identity (just as one may profess a belief or a faith). The *bel esprit* was always accused of wearing his role on his sleeve, as a label: to him, *esprit* was something to be displayed. For La Bruyère, Voltaire, and Duclos, the *bel esprit* was someone who was unable to give himself up entirely to his creation, a self-conscious writer who made a show of his craft or a bad actor who let his own voice smother that of the character. *Esprit* moved the audience's attention away from the object toward the subject of enunciation and was thus an effect of *amour-propre,* the root of all evil. That is why the attacks on Marivaux's style often involved a critique of the author himself. Morality and aesthetics thus converged to condemn a certain form of theatricalized self-consciousness.

Illusion Rediscovered

In a letter intended to mollify his longtime rival, Voltaire made the following appraisal of Marivaux's theater:

It is true that I sometimes wish that he had a style less polished and that he treated more noble subjects. . . . I would disapprove of his representing the passions with too much detail and of missing the pathway to the heart by taking roundabout ways. I would like his *esprit* even more if he were willing to show less of it! Indeed, a character in a play ought not to appear witty [*spirituel*]; he must be so despite himself and without being aware of it.[44]

Ironically, in his dealings with the Théâtre-Français Marivaux had advocated the type of unselfconscious acting required by Voltaire, one similar to that of the Italian actors, who were successful because they were able to play as if the spectators were not there. "They never seem to be conscious of the implications of what they say, and yet the spectators are." But he never got his wish because he encountered the resistance of the French actors: "Despite my repeated efforts, the French actors' obsession with appearing witty [*montrer de l'esprit*] was stronger than my humble remonstrations, and they preferred, out of vanity, persistently to misinterpret the text rather than to appear the dupes of their role."[45] But Marivaux was fated to provide fodder to his critics and to see his own ideas turned against him. To Voltaire, Marivaux's characters lacked an independent, all-rounded life and were nothing but a vehicle for the author's vain display of *esprit*. While enthusiasm carries the genius beyond himself and into his character, *esprit,* vampirelike, drains the life out of one's own creation and forces the audience constantly to face the author's insignificant self. In his *Lettre sur l'esprit* Voltaire made that point again, this time selecting his gallery of bad examples from Corneille, Racine, and Fléchier: "All that flash . . . is not suited to a serious work, which must absorb the audience. What happens, then, is that while all the audience wants to see the character, the author usurps all the attention."[46]

Such vanity has the unfortunate result of leading the writer to sacrifice the *faith,* the belief in the illusion he has created, for the sake of the *admiration* he craves. Without such illusion, however, there can be no real emotion on the part of the spectator. In that respect, Voltaire's position echoes that of Diderot and harks back to the aesthetic tenets of early classicism, which, in turn, borrowed heavily from the theatrical poetics of the Italian Renaissance.[47] In 1623 Jean Chapelain wrote in his *Préface à l'Adonis du Chevalier Marin* that catharsis *(purgation)* required that the spectator undergo an emotional event that he could not experience without immersing himself in the truthlike illusion of the spectacle: "[The willing suspension of disbelief] is followed by faith or confidence in the subject; that is of crucial importance, because wherever belief is lacking, attention and affect are lacking too; and where there is no affect, there is no emotion and, as a consequence, no purging of the human passions, which is the function of [dramatic] poetry. Faith, therefore, is absolutely necessary to the theater."[48] It was because he was unable to sustain such faith that the *galant* and *précieux* Corneille found no grace in the eyes of Mirzoza, the sultan's favorite and a brilliant critic in Diderot's Oriental fantasy *Les bijoux indiscrets:*

> "I do not know the rules," continued the favorite, "much less the learned words by which they are expressed; but I do know that truth alone can please

and touch an audience. I also know that perfection in a play consists in an imitation of an action so perfect that the spectator, continually deceived, imagines himself part of the action itself. Now, is there anything similar to this in the tragedies you have just praised to us?" . . . "At least, Madame," replied Selim, "you will not deny that if the episodes distract us from the illusion, the dialogue brings us back to it. I do not know anyone who understands this better than our tragedians." "Then nobody understands it," retorted Mirzoza. "Their bombast, glibness [*esprit*] and ostentation [*papillotage*] are a thousand miles from nature. The author may try to hide in vain, but my eyes are keen and I incessantly see him behind his characters. Cinna, Sertorius, Maximus and Aemilia are Corneille's speaking trumpets on every page."[49]

The self-conscious brilliance of the style is said to rip the veil of illusion and to prevent the spectator from being drawn into the emotions of the spectacle. Toward the end of the century such a concern for the integrity of theatrical illusion will prompt the proponents of the *drame* to do away with verse, which raises distracting applause for authorial skill. Ironically, Voltaire saw the tables turned on himself when his turn came to become the target of the by now ubiquitous critique he had once formulated against others: "Monsieur de Voltaire has become *epic* in his *Oedipe* and his *Alzire*, in *Sémiramis*, in the first scene of *Orosmane*," wrote Mercier, "seduced by a pompous elocution that is applauded by the parterre. His confidants are often given the best lines because he likes to be admired, but as soon as the verse forces us to admire the poet, the verse for sure has killed the character. And then what is left of illusion?"[50]

Theatricality on the stage and in the act of writing had been a constant feature of the genre of the burlesque and the mock-heroic literature illustrated by Sorel and Scarron, which Marivaux had illustrated in his youth with *Pharsamon*, *Télémaque travesti*, and *L'iliade travestie*. The burlesque was an eminently self-conscious genre that relied upon a comic reflection on the forms of writing and on fictional conventions. It aimed less to be believed by the reader than to cautioning him or her against the dangers of such belief, because the purpose of this literature was precisely to undermine the power of illusion conveyed by the genres it parodied, such as the epic poem or the heroic, sentimental novel. A good example of such a display of self-consciousness in the burlesque novel is illustrated by Marivaux's delightful preface to *La voiture embourbée*, which parodistically embroiders on the conventions of *captatio benevolentiae:*

> This is a pleasant and amusing book; the transitions are effortless, there are many original surprises. If this is so, we have here a good book. But who

says so? It's me, the author. Oh, people will say, how quaint are those authors with their prefaces full of praise for their own works! But you, reader, how difficult you are! You absolutely require a preface, and then you protest when the author says what he really thinks of his book. You must agree that if he thought that the book was no good, he would not have it published. I agree, you reply. But an attitude of reserve, perhaps even of humility, must, when he speaks of his book, throw a veil of decency upon his real feelings. Let him be vain and fearless (for being contemptuous of a work one is about to publish is worthy of a madman); but being proud of one's work and announcing it modestly: that should be the conduct of a prudent author who, unable to hide his satisfaction completely, would wear a mask of reserve in order to avoid the ridicule of having his feelings made public. Fine. I agree. I was wrong. I have spoken too openly; I am going to put on a mask. Now, my reader ought to know that in publishing this story I am not so conceited as to think that I am offering him anything special; some friends, flatterers, no doubt, have forced me to publish it, but . . . But enough! will cry some cranky misanthropist. . . . I cannot stand this phony humility, this ridiculous combination of hypocrisy and conceit that afflicts most authors. I much prefer an open expression of conceit to the detours of bad faith. And as far as I am concerned, Monsieur the misanthropist, I'd rather publish a book with no preface than sweat and please no one.[51]

The theatricalization of the author involves that of the reader and of the act of writing. At a time in which, as Christian Jouhaud puts it, "every action was also a demonstration of the capacities of its agent, hence a confirmation of his social and symbolic status," this approach was particularly suited to the satirical staging of the writer's uncertain advance in a world that was rife with danger.[52] The dialogue between "author" and "reader"—both textual effects— prefigures many of the themes that appear in Marivaux's subsequent works, especially in the journals; it enacts a strategy of preemptive strike. The fictional author is represented as ludicrously paralyzed by a self-reflexive mood; all his statements revert to questions of authorial intent and to the conventions of literary discourse. This aspect of the burlesque will flourish, as we know, in Sterne's *Tristram Shandy.* It is a peculiarity of the burlesque that the reader is faced with an avowedly incompetent author: unable to tell a story straightforwardly, the author does little more than write about writing; his acute self-consciousness appears as a sterile exercise. The author can never control his multiple reflections in the eyes of others: the more he protests, answers, and preempts objections, the more he becomes mired in his own argument and in countless digressions. The audience is embodied in a multitude of voices contesting one another. Such dialogism anticipates the multiplicity of characters who, in turn, take the stage in Marivaux's journals, none speaking unequivocally for the author and each representing at least one side of him. But more important, the theme of the author's *amour-propre* is woven into a reflection on the nature of illusion, embodied in the image of the mask (particularly the mask of false modesty, which in his eyes fares worse than straightforward vanity), a central theme in Marivaux's work. Even the character of the misanthropist, the intolerant rigorist who preaches sincerity to others but is unaware of his own latent hypocrisy (here Rousseau comes to mind), resurfaces in a more developed form in his subsequent work.

The language of the burlesque was the vehicle for an ironic reflection on the act of writing, in which the author's ineptitude necessarily turned him into the sole protagonist. But when, in *La vie de Marianne,* Marivaux imported those themes from the burlesque to the serious novel and to journalistic writing, he overstepped a boundary. He was seen as drawing on a tradition that was increasingly being portrayed as unseemly. What had been a widespread literary practice was now seen as a personal vice and a breach of the pact of illusion that novelists had been observing since the times of Du Plaisir. In the *Sentiments sur les lettres et sur l'histoire, avec des scrupules sur le style,* composed in 1683 in the wake of the success of Mme de Lafayette's *nouvelle historique,* Du Plaisir had formalized the new rules illustrated by the *nouvelle,* which set it apart from the *roman* or *poème héroïque,* which had fallen out of favor (of course, the decline of the *roman héroïque* had been accompanied by a parallel decline of the burlesque, which was the flip side of the heroic style). Thus, Du Plaisir had recommended that the novelist conceal any sign of his presence and avoid interfering with the narrative and the dialogue of the characters:

> The novelist must everywhere appear polite, but he cannot appear witty [*spirituel*]. He cannot give free rein to his *esprit;* in other words, he cannot enter into lengthy reflections. . . . The author must seem witty despite himself; that is to say, he must use all his resources [*tout son esprit*] in order to compose a spontaneous conversation that gives the impression that it is the characters who speak, not him.[53]

The new emphasis placed on the illusion of reality in the novel paralleled the major turn that some forty years earlier had transformed the French theater and the spectatorial response to the stage. That transformation had been accompanied by the formalization of rules intended to preserve the integrity of verisimilitude or illusion in the theater. It was for the sake of illusion (the term *vraisemblance* was preferred over a word that smacked of demonic possession, deceit, or optical trickery)[54] that all consciousness of acting and of the presence of spectators, all awareness of the conventional character of stage rules, had to be suppressed. Thus d'Aubignac wrote:

> The author should arrange everything as if there were no spectators, which means that all the characters must move and speak as if they really were kings, not Bellerose or Mondory; as if they were in Horace's palace in Rome, not in the Hôtel de Bourgogne in Paris; as if no one heard and saw them but those who were on the stage with them and inside the [fictional] space represented. . . . This must be scrupulously observed, because any interaction with the spectators is a flaw.[55]

The spectator had to be made to feel that he was witnessing an actual event, not watching a spectacle. The world on stage must be autonomous and self-enclosed, emancipated from all explicit or figurative reference to an author, a spectator, and a theatrical setting. The theoreticians believed that it was this very distanciation and the bracketing of all awareness of fictionality that allowed the spectator to be drawn into the spectacle, transported out of his body, so to speak, onto the scene. Thus, all metatheatrical elements, such as the prologue addressing the audience, the actor's asides *(apartés),* the *stances* and the lengthy tirades, which were frequent in the baroque theater of the early seventeenth century (until approximately 1730), had to be suppressed.[56]

In that context we can better understand the disapproval felt at the time of its publication for Marianne's first-person theatricality, for her continuous reference to an audience, and for her divided self, all of which were manifest in her tendency to double the narrative with extensive commentaries. To its critics, those features were the effect of an unwanted awareness of fictionality; the narrator, however, presented them as precisely the opposite, that is, as proofs of the narrative's authenticity. Only true memoirs (or a truly original novel, for, of course, that was the drift) could be written in such an unfashionable style: "If that were an invented story, very likely it would not have the form it has. Marianne would not make such lengthy and frequent reflections; there would be more facts and less morals; in other words, it would be more in line with today's established taste. . . . People expect adventures, and adventures only; but Marianne, in writing hers, did not care for that."[57] Moreover, as *Marianne* was published in installments, its author had plenty of time to incorporate the criticism of the novel into his text (a device also amply exploited in his journals). Thus, to add insult to injury, in answering that criticism Marianne not only commented on her adventures but also commented on the critics' commentaries. It is not surprising that to his critics Marivaux's dedication to such poetics must have looked like perverse obstinacy.

In fact, Marivaux's writing alternates between preserving and suspending the illusion of verisimilitude, between, on the one hand, the belief in the impenetrable integrity of the fictional world and, on the other, the pleasure of puncturing that perfect façade through a suggestive reflection on the conditions that make illusion possible and the investigation of the moral status of illusion for both reader and writer. Marivaux never ceased to explore the interpenetration between reality and fiction, truth and verisimilitude, both in the realm of literature and in that of personal character. In the eyes of his critics, however, this interest was imputed not to the writer's choice of a poetics but to a peculiar defect of his nature, that is, to an excessive *amour-propre.* Marivaux shared this belief that mimetic illusion was inseparable from the issue of the moral illusion created by *amour-propre.* In the Augustinian tradition he draws from, *amour-propre* is associated with fiction and spectacles. In the grip of vanity, we turn ourselves into objects to be beheld, and by relying upon a wealth of exempla gleaned from our readings, we create a fictional self that feeds parasitically upon the real one, which we nurture and worship like an idol. *Amour-propre* leads us to replace the bleak reality of our wretched selves with self-aggrandizing fictions and to legitimize them through the mediation of the audience we have duped, the greatest dupe being, of course, ourselves, for the self, dissociated in the roles of actor and spectator, is the ultimate theatrical stage and the privileged audience for its own antics.[58] Self-reflexivity is the fundamental mode of existence of *amour-propre,* which is no more than conscience's obsessive self-mirroring and folding back upon itself—self-awareness run amok. *Amour-propre* is an essentially theatrical *form.*

The Disenchanted Spectator

Throughout the journals, Marivaux mingles discussions on style and authorial intention with anecdotes illustrating the vanity of various characters, in particular coquettish young women. Many of those stories raise the issue of self-deception and self-theatricalization, with characters who deceive others by deceiving themselves first. The narrator takes full advantage of the freedom offered by the genre and goes back and forth between the metanarrative analysis of his poetics and the narratives of various characters, who are sometimes embedded in his discourse and sometimes speak in the first person. Meaning thus emerges from the juxtaposition of jarring elements. By alternating discussions on the conditions that make illusion possible with anecdotes illustrating the perverseness of illusion as such, the narrator never allows the reader to become a passive recipient. While becoming involved in the pathos of the characters, the reader is on the alert, encouraged to pay close attention to the context of enunciation.

Thus the various anecdotes on the vanity of women have a figural function: they are emblematic of the authorial situation. A striking example appears in the much-quoted passage that opens the first issue of *Le spectateur français,* published in May 1721. The narrator presents himself as a misanthropist, a world-weary old man cut from the same cloth as the narrator of La Bruyère's *Caractères,* that is, a Christian orator who wants nothing for himself but the moral improvement of his readers: "Neither the orator nor the writer is able to conceal the joy he feels in being applauded; but they ought to blush if they aim at nothing but praise in their speeches and writings. . . . We should speak and write only in order to instruct."[59] Similarly, Marivaux's *Spectateur* likes to observe others but has no wish to be seen; he is above the social and the literary fray:

> Be as it may, I wish my reflections to be useful. Perhaps they will be; it is only for that reason that I am publishing them, not in order to prove that I am talented [*si l'on me trouvera de l'esprit*]. . . . Besides, my advanced age, my travels, an old habit of living only for listening and watching, my experience: everything has softened my *amour-propre* and made me indifferent to the many small pleasures that people draw from vanity. So that should my friends tell me that I pass for a *bel esprit,* I would not be pleased. On the contrary, were I to realize that someone had profited from my reflections and been cured of some flaw, that would really touch me and give me the kind of satisfaction that I could truly appreciate.[60]

The narrator then proceeds to recount an episode of his youth that he presents as a foundational experience and the source of his current misanthropy. When he was seventeen, he gave his affections to a young woman who seemed to him as attractive as she was simple and unaffected:

> I was sure that she was so unaware of her good looks that she ignored them completely. I was so naïve in those days! What a joy, I would tell myself, to be loved by a girl who does not wish to have lovers, since she is beautiful without paying any attention to it, and therefore she is not vain! . . . Was she sitting or standing? talking or walking? She always seemed unconscious of how she looked.[61]

What a treasure this girl is who is entirely devoid of *amour-propre* and has no notion of the coquette's derivative sense of identity. Unlike the coquette's, her existence is autonomous: she does not need others because she does not need to be seen in order to feel that she exists. Rather than searching into their eyes for that precious reflection of their love that can never quite fill the coquette's inner void 'and inexhaustible need, this girl allows herself to be the purely passive object of someone else's gaze: she ignores the reciprocity of desire. Marivaux, a great parodist of Fénelon, was familiar with the portrait of Antiope, the future wife of Télémaque and the epitome of the Christian spouse: "'What touches me in her,' said Télémaque, 'is her silence, her modesty, and her privacy, . . . her contempt for vain ornament, her disregard and ignorance of her beauty. When Idoménée [her father, the king] takes her hunting, she is skilled and majestic with the bow, like Diana surrounded by her nymphs. Everyone admires her, but she is the only one who does not see it.'"[62] Unlike Télémaque, however, disappointment awaits our Spectator:

> One day in the country, I had just left her, but a glove that I had forgotten made me come back. I saw that beauty from afar: she was looking at her mirror, and I saw, to my great surprise, that she was rehearsing to herself all the poses that her face had taken during our encounter. Some of the expressions that had seemed so spontaneous were in fact tricks of the trade. I could see that her vanity would select some and reject others; she recorded those little expressions much like a woman would record a musical tune. . . . She saw me from afar, reflected in her mirror, and she blushed. Ah! Mademoiselle, I beg your pardon; until now I attributed to nature a charm that you owe to your skill alone [*votre industrie*]. . . . I have just seen the machines of the opera. The spectacle will always interest me, but I will be less touched.[63]

Chance, an unexpected and trivial accident, dissipates the illusion created by the artful girl. The lover discovers that what he mistook for nature was a mask, the product of the most refined and calculated art. The discovery is staged so as to bring to our attention the complexities inherent in seeing and being seen. The girl is looking at herself in the mirror, through the projection of her lover's gaze, which she has internalized; she is performing, for his future enjoyment and for her satisfaction, perfecting the spectacle she has just offered him. But suddenly she sees reflected in the mirror the real gaze of her flesh-and-blood lover, and his all-too-real appearance shatters the delightful intimacy with her image. As for the Spectator, his own irrelevance is fully revealed to him when he discovers that he was not a protagonist but only an accessory in the girl's staging of a fiction. The ingénue is a consummate actress whose artful exploration of physiognomy anticipates Diderot's conception of acting in *Paradoxe sur le comédien*. Rather than being the passive object of the other's gaze, the coquette is the stage director in a comedy of innocence that turns the tables on the spectator-seducer. But she is, in turn, caught unaware and put to shame. Her plight brings to mind the description of artifice exemplified by Castiglione's courtier, who must conceal the effort with which he has turned himself into a living work of art. That is necessary because everybody dislikes effort and affectation, which are "contrary to that pure and lovely simplicity which is so attractive to the human soul. . . . In everything that he must do or say, let him, if he can, always be prepared in advance, but pretend that everything has been improvised." Like the *beaux esprits* denounced by La Bruyère, Montesquieu, and Marmontel, the apparent spontaneity of the courtier and the coquette is always secretly scripted before being publicly staged, a duplicity that to Castiglione seems perfectly acceptable, even recommended: all that matters is concealing one's game well. "The truest art is that which does not seem such; above all, it must be hidden, for if it is discovered, one loses face entirely and is no longer respected."[64] Which is exactly what happens when chance exposes the coquette's effort and ruins the effect of her art. The severity of the humiliation she endures from her lover shows that neither the coquette nor the artist (nor the courtier, for that matter) can be exposed without losing face and being put to shame.[65] Indeed, the formerly enchanted Spectator feels nothing but horror for backstage goings-on. Mercier will go so far as to suggest that the theater-lover would be as profoundly disturbed by a glimpse of what takes place behind the scene as a lover who uncovers a cancer on the breast of his beloved.[66] The more powerful the sway of illusion, the more bitter the disappointment at the discovery that the artist's technique has inadvertently turned itself into spectacle. On all counts it is a fiasco.

One might think at first that the message conveyed by the Spectator's anecdote consists in the rejection of artifice and the praise of artlessness. That is how most critics have read it, and some have read this episode as an autobiographical confession. Its meaning, however, is quite different. The allegorical status of the Spectator's story is evidenced by the starkness of the dichotomy between nature and artifice. Seldom in Marivaux's *oeuvre* do we find such a blatant opposition between nature and the mask. Indeed, Marivaux is typically fond of filling the gap between the two with a subtle analysis of the degrees that lead from one to the other. In his work, nature and artifice usually stand in a dialectical relationship with each other. This anecdote, in contrast, presents such a caricatural image of the social and erotic comedy that it betrays its ironic nature. Indeed, the coquette is both the artist and the work of art, the producer and the product of illusion. The spectacular aspect of the illusion-producing artifice is evoked by the reference to the machines of the opera, the emblem of unrestrained deceit and imposture. The machinery of spectacles is the ultimate form of the strategic manipulation of illusion. To which we may add the word *industrie,* which smacks of imposture and cheating.[67] Did Marivaux intend to present his denunciation of the artifice of illusion in a manner as unmitigated as possible? In fact, the juxtaposition of the Spectator's denial of *esprit* with a tale that bluntly exposes the artifice that lies hidden beneath the show of modesty and self-effacement is more likely meant to do the opposite, and to raise in the reader a suspicion of the Spectator's own words.

Marivaux proceeds, throughout the journals, by sudden reversals that undermine the credibility of the narrator and aim at involving the reader. "It will always interest me, but I will be less touched," said the Spectator at the discovery of his beloved's duplicity. The same words could be put in the reader's mouth once he realizes that he has become the dupe of the narrator's artfulness. By drawing the reader's attention to the machinery of illusion, to its technique, to the act of writing, and consequently to himself qua author, the coquettish Marivaux is supposed to prevent the arousal of emotion in the reader. Like a woman locked in an exclusive relationship with her mirror, the author is unable to engage in anything other than a narcissistic reflection in his own writing: "We can see those authors, drawn to frenzy by their desire to seem brilliant, . . . constantly admiring themselves in everything they say, as if writing were a mirror that preserved the flattering image of their *esprit,*" writes an anonymous contributor to the *Mercure.*[68]

But Marivaux's apparent denunciation of illusion is in fact a denunciation of those who profess to expose the deceit of others. His target is not the accused but the accuser—his mood of suspicion, his uncompromising rigorism, and the naïve faith in the possibility of unmediated representation. The Spectator was too proud of his authorial modesty and too demanding of the modesty of others to be truly innocent of the vice he condemned in others. One of Marivaux's most persistent, indeed obsessively repeated, motifs is a dislike for moral rigorism, self-flagellating humility, and unforgiving misanthropy. What better way to ridicule such pretensions than to use a story that seems to indict the duplicity of others but in reality exposes the duplicity that lays in the moralist himself? In the wake of La Rochefoucauld, Marivaux believes that it is precisely when *amour-propre* seems to be working against itself that it savors its most delightful triumph.[69] False modesty always fares much worse with him than the open and straightforward confession of one's own vanity. (Thus he follows in the steps of the Jansenist Pierre Nicole, for whom the simulacrum of virtue was far more perverse than the outright absence of virtue and all seemingly good theater was worse than vulgar farce.) In the words of Marivaux's most iconoclastic embodiment of the author, the title character of the *Indigent philosophe:*

> I would never be done counting hypocrites; there are too many of them; there is nothing but them in life. As I say in my book, genuine humility is perhaps nothing but a mask among men. True, there are some masks that cannot but be mistaken for the real face. . . . Do you hear me, all of you, the spitting image of sincerity, do not brag about your virtues! I would not want to be like you; you are all frauds, with your parade of severity for human weaknesses. Perhaps you are even more contemptible than the others.[70]

The numerous references throughout the journals to false modesty, and particularly to the false modesty of authors, deserve to be considered with attention. They are part of an ongoing apology for the aesthetics of *bel esprit* and modernity, which, in the eyes of its critics, is associated with the ethos of vanity and with misplaced theatricality. This apology is complex and multi-layered, and it covers much of the writings in Marivaux's journals, which may be seen as a laboratory for his aesthetic ideals and a reflection on writing and on the role of literature in the social constitution of reality. Marivaux invites the reader to reflect critically on the role of the imagination in the construction of the self and of reality. Illusion and deceit penetrate reality through and through, and it is the function of the artist to devise increasingly finer tools for deconstructing their effects. But in his painstaking denunciation of illusion Marivaux arrives at conflicting outcomes. On the one hand, he hopes to find that kernel of authenticity that forever escapes even the severest scrutiny. On the other, he is committed to embracing the imperfect, deceptive, and hopelessly unstable character of a human nature that is separated from itself, never ceases to reinvent its identity, and cannot help but mask itself, even in the most intimate moments. In Marivaux's theater the tension between truth and mask finds a dialectical solution in the happy denouement. By enacting, and overcoming, illusory appearances, the theater portrays self-deception as a step on a path toward self-discovery. But in his prose writings this tension never finds a clear resolution. The alternation between those two moods constitutes the core of Marivaux's irony, or to put it differently, of his attitude of charity toward a flawed and protean human nature. In the sphere of human agency the only type of truth that is available to us is approximate and tentative; demanding a more rigorous one would amount to an even worse kind of self-deception. In that respect, one could see Marivaux's morality as a kind of Augustinianism lite: the acceptance of human dualism opens onto an ironic acceptance of worldly immanence rather than onto a refuge in transcendence.

Marivaux's own idiosyncratic brand of extreme fastidiousness and disenchanted tolerance for deception in moral life is paired with a desire to take apart the mechanisms of illusion in the aesthetic realm. Although his extraordinary sensitivity to masking and self-deception emerges to a great extent from the Augustinian mood of suspicion about the nature of our moral drives, Marivaux ends up undermining some of the most cherished moral and aesthetic beliefs held by the ancients and by all those who reject the mood of heightened awareness that he is promoting. In Marivaux, as in the other writers and artists of the *goût moderne,* notably Dufresny, Montesquieu, Crébillon the younger, and the Diderot of *Jacques le fataliste,* the reflection on the role of illusion in moral life is accompanied by a parallel reflection on the processes of production of illusion in the novel and the theater. While the reader becomes aware that his perception of the real is coextensive with his activity as a consumer of fictions, he is also invited to take an active role in the constitution of meaning and to reflect upon the spectatorial function. The *goût moderne* conceives the social realm as unstable, evolving, and unhinged from its religious foundations. The undermining of moral and religious authority leads it to see the work of art as a project in the making, as the result of an interaction between the artist and the audience in which the former does not necessarily claim precedence over the latter. All of that was unacceptable to the neo-ancients, who defended a hierarchical, didactic, and sacralized conception of the relationship between the artist and the audience. The aesthetics of the moderns was also rejected by those who, like Voltaire and the Diderot of much of his Salon writings, wished to introduce an ethos of energy and passion that was presented as the recovery of a lost state of grace.

3 | *The Sly and the Coy Mistress*

Style and Manner from Fénelon
to Diderot

*Something is needed besides skill for the work of art to have an impact;
for speculative ideas to become sensate and keep their promise; for rules
to turn into living examples; for knowledge to turn into action and
words into things.*

—Guez de Balzac

Find the thought first; the style will follow.

—Diderot

*As Buffon said, "All the spiritual beauties to be found in a beautiful
style, all the relations of which it is made up, hold a truth that is more
precious for the public mind than those that constitute the subject
matter."*

—Proust

Divine Mimesis

The dictate on the author's modesty was sanctioned by three distinct but
interrelated discourses: moral, aesthetic, and worldly. Modesty and unaffectedness (or should we say the affectation of modesty) were as suited to a good
writer as they were to the *honnête homme* and to a beautiful woman. Being a
bel esprit transcended what today we call being a writer; it fell into the murky
category of the things one cannot take credit for without ridicule, such as being smart or seductive.[1] As the abbé Bouhours's Ariste put it, "'I have too bad
an opinion of myself to fancy myself an acceptable model of *bel esprit*. I lay no

claims to it, and I would feel ridiculous if I did.' 'Indeed, one must make no claims to it,' Eugène replied. 'Those who wish truly to be a *bel esprit* ought not to be too satisfied with themselves. If I were to add one last touch to your portrayal, it would be modesty. It is a quality that enhances all others and that is becoming both to beautiful women and to *beaux esprits.'"*[2] Modesty, however, was far more than a question of authorial and social propriety. It involved a particular conception of representation and a theory of the passions: *amourpropre* was a passion that led to deceit and illusion, and as such it influenced both morals and aesthetics.[3]

In the closing years of Louis XIV's reign, well before Voltaire and Diderot took up the fight, one of the most eloquent advocates of a return to the sublime eloquence of the ancients was François de Salignac de la Mothe-Fénelon, bishop of Cambrai and tutor of the Duke of Burgundy, the heir apparent to Louis XIV. Marivaux was well acquainted with Fénelon's work. His *Télémaque travesti* (1713) was a burlesque rewriting of Fénelon's own Christian rewriting of Homeric epics, *Les aventures de Télémaque* (1699), a bestseller in the eighteenth century and the century's most frequently reedited book. Marivaux's parody did not necessarily exclude admiration for an author who, despite his disgraced exile to his diocese of Cambrai, was, even after his death in 1715, among the guiding lights of the circle of Mme de Lambert (which Marivaux frequented regularly until Lambert's death in 1738). The most openly Fénelonian of Marivaux's writings is probably *L'éducation d'un prince,* one of his last works, which appeared in the *Mercure* in 1754. There Marivaux ventured to take the mantle of mentor to the young prince, the same role he had once parodied in *Télémaque travesti* with his portrayal of the rustic pair Brideron, the gaudy farmer, and Phocion, his dim-witted uncle and guide. Though Marivaux may have felt little sympathy for Fénelon's reactionary stance against the moral economy of the moderns, he may have been drawn to Fénelon's writings on the mysticism of *pur amour,* to his pedagogical thought, to his reduction of political struggles to the terms of individual, moral conflicts, and, most of all, to the thematics of benevolent, sentimentalized authority.[4]

In the Academy session of 26 May 1714 Fénelon proposed a wide-ranging project of reform of religious eloquence, poetry, and theater. His proposal was published as *Lettre à l'Académie,* or *Rélexions sur la grammaire, la rhétorique, la poétique et l'histoire.* Inspired by Augustine and by Roman and Athenian oratory, Fénelon advocated the return to a simple and sublime eloquence. The task of the orator was not simply *delectare,* to give pleasure, but *movere,* to raise passion for the *patrie* and incite the audience to take action in the civic realm.

The underlying motivations for such reform were political. Although he was a staunch monarchist, Fénelon found in the republican ideal a powerful tool and a metaphor for expressing his disaffection with absolutism, a feeling he did not hide: his disapproval of Louis XIV's absolutist policies found ample expression in *Les aventures de Télémaque* (a pirated edition of which was published without the author's approval). The book infuriated the king and compounded the earlier disgrace that Fénelon had suffered for his association with Mme Guyon's mystical heresy. Those travails, and much misunderstanding about his true ideas, gave him a place in the revolutionary pantheon.[5] At the opening of his work Fénelon forcefully stated a Longinian idea that was to become a philosophical leitmotif: there was a causal connection between liberty and eloquence, between the establishment of absolutist rule in France and the decline of public speech.

> Among the Greeks, everything depended on the people, and the people depended on speech. They were led by able and fervent rhetoricians. Speech was a great resource in peace and war. . . . Discourse no longer has any such power among us. Assemblies are nothing but ceremony and spectacle. There no longer are any vestiges of powerful eloquence, of our ancient parlements, of our Estates General, of our councils of notables. Everything is decided in secret in the cabinet of a prince or in some secret negotiation.[6]

Fénelon finds in the republican *patrie* and in the *vertu des païens* a secular equivalent of the Christian mystical body. A dominant theme of antiabsolutist literature from Corneille to Montesquieu to Rousseau, and a major educational tool in the Jesuit and Oratorian *collèges,* the Christian appropriation of ancient history greatly contributed to shaping the myth of republican virtue advocated by the Revolution.

The majority of Fénelon's writings on rhetoric and style contained impassioned diatribes against the aesthetics of *bel esprit* and *galanterie:* "The eloquence of the ancients only aimed at persuading and arousing the passions. They had no use for *bel esprit.* . . . How feeble, indecent, and debased their discourse would become if it were burdened with witticism and wordplay!"[7] Fénelon's hostility toward *esprit,* the language of modern worldliness, was a result of his conflict with the urban, luxury-oriented society that flourished under absolutism. His admiration for the early republics, for epic poetry, and for ancient oratory were all part of his dream to reform French society according to the archaic utopia of an agrarian and patriarchal order that bore only a partial resemblance to the early republics. The ideal societies of Bétique and Salente, portrayed in *Les aventures de Télémaque* (which greatly influenced Rousseau and Montesquieu), presented a republican-Christian utopia in which social mobility was forbidden, commerce was rudimentary, the economy was frugal, women were relegated to their domestic activities, and only male citizens were allowed to play an active role in an oligarchy regulated by a strict and visible hierarchy. Because of his critique of an absolutist culture geared toward the production and consumption of luxury goods, his nostalgia for the poetics of the ancients, and his advocacy of the pedagogical and political role of literature in society, Fénelon exercised a great influence on Diderot, who too hoped to revive ancient eloquence and to rescue it from the "decadence" it suffered under the combined influence of absolutism and market society. Many of the themes we encounter in Fénelon's battle against *galanterie* are recycled by Diderot in his critique of the *goût moderne*. In his inaugural speech to the Academy in 1683 (where he replaced the *galant* Pellisson) Fénelon celebrated the revival of antiquity in the visual arts and in literature by noting that "we have finally understood that we must write as Raphael, Carraccio, and Poussin painted: not for the sake of pursuing astonishing fancifulness and putting one's imagination on display through brushstroke virtuosity, but for the sake of painting after nature."[8] The frugality and restraint of a morally reformed society are thus reflected in an art that makes judicious and guarded use of its stylistic powers.

Hoping to raise society to the pitch of Christian, heroic self-abnegation, Fénelon was searching for a language capable of inspiring the people with a passion for the community and a disinterested love of goodness. The orator must embody the qualities he wants to impress on the people: "I am seeking a serious man who would speak for me and not for himself; who would labor for my salvation and not for his vainglory."[9] The parallel between Cicero and Demosthenes exemplified those qualities. Writing at the dawn of the empire, Cicero was an opportunist who endorsed the tyranny of Octavianus and put his oratorical talent at the service of his career. In contrast, the Greek Demosthenes, the citizen of a republic, was willing to forgo his authorial pride and devote himself to inspiring his audience with a passion for the *patrie*. "Cicero's art is astounding: but it shows through. The orator never loses sight of himself, even as he is thinking about the fate of the republic, and neither does the audience. Demosthenes seems to go out of himself and see only the *patrie*. He does not pursue beauty; he finds it without searching for it. He is above admiration."[10] The beauty of Cicero's language is an effect of the orator's *amour-propre:* the audience may admire it, but it cannot be persuaded by it. The good orator, on the contrary, does not seek beauty, which is useless, but only efficacy; he becomes a pure instrument of truth, which speaks through him in an unadulterated flow. The poet and the orator must erase from their work all marks of their own individuality. Only then can language convey the vivid presence of the object and raise the audience's emotion: "The poet disappears; we see only what he makes us see, and we hear only those he lends a voice to. That is the power of imitation and painting."[11]

The same principles that rule spiritual life must also preside over the composition of the artwork. Indeed, all human activities are seen by Fénelon through the prism of a strict economy of selflessness in which the individual devotes himself to the glory of his community. The matrix of this relationship lies in Fénelon's mystical conception of *pur amour,* a doctrine rooted in the Augustinian principle of the alienating effects of *amour-propre* and in the doctrine of the two loves (the postlapsarian soul is torn between the love of God and the love of himself).[12] But it diverged radically from Jansenism because it upheld the possibility of redemption through human action and aspired to reach in this life a perfect state of union with God. Through the cultivation of a mood of indifference toward one's affects and passive abandonment to God's will, the self is purged of its passions and anxieties and is able to recover a prelapsarian kind of happiness. The soul must alienate itself from its volitions and self-interest so as to become enfolded in the embrace of God's will. To reach that state, Fénelon recommended curbing the passions by inner discipline, yielding to a love that transcended the self, and persevering on that path with *no* thought of a reward:

> We may love God with a pure charity untainted by all self-concern. . . . Neither fear of punishment nor desire for reward may have any share in this love. We no longer love God for the sake of the merit, the perfection, the happiness we find in loving him. We would love him just as well even if, by an impossible supposition, he were unaware of our love; even if he wanted to make eternally unhappy those who loved him.[13]

This lesson will not be lost on Sade's Justine, whose piety is constantly "punished" by God or by fate.[14] The ultimate sacrifice to God would be desiring one's own damnation. Such a paradoxical possibility was briefly considered but forcefully rejected as heretical by Fénelon (who had to submit his doctrine as a series of propositions to the pope's approval), yet one feels that the gap between Fénelonian self-denial and its heretical upshot is not so wide.[15] Such spiritual abnegation may be extended to all aspects of life, but especially to politics and the arts. That is the conception of kingship conveyed by *Télémaque,* the educational novel that apparently succeeded in turning the violently assertive Duke of Burgundy into a dedicated and obliging dauphin. A model to all citizens, but especially to the orator and the artist, the king, Christ-like, embodies the sacrifice of the self to the community: "He belongs to all the people he governs. He is never allowed to belong to himself. . . . He is the slave of those over whom he seems to be lording. He was made for them. He gives himself entirely to them, he is burdened with all their needs."[16]

All art molded after eloquence aims toward pathos and persuasion and hence requires visual energy *(enargeia),* something that can be achieved only through the self-abnegation of the artist:

> [In Virgil and Homer] we find simple things, nature is everywhere present, but art is hidden everywhere. You will not find one word serving the poet's *bel esprit.* The poet prides himself on disappearing so as to plunge you into the things he paints, just as a painter is concerned with putting before your eyes the forests, the rivers, the mountains, the perspectives, the men and their adventures, their actions, their passions, but without allowing you to see the brushstrokes. Artistry is vulgar and wretched when it is displayed.[17]

The audience must be drawn into the representation; it must enter into it and be literally possessed: the tragic spectacle, following the classical theory of imitation, is an out-of-body experience *(transport),* a kind of alienation.[18] When reading Virgil's evocation of the fall of Troy, we are transported to the middle of the fire: "We think we are in the midst of Troy, gripped by horror and pity."[19] We are not spectators to a fiction but witnesses to a tragic action. Horror and pity are predicated upon the audience's capacity to forget that this experience is mediated by linguistic, conventional signs: all awareness of the medium that conveys it must be suppressed. In that respect, Fénelon's conception of the arts (poetry, oratory, and painting) is the correlative of the theatrical doctrines elaborated in the seventeenth century by d'Aubignac and Chapelain, which in their turn reflected rhetoric's longstanding desire to merge with painting and action. The conventional signs of language must have the same visual presence *(enargeia)* as natural signs.[20] In no way must the material conditions of the performance interfere with the object conjured by the representation—a radically antitheatrical stance that foreshadows Diderot's own battle against theatricalized mannerism, his split between the materiality of the art medium and the ideal of art: "The beauty of the ideal makes an impression on all men, while beauty of handling [*faire*] appeals only to the connoisseur; if it makes him dream, it's always of the artist and his art, not of the thing itself; *he always remains outside the scene and never enters into it.* True eloquence does not call attention to itself. If I tell myself you are eloquent, then you are not eloquent enough."[21]

The touchstone of the work of art is the emotion it produces in the beholder, just as in oratory it is the action it spurs. The eloquent discourse disappears as a sign, while its object is reincarnated as vivid presence, and the verb is made flesh: "Demosthenes seems to part with his own self and see nothing but the *patrie*. . . . He uses language as a modest man uses his clothes: to cover himself up. He thunders, he fulminates. It's a torrent that carries everything away. We cannot criticize him: we are captured. We pay attention to the things he says, not to his words. We lose sight of him."[22] Demosthenes' speech consumes itself and its author on the altar of the real so as to leave nothing in the audience's mind but the experience of an emotion so intense that it erases all memory of the words that conveyed it. Not signs or colors but a pure, disembodied presence. The purging of the author's subjectivity from his work recalls the process whereby the soul empties itself of its emotions in order to achieve a state of passivity and total acceptance of divine will. God traces his characters upon the docile, receptive soul, which no longer holds any traces of its individual interest, with a kind of divine mimesis:

> The soul that is moved by self-interested love (the least perfect kind of love) is still troubled by a trace of apprehension for itself that makes it less weightless and nimble when the waft of the inner spirit nudges it. Turbulent waters are dull and cannot reflect the likeness of the objects that are close to them, but still water, like an untainted mirror, receives unadulterated the images of many objects and keeps none. The pure and peaceful soul is the same. God impresses his image on it and on of all the objects he wants to impress. Everything is imprinted, and everything is wiped away. The peaceful soul has no form of its own, but it receives all the forms that grace bestows on it. . . . Only pure love grants such peace and such perfect compliance.[23]

In a state of complete surrender, the soul feels as light as a feather; it floats with the tide of a reality willed by God. The pure soul is like a pool of still water or a mirror faithfully reproducing the divine likeness: devoid of all form or substance of its own except a capacity to reflect, neutrally, the flow of images that stream before it or any sentiment willed by God. This supreme impressionability allows the soul to assume all forms without retaining any. The receptive soul has emptied itself of the peculiarities of character and has become universal. The principles of mimesis thus coincide with those of pure love.

Only self-surrender enables the artist to reproduce reality with all the vividness of a sustainable illusion, because then it is God who holds the pen or the brush. Unlike Burke's and Sade's notions of the sublime, which reside in the unlimited flight of an imagination out of bounds with the real, the Fénelonian sublime consists not in a break with reality but in the complete surrender of the self to a divinely inspired nature.

Fénelon conceives art, whether verbal or visual, as a reproduction or simulacrum of the object experienced by the senses; discourse, bypassing the mediation of conventional signs, conjures a visual replica of the object. In classical rhetoric from Quintilian to Longinus language's drift toward the visual signals the presence of the sublime: *images* or *peintures (hypotyposis* or *evidentia)* occur when figures of speech bring vividly to the mind's inner eye *(phantasia)* the image of an object that the eye does not see: "In a moment of extraordinary enthusiasm and transport of the soul, we believe we see the object of our discourse, and we put it before the eyes of those who are listening to us."[24] In Longinus, images are a powerful and dangerous tool for taking possession of the listeners, for raising violent passions capable of turning any audience into a lynching mob; transcending reason and persuasion, images allow the orator to dominate and captivate.[25] For Longinus, the ultimate example of a rhetorical image is not verbal; it is the actual display of the object before a crowd: Caesar's blood-stained tunic or the alleged criminal himself, who is paraded by the orator in front of a mob driven to bloodlust by his fiery eloquence: "If, in those circumstances, anybody were to show them the author of such offense, that would be the end of him. That unfortunate individual would be massacred on the spot, before he even had the time to open his mouth."[26]

If the power of discourse is to be measured by the effects of *movere,* then language must give way to silent display *(ostendere).* In focusing on the action-laden value of iconic and deictic images, Fénelon seems to be reaching toward silence, toward the holocaust of discourse, for the sake of sublime terseness. The one aspect that Fénelon wishes to exclude is poetry's capacity to raise and deepen the consciousness of its own activity. Aesthetic pleasure is distracting and must be suppressed: there can be no awareness of the medium, but only a self-forgetting, trancelike ecstasy immediately translatable into emotion and action, for the telos of all poetic language is persuasion, and its ultimate meaning is the action that it summons. The ability of art to represent an object at the same time that it represents itself as the process of representation is to Fénelon utterly unacceptable. In describing discourse purely as picture or replica, he denies the consciousness of the poetic vehicle: a good painting, like an eloquent discourse, leads the beholder to repress the awareness that he is contemplating a work of art and to feel as if he were responding to the thing itself.[27] Sublime simplicity, which does not cease to haunt all subsequent reflection on art, is the dream of an art so perfectly purposeful that it may be graced with the obviousness of nature, an art object so necessary that it may become a living thing among others: "The naïf is very close to the sublime; it may be found in everything that's beautiful: in an attitude, a gesture, a drapery, an expression. It is the thing itself, the pure thing, without the slightest alteration. Art is no longer present."[28]

Two things are thus required of the author: that he make himself absent from his work and that any trace of technique be carefully hidden. Those requirements are one and the same because technical virtuosity is rooted in the author's *amour-propre,* in the sensual and corrupt desire *(concupiscence)* that makes us love the creature more than the creator. Those claims must be placed within the larger context of the suppression of theatricality on the stage and in the novel that theoreticians relentlessly advocated in the early seventeenth century. The purging of the author from the tribune, from the pulpit, and from the page was part of a general attempt to endow the fictional world with a life of its own, with a hallucinatory effect, and to explore the power of language to entice and captivate. In the theater and in the novel such reform, which emphasized the power of fiction to enchant the recipient and to allow him to reach beyond himself, had the result of enhancing the autonomy of the fictional world and the spectator's pleasure, but in the Christian-republican utopia of Fénelon it also aimed at reforming and regenerating the audience, touching it with the grace of the sacred word. In both cases the audience was drawn into the discourse so as to emerge transformed.

Successful art aimed at its disappearance: *ars artem celare.* It was art's triumph, and the effect of the sublime, to conceal itself behind its very success: "How does the orator conceal the figures he employed? He does it, of course, through the overpowering splendor of his idea. In the same way as dimmer lights vanish under the glow of the sun, so all the subtleties of rhetoric disappear under the majesty that overwhelms us."[29] Fénelon wrote of Raphael that "far from making his skill visible to us, he tries to hide it. He would like to deceive the spectator and have him take his painting for Jesus Christ himself transfigured on the Thabor."[30] Writing in the second half of the eighteenth century, when classical doctrines were being resurrected to counteract the perceived excess of the *goût moderne,* the abbé Laugier resumed the same conception of mimesis as trickery or illusion: "What is the end of painting? To give us a representation of the object so truth-like as to trick the mind into the illusion of believing that what it is seeing is the thing itself."[31] One of the dialogues in Fénelon's *Dialogues des morts* features a conversation between Poussin and Parrhasius, the legendary Greek painter of a much-quoted parable by Pliny: Zeuxis, his rival, had deceived birds into taking for real his painted grapes but was in turn deceived by Parrhasius into taking for real a painted curtain.

Identifying the morality of art with its capacity to deceive would have seemed especially perverse to Plato, who, in the *Republic,* reserved a special blame for *skiagraphia,* theatrical decoration that produced illusion and trompe l'oeil by twisting perspective and falsifying the real proportions of objects.[32] More relevant to our purpose, it was also antithetical to the Aristotelian conception of representation. In the *Poetics* Aristotle had pointed out that audiences are capable of experiencing pleasure in contemplating a theatrical or pictorial representation of an object that they may find repulsive or painful in real life:

> The sight of certain things gives us pain, but we enjoy looking at the most exact likeness of them, whether the forms of animals which we greatly despise or of corpses. The reason is that learning things is most enjoyable, not only for philosophers, but for others equally. . . . Hence they enjoy the sight of images because they learn as they look. . . . If a man does not know the original, the imitation as such gives him no pleasure; his pleasure is then derived from its workmanship, its color, or some similar reason.[33]

Aristotle was not primarily concerned with the moral status of art but rather with art's potential to enlighten the mind about its own process of apprehending the world. No aesthetic pleasure is possible without the knowledge that what we are beholding is a representation, all the more so when the referent of that representation is perceived as repellent, hateful, or distressful. Such a realization was implicit in Diderot's befuddled appreciation of Chardin's still life *La Raie* (The Skate). The painting seemed to have no object other than the celebration of the artist's ability to flirt with the abject quality of the real: "The object is revolting, but it is the very flesh of the fish, its skin, its blood. Beholding the thing itself would not affect us any differently. Monsieur Pierre, look at this painting carefully when you are at the Academy: learn, if you can, the secret of redeeming through talent the revulsion we feel for certain objects. . . . Ah! my friend [*to Grimm*], to hell with Apelle's curtain and Zeuxis's grapes!"[34] Instead of being tricked into illusion, the Aristotelian beholder is able to distinguish the qualities specific to the representation from the qualities inherent in the object represented. It is precisely from the *awareness* of such a distinction that he draws a pleasure that is both cognitive and aesthetic. The flickering awareness dividing the spectator's attention between the art form and the object was something that Diderot never ceased to explore.[35] Such a multilayered response to artistic representation was not possible, however, within a conception of mimesis that sacrificed all cognitive dimension to the necessities of emotional enthrallment. To Fénelon, the artist was nothing but the mouthpiece of God: his work had to disappear behind the celebration of the glories of divine work.[36]

In a passage in his *Dialogues sur l'éloquence*, A, Fénelon's spokesman, attempts to undermine B's admiration for a prelate's preaching style. A simulates ignorance: he has missed the sermon, and he wishes his companion to recount exactly what the preacher said. B is embarrassed: he is not capable to summarize the sermon and do it justice. "They are thoughts so subtle [*pensées si délicates*], they rely so much on the turn of phrase and the refinement of the expression [*finesse*] that their immediate seduction cannot be rendered afterwards. Were one able to do it, one would be forced to employ other terms, and then it would no longer be the same: the idea would have lost its grace and its force." That was the cue that A was expecting: "Then, Monsieur, it is a fragile beauty that disappears on touch. I would much prefer a discourse that had more body and less spirit."[37] A's irony inverts the terms of the debate; B's "force" of expressiveness becomes "fragility," and A plays on the double meaning of *esprit:* far from being spiritual, *esprit* belongs to the realm of the body, to the materiality of language, to everything that Fénelon casts off in favor of incorporeal expression. A thus rejects the concepts of *délicatesse, finesse,* and *grâce,* which belong to the constellation of *agrément* and *je ne sais quoi,* which constitute the core of the aesthetics of *galanterie* and *bel esprit:* they are nothing but the expression of the speaker's corrupt desire, which separates the audience from truth.[38] Fénelon's stringent conception of linguistic humility veers toward the disappearance of language.

Bare Essentials

Fénelon's self-defeating approach was by no means exceptional within the theory of representation of his time. The Port-Royal *Logic,* for instance, held not only that the signifier had to be transparent to the signified, erasing all idea of mediation, such as the *idea* of the representation *as a sign;* it also aimed at reaching an elusive and spiritual eloquence that did not need the support of rhetoric and linguistic conventions. The same yearning after an intangible and pure expressiveness—which is the inner core of art, once art has discarded its visible trappings—goes for painting. In the tradition of *ut pictura poesis,* color is to drawing what rhetorical ornament is to narrative structure *(fabula).* Neither the painter nor the poet ought to pay too much attention to color; rather, he should pay attention to conception and composition. The paradox here is that hypotyposis, language's capacity to make the referent virtually visible to the mind's eye, is achieved, not by the skilful use of figures, as Longinus and Quintilian had argued, but without them. Arnauld and Nicole argue that incorrectness and disregard for the rules of language and art are preferable to flawless mastery:

> Accuracy of language, the use of figures, are to eloquence what color is to painting: its lowest and most material part. The main thing is to conceive forcefully, to express things so as to bring to the auditor's mind a lively and luminous image: one that would present not only present things *naked as they are* but also the very act of conceiving them. All that may be found in people whose language is not very accurate and who have a scarce sense of rhythm but rarely in those who pay too much attention to words and ornament, because such concern weakens the force of their thought. Similarly, painters have noticed that those who excel with color do not normally excel with drawing; the mind is not capable of mastering both, since one undermines the other.[39]

Pure conception disembodied from its material, linguistic support, the substance of the idea, standing for the "naked" object (the object as God conceives it, untouched by human interest and linguistic equivocations), commands the cultured audience's attention, whereas the ignorant populace is attracted by the superficial brilliance of color and verbal "ornament." The pleasure of language (dismissed as a flimsy concern for formless surface) is equated with the dazzling seduction of a canvas's bright coloring. The association of *bel esprit* with color in painting was commonplace through the eighteenth century: "a *bel esprit* is a painter who neglects drawing and is attracted only to color."[40]

Eloquence must not only describe things "naked as they are," in their poignant lifelikeness; it must also, following Aristotle's conception of metaphorical *energeia,* represent "the action of the mind as it conceives them." Arnauld and Nicole, as well as Fénelon, favored the depiction of thought in the stages of its formation, the seemingly unfinished and unpolished sketch, rather than the effect of completion. In their desire to return language fully to its redeeming function, however, they deprived it of the means of doing so. The language they prescribed was puritanically stripped of its sensuous body. That was all the more paradoxical as it was in the name of expressiveness and pathos that they were drawn to undercut the powers of figurative language. To Fénelon, it was inconceivable that the transmission of a spiritual experience should in any way be the result of the skill of the orator and his mastery of a craft.

Fénelon's impassioned defense of the sublime simplicity of the ancients involved a wholesale rejection of rhetoric and of the materiality of the linguistic medium. Adopting a kind of Cliff Notes approach to poetry, he proposed to rewrite the powerful hypotyposis in Théramène's speech in Racine's *Phèdre* as a telegraphic two-line information:

> Nothing was less natural than the narrative of Hippolytus's death at the end of *Phaedra*, which otherwise has great beauties. Théramène, who comes to Theseus with the news of the tragic death of his son, ought to say those two words only, lacking even the strength to utter them distinctly: "Hippolytus is dead. A monster sent from the bottom of the sea by the wrath of the gods has killed him. I have seen it." Would a man in his position, shocked and terrified, waste his time with the most fatuous and pompous description of the dragon's figure? . . . How distant is Sophocles from such a misplaced elegance, so contrary to truthfulness! He has Oedipus utter only broken words. . . ; it's more a groan or a scream of pain than a discourse. . . . That's how nature speaks when it succumbs to sorrow. Nothing could be farther removed from the glittering phrases of *bel esprit*. Hercules and Philoctetis speak with the same straightforward and intense grief.[41]

Fénelon favored an atticism that found its canonical models in the frequently cited examples of sublime economy in Corneille's plays.[42] In its search for the ultimate dramatic expressiveness, language surrenders to an emotion that overrides all verbal expression. "The sublime," wrote Boileau, "may be found in a single thought, a single figure, a single turn of phrase."[43] Sublime words act without mediation upon the body of the auditor, inflicting upon it an emotion that makes all other language seem irrelevant or redundant: "The sublime overwhelms us and weighs down on us with all its force; it deprives us of speech and reduces us to tears."[44]

Fénelon's stance against *esprit* in classical theater prefigures and very likely inspires Diderot's own desire for dramatic reform: they share the same hankering after the "simplicity" and the straightforwardness of the ancients, illustrated by Sophocles' wailing heroes, the same desire to disarticulate the structure of the verse so as to bring out overpowering, nonverbal expressivity. In the wake of such critique, and inspired by Sophocles' example, Diderot went all the way, at least in his theory, toward overcoming the conventions of dramatic verse. He called for bringing to the stage inarticulate cries and guttural groaning: "What is it that affects us in the spectacle of a man moved by a great passion? Is it his speech? Sometimes. But what always moves us is cries, inarticulate words, broken utterances, some monosyllables that erupt intermittently, a kind of moan deep in the throat, breaking out between the teeth."[45] To Diderot, the tableau of the suffering body exposed to the spectator was far more powerful than any verbal, poetic mediation. That belief spelled the death of poetry. Since the seventeenth century the highest kind of poetry had been drama. But when drama was subsequently pushed in the direction of stronger expressivity and persuasion, there emerged a danger of subsuming all poetry under the category of persuasion. To Diderot, the most effective form of dramatic persuasion consisted in the communication from one body to another; on the stage, the immediate contagion of the passions would thus supersede the mediation of poetic language.[46] The sublime was a counterlanguage.

The sublime rose high but aimed at remaining firmly grounded in the ordinary experience whence it emerged. There was a question, however, that few, if any, openly dared to ask: could it be that the search for the sublime would result in the trivial and the dull?

A few years earlier, in the *Lettre sur les sourds et muets* (1751), Diderot had tackled the issue of the function of poetry in drama in much the same terms as Fénelon. With characteristic deviousness, however, weaving a web of multiple references and creating a chamber of echoes among his various sources, Diderot concealed himself behind another great teacher and rhetorician, the Jesuit Charles Porée (1675–1741), a professor of rhetoric at the Collège Louis le Grand and a dramatist for the students' theater. Diderot's personal appreciation of the problem at hand remains elusive and ambiguous:

> But if we were taught at Louis le Grand to notice all the beauties of this passage of Racine's tragedy, we were also warned that they were out of place in the mouth of Théramène and that Theseus would have had some reason to stop him and say, "Enough of my son's chariot and horses; tell me about him." It was not thus, the celebrated Porée would tell us, that Antilochus announced the death of Patroclus to Achilles. Antilochus approaches the hero with tears in his eyes and tells him in a few words the terrible news: "Patroclus is no more; they are fighting for his body. Hector has his armor." There is more sublime in those two lines by Homer than in all of Racine's pompous declamation.[47]

Antilochus's superbly dull message, with its tripartite, paratactic structure, is a close replica of Fénelon's amended speech of Théramène. The banality of the expression passes for a sublime example of reticence bordering on aposiope-sis.[48] Presumably the actor and the spectator must complement such terseness by adding accent, tone, and gesture. In *The Salon of 1767* Diderot notes that while language is limited in its expressive resources, it is the "variety of accents" that "compensates for the paucity of words. . . . The number of words is lim-ited, while that of accents is infinite; this is why each one of us has his own individual language and speaks as he feels, is detached or ardent, agitated or placid; is himself and none other than himself, although at the level of idea or verbal expression he appears to resemble another."[49] Paradoxically, however, in the same text that theorizes the "hieroglyph" and the emblematic dimension of a poetic language in which sound and image, mysteriously and ineffably, converge, Diderot confronts the issue of the appropriateness of poetry to dra-matic persuasion or verisimilitude in terms that are far from new or original.[50] Not surprisingly, he will never be able to bring a coherent resolution to the intractable problem of the relationship between stylistic texture, poetic imagi-nation, and verisimilitude: "The truth! The truth!" cries the narrator of *Jacques le fataliste,* "but the truth is dry and dull." The problem of how to infuse new life into the conventional codes of theatrical and literary propriety comes back to haunt all of his subsequent works, especially the Salon writings. Diderot's mistrust of rhetoric, his flight toward unmediated forms of expression emanat-ing directly from the body, is rooted in his misgivings about language as an unpredictable and uncertain vehicle of communication: "Why is it, I said to myself, that the most general, the most revered, the most widely used words— law, taste, beauty, goodness, truth, custom, morals, vice, virtue, instinct, mind, matter, grace, beauty, ugliness—though uttered so frequently, are so little un-derstood, so variously defined?"[51] The philosopher, the ordinary man and the child all speak the same words and seem to agree about their value and use, yet they could never agree on their meaning. Diderot's skepticism about the incongruity between linguistic meaning and use, his fear that language did not reflect reality but rather contributed to skewing its perception, was to resonate throughout the Enlightenment.

While the Fénelonian critique of language relied largely upon classical themes of oratorical propriety and efficacy that went back to Quintilian and even to Cicero himself,[52] it would find a special political resonance in the dis-course of prerevolutionary radicalism, among writers such as Jacques-Pierre Brissot, Jean-Paul Marat, and Jean-Louis Carra. There was a continuity be-tween the traditional, moral critique of stylistic refinement that Fénelon il-lustrated and the new "unmasking" of stylistic hypocrisy in manners and language. The former provided the revolutionary writers with a set of prefabricated arguments ready to be filled with new meanings. In the 1780s numerous tracts about ministerial policies would invoke a war on style. The people were warned to be on their guard against the trickery of elaborate or "moderate" style, against the "abuse of words," which led to the abuse of things. The public was encouraged to mistrust the use of uncertain language and to define precisely the meaning of words so as not to be misled by the false political arguments of their deceitful, rhetorically clever foes:

> Today above all, when a universal morality seeks to purify its language and to fix once and for all our ideas on the true nature of good and evil, of justice and injustice, it is of the utmost importance not to evade the positive meaning of words, for fear of leaving the mind in a state of uncertainty. . . . The language of truth cannot allow, in the direct construction of its sentences, any vague and uncertain nuance.[53]

Such tendencies were deployed in full force during the revolutionary years. Sophia Rosenfeld has analyzed the revolutionary "logomachy," the crucial role played by debates about the meaning and the use of words in public discourse. In the wake of the Enlightenment search for a universal language of gesture rooted in nature (illustrated by Diderot, Condillac, and Rousseau) the revolutionaries believed that if they were able to stem the proliferation of ill-defined and misunderstood words in the public arena, they would sooner be able to reach a rational and enlightened consensus on the goals of the Revolution. "The prevention of semantic subversion and the definition of the language of politics" was thus one of the essential tasks of the many *sociétés* that flourished in 1789, on both the right and the left, such as the Société des Amis de la Révolution, later renamed the Société des Amis de la Constitution, the forerunner of the Jacobin Club.[54] Those philosophes who had previously published works on stylistics, grammar, and criticism, such as Jean-François La Harpe and André Morellet (who styled himself "Le Définisseur"), worried about the dangers that democratization would bring to language, fearing that conceptual errors and misuse of rhetorics would lead to linguistic demagoguery and social conflict. At the height of the Terror, however, even the mastery of political discourse and its correct use became suspect: linguistic ability became a sign of counterrevolutionary intentions, of overcivilization, duplicity, and attachment to aristocratic mores. In their pursuit of a masculine and virtuous "laconism," the Jacobins, who had become suspicious of the linguistic reforms they previously had promoted, yearned for a language of action and energy—such as that which Diderot had advocated in the drama—based on natural signs and symbols that would appeal to the emotions directly.[55]

Against Style

Most of Marivaux's writings on style and elocution in the journals contended with the critique raised by Fénelon and the new wave of the ancients. To be sure, Marivaux was fascinated by courtroom eloquence and by the rhetorical power of persuasion, but he did not turn the rhetoric of pathos into the ultimate touchstone of the work of art.[56] Humility, transparency, expressiveness, exactitude in the choice of words, faithful reproduction of thought processes—those issues were very much on the mind of an author who was drawn to theorize upon his art both because of his own disposition and in order to respond to his critics' persistent attacks. "All those discussions on style are nothing but verbose ramblings that ignorance and malice have put in fashion; their purpose is to disparage those works that fall outside the trodden path. . . . You accuse an author of having a style that is precious; what do you mean? What do you mean by style?"[57] Refusing to separate thought and linguistic expression, Marivaux argued for the emancipation of language from the tyranny of custom and genre; he also reintroduced the author into the representation. The artist's responsibility to himself comes before his responsibility to the public. Pathos, the persuasive effect of discourse on the audience, is thus subordinated to ethos, the expression of the mental disposition of the orator. Style is consubstantial with thought because style is above all a matter of perception and vision, the author's own. Style is the expression of the subjectivity of the artist, that is, of his *amour-propre* (or *concupiscence*), the fundamental drive that shapes his sensual grasp of the world and binds him to a form. "*Amour-propre* stands to the mind [*esprit*] as form stands to matter. Every mind has *amour-propre,* and every portion of matter has its form."[58] Thus, it is the writer's function to fashion a style capable of expressing, with the utmost precision, the peculiarities of that vision:

> But is it true that [the author] thinks incorrectly? That's what needs to be proven, for if he must submit to a critique, it must be to that one, and not to charges about style. Style is nothing but the accurate mold of his thought; perhaps his style is charged with being bad, precious, and affected only because the thoughts it expresses are hard to grasp and have been shaped by idiosyncratic connections of ideas.[59]

Marivaux was painfully aware that originality of expression would be equated by critics with affectation and mannerism. But to his eyes, the relationship between thought and language was not arbitrary: asking a writer to make himself accountable for the peculiarities of his style meant inviting him to explore the nature of that relationship. To support his argument, Marivaux proposed a stylistic reduction similar to Fénelon's and Diderot's attempts to rewrite poetry in a rhetorically poor manner. He selected a canonical author and a well-known witticism, "The mind is often [*sic*] the dupe of the heart":

> It was M. de la Rochefoucauld who said that. Let us imagine that it was written by a contemporary; wouldn't everybody accuse him of being precious? Very likely. Why not write, a critic would say, that the mind is often misled by the heart, or that the heart deceives the mind? It is the same thing. No, it is not. It is no longer the author's exact thought; you weaken and diminish it. The style of your thought (since you insist on style) only conveys a platitude. The style of that author conveys something more original and more subtle.[60]

Marivaux's modern bent persuaded him that the formation of ideas was dependent on language's capabilities and that frames of thought and expression would vary with time, manners, and rhetorical tradition. Thought and language were historically and culturally determined; they were dynamic forces that evolved along the same axis: "If France saw a new generation of people whose minds were even more refined than those of today, there would be a need for new words, new signs to express the new ideas that this generation would be capable of producing."[61] Marivaux replied to the attacks against neologism and linguistic experimentation by defending the right of the writer to create new tools for expressing his original perception and for answering the new and multiple solicitations of a constantly evolving reality. To him, linguistic evolution was the corollary of an increased refinement in the apprehension of the real:

> The man who reflects much meditates on the subjects he treats: he penetrates them and observes things of an extreme complexity that everybody will be able to understand after he has formulated them, though at any time only very few people have been able to observe them. That man will necessarily express those observations with a combination of ideas and words very rarely seen together. But see how critics will take advantage of the inevitable strangeness [*singularité*] that this will bring to his style! How affected [*précieux*] it will it be! And also, why does he bother to think so much and to observe, in what everybody sees, aspects that only a few can notice and

that can be expressed only through a style that will necessarily appear mannered?[62]

Unlike most of his contemporaries, Marivaux broke with the scholarly (and Longinian) tradition of *inventio* and the emulation of great models that was taught in the colleges and was seen as central to all creative processes. Writing to him originated in the writer's sensate body, in his peculiar perception, as well as in the historically determined manners of a particular society:

> Should a young writer be the copier of those [great] authors' style? No, for that style has an undefinably ingenious and subtle quality, the literal imitation of which would turn him into a monkey, would force him to become affected [*courir après l'esprit*], and would rob him of his naturalness. . . . Either his organs steer him toward another kind of ingeniousness, subtlety, and dignity or the quality that he would like to imitate is present in those authors only as a function of the kind of manners they have depicted. He should therefore nurture his spirit with what he feels is good in them, but then he should let his own spirit follow its natural posture [*son geste naturel*].[63]

Ingeniousness, the mind's spontaneous and creative effervescence, is for Marivaux the essence of an author's style and the core of his vision, what makes his style what it is *(son geste naturel);* as such, it cannot be imitated nor reproduced. What the young author may try to replicate is not the product but rather the process of production, the creative drive or the vital sparkle that animated the original. At a time, however, when *particulier* or *singulier* did not mean "original," but "eccentric," "awkward," or "ridiculous," when *singularité* was a label affixed to any discourse that took liberties with linguistic propriety and the tyranny of conventional use, all that academic thinking saw in stylistic experimentation was an imagination unruly and out of bounds. The academies saw no cognitive or aesthetic value in such adventures.

Despite Buffon's famous phrase "Style is the man himself,"[64] the chevalier de Jaucourt recommended, in the *Encyclopédie* article "Style," that in order to find a style an author ought to read the best writers, imitate their best models and try as much as possible to emulate great geniuses. For most people, *style* did not denote the expression of an individual voice but rather the encoded and formulaic encounter of subject matter, audience, and genre: each commanded its own stylistic propriety and its own lexical patrimony.[65] Style was not primarily a matter of self-expression on the speaker's part but one of conformity between a discourse and the object it represented. It was not until 1798 that the *Dictionnaire de l'Académie* associated style with the expression of an individual author: "When we say that a writer has no style, we mean that he has no manner of writing that belongs to him." To Voltaire and d'Alembert, style indicated such qualities as propriety or decorum *(la propriété des termes)*, nobility and elegance, and "pertinence with the subject-matter."[66] In the *Discours préliminaire* to the *Encyclopédie,* d'Alembert professed his admiration for Voltaire's unfailingly correct style, for the economy of his "color" (rhetorical figures and ornament), which was "appropriate for each thing," and for "the art of . . . never being above nor below his subject."[67] Writers traveled within a literary landscape already mapped out by tradition and by the emulation of great models.[68] Marivaux's historicized conception of language and style was attacked, with a fervor verging on panic, by Voltaire:

> That desire to dazzle and say in a new fashion what other people have already said is the source of new expressions and affected thoughts. Those who cannot impress by their thoughts try to do so by their words. . . . If we kept doing that, the language of Bossuet, Racine, Pascal, Corneille, Boileau, and Fénelon would soon become obsolete. Why neglect a current expression in order to introduce a new one that means exactly the same thing? A new word may be forgiven only when it is absolutely necessary, intelligible, and easy on the ear. We are compelled to create new ones in physics; a new discovery, a new machine, demands a new word. But do we make any new discoveries in the human heart? Is there a greatness other than that of Corneille and Bossuet? Are there passions other than those that have been handled by Racine and touched lightly upon by Quinault? Is there an evangelical morality other than that of the père Bourdaloue?[69]

To Voltaire, *bel esprit* meant the undermining of the tradition handed down by the great men of *le Grand Siècle;* it meant the sin of neologism, the nightmarish creation of new linguistic terms and expressions, which risked breaking down the organic relationship between words and objects. But above all it meant the disappearance of a national identity transmitted by the canon of great writers and the loss of all vital connection to that tradition; the inevitable alteration of the fundamental mapping of the human passions that they had drawn; the bastardization of morality; and ultimately, the decline of the culture that grounded the French self. In fact, style was seldom seen in terms of self-expression; rather it was seen as a collective, national phenomenon, symptomatic of a nation's cultural identity. Innovating literary language or tampering with the style of the great classics meant altering the identity of the French nation, which rested upon its canon, and risking the loss of France's cultural predominance. Hence, any discussion of style, taste, and pictorial manner quickly veered toward a discussion of the politics of the arts and the state of civilization in the nation at a given time.

Marcel or Suzanne?

In Diderot's Salon writings and in the *Essais sur la peinture, goût, tact fin,* and *finesse* gravitate in the semantic orbit of *style,* and *manner* is often meant as a synonym of *style* in painting.[70] *Goût* and *tact fin* are rooted in temperament and refined by experience. Pertaining both to aesthetic judgment and to artistic production, they are relevant to the artist as well as to the beholder of a work of art.[71] All representation, be it pictorial, plastic, or verbal, must be, not a mimetic reproduction gathered from the passive observation of nature, but the result of a creative act that culminates in the *idea;* it is a conceptual insight into nature and the intuition *(tact fin* or *goût)* of the necessary concatenation of laws that rule nature. Whether nature is intended as an idea or as a phenomenon, for Diderot—in line with his Renaissance predecessors—art is the product of an intuitive knowledge that is akin to the scientific understanding of nature's laws.[72] The workings of the imagination thus coincide with nature's hidden structure. It is such understanding that informs works such as Vernet's landscape paintings. In praising them Diderot finds accents that are close to Fénelon's:

> There are no more buildings here than are necessary to enrich and animate the scene; intelligence, and taste, and art, have seen to the effectiveness of their distribution, but the resulting effect is achieved by concealing the artistry. . . . Everything is true. One feels it. We reproach nothing, we miss nothing. We take pleasure in everything. I've heard people who have long frequented the seaside say that they recognized on this canvas this sky, these clouds, this weather, this entire composition.[73]

The miraculous balance achieved by Vernet and Chardin transcends the distinction between nature and art, between the object and its representation, upon which rest all notions of mimesis. When confronting the demiurgic power of their works, Diderot reacts with the same *émerveillement,* the same stunned and enthusiastic admiration that he showed in his reading of Richardson: "His compositions preach the grandeur, power and majesty of nature more compellingly than nature herself: it is written: *Coeli enarrant gloriam Dei,* but it's Vernet's skies, it's Vernet's glory."[74] Such achievement, however,

is a fragile miracle, one that is constantly threatened by the powers that converge to undermine the work of the artist: the marketplace's pull toward mediocrity;[75] the corruption of taste that is brought about by the degradation of
morals and by the progress of reason and philosophy; the influence of artistic
codes and techniques that weigh heavily on the artist who finds himself the
last link in a long evolutionary chain. "There is a traditional technique that
the man of genius has bowed to; it is no longer after nature but after such a
technique that he will be judged." The iconoclastic Diderot does not hesitate
to tell Grimm that the "technique" he has in mind is Racine's.[76] When the taste
of a nation—or of a particular artist—has peaked to perfection, it is as if one
were standing on a razor blade. Holding one's balance becomes impossible; a
fall into mannerism, the modern form of barbarity, is fated to happen:

> At the origin of societies one finds art that's crude, discourse that's barbaric,
> and morals that are countrified; but these things tend to work together in
> favor of perfection, until the grand style [*grand goût*] is born; but this grand
> style is like the edge of a razor on which it's difficult to maintain one's foot-
> ing. Very soon, morals decline; the empire of reason extends its boundaries;
> discourse becomes epigrammatic, clever, laconic, sententious; the arts are
> corrupted through refinement. The ancient routes are blocked by sublime
> genres one despairs of ever equalling. Poetics are composed; new genres are
> envisioned; the singular, the bizarre and the mannered make their appear-
> ance; from which it would appear that mannerism is a vice that occurs in a
> highly civilized society [*société policée*], one in which good taste tends toward
> decadence. . . . These copyists of a bizarre model are insipid because their
> singularity is secondhand; their vice is not their own; they're the apes of
> Seneca, Fontenelle, and Boucher.[77]

The same fall into decadence may threaten an individual artist. In his masterpiece, *Le miracle des ardents,* Gabriel-François Doyen already shows signs of
straying into dreaded mannerism: "He is on the edge; one step further, and
he'll be smack in the middle of racket and disorder," the same racket and disorder *(fracas, tapage)* that also characterize the paintings of Boucher, the perfect
embodiment of modern mannerism.[78] To Diderot, art, like civilization, is cyclical: out of the barbarism of early ages slowly and gradually emerges the grand
style and taste *(grand goût)*. Style thus gradually becomes self-conscious and
self-regulated. Quickly reified, copied, and circulated in countless academic
lectures, discussions, manuals, and schools, it is bound to degenerate into rep-
etitious codification and affectation.[79] The sublime embodiments of ancient
art lose their exemplary status, their power to stimulate and inspire. Emulation

gives way to slavish imitation on the one hand and to a search for the bizarre and the titillating on the other. Only a violent and bloody return to barbarity could prevent the civilized world from sinking further into mediocrity and calculated bizarreness. As things stand in modern times, a civilized nation, much like an aging libertine in need of increasingly potent stimulation, has developed a taste for provocatively offered, alluring flesh, such as that provided by the paintings of Boucher, Lagrenée, Baudouin, and Fragonard: "The passionate young man is not demanding in his tastes. He seeks immediate gratification. The old man is less in a hurry. He waits. He selects. The young man wants a woman. Sex is enough for him. The old man wants a beautiful one. A nation is old when it has acquired taste."[80] A nation is old when it becomes capable of inventing love and deferred gratification, when a woman is no longer the same to a man as any other woman, when it comes to regard the aesthetic as an absolute value, independent from any considerations of purpose.

Diderot's conception of artistic decadence thus is not far from Rousseau's semimythical account of the emergence of a "mirror stage," in which primitive human beings become aware of the presence of others and of the reciprocity of beholding, in which they abandon their previous existence as autonomous individuals and subject themselves to living under the alienating gaze of others.[81] The moment when primitive humans begin to conceive themselves as objects of other people's attention and to value themselves as by-products of other people's opinion signals the rise of individuality and morality; of love, of deferred fulfillment, and of women's power over men. By the same token, those gestures set off corruption and inequality. But what is there in common between Rousseau's parable on the origins of civilization and Diderot's conception of academic mannerism? What links Rousseau's political myth of origins to Diderot's portrayal of social manners, decadent sexuality, and artistic corruption? In all of those spheres—political, artistic, social, sexual—distinct as they may appear at first, a crucial role is played by theatricality and theatrical self-presentation. Theatricality (with its corollary, inauthenticity) is the underlying feature that makes them all interdependent.

"Every individual who seems to say to you: 'Look how well I weep, how well I get angry, how well I entreat,' is false and mannered"; that is, every individual who is aware of being a spectacle to others and who positions himself to his best advantage is false and mannered.[82] When a character is not in the hold of a strong emotion or an absorbing action, when his attention is divided between his task and his awareness of the presence of a spectator, his gesture and posture veer toward mannerism. That is true of the academic model, who styles and positions his body so as to resemble closely the ancient statues that fashion the taste of the Academy's students: "All these studied, artificial, carefully arranged academic poses, all these movements coldly and ineptly imitated by some poor devil, and always the same poor devil, who is paid to appear, undress, and let himself be manipulated by a professor three times a week, what do they have in common with postures and movements in nature?"[83] That is true of all the pupils of François Marcel, the century's most famous dance master and choreographer of courtly ballet, with whom Diderot is so taken that he grants him the dubious favor (also enjoyed by Marivaux) of coining a verb after his name:

> Should you lose all feeling for the difference between a man presenting himself in company and a man acting from motivation, between a man who is alone and a man being observed, throw your brushes into the fire. Your figures will be academized, denatured, affected. Would you like to get a sense of this difference, my friend? You are alone at home. You are waiting for my copy, which is late. You are reflecting on the determination of sovereigns to be served on time. You are sprawling on your cane chair, your arms resting on your knees, your nightcap falling over your eyes, or your hair down and dishevelled; your dressing gown is half open, falling in long folds on both sides: you are utterly picturesque and beautiful. The Marquis de Castries is announced; suddenly the cap is pulled up and the dressing gown drawn closed; my man straightens up, composes his limbs; he becomes mannered, *Marcelized*, making himself presentable for the arriving visitor, but quite dull for the artist.[84]

Addressing first the artist and then his friend Grimm—as Diderot imagines he might be at the very moment those lines are being written—Diderot draws a little sketch that dramatizes the difference between the philosophe alone in his cabinet and the philosophe in the company of someone else—but not just anybody, for the visitor is the marquis de Castries, Grimm's most influential patron. The sketch is at once a study on mannerism and a social satire. Grimm first appears in all the unstudied glory of the solitary man of talent cogitating in his cabinet, hair tumbling down his shoulders, his gown baring his chest, in the manner of antique statues, folds draped like a toga (he is as "picturesque and beautiful" as Diderot in his old dressing gown),[85] an Epictetus living in austere poverty, slouched on a cane chair. But at the marquis's imminent arrival the philosophe, answering the call of his patron and that of worldly ritual, lowers himself into the obligatory mimicry of sociability and forces his body into the gracious movements and the conventional bearing taught by the dance master. No longer a man entirely absorbed in action or meditation, Grimm has become slightly ridiculous in his polite alienation—perhaps a fitting illustration for d'Alembert's rant against worldliness in the *Essai sur la société des gens de lettres et des grands* but not a worthy model for the artist.

The same theatricality that Diderot finds objectionable from the standpoint of artistic representation is also the source of much that he finds morally offensive in modern manners and art: "Manner in the arts is the same as hypocrisy in manners. Boucher is the greatest hypocrite I know."[86] If theatricalized mannerism makes the philosopher look unnatural and ridiculous, theatrical self-consciousness makes the women in Boucher's and Lagrenée's paintings appear obscene:

> A nude woman is not indecent. It's a woman with her skirts tucked up who is. Imagine the Medici Venus is standing in front of you and tell me if her nudity offends you. But shoe this Venus's feet with two little embroidered slippers. Dress her in tight white stockings secured at the knee with rose-colored garters. Place a bonnet on her head, and you'll feel the difference between decent and indecent quite vividly. It's the difference between a woman seen and a woman displaying herself.[87]

Any reciprocity between the beholder and the object of representation risks blurring the separation between the two, sending the beholder back to his dreary reality and preventing him from being absorbed in the picture or the fictional space.[88] Much like Marivaux's indignant Spectator (see chapter 2), Diderot's spectator draws pleasure from capturing a woman while she is unaware of being watched. As with Fénelon's virtuous Antiope, her obliviousness to other people's attention leaves her exposed and available to their gaze. Like the "savage," "she is unselfconsciously naked."[89] Like the cavalier d'Arpino's *Suzanne au bain,* in her attempt to block the view of the old men she holds up her clothing on the side facing them, thus unwittingly "leaving her nudity completely exposed to the view of the spectator looking at the painting."[90] Diderot is quite besotted with this picture of Suzanne and keeps coming back to it over the years. His appreciation is a living illustration of the fact that the last thing a voyeur ever wants is to deal with an exhibitionist: when Diderot creates a clandestine theater for himself, he does not like to find the stage occupied by actors in search of an audience.[91] A woman looking back at him or, what amounts to the same thing, a woman scantily decked in provocative finery (we cannot but be seduced by Diderot's expert description of lingerie and shoes), consciously summoning the spectator's attention, is perceived as indecent and profoundly distasteful. Is that because, as René Démoris has suggested, those women's explicit and deliberate erotic appeal no longer allows Diderot to ignore his own scopic desire?[92] That may well be; Diderot, however, is far from ignoring it: "I am looking at Suzanne, and far from feeling horror for the old men, perhaps I have desired to be in their place,"[93] that is, in their place *inside* the painting. But for such transference to occur, Diderot must bracket not only all awareness of pictorial manner but also all reference to himself as the self-conscious spectator to an erotic scene. In order to enjoy the painting, both as an aesthetic and an erotic object, Diderot does not want to be invited: he wants to break in. "Lairesse maintains that it is all right for the artist to introduce a spectator into the scene he paints. I don't believe it. . . . That would be in as bad taste as an actor addressing the parterre. . . . When Suzanne in hiding behind her clothes from the old men's gaze is exposed naked to my eyes, Suzanne is chaste, and so is the painter: neither knows that I am there."[94]

At the core of Diderot's reflection on stylistic mannerism in the arts we find the ever-present duality of the coquette and the ingénue, of the sly and the coy mistress. This very duality characterizes another Suzanne (the name is very likely not accidental), the most memorable of his female characters, Suzanne Simonin, the *religieuse*. Readers noting the discrepancies in her story, as well as the canny use she makes of her body for rhetorical purposes and for the spectatorial arousal of emotion, have often imputed them to duplicity. Indeed, Suzanne proves to be both an extraordinarily savvy and self-conscious manipulator of images in a spectacle of innocence and an oddly naïve, unselfconscious narrator. But rather than invoking character duplicity, it is to Diderot's eroticism of spectatorship that we must turn for an explanation. The fact is that the *religieuse*'s otherworldly unawareness of the nature of her relationship with Mme d'Arpajon, the lesbian mother superior, makes her all the more available to the game of seduction that she "naïvely" reports to the appreciative spectator, the marquis de Croismare. Hence the necessary—and narratively implausible—sexual ignorance of Suzanne, which strangely persists in her correspondence, even after the events that she narrates retrospectively have fully unfolded. But Suzanne, like her namesake in the cavalier d'Arpino's painting (and unlike Boucher's coquettes), must be completely ignorant and completely innocent even as she is actively involved in the sexual act to which she has made the marquis a party and an accomplice. Even more crucial, her ignorance and innocence must be fully preserved throughout her narrative of the event: like the biblical Suzanne, Suzanne Simonin exposes herself naked to the marquis's eyes, but in order to maximize his pleasure and his good conscience, she must appear unaware that she is doing so. This obdurate innocence, implausibly persisting in the midst of flagrant initiation, is also what characterizes many other thrilling ingénues, from Molière's Agnès to Mlle Éradice in *Thérèse philosophe* to Laclos's Cécile Volanges.

The coquette is declared abhorrent by Diderot, whose indignation is fueled by the anxiety of having to relinquish his self-control as a male, as a patriotic philosophe, and as an art critic, an anxiety that comes forth in his unwitting and irascible surrender to the seduction of Boucher's paintings, with their irresistible virtuosity and unabashed grace and their enticing female nudes (which, in the words of the Goncourts, who had read Diderot, are never "nude" but always "undressed").[95] But the coy girl is seen by Diderot as his own salvation, the salvation of modern art and of the nation: if only art were able to discard its stylistic theatricality in order to recover an untouched, unselfconscious grace; if only the nation were able to reform its lewd and mediocre taste in order to restore the *grand goût*. Indeed, Diderot devotes many pages to exposing his fascination for the daughter's sacrifice and the young virgin's martyrdom. Iphigenia, both in painting and in poetry, is his persistent obsession (Suzanne Simonin, sacrificed to parental self-interest and to religious fanaticism, is the modern equivalent of Iphigenia, sacrificed to her father's ambitions and to the reason of state).[96] For who could better defeat theatricality than the meditative, suffering virgin brought to the sacrificial altar? Who could give a more powerful example of selflessness and civic responsibility than Iphigenia, far more forceful in her filial devotion than the irresolute Agamemnon?[97] What better way to redeem the violence inherent in the voyeuristic appeal of erotic painting than to replace it with the purified, sanctified violence of martyrdom?[98]

Unlike the lustful old man holding in wait for a beautiful woman whom he had turned into the emblem of an aging and corrupt nation, Diderot proudly confides to Grimm that in his old age he has discarded all taste for coquettes and self-confident libertines of times past. What he favors now—a sure sign of his amended ways—is young, innocent, and shy girls:

Each of life's stages has its tastes. Sharply outlined vermilion lips, an open, smiling mouth, beautiful white teeth, a provocative gait, a confident gaze, beautiful full cheeks, a turned-up nose prompted me to hot pursuit at age eighteen. Today, when vice is no longer good for me and I'm no longer any good at vice, it's the young girl with an air of modesty and decency, a restrained gait, a hesitant gaze, walking in silence beside her mother, that attracts my attention and charms me. Who has good taste? Myself at eighteen? Myself at fifty?[99]

What Diderot the philosophe and the paterfamilias truly likes in his mature years is not the provocative gesture and the inviting gaze of Boucher's coquettes but the retiring passivity and vulnerability that he sees in Greuze's portrayals of self-absorbed, tearful girls; not mannerism but nature in all its untarnished purity; not vice but ever-alluring virtue.

Sade liked them too, but he knew better.

4 | Capturing Fireside Conversation

Diderot and Marivaux's Stylistic Challenge

Poets represent the fountain of the Muses gushing forth under the foot of the legendary winged horse, . . . that is how thought must spring out of the writer's mind.

—Mercier

I do not compose, I am not an author; I read and I converse; I ask questions or I reply.

—Diderot

Parabasis

The core of Marivaux's *oeuvre* and of the seduction of his poetics lies in the disjunction between the surrender to the lure of the fictional world and an attitude of distrust toward all manifestations of inauthenticity and fictionality. Well before Rousseau, Marivaux was the writer who devoted the most attention to analyzing the contamination of reality by fiction. All of his novels, including his youthful experiments and his two mock-heroic epics, explored the troubling role that rhetoric played in personal identity and in the construction of reality. In that respect, Marivaux differs from Diderot and from other philosophes like Mercier, who felt that the sentiments that we experience through fiction enhance our sensitivity to the moral dimension of the real. In his praise of the reader's response to Richardson, Diderot saw no fundamental separation, but rather interpenetration, between the emotions created by fiction and those the reader would experience in real life: "My soul was kept in constant turmoil. How good I was! How fair-minded! How satisfied was I with myself! When I was finished reading, I felt like a man who has spent an entire day doing good deeds."[1] The admiration the reader feels for the moral beauty embodied in the characters with whom he empathizes is reflected back upon himself and leads him to a virtuous emulation, for emulation is a fundamental aspect of the sublime mode of cultural appropriation, the sacralization of the audience's dependence on its heritage and on the culture produced by the great men of the past, who ground the audience's identity. Thus, the appreciation of fictional virtue prepares the reader to engage ethically with the real. In a similar vein, Mercier waxed enthusiastic about the formative role played by fiction, and most notably by theater, in shaping the sensitivity of the public: "What is dramatic art? It is the art that most activates our entire sensitivity; that sets in motion those rich faculties we have received from nature; that opens up the treasures of the human heart, makes pity and commiseration fruitful, teaches us to be honest and virtuous."[2] The philosophes were so confident about their moral excellence and the sacredness of the writer's function in society that they reconfigured the impact of fiction according to the model of religious eloquence. The response they summoned from their audience was similar to that elicited by the sacred text. The writer, "bard of humanity, painter of manners, profound moralist, enthusiast of virtue, benefactor of the *patrie* and the world," could do no wrong; indeed, he could achieve nothing but miracles.[3] Readers were invited to embrace the text wholeheartedly and to bring it into their lives in the same way as the readers of a devotional text might hope to imitate the life of Christ.

But in the early decades of the eighteenth century the novel was not an analogue of religious experience but rather a rival to it. To Marivaux, who felt that the writer enjoyed no such mandate to save the world, the literary text was a thing to be used with caution. The seduction of the written word was a phenomenon not to be taken lightly, for all emulation was potentially disastrous. Reading was a form of melancholy that might lead to obsession and madness. Indeed, many of Marivaux's readers are *visionnaires,* like the characters in Desmarets de Saint-Sorlin's eponymous play (i.e., precursors of bovarism). They are relentless builders of sand castles, delusional enthusiasts who mistake fiction for reality and are oblivious or even hostile to anything that might puncture the beautiful bubble of their fantasy. Marivaux's early novels are a reflection on the powers of fiction, offering a burlesque representation of reading and readers in the tradition of *Don Quixote.* By turning the reader into the subject of the novel, they offer the empirical reader an unflattering and deformed likeness of himself, which he cannot but try to preempt. These works celebrate fiction's power to seduce; at the same time, they caution the audience against the consequences of that seduction, much as Rousseau does. Indeed, while Rousseau's works elicited from the public the sacralized, transformative type of reading that the philosophes advocated, they also led the reader to question the effects of imitative response. In *Emile* the young Sophie, Emile's future bride, has become a true *visionnaire:* she has lost her sanity by falling hopelessly in love with Fénelon's fictional Télémaque, a paragon of perfection. "Sophie loved Télémaque; she loved him with an incurable passion." For a moment Rousseau is tempted to drive his heroine to a tragic end that foreshadows that of Emma Bovary: "Shall I bring this sad tale to its catastrophic conclusion? . . . Shall I depict the unfortunate girl, whom [her parents'] persecution has attached even more to a figment of her imagination, slowly descending into death, and into her grave, at the very time she is expected to go to the altar? No, let us set aside such gloomy thoughts."[4] Indeed, more fortunate than Emma, Sophie is rewarded by Rousseau with marriage to a man whose perfections equal those of the imaginary Télémaque.

In Marivaux's *Télémaque travesti* too Fénelon has sown mayhem in young minds. Unbridled emulation drives the young farmer Brideron and his uncle Phocion, both avid readers of romances, to the brink of madness: "Having pronounced those words that hastened in his mind the progress of madness, he opened the book and gave it to his nephew, who, accustomed by his uncle to enthusiasm and high-mindedness, devoured the story of Télémaque. He read it over and over and took from it the dose of noble and extravagant feelings necessary to forming the project of going out to seek adventures."[5] All of Marivaux's early works are full of such delusional readers. They all focus on flawed and ridiculous imitation; indeed, they make the very notion of imitation appear ridiculous. The burlesque is in fact the ostensibly awkward and deformed imitation of a text that is already the mediocre imitation of a previous work. In fact, neither *Télémaque travesti* nor *Homère travesti* directly parodies an ancient epic; rather they are grotesque rewritings of rewritings they expose as flawed: the first, as we know, mocks Fénelon's interpretation of the fifth book of the *Odyssey,* while the second is a parody of Antoine Houdar de la Motte's own free translation and adaptation of the *Iliad.* Thus Marivaux, a writer who valued originality above all, started his career by dipping his pen into the fount of commonplace, as if wishing to exorcise all forms of derivative writing and the sanctimony of literary cults.

The specter of inauthenticity, which raises its grotesque head in the early works, never ceases to haunt the productions of his maturity, albeit more elusively. The early characters—the Pharsamons, Clitons, Briderons, and Phocions—constructed their identity in a parasitical way, following fictional models; they formed an ideal image of themselves and tried, very clumsily and ineffectively, to act it out. Marianne and Jacob are far more successful in peddling their imaginary identity with others, but they are treading a fine line between the burlesque and the sentimental. In other words, they invite a reading that is suspended between an awareness of dissonance and absorption in unmediated emotion, between successful imitation and grotesque failure. They are theatrical creatures, always aware of their situation as objects in other people's eyes, always divided between involvement in their own feelings and the perception of their effect on the interlocutor. "When this lady looked at me," writes Jacob, "I would become self-conscious; I would adjust my gaze, look at her in a caressing way; and yet, I could not have given any reason for that: I was acting out of impulse, and impulses are not rational."[6]

In a classic article, Jean Rousset has brilliantly shown that Marivaux's narrative voices are always split between a subject and an object, a protagonist and a spectator, a then and a now.[7] The same goes for his plays, even though in the theater the spectatorial function is projected onto the masks of the *commedia dell'arte*, onto the valets, who, by playing the role of mirror to their masters, introduce a note of comic dissonance into the language of *galanterie* spoken by the protagonists. "The one who is acting and the one who is looking are not the same person," argued Dorval in Diderot's *Entretiens sur Le fils naturel.*[8] That is not necessarily true for Marivaux's narrative prose; actually it is very seldom true for his work. Writing in the first person, Marivaux develops, through the mask of his narrators, a hermeneutics of deception. Like Marianne, all his characters are pursued by the threat of inauthenticity: "This beginning seems to announce a novel, yet this is not one; I am telling the truth just as I learned it from those who raised me," Marianne declares.[9] However, the stories they tell, replete with the clichés of the baroque novel—improbable coincidences, unexpected recognitions, far-fetched situations—defy the verisimilitude they claim to respect. Their allegations of truth are undermined by signs that raise the reader's suspicion, as if to demonstrate that the only law the novel respects is one internal to fiction.[10] Thus, most of Marivaux's narrators are unreliable. They do not so much undermine our belief in their *presence* as expose the illusions they live by. In other words, the tight coherence of their rhetorical project and the vividness of their linguistic characterization are able to command the reader's attention and draw him or her to their reality, but such reality appears deceptive, and the characters, self-deceived. All of Marivaux's novels present some hermeneutic conundrum.

Both in Marivaux's theater and in his novels the audience is driven to know and understand more than the character himself is able to know, which is the fundamental structure of irony, both comic and tragic. *Le paysan parvenu* in particular shows the cracks between the naked reality of human desire and the rhetoric that conceals it; it shows the inconsistencies between what the characters do and the stories they tell themselves in order hypocritically to comfort one another. The novel's burlesque quality lies in such incongruities. For instance, when the mature demoiselle Habert decides to marry the nineteen-year-old Jacob, whom she has met just three days earlier on the Pont-Neuf,[11] she relies upon arguments drawn from her religious devotion in order to interpret the meeting as a miraculous sign of God's will. If she can see the attraction she feels for the vigorous young man as being divinely inspired, then that is a sign that her marriage has been decided in heaven and that in satisfying her lust she will also be doing God's work. The burlesque lies in the discrepancy between what she does and what she says; between what she believes and what she unwittingly betrays to others; between the "low" reality of her sexual desire and the "high," noble language of religious faith that legitimates it. Such dissonances become the structuring principle of a novel that has been read as a "realistic" account but that in fact shows insidiously the signs of its implausibility.[12] Marivaux thus invites the reader to observe, not what is narrated, but the process of narration, the rhetorical value of mental structures and stereotypes, or, to put it differently, the ideology conveyed by language. Indeed, the language of Jacob, redolent with hypocrisy and the ferocious stupidity of popular aphorisms, is a not-too-distant precursor of *Le dictionnaire des idées reçues.*

All of Marivaux's work demonstrates this tension between the irresistible seduction of discourse and critical resistance to it, between belief in the internal coherence of the fictional world *(vraisemblance)* and a mood of suspicion toward its authenticity. Its comic power and discursive critique emerges from those structures of destabilization and disjunction. Such an attitude was practiced by the moderns, often as a tool of satire and philosophical irony. But it was perhaps never theorized as clearly as in Baudelaire's essay *De l'essence du rire,* which deals largely with the comic effect of the characters of the *commedia dell'arte* (as we know, one of Marivaux's sources of inspiration). Laughter is "a phenomenon [that] comes into the class of all artistic phenomena which indicate the existence of a permanent dualism in the human being—that is, the power of being oneself and someone else at one and the same time."[13] The source of the comic effect resides in the spectator who laughs, and not in the object that provokes laughter; that is why only a "philosopher" is capable of laughing at himself, for he is a man who "has acquired by habit a power of rapid self-division and thus of assisting as a disinterested spectator at the phenomena of his own ego."[14] Understanding the functioning of such duplication is essential for understanding the nature of Marivaux's irony and that of the moderns.

Irony is a relationship between two simultaneous modes of experience that lead to a disjunction in the subject's consciousness. Such a disjunction is the essence of theatricality. A perceptive reader of Baudelaire, Paul de Man highlighted that quality in his commentary on Baudelaire's rhetoric of irony, which he juxtaposed to a text by Friedrich Schlegel that describes irony as "a permanent parabasis" (eine permanente Parekbase).[15] Now *parabasis* is the movement of the actor confronting the spectators and advancing toward the front of the stage; in Greek comedy it was the discourse of the coryphaeus in which the author presented his personal opinion to the public. Parabasis is thus the equivalent of the infamous *esprit,* the author's or the narrator's intrusion on the fictional stage, exploding its integrity and preventing illusion from taking hold. Irony emerges as an essentially theatrical phenomenon. Like parabasis, it deflects attention from the content of the discourse to the scene of writing; it introduces discontinuity without, however, breaking the unity of the work of art. Even this "complete interruption and dissolution" of the performance does not harm the unity of the comedy, whose essence lies, Schlegel argues, in its destabilizing all purpose and intention.[16] Such displacement, de Man suggests, undermines the effect of reality and reminds the audience that the essence of fiction does not reside in its correspondence with reality but in its power of negation. "Irony divides the flow of temporal experience into a past that is pure mystification and a future that remains forever harassed by a relapse into the inauthentic. It can know this inauthenticity but can never overcome it. . . . Irony [and allegory] are united in their common demystification of an organic world postulated in symbolic mode of analogical correspondences or in a mimetic mode of representation in which fiction and reality could coincide."[17]

Phenomenology of the Coquette

The threat that lurks behind the ironic structure of a disjunct consciousness is that of inauthenticity. That was not fundamentally a problem within a Romantic perspective, which saw the essence of art, not as mimesis, but as the negation of nature, a position endorsed by Schlegel, Baudelaire, and de Man. But it was certainly an issue for Marivaux, who labored within a mimetic conception of representation and an Augustinian prejudice that identified self-consciousness with the inauthenticity of *amour-propre,* that diabolical mirror. The moment that triggers theatrical self-awareness, when the self is divided between its immediate experience and its becoming a spectacle to itself, suggests the danger of dissolution, the flight into the immateriality of a solipsistic fantasy, and the loss of contact with authentic emotions, a danger that is all the more pressing as reality is willed by God, whereas fantasy carries the imprint of demonic simulation and deceit. Rather than abandoning himself to God's benevolent gaze, the theatrical self, like Malebranche's *bel esprit,* turns into a self-conscious performer, thus becoming a god to himself. But what is the real, and can it be experienced without the duplication of theatricality? Hardly, Marivaux suggests.

Hence his fascination with the character of the coquette. Vanity, *vanitas,* is also evanescence and emptiness. The coquette is always eagerly trying to grab a reflection of her image in the eyes of others in order to buttress her fragile hold on herself and on her own experience, using that image as a bulwark against the threat of nonbeing. The protagonist of *Lettres contenant une aventure* takes to the privacy of her room so as to collect herself and to recapture, in front of her mirror, those precious moments that escaped her grasp when she first experienced them: "When the time came to go to bed, I rushed to my room to undress and to have a look at myself: yes, to look at myself, because I had a new appreciation for my face and I was eager to prove to myself that I was right."[18] Immediate experience does not elicit as much pleasure as the moment of recollection in the solitude of her room, when she relives the recent past and recreates it in the private theater of her imagination; like Baudelaire's artist, she is at the same time a spectator and a protagonist. It is therefore the reciprocity of spectatorship that we maintain with others (or with our theatrical self) that produces a semblance of continuity and coherence within an experience that otherwise would be nothing but a "bundle or collection of different perceptions" and fugitive moments rapidly succeeding one another and leaving no trace in memory.[19] It is only the spectatorial relationship, with ourselves or with others, that enables us to hold on to the fleeting moments of our existence. In a famous passage from the *Spectateur français* a former coquette thus describes the fragmented state of a conscience that abandons itself to the flow of unmediated experience:

I am, at the moment that I am writing this more than seventy-four years old. I have been living for a long time. A long time? Alas! I am mistaken. To be exact, I live only in the present, which is here now and then is gone. Another moment comes—it has already flown away—and it is as if I had never been. Could I not say, then, that my life has no duration but is always beginning? Young or old, we would all be the same age. A child is born at the precise moment when I am writing this, and if I am right, no matter how old I am, he would already be as old as me. That is how I see it, and if it's true, what is life, then? An eternal dream, but for the moment that we are enjoying now, which quickly vanishes too, like a dream.[20]

From the standpoint of the immediate quality of the lived sensation (the here and now, the *ecceitas*) a child and an old woman experience the same feelings and have the same sensations: they have the same experience of redness, of pain, of hunger, of pleasure, and so on. Reduced to a mere succession of instants, deprived of the awareness of memory and the continuity of consciousness (which to Hume lies in the rhetorical connectedness of contiguity, resemblance, and causality) they would be very similar because there would be no individuality. Georges Poulet found here grounds to expostulate eloquently on the inner emptiness of characters devoted entirely to the enjoyment of a timeless and inconsequential sentiment of existence.[21] In fact, the connection between Marivaux's phenomenology, his ethics, and his aesthetics of *esprit* still remains to be explored.

Marivaux draws characters who, while they yearn to surrender to the lure of the moment,[22] are torn between their subconscious emotions and their formalization, between the immediacy of the moment and the frozen commonplaces of language. Language often forces them to express those elusive states of mind through concepts and signs that are not flexible enough or are informed by rigid and stereotypical thinking. Marivaux's pursuit of *esprit* is therefore a way to challenge a language and a philosophical system that hampers, more than it serves, our knowledge of moral life; it is an attempt to push language to the limits of its expressive powers so as to compel it to account for the infinitely small, continuously evolving metamorphosis of the emotions.

In the wake of the discoveries of empiricist and sensationalist philosophy, Marivaux maintained, throughout his *oeuvre,* a reflection on the phenomenology of the passions, that is, on the various states of consciousness and on their relationship to linguistic expression. In particular, he believed that there existed several degrees of consciousness and that the awareness of the emotions had many shades of clarity and definition (Leibniz's and Malebranche's

pensées imperceptibles or *perceptions insensibles*). Exploring the intersection between ethics and epistemology, Marivaux was always looking for better ways
to describe the murkiness of consciousness. At stake was the principle of ethical responsibility, which was crucial to the Augustinian phenomenology of
amour-propre. For instance, to what extent can one be held accountable for
a duplicity that is innate, "mechanical," and unconscious? May a person be
called a hypocrite who is not aware that he or she is dissimulating? As in the
case of Marianne, can one be at once, and *almost* in the same respect, sincere
and disingenuous, spontaneous and cleverly calculating? Marivaux raised the
issue again and again with respect to innate female vanity, one of his favorite
subjects. He also drew unexpected dramatic potential from the theatricalization of half-conscious states of mind in his plays, most notably those that are
reducible to what d'Alembert disapprovingly called "that eternal surprise of
love,"[23] those exceptional moments when the self must face unforeseen and
threatening emotions emerging from its subconscious that painfully clash with
its convictions and with socially enforced rules.

In the *Spectateur français,* the old woman, once a coquette, confronts those
problems in an autobiographical sketch in which she recalls her dealings with
a married man. Even while she believed that she was discouraging his atten-
tions, she says, she was confusedly aware that subtle signs in her behavior were
sending him the opposite message and drawing him closer to her. "I was a
woman," she notes, "and one cannot be a woman without being a coquette.
Do not tell me that such vanity was in any way remarkable. It was the least
that a woman could do. Indeed, it was nothing more than an instinctive and
mechanical kind of vanity. Really, when reflection enters into it, then we are
in trouble!"[24] May a woman call herself virtuous who harbors such conflicting
drives and who is so confused about her motivations and the consequences of
her behavior? To what extent are we able to know and name states of mind
that are so intricately woven with contradictory feelings and moods? Is there a
language that can discriminate ever more subtly between those moods?

Awareness was an important issue to Marivaux because it cast its own peculiar light on the emotions. The object that is illuminated by the mind is no
longer the same as the one that remains in the shadowy unconscious. Emotions are not fixed and stable entities; they are transformed when placed under
scrutiny and named. Discursive imagination and reflection lend a form to the
previously undifferentiated mass of experience and thus alter it. Inauthenticity, therefore, may be the price to pay for consciousness and a stable identity.
The coquette lives an imaginary life in her own mirror and in the eyes of oth-

ers because her own immediate existence and her core individuality escape her grasp. Like the Spectator's duplicitous girlfriend, the coquette is able to master a technique for producing a mask, a simulacrum of life and the semblance of spontaneity. But all that a mask can do is reproduce the appearance of a life frozen in time and threatened by affectation and artifice. Those who live imprisoned behind the mask are unable to know themselves, to be creative, and to evolve, for the only truly authentic moments are those that escape the grasp of self-theatricalization and the reach of language. Those moments are full of risk. Marivaux's theater is rife with situations in which a character is utterly lost and confused, in which all he or she can say is, "I do not know what I am doing," for Marivaux's theatrical characters—counter to the trite conceptions included under the name *marivaudage*—are most of the time unable to know what they are saying, to put into words the disturbing and embarrassing cluster of emotions that drive them out of their wits and their language. Ironically, it is precisely the characters who under normal conditions are the most verbally deft and astute (most often women) that end up inarticulate or speechless when a crisis develops. Yet, it is out of such confusion that the most dramatic transformation takes place and the action moves forward toward its conclusion.

Even the coquette may experience such moments when she surrenders to a chance event, to an accidental encounter that, defeating her plans, leads her to experience the unexpected and to succumb to disruptive emotions. In *Lettres contenant une aventure* a woman recalls: "But my dear, the funny thing in this story is that in the midst of it I had an accident that I had not anticipated. I took my share in the pleasure of a reconciliation that I had planned out of *coquetterie;* I mean, my share of love: it was no longer vanity, it was tenderness."[25] Unlike what happens to Crébillon and to Laclos's libertine self, chance may undo the web of strategies, but the self does not come undone because of it. Marivaux rarely reserves a cruel punishment for the character who risks authentic emotion: in his work, libertine chance *(occasion)* is rife with emotional self-discovery, not sexual humiliation. Indeed, authenticity is often equated by him with unreflectiveness, and not only in the realm of romantic love.[26] Virtues, for instance, generosity, are such only to the extent that they are unreflective and unconscious. Referring to her benefactor, Marianne observes: "Mme de Miran never cared to think whether she was being praiseworthy or not. She was never generous because of the beauty of it, but only because you needed her to be so."[27] Unaware of the symbolic value of her action, Mme de Miran does not translate the gratitude of her beneficiaries into prestige capital for herself; essentially untheatrical, she has no *amour-propre*. That conception responded to the tenets of the Augustinian phenomenology of *amour-propre*. As Pierre Nicole argued, God made it impossible for us to know the source of our motivations with any certainty: awareness of our own virtue would inevitably translate into a feeling of pride, thus spoiling the act. Knowing oneself as virtuous is the same as ceasing to be so; emotions vanish or are denatured by cognition: "Knowledge of their humility makes them proud, and knowledge of their pride makes them humble."[28] Everything good turns to dust under the light of self-scrutiny; conversely, the knowledge of one's own wickedness may turn it into goodness. Self-awareness always alters the nature of that which it reflects.

The challenge set by Marivaux's narrative is how to represent immediacy, how to account for the interval between two states of consciousness, between surprise and knowledge, immediate sensory experience and its processing by the mind. Marivaux is the poet of thresholds, the narrator of passage and processes of change: this preference affects his theater but also the structure of his novels. The need for closure is subordinated to the description of transient states; the novels end when the action is still heavy with the promise of its fulfillment because its completion no longer interests the narrator. Marivaux's characters confront the difficulties of expressing, in the first person, the surge of emotion just before the mind takes hold of it and language alters it beyond recognition. It is necessary, therefore, to push language to its expressive limits, breaking out of the mold of trite expressions, forcing thought out of its familiar tracks. The moment of surprise, that fundamental mode of the rococo aesthetics, is the mind's response to the flow of experience and its effort to make sense of it. Therein lies the key to the concept of *esprit*, which remained so controversial during Marivaux's time.

Against Consciousness

Marivaux's poetics wavers between two distinct but complementary modes, both of which are facets of the aesthetics and the epistemology of *esprit*. On the one hand, Marivaux displays on the page characters who are highly conscious of the difficulties of self-expression. They confront the written medium with a critical eye: either with a burlesque emphasis on their awkwardness and lack of experience (as in the early novels) or with an overstated claim on their sincerity and absence of artifice. Either way, the narrative persona ironically distances itself from its own words and from the tools of rhetoric. The referential content is sometimes eclipsed by the focus on the materiality of language and on narrative conventions. On the other hand, Marivaux's narrators dream of a purely unmediated discourse flexible enough to express half-conscious modes of thought, a discourse that would portray characters chiefly as sensitive human beings and not as wily, self-conscious, and rational creatures. Both tendencies are present in his work, sometimes simultaneously, jostling for the spotlight. Even while enmeshed in the tangle of rhetoric, his characters yearn for the unattainable: an entirely spontaneous and unselfconscious discourse that would transfer onto the page a stream of emotions or a train of thought. The alternation between those two approaches, between a theatrical mode and a self-absorbed, spontaneous, and negligent mode, is at the core of Marivaux's irony. Never unadulterated and straight, always pulled between those two poles, the narrative voice is aware, somehow, that its yearning for unmediated transparency will inevitably lead to a leap into theatricality.

In the journals, the duality of *esprit* is expressed in the multiple personalities of the fictional author. Though he claims to utter the truth and nothing but, the author speaks through several masks and voices. One of them is that of the professional author who never stops reflecting upon his craft and who is painfully squeezed by the politics of the literary field. He knows that each and every word might be dissected and parodied by other authors and other professional critics, that his discourse will be quoted out of context, perhaps appropriated. For a work of art is also a means for positioning its author within a community; it leads to the formation of networks of solidarity and rivalry, literary production and responses being inflected by complex relations of power. Marivaux introduces as a counterweight a second persona, who devotes a great deal of energy to protesting that he is by no means an author: "Reader, I do not want to deceive you; I warn you that what you are about to read was not written by an author"; "I want to be a man and not an author"; "Here is what you are about to read, written in the style of a man who has written down his thoughts as they came along; who only strove to see them plainly, to express them with clarity, without altering anything of their abrupt frankness."[29] Already the narrator of *Pharsamon* declared, "Should you take me for an author, you would be wrong. I am having a good time, that's all. . . ; I am not playing games with you, I am not an author; I spend my time telling fibs, and that's better than doing nothing." And the fictional editor of *La vie de Marianne* protested that Marianne "is not an author: she is a woman who thinks. Marianne has no model present to her mind"; in fact, her style is not that of the novel but her own.[30]

To be sure, such pretense was a tool in the writer's professional wares at a time when it was commonplace to introduce fiction under cover of a confession or a memoir.[31] However, the claim is frequent enough to suggest something more than the simple observance of a convention. Rejecting his role as an author, the writer enjoys complete freedom; solitary and rebellious, he is released from his dependence upon the audience and from the need to answer the expectations implicit in the pact of reading: "I am not promising you anything, I guarantee nothing. Should I bore you, I did not say that it would not happen. Should I interest you, I am not committed to it and I owe you nothing. Things being this way, whatever pleasure I grant you, take it as a present; and if by chance I teach you anything, I am magnificent, and you find yourself showered with my blessings."[32] Following the inspiration of the moment—the libertine *occasion* or chance—the narrator lives in a purely contingent present. He is independent and sovereign. "I am extremely poor, I am picture-perfect poor since my clothes are in tatters and the rest of my possessions are in keeping with them. God bless, that does not prevent me from laughing, and I laugh so wholeheartedly that I want to make others laugh too."[33] Extreme poverty and royal magnanimity come together across the spectrum of human relations of reciprocity and exchange because both pretend to ignore agonistic exchange and the logic of the countergift.[34] Laughter supposes the carefree rejection of social interaction, of subjection to others and to literary conventions. The pauper's destitution and his alleged exile five hundred miles from France (it later turns out that he lied about that) indicate the author's emancipation from the world of letters and the milieus frequented by the *beaux esprits*.

It is exchange, of course, that regulates the pact of reading and that can never be entirely suppressed. The author nonetheless does his best to bracket any awareness of it. As if following Diderot's injunction to play "as if the curtain had not been raised," the author entertains the possibility of enjoying perfect autonomy, writing entirely for himself, with no audience in sight: "At the moment I am writing this that you are reading (if you are reading me at all, for I am not sure that this kind of memoir will ever reach you or that I will have any readers)."[35] And again: "I do not remember that in writing these thoughts I ever dreamed that they would be read; except that now I seem to be thinking of it, since I take the trouble of saying that I never thought of it. And yet, what did I write them for? Was it for me alone? But does one write for oneself alone? I have trouble believing it. Is there a man who would put his thoughts down if he did not live with other men?"[36] It is, however, impossible to deny the reciprocity of interaction. Every utterance is a speech act addressing some audience, indeed creating its own audience. The "I" is shadowed by a "you" that it can never cast aside: theatricality or dialogism—the double rebound of anticipated response—is the inescapable fate of all expression. The more the reader is confronted, and his existence denied, the more tightly the author remains locked in an intimate relationship with the being that his words cannot fail to conjure up. The Indigent, nonetheless, goes as far as he possibly can toward the pursuit of an autonomy that emerges comically as a horizon forever receding. Such lightheartedness is the precondition for the self to become receptive to the flow of sensations and experiences. The prize the author seeks for suppressing his awareness of the audience and of social dependence is a better grasp of himself and of the nature of his impressions. Following a kind of *écriture automatique,* he hopes to descend into himself in order to discover a form of authenticity that is guaranteed by chance encounter, not by the self-conscious rules of the literary trade: "I am unable to create; all I can do is grab hold of the thoughts that chance fills me up with [*les pensées que le hasard me fait*], and I would be sorry to add to them anything of my own. I do not care to examine whether this or that is clever or not. I only try to record accurately whatever strikes my imagination, according to its own bent and that of things."[37] A passive receptacle, the author is pregnant with the impressions that the real, here identified with random chance, imprints on his mind: like a child or a woman, whose brains are soft and humid, he receives the flow of impressions without holding to their form for long.

It may seem paradoxical, however, that the author's wish to remain true to the self and to its mode of apprehension of the world should require emptying that self of all intentionality. Subjective intentionality has been framed in terms of alienation: it is a source of error and prejudice, laden with the dregs of language and literary codes. The author sees only contrived artifice in the effort and the attention that ordinary writers devote to composing their essays according to a preconceived plan. The receptiveness he seeks is accompanied by the need to disengage himself from his own intentions and will, to emancipate himself from all expectations from the world of letters. Seeking to embrace the world of sensations, the author refuses to impose on it any concerted order: a true libertine, he welcomes confusion and surrenders to chance. Marivaux's earlier journalistic venture, *Lettres sur les habitants de Paris,* already illustrated the same drifting journey *(dérive),* the desire to go with the flow: "I keep going, following chance, and I stop when I like it. In one word, this work is the product of a libertine mind, which does not deny itself anything that may gratify it along its journey."[38] One should write as if no one had ever written before, because what matters most is being true to one's peculiar experience and avoiding following any models. "Being natural . . . means refusing to mold one's thought according to anybody else's outline, but on the contrary, faithfully resembling oneself. . . . Thinking naturally means keeping true to the original turn of mind [*esprit*] that we have inherited. Just as every face has its own physiognomy, so every mind carries its own specific difference," which must be discovered and preserved.[39] Thus Marivaux lends a new credibility, drawn from the language of empiricism, to the ancient myth of divine inspiration that manifested itself in the poet's gift for improvisation, of which Fénelon's conception of *pur amour* provided a Christian version.[40]

In that respect, both Marivaux and Fénelon were treading the same path: no claim to spontaneity could be entirely unmediated, nor could it escape the hold of literary tradition. In this case, the tradition is represented by Montaigne, who was Marivaux's favorite among the small number of authors for whom he professed unconditional admiration.[41] He was a kindred spirit and an ally in the contest for stylistic freedom and the right to originality; had he lived long enough to attract the attention of the *Dictionnaire néologique*, perhaps he would have suffered a fate similar to Marivaux's: "Had Montaigne lived today, how much blame his style would have attracted! For he did not speak French, nor German, nor Bretton, nor Swiss. He thought and expressed himself in agreement with an original and refined mind. Montaigne is dead, and he gets his due; it is precisely the originality of his mind—and as a consequence of his style—that is admired today."[42] Following his lead, Marivaux's narrator would like to write in a language consubstantial with himself and with his own experience, emancipated from the rules of the literary establishment. "He knows what he is saying, but he does not always know what he is about to say," wrote Guez de Balzac of Montaigne at a time in which a noble *sprezzatura,* that is, nonchalance or negligence, was the most precious value bequeathed by the ancients, notably by the Ciceronian notion of *neglegentia diligens.*[43] Such qualities transcended the distinction between the ancients and the moderns and were heralded by both. Marivaux and Montesquieu, however, typified the *goût moderne* in the emphasis they placed on the association between feminine, erotic seduction and the seduction of a negligent style. (The identification of rhetoric with feminine ornament was also a classic motif, but the moderns revived that commonplace with a positive spin.) "Nothing pleases us more in finery than the negligence, or even the disorder, that conceals all the attention to detail that vanity, not propriety, required; the mind never has more grace than when what one says is spontaneous and not contrived."[44] In the wake of *galanterie* the written word took as its model the living voice of conversation, the extemporaneous surge of oral improvisation. The writer, Montesquieu noted, was formed both in the solitude of the cabinet and in worldly conversation: "In the cabinet we learn to write with method, to reason well, and to discipline our reason. . . . In a social gathering, in contrast, we learn to develop our imagination. . . . There, we are thinking beings for the reason that we do not think; that is to say, we run into the ideas that chance offers us, which are often the good ones."[45] The imagination, in its creativity and originality, does not deploy itself in solitude and tranquil recollection but in the chance encounter that takes place in oral interaction—an attitude that goes a long way toward explaining the lure of conversation to eighteenth-century writers.[46]

Self-reflexivity and irony, however, are never quite absent from the discourse of an author who constantly *says* he is negligent and unaffected but who dramatically fails to shed the self-consciousness that prevents him from actually being so. His many references to simplicity and transparency can hardly avoid appearing emphatic and ostentatious, and the author does protest too much for the reader to take such unaffectedness at face value. The author finds himself in the bind described by Montesquieu: "But how can one work at being natural?"[47] What is more, how credible a claim of spontaneity and authenticity uttered through a series of masks or dramatis personae may be? Many of the first-person characters who emerge from the pages of the journals claim the status of authorship, or, more humbly, that of simple and unaffected humanness. Yet, in the polyphonic choir produced by this motley crowd (the misanthropist, the cynical philosopher, the picaro-Harlequin, the drunken actor, the posthumous *homme d'esprit*) we can never hope to find the author's "authentic" and unmediated voice. In order to lend his characters the veneer of "authenticity" the journalist draws upon conventions: the treasure-trove of the "chest full of papers";[48] the letters written to a provincial lady *(Lettres sur les habitants de Paris);* fake memoirs and stolen correspondences in *Le spectateur français,* to name a few.

Ultimately, none of those voices are able to let the consciousness flow unadulterated. Marivaux's prose writing—in the novels and in the journals—is unable to resolve the paradox of self-consciousness: Spontaneity cannot be *said* nor willed. It can only be performed. It can only *happen* in the language of drama.

In Search of Voice

Surprisingly, the challenge Marivaux was facing in his search for a new relationship between language and states of consciousness was not unlike the challenge his rival Voltaire confusedly formulated in his longstanding crusade against *esprit*. If we want to understand the context of Marivaux's search for a new fictional language, we must turn to Voltaire's own, lifelong struggle against bad taste:

> What we call *esprit* may sometimes be a new comparison or a fine allusion; here it is the misuse of a word that is used in one sense but suggests another; there it is a delicate relationship between two ideas seldom encountered; it is an unusual metaphor; it is the search for a meaning that lies hidden in an object but nonetheless exists. . . ; it is the tendency to develop one's thought halfway so as to suggest the rest. I would say more about *esprit* had I more of it; but all that glitter (not to mention fake glitter) is not suited, or is rarely suited, to a serious work, one that must hold the audience's attention. The reason is that the author shows through, while the audience wants to see the character. Now, the character is always in the grip of passion or danger. Danger and passion are not after *esprit*. Priamus and Hecuba do not compose epigrams while their children are being massacred and Troy is in flames. Dido does not grieve in madrigals while going to her martyrdom. Demosthenes does not have pretty thoughts when he prods the Athenians to war. If he had them, he would be a rhetorician, not a statesman.[49]

The *Lettre sur l'esprit*, of which this is an excerpt, was very likely written in self-defense.[50] As we saw in chapter 2, the grievances Voltaire expressed against *esprit* throughout his *oeuvre* were not especially original; rather, they were the echoes of previously established fault lines in the literary landscape. In this text, however, something else is at play. Beyond the tired arguments that resurface time and again we may discern a new restlessness. What really struggles to come out of Voltaire's recurring admonitions is the need for a new theatrical and poetic language. But like a man facing a danger in the dark, Voltaire strikes right, left, and center, striking down the language of literature indiscriminately and blindly. Down with the use of new metaphors! Down with surprising and discerning comparisons among new ideas; down with ambiguity and complexity of meaning, with polysemy of all kinds; with allusion and reticence. In other words, down with many of the traits that have made Voltaire's own prose, in such works as the *Lettres* and the *Contes philosophiques,* so effective. There is a terrible irony in his position. As Lionel Gossman has remarked,

Voltaire proposes a standard of value that renders his own work minor and irrelevant. As a dramatist and a historian, he upholds a classical ideal in light of which the portion of his *oeuvre* that we value most—his *Contes,* his dialogues, his correspondence, his light verse—must necessarily appear as "marginal and inconsequential."[51]

The failings of modern *esprit* cover a territory that is vast indeed, perhaps too vast. For once he has purged his prose of it, what is the writer left with? We find Voltaire in a bind similar to the one confronted by Fénelon. Once again, what we encounter is a kind of linguistic and stylistic virtue turned terrorist. It is also worth noting the slippages of a text that starts by referring to modern prose, continues with allusions to modern theater, then to Homer and Virgil's epic poems, only to end with the obligatory Demosthenes, that is, with a "statesman," not a "rhetorician," God forbid. Where would Voltaire situate himself in relation to such weighty tradition? The author must disappear, we are told, so as to let the characters speak. But what will be their language? Voltaire wishes he could set himself free from the theatrical and linguistic conventions that burden any ambitious and successful tragedian. But what will he replace them with? In what voice does passion speak when it flows spontaneous and unshackled from literary codes and rules? In the grip of a powerful emotion, he insists, the heroine does not speak in epigrams and madrigals. True enough. But neither does she speak in verse. Does that mean that tragedy should reject verse altogether? That is a step that Voltaire does not even consider.[52]

In reality, the dissatisfaction Voltaire so confusedly expresses here is very close to that which Diderot conveys in his many writings on dramatic language, and most forcefully in the *Paradoxe sur le comédien*. Contrary to current opinion, the *Paradoxe* is not primarily the paean to the rigid codification of theatrical gesture and to the rejection of sensitivity in acting that it is taken to be. The *Paradoxe* is an extended *persiflage,*[53] a rhetorical ambush, another example in a long list of Diderot's deceptions and decoys. It is a clever set piece in which Diderot pretends to extol the virtues of calculated artifice in acting so as to expose the intolerable artifice that dramatic language has become in his day and the decadence of a theater that has lost all power to express the real emotions of ordinary human beings. "The likeness of the passions on the stage is not, then, its true likeness; it is but extravagant portraiture [*portraits outrés*], caricatures on a grand scale, subject to conventional rules."[54] The sensible (and relatively banal) argument that Diderot makes in favor of a controlled use of the emotions in acting is pushed to the extreme so as to highlight his conviction that the dramatic style prevalent in his day has grown hopelessly out of touch with the actual experience of spectators and with the new dramatic genre that Diderot wishes to promote.

On the one hand, Diderot points out, the simple tone of the *sermo familiaris* would seem misplaced in the theater: "But now transfer your easy tone, your simple expression, your informal bearing, your natural manner, to the stage, and you will see how paltry and weak you will be. You may shed tears: you will be ridiculous and the audience will laugh. It will not be a tragedy that you enact but the fairgrounds parody of a tragedy [*une parade tragique*]. Do you suppose that the dialogues of Corneille, Racine, Voltaire, and Shakespeare may be delivered with your conversation voice and your fireside tone?" On the other, theatrical grandeur would appear ridiculous in an intimate setting because such grandeur is not rooted in nature: "When by a long stage habit one keeps the stage's emphatic accent in society and struts around as Brutus, Cinna, Mithridates, Cornelia, Merope, Pompey, do you know what one does? One couples with a soul small or great, exactly as nature has cut its measure, the outward signs of an exalted and gigantic soul that is not one's own. The result is ridicule." To which his interlocutor replies: "What a cruel satire of actors and authors is this you are making, *innocently or by design!* . . . I do not think that the expression of true grandeur can ever be ridiculous."[55]

In fact, Diderot suggests, the putative incompatibility between ordinary language and theatrical speech, between the "fireside tone of conversation" and the "stage accent," is not an ontological, necessary fact of the divide between reality and representation. Rather, it is a fact contingent on the theatrical conventions tied to a given time and place, one that authors and theater lovers ought to be able to put into perspective. It is a situation that may seem inescapable and God-given only to a theatrical culture that has lost its true function and identity. Corneille and Racine, revered as they are, are the practitioners of an art in which "bombast, *esprit* and *papillotage* are a thousand miles from nature;"[56] of a style burdened with an emphasis inherited from the Spanish baroque ("the rodomontade of Madrid"), "overblown bombast in Corneille's manner."[57] They have succumbed to a theatrical language that, frozen into a "three-thousand-year-old protocol," has lost its capacity to move the audience. Diderot's expressions mercilessly emphasize the caricatural, camp quality of contemporary acting: "Leave those hippogriffs on the stage, with their action, their posture, and their screams. They would make a sorry figure in history; they would incite laughter in a circle or in any other social gathering."[58] It is highly unlikely that Diderot, who did in fact remove the theatrical scene from the stage and bring it to the intimacy of the drawing room and the social gathering (and, indeed, to the fireside), would have endorsed the idea of a theatrical style so outrageous and outlandish as to appear ridiculous and misplaced in those intimate settings. In reality, his critique of theatrical declamation and gesture has always been unequivocal, radical, and devastating: "Have people ever spoken the way we declaim? Do princes and kings walk any differently from a man who walks well? Do they ever gesticulate like madmen or lunatics? Do princesses speak in a shrill whistling tone?"[59]

Like many of their contemporaries, Voltaire and Diderot rejected a language and a style that they had inherited from the seventeenth-century conversation of the *précieux*, a language that in their eyes had become too perverted by the "luxury" of rhetorical ornament, too contrived, and too morally tainted to represent the passions that "republican," regenerated audiences ought to experience. "It would be desirable," wrote d'Alembert, "that those among our writers who attempt, whether in the theater or in another art medium, to portray their own age would not limit their efforts to borrowing its jargon. They believe that they are writing the history of man, but they are only writing that of language. It is from this tortuous, inappropriate, and barbaric language that many claim today to recognize those authors who frequent what goes under the name of good company."[60] Artistic expression had to be dislodged from its dwelling within polite society and purged of the ambiguities, the self-indulgence, and the uncertainties of modern existence: it had to recapture the intensity of an earlier, mythical time. Like Fénelon before them, Voltaire and Diderot doggedly pursued and tracked down the so-called *esprit,* the ubiquitous impropriety that seemed to betray the trace of mannerism and the failure of fiction to move and persuade. But neither of them succeeded in finding the radically new manner and style that they were calling for. Neither was able to implement a theatrical language flexible enough to embody the new passions, the new morality, and the new characters that they wanted to bring to the stage.

Rather than trying to capture the accent of the present, Diderot and Voltaire sought their inspiration in the revamping of the ancients, a move that Mercier pitilessly termed "Voltaire's face-lift" (le retapé de Voltaire).[61] They turned their eyes toward the fabled "simplicity" and the sublime stylistic economy of a heroic age that they hoped to revive: "If the day comes when a man of genius dares give his characters the simple tone of antique heroism, the actor's art will assume an entirely new difficulty," wrote Diderot.[62] "It is not what we call *esprit,* it is the sublime and the simple that constitute real beauty," noted

Voltaire, in a rebuff to Corneille (Voltaire was the author of a multivolume, line-by-line, severe appraisal of Corneille's complete theater).[63] In Diderot, the desire to recapture the energy that imbued ancient works of art was countered by his bitter conviction that their greatness was out of the moderns' reach: "To put it in a nutshell, it seems to me that the masterpieces of the ancients will always attest to the sublimity of artists of the past and eternally guarantee the mediocrity of future artists. I am sorry about that."[64] Trapped in the logic of emulation that he had learned in the college *inventio,* Diderot was obsessed by ancient models, which haunted him like a bad conscience or as a constant reminder of the present's artistic inferiority. Only the sacrifice of their vanities, the trauma of civil war, and a return to the primitive sources of civilization could save the French from themselves, their jargon of politeness, their whigs and their silk costumes: "If our painters and sculptors were henceforth to be obliged to draw their subjects from the history of modern France—I say modern, for the first Franks retained in their mode of dress something of the simplicity of antique garb—then painting and sculpture would soon fall into decadence. . . . I'd very much like to know how the artists of several thousand years hence will depict us."[65]

In their search for expressive intensity and the stark simplicity of primary moral conflicts, the philosophes tended to mistake preachiness for pathos, melodrama for tragedy, and the expression of philosophically good intentions for the representation of the real. They thought that art ought to disdain the space of ordinary interaction and conversation and instead stake out the ground of the extreme and the extraordinary, that it ought to embrace the violently melodramatic spectacle of terror and death:

> In general, the more a people is civilized and polished, the less its manners are poetic; everything weakens when it softens. When does nature prepare models for art? It is when children pull out their hair around the bed of their dying father; when a mother uncovers her bosom and begs her son for the sake of the breast that nourished him; when a friend cuts his hair and spreads it on the cadaver of his friend; . . . when disheveled widows, whom death has robbed of their husbands, tear their faces with their nails.[66]

Poetry, to Diderot, wore the intensely distasteful, messy face of disheveled mourners, such as eighteenth-century urban France would never see. (It would be worthwhile exploring the reasons behind Diderot's curious obsession with the funereal, hair-rending practices of the traditional Mediterranean world.)

From Tragedy to Marivaudage

In the end, for all their emulation of the ancients, the neoclassicists could not inject one jolt of energy into the carcass of tragedy. The experiment of the modern *drame* (which the revolutionary stage would revive) yielded for the time being only partial success and much promise of future kitsch. In one of the most scathing chapters of his *Tableaux,* Louis-Sébastien Mercier juxtaposed the crowning of Voltaire's bust on the stage of the Théâtre-Français, at the end of the performance of *Irène* (Voltaire's last and greatest triumph) to an event of a very different kind that occurred three months later. Mercier declared that it was no longer Voltaire but the humble fairgrounds actors, headed by the lowly Janot, who now carried the enthusiasm of Parisian audiences. "Janot acted in a farce that, more successful than *Irène,* only enjoyed five hundred performances. The language of the people's lowest class was portrayed just as it was; and the actor's artless manner, his steadfast expression, formed a tableau that, no matter how lowly, had a quality that one rarely encounters on the French stage: the accent of perfect truth."[67]

It was that same truth, embodied in the "voice of the people"—not that of the lower classes (which were still confined, with the possible exception of the *drame,* to the *poissard* jargon of the farce), but that of the educated, worldly bourgeoisie—that Marivaux sought to bring to the stage. And it was in the theater, rather than in the journals, that he succeeded in carrying out Montaigne and Pascal's wager: writing like a man (or a woman), not like an author; writing in the voice of intimate conversation, capturing the flow and the spontaneity of the *sermo familiaris.*

> We are accustomed to the style of authors because they have their own. We almost *never write as we speak.* When we arrange our thoughts, we give them a twist. Everywhere there is a taste for uniformity and evenness that we do not notice because we have grown accustomed to it. But if, by chance, you abandon that style and bring to a work of art, to a play, the ordinary language of men, you will be sure to make an impression. If you are successful, you will be very successful, all the more so as you will be perceived as new. But should you do it again, the ordinary language of men will no longer seem so, because it has been appreciated, not as such, but as your own: people will say that you are repeating yourself. I am not suggesting that I have been in that situation myself, though it is true that I have tried to capture the language of conversation, the diverse and intimate accents that flow through it. But I do not claim that I have succeeded.[68]

Marivaux, with his habitual taste for paradox, understood why his critics blamed him for obsessively focusing on "that eternal surprise of love."[69] The style of an author was perceived as "natural" only as long as it followed the expectations of the public and the ruling conventions. Any departure from such codes, any attempt to break the riddle of "the ordinary language of men," to reproduce the rhythm of actual conversation, would be jarring and disconcerting to an ear accustomed to taking the stage jargon for real. Such an attempt would be perceived as peculiar to an author, not as faithful to the culture he was trying to portray. Diderot echoed that problem when he noted, some thirty years later, in the *Paradoxe* how ridiculous the speech of Merope and Cinna would sound in the salon and, conversely, how inappropriate the language of conversation would sound on the stage. To a certain extent, that was and always will be the case. What we accept as "natural" and "realistic" in the cinema and on television today is different from what we take for natural in our daily interactions: both languages seem "natural" to us only because we are unaware of the subtle differences that we edit out so as to become inured to the perception of a distinction between the two.[70] And, of course, the audience's greater or lesser awareness of the linguistic conventionality of a text depends on its historical relationship to it. The farther removed we are from it in time, the more slanted our perception will be by our preconceptions about what may count as "natural" or "mannered" in a given period and place (we must remember that Racine's and Molière's language had greatly aged in Voltaire's time). However, as Marivaux paradoxically suggests, the two poles—the immediate present and the distant, canonized past—end up converging: to an audience hearing it for the first time, the language of contemporary conversation, which he had tried to capture in its spontaneous outpouring, might have seemed just as contrived as Corneille's poetic idiom.

That foreword accompanied the publication of one of Marivaux's most original plays, *Les serments indiscrets*. The play's opening night, at the Théâtre-Français, had been a disaster, probably orchestrated by a cabal mounted by Voltaire (who was eager to make the stage available for the presentation of his new tragedy, *Zaire*). A few months earlier, in an epistolary allusion to the possible flop of his rival's play, Voltaire had basked in a bout of schadenfreude: "We are going to have this summer a prose comedy of the Sieur Marivaux, under the title of *Les serments indiscrets*. You may bet that there will be much gibberish [*métaphysique*] and scarce taste and that the cafés will applaud, while people of taste will understand nothing."[71] Voltaire, like most of his contemporaries in the world of letters, remained deaf to the originality of Marivaux's theatrical language.

And yet, rather than follow the timeworn protocol denounced by Voltaire and Diderot, Marivaux had tried to bring to the stage the revealing rhythm of actual conversation as he knew it: "Among people of taste [*gens d'esprit*] conversations are much more animated than we usually think, and . . . all that an author can do in order to imitate them will never come close to the animation, to the spontaneous and sudden outbursts of fancy that they put into it."[72] Conversation to Marivaux was not the contrived and theatrical exercise in self-invention that Marmontel, Crébillon, and Diderot satirized.[73] Indeed, he did not emphasize the rhetorical virtuosity that the salon guests had learned in the colleges, the crossfire between the interlocutors and the verbal brilliance that constituted *esprit*. Quite the contrary. We would be hard pressed to find in his plays the verbal playfulness that characterizes a Crébillon or a Laclos. His characters seldom show Valmont's or Merteuil's ironic detachment and control over their expression. Most of the time, the occasional *pointe* is made by the valets, not the masters, who are too involved in their own emotions to be able to distance themselves from their language. Indeed, it is often the contrast between the verbal playfulness of the valets and the embarrassed silences of the masters that drives the action. Merteuil and Valmont use language as a weapon pliable to their will. But in Marivaux's theater, language and will are at odds. His characters, even when they make up phrases and speeches, always allow the spectator to see, through the mask, their humanity and vulnerability. Whatever they may say, we are able to hear something else.

Damis and Lucile, the young lovers of *Les serments indiscrets;* the countess and the marquis, the aging and awkward suitors in *Le legs;* Araminte in *Les fausses confidences;* and Hortense in *Le prince travesti* are not in control of what they say and show of their emotions. Their language is revealing, not because of the meaning that it conveys, but because of what it betrays of their passions; not by what it says, but by what it suggests in oblique and devious ways; by its reticence and silence. Through repetitions and *reprises,* the rebounding of one word from a character to another, embarrassing pauses, interruptions, hysterical petulance, slips of the tongue, the characters always show more than they wish to; language leads them astray, much against their will, to strange and dangerous places where they would rather not go. Marivaux was alone among his contemporaries (with the possible exception of Crébillon) to explore the many ways in which the subconscious peeks through the carefully wrought structure of verbal and social conventions and the codes of politeness and *galanterie*. Language to him was a living thing; it had an existence of its own, independent of the speaker's intention. Thus, it was only in the theater that Marivaux was able to overcome the spectatorial self-awareness that pervaded his novels and his journals. While in the narrative works the spectatorial function was internal to the protagonists, in the plays it was divided among a bevy of subordinate characters (parents, friends, and servants, who played, in turn, the role of obstacles or facilitators), thus leaving the protagonists free to become ensnared by their passions and liberated from burdensome self-consciousness. It was thus in the theater that Marivaux was the least self-consciously "theatrical."

Another aspect of Marivaux's reworking of theatrical codes was the transgression of the boundaries of genre. A fact that his contemporaries were unable to grasp was that through those dislocations of the language of *galanterie* and courtship Marivaux had succeeded, where would-be reformers of the theater had not, in doing the unthinkable, namely, marrying the language of high tragedy to that of the Italian farce—not in the clashing, contrastive manner of parodists, but in his own seamless, harmonious, and invisible synthesis. Neither comedies based on character like those of Molière nor moral and social satires like those of Lesage, Dufresny, or Dancourt, Marivaux's plays seemed to resist all description. No one had come to the realization, undoubtedly because it would have been unimaginable, that the genre that came closest to them was not the contemporary comedy of manners but the great classical tragedy of Corneille and Racine.

What Marivaux did was borrow the structural elements that defined tragedy and translate them into the language of comedy and into the idiom of the contemporary polite world. True, there was nothing "tragic," in the sense that we intend today, about Marivaux's theater, for by and large his plays had a happy ending. But Corneille did not define tragedy by its catastrophic outcome: he defined it by the existence of a confrontation between conflicting passions during an extraordinary and intense encounter between the characters and/or within the characters themselves as a result of such an encounter.[74] The focus of Corneille's plays was not the calamitous consequences of unruly passions, as had been the case for earlier tragedies, but the passional event itself. Similarly, the nexus of Marivaux's comedies lies in the dramatization of a conflict resulting from the clash between contrasting passions. They may not be grand and imposing ones, but they are equally absorbing and conducive to a paroxysm of anguish: love and pride *(La surprise de l'amour, La double inconstance);* desire and shame, or fear of losing one's freedom and autonomy *(Les serments indiscrets*; *Le jeu de l'amour et du hasard)*; or, even more comical, as is the case in *Le legs,* a longing for companionship running afoul of insurmountable timidity and fear (with a sprinkling of avarice, which receives a far less ridiculous treatment at Marivaux's hands than at Molière's). All of those feelings take hold of the heroes and tear them apart, with varying intensity, in agonizing, if comical, tension. Marivaux succeeded in adapting those conflicts within a discourse of *galanterie* that he had inherited from Madeleine de Scudéry and Corneille but that he subjected to the attenuations of irony and a benign, libertine distancing. Thus, his heroines are young coquettes and ingénues, but they preserve something of the troubling pathos and vulnerability of Racinian heroes and heroines. At the peak of the crisis—just before the abrupt resolution that will transform her relationship to herself and to the world—when the heroine has lost her moorings and her identity, her cry of embarrassment and anguish, "Je ne sais plus où j'en suis" (I no longer know what I am doing / who I am), is perhaps no less poignant than that of Mithridates: "Qui suis-je? Est-ce Monime? Et suis-je Mithridate?"[75] In *Arlequin poli par l'amour* Silvia's despair for having put Arlequin's life into the hands of the jealous and all-powerful Fairy is not unlike that of Monime, who has been tricked into revealing her love for Xipharès to his all-powerful rival Mithridates, or that of Atalide, who has unwittingly betrayed Bajazet to her equally all-powerful rival, Roxanne. (The same structure occurs again, in the upper register, in act 3, scene 5, of Marivaux's *Le prince travesti*.) When Silvia gives up her love in order to save Arlequin, her sacrifice is no less heroic than that of Racine's heroines, though it is of far shorter duration, for evil is defeated in the end.

Marivaux's bourgeois Silvias and Angéliques are at least as proud as the princely Chimène and Emilie; like them, they want to test whether their lovers are worthy of them: as in Corneille's tragedy, love is a relationship of rivalry. To do so, the women engage their adversaries (the various Dorantes, Lélios, Damis, Lisidors) in an all-out battle of wits and pride, in which the *aveu,* the confession of love, is the main stake. (We are reminded of the importance of the *aveu* in such plays as *Le Cid, Mithridate,* or *Bajazet.*) Betrayal, jealousy, cruelty, and deceit, the motors of tragedy, do make their appearance in Marivaux's comic world, but in the final revelation they are neutralized, or they turn out to have been illusory. Those who seem briefly to succumb to such evils, like Angélique in *L'épreuve* or Mme Argante in *Les acteurs de bonne foi,* see their suffering vanish in a flash when their tormentors take off their devilish masks and are revealed to be benign fathers, mothers, prospective husbands. (Whether in reality they are entirely benign remains an open question, and a tribute to Marivaux's inexhaustible well of ambiguity.) Furthermore, the structure of tragic irony—the hero's blindness about his fate or his passions, which is a source of pathos in tragedy—becomes in Marivaux an endless source of comical awareness, as the spectator is given an insight into the characters' motivations that they are unable to have themselves (an insight mirrored by that of the spectatorial eye of the valets and soubrettes).

The much-criticized stretching of time in Marivaux's plays, the narrow focus on the slow and convoluted unraveling of the emotions (which had Mme du Deffand complain that "Marivaux makes us run around for miles within the confines of a single parquet leaf"),[76] may be best understood when placed alongside the equally maniacally detailed treatment of the passions in tragedy. As Jean-Marie Apostolidès puts it,

> The tragic time is that of the intimate experience, that of a history lived through the subconscious. That is why it appears as the drawn-out suspension of a brief moment. The thing that in ordinary life would take a few seconds, perhaps a few minutes, to formulate and communicate is leisurely explicated in Racine. All the vacillations of the mind, all the movements of the heart, are registered, analyzed, dissected in lengthy *tirades*. Tragedy is not a temporal shrinking but rather a stretching of time, thanks to rhetorical procedures that may be compared to cinematographical slow motion. The fluctuations of the hero's heart and mind are presented as a closeup; we are able to perceive their microscopic movements, which, when added up, result in an action that takes place outside the spectator's purview. Racine is less interested in the act than in the minute mechanisms of the heart that prepare and follow the act, and that the author takes apart before our eyes, from one play to the next, with unswerving patience.[77]

All of which may be said of Marivaux's theater. The fact that in his plays action was carried out through dialogue led d'Alembert to comment quite obtusely: "It is true that they have no action to speak of; all there is, is dialogue without a plot."[78]

It had not occurred to d'Alembert that it was precisely in his treatment of speech that Marivaux's plays came closest to the ideal of *le Grand Siècle*: speech is action, the plot is carried out by the dialogue, and the time of the performance overlaps as closely as possible with fictional time.[79] But by the end of the eighteenth century the ideals of seventeenth-century theater had been entirely lost in the fog of history (or perhaps in the fallacious familiarity of endless confrontation and emulation). The extent of the misunderstanding may be measured by La Harpe's acidic assessment of Marivaux's poetics:

"The crux of his plays is nothing but a word that must at all cost be uttered at the end, though everybody has known it since the beginning"—one could find no better description for the plot of Racine's *Bérénice*—"obstacles spring merely from his dialogue; instead of weaving a plot, he endlessly unravels a declaration or an avowal [*aveu*]."[80] The most significant distinction between classical tragedy and Marivaux's comedy lies in the disarticulation of the *tirade*, which in Marivaux is replaced by a lively dialogue, by the exchange of replies bouncing from one interlocutor to another. But the same attention is lavished upon the minute analysis of the evolution of the passions, which for being subdued—or, as Hume would say, moderate—are no less dramatically significant. Marivaux's painstaking detailing of the dynamics that drives ordinary people in their ordinary moments of crisis (the choice of a husband for oneself or for a child, the life-changing arrival of a new neighbor, the breaking of a contract, the sacrifice of one's longstanding habits), raised such ordinariness to the level of a representability that, for the first time, transcended the traditional divide between the comic register (reserved for the pedestrian, concrete aspects of life) and the dignity of poetry (reserved for highly disciplined passions removed from the sensuality and the triviality of the present).

Marivaux thus almost alone succeeded in achieving a cross-fertilization between the traditional, courtly forms of high culture and those of the satirical, popular theater. He did that for the benefit of an elite audience that was no longer eager to embrace the upright, reformed taste of courtly classicism (which remained popular among the lower bourgeoisie), preferring to recognize itself in the dynamic language of conversational *galanterie* and in the ironic deflections achieved through the juxtaposition of *galanterie* and the irreverent theatricality of the Italians and the fairgrounds.[81] The marriage of high and low culture also responded to the aesthetics that had been formulated almost a century earlier in the circles of Madeleine de Scudéry and Mme de Rambouillet, among the elites who had found in the pastoral fantasy of *L'astrée* a welcome respite from courtly constraints and from more martial—and highly stylized and tragic—forms of heroism. In fashioning a coherent aesthetics out of the apparently unreconcilable elements of tragic passion and farce, Marivaux was able to bring to the official stage and to the public of the Regency the kind of synthesis that Watteau had been producing during the same years in the portrayal of the *fête galante*, with its metaphorical use of masks, the intimate, pastoral scenes of nobles and wealthy bourgeois engaged in the "improvised form of ritual leisure" of amateur theater and *parades*.[82]

5 | *Grace and the Epistemology of Confused Perception*

> *What's happening to us now is the same that happened the century following that of Augustus. The likes of Lucan overtook Virgil, and the likes of Seneca, Cicero. The Senecas and the Lucans had fake glitter; they bedazzled the people, who rushed to them because they seemed new.*
>
> —Voltaire

> *In some texts, words are* sparkling; *they are distracting and incongruous apparitions.*
>
> —Barthes

More Dazzling than Enlightening

In chapter 2 we explored one facet of *esprit*, namely, the *bel esprit* in its social dimension as a ridiculous author who turns his craft into a self-promoting enterprise. But *esprit* was far more than a snob's career move. It was above all a style and a mode of vision, a concept that was both cognitive and aesthetic. Historically speaking, *esprit* was associated with the poetics of *acumen* and *ingenium* (Voltaire defined it as *raison ingénieuse*),[1] which, from the sixteenth century on had been expelled from the national body of French literature and identified with the conceit *(concetto)* that characterized the baroque poetry and poetic treatises that flourished in Italy and Spain, with the works of Ludovico Ariosto, Torquato Tasso, Luis de Góngora, Baltasar Gracián, Emanuele Tesauro, and Matteo Peregrini.[2] But the genealogy of *esprit* goes further back. Latin poets such as Seneca, Martial, and Lucan, infamously born in Roman

Hispania, had been diagnosed, by several generations of French writers (notably by Montaigne, Guez de Balzac, Boileau, Bouhours, and Voltaire), with the same disease as their progeny. *Esprit* was a miasma that one breathed with the air of southern climates; it traveled fast and tended to spread its infection. French authors from Ronsard to Voiture to Corneille, not to mention the practitioners of *préciosité* and *galanterie,* were seen as suffering from its effects. In the eyes of their detractors in the early eighteenth century, *esprit* was a great many things, but most of all it was a delirious language that had lost all referential function, an empty parade of refinement and virtuosity, the search for artificial similarities between disparate objects, the evanescent sophistry that emerged from a mind drawn to "weighing insect eggs on a bed of spider webs."[3] Morvan de Bellegarde, a harsh critic of the culture of *esprit,* detailed in a text published in 1702 an extensive list of offenses, all symptoms of a generalized decadence of taste:

> Good taste has its tribulations, much like philosophy. Until recently taste in France was very depraved: *phébus,* preciosity, buffoonery, had banished good sense. Witticism [*pointe*], equivocations, wordplay had replaced true beauty in writing. Set rimes [*bouts-rimés*], burlesque gibes, dreary jokes delighted the populace and the court. Reason was buried and smothered under a hodgepodge of bad productions. It was only after many trials and countless combats that good sense recovered its rightful place.[4]

Readers familiar with the *Art poétique* may find here an echo of Boileau's opposition between *pointe* and *bon sens,*[5] as well as of his abhorrence for anything resembling semantic polyvalence, such as *equivoque,* which truly sets Boileau over the top.[6] *Esprit* is described by Bellegarde as a multifaceted linguistic phenomenon and as a kind of contagious disease that seeps through the world of letters from the lower strata of the populace to the upper echelons of the court; from the "turlupinade" that rules the stage of the popular theaters[7] to the "bouts-rimés" that are the amusement of worldly circles. Worldly *galanterie* and the people's burlesque amusements are fertile grounds for a linguistic intemperance that shares the same depravity. *Marivaudage,* the label that was affixed to Marivaux's language toward the end of the eighteenth century, "metaphysical jargon," a "mixture of burlesque and common language,"[8] clearly belonged to the same phenomenon.

Following the Pascalian notion of *finesse,* however, *esprit* indicated a kind of penetrating vision that suddenly illuminated a multiplicity of occult relations between objects, a form of perception that, unlike the *esprit de geométrie,* was able to bypass all the stages of a rigorous and demonstrative reasoning.[9] Thus the latin word *acumen* (in Italian *acume* and in Spanish *agudeza*), aptly translated in French by *pointe,* meant not only "witticism" but also the sharp edge of penetrating, "acute" intelligence. If *esprit* had anything to do with conceits and figures of speech, it was because its prompt understanding could hardly be reduced to a systematic, step-by-step demonstration; it was better suited to the coming together of metaphorical thinking.[10] *Esprit* relied upon a form of judgment that eluded expression because the steps it took were too many and too small to rise above the threshold of awareness.[11] Marivaux thus associated *esprit* or *bel esprit* (often used as synonyms) with the domain of intuition *(sentiment),* immediacy of feeling, subtlety *(délicatesse),* and all that was ineffable in the mind and in personal character. In her portrait of Mme de Miran, Marianne expressed the difficulty of putting into words her intuitive knowledge of someone's character:

> I know the people I live with much better than I am able to define them. There are things in them that I do not know well enough to tell, and that I perceive for myself, not for others. They are objects of intuition [*sentiment*] so complex and of such delicate makeup that they get blurry as soon as reason examines them. I do not know how to get hold of them in order to express them, so that they are in me but do not belong to me. Have you ever felt the same? It seems to me that on many occasions my soul knows far more than it can say and that is has a mind of its own that is far superior to my ordinary mind.[12]

Sentiment is for Marianne an unselfconscious mode of thought eliciting a confused representation drawn inferentially from the minute perceptions that constitute experience and all but impossible to reproduce verbally.[13] Marivaux points out in his journals that a different type of rationality regulates *sentiment;* just because we are not aware that we are making a reflection does not mean that reason is not involved: "What is *sentiment?* It is an instinct that guides us and makes us act unreflectively by presenting us with something that affects us. It is not developed in certain persons as it is in others. . . . Yet, it is the same as the mind [*esprit*] but more or less confused."[14] Not only does *sentiment* enable one to perceive beauty but it is an effective tool for understanding the intricacies of social relations. In fact, *goût, finesse,* and *délicatesse* denoted in the seventeenth and eighteenth centuries a kind of empirical judgment that could be applied not only to the appreciation of aesthetic objects but also to discernment in worldly interaction. The domain of the aesthetic and that of worldliness were coextensive: the same type of rationality informed aesthetic judgment and the capacity to find one's way through the social labyrinth, to the ability to regulate behavior and to interpret that of others, to the perspicacity that allowed one to position oneself within the social sphere. In the seventeenth century, aesthetics and ethics were closely connected under the combined patronage of such intractably evasive concepts as *goût* (taste) and grace. In the writings of Méré, Madeleine de Scudéry, and Bouhours key terms such as *délicatesse, finesse,* and *je ne sais quoi* (as we shall see, akin to grace) were tools employed in the definition of social ideals such as *honnêteté* and *air galant.* Only secondarily were they used to explore the still uncharted domain of taste and aesthetic appreciation, which was not yet emancipated from other kinds of value. In Marivaux, aesthetic judgment and the understanding of social behavior are both rooted in the faculty of refined intuition. Marianne, in fact, does not miss any opportunity to suggest that her heightened sensibility and sharp understanding are the products of an aristocratic nature.[15]

The author *bel esprit*—who united elegance of expression, intensity of emotion, and clarity of reasoning—could not fail to demonstrate that he possessed, more than anyone else, a highly refined cognitive ability drawn from sensation. His vision was the result of sensibility and a subtle balance of the humors:

> A *bel esprit* is not an artisan geometer but a born architect who, while meditating on a building, is able to see it rising before his eyes complete in all its various parts. He imagines and perceives its totality thanks to a reasoning that is imperceptible and instantaneous. . . . In other words, a *bel esprit* is blessed with a disposition that gives him a fine and precise intuition of all the things that he sees or imagines.[16]

The metaphor of architecture allows the *bel esprit* to argue for the superiority of *sentiment,* a prompt and discerning judgment that does effortlessly what would otherwise require painstaking and slow laboring on the part of the master *géomètre.* While the latter is defined as an *ouvrier,* a craftsman devoid of any intellectual creativity, the *bel esprit* is able to conceive a whole building as a perfectly achieved form and also to have an intuitive, analytic knowledge of all its separate components. Those who accuse the *bel esprit* of being nothing but a craftsman who makes a trade of his art do not understand that he is an intellectual, "a sensitive man, a man whose organs are most refined" and who "carries his sight and his intuition further than ordinary men."[17]

Marivaux employs here a language drawn from modern, empiricist epistemology, while also relying upon the traditional language of the ancient physiology of the humors, which the abbé Bouhours had illustrated in his widely circulated essay on the *bel esprit.* Following Bouhours, the *bel esprit* draws his superior epistemic capacities from "a well balanced and proportioned head, of a well-tempered brain filled with a refined matter, a clear bile made stable by melancholy and smoothed by blood." The physiology of *esprit* is more complex, however. On the one hand, *esprit* is the product of a balanced temperament and a human being who is perfectly mediocre in the Aristotelian sense. On the other, it is a creative energy, pure virtuality resulting from the spiritualization of matter in the brain. It is a sort of elixir, the effusion of matter distilled into its quintessential components emanating a kind of light, or enlightenment:

> The spirits of blood and bile smolder in the brain in the same way that hot vapor may blaze in a cold and moist cloud. The burning spirits spread to the head a dry radiance that, according to Heraclitus, makes the soul wise and bright. And since among corporeal objects nothing has less matter and more virtue, nothing is purer and more energetic than those spirits; the flame that emanates from them is the finest, the most vibrant, and the most ardent that exists in nature. It is this flame that at once enlightens reason and fires the imagination, that makes the species of things visible to the soul and reveals them to it in their true light. In one word, it is in the light of this splendid fire that the understanding discovers and contemplates the most obscure truths.[18]

In 1756, in his article "Esprit," Voltaire appeals to the same tradition when he describes *esprit* as "the most subtle part of matter" and as the energy that creates movement and life: "Those spirits that we believe run through the nerves are a subtle fire." *Esprit* is the spontaneous efflorescence of the mind's creative energy and inventiveness.[19] That sense was present in the Latin word *ingenium*, which was often translated in French by *esprit*. In his dictionary, Furetière defined *ingénieux* as "that which has *esprit*, which is made with *esprit*."[20]

In the writings of sixteenth-century Italian theoreticians the etymology of *ingenium* was ascribed to the verb *in-gigno* (from *genus* and *generare*). One of its cognates was a term that frequently appeared in theological discourse, that is, *ingenitus,* "the unengendered and uncreated," which denoted the Father. (Those early masculine connotations, also contained in the image of *acumen* and *pointe,* will turn effeminate, thus sterile, once the ideal falls into disrepute.) *Ingenium* was thus the primal, creative force of intelligence, its inventive drive, and a reflection of our divine nature. A virtue, or creative energy, *esprit* is also the flame that enlightens the mind and allows it to see the true nature of things and of their species, revealing the hidden qualities of objects and the multiplicity of their relations. The notions of creative drive and clarity of vision are both contained in the concepts of energy and virtue associated with *ingenium*. The Greek term *energeia* was translated by the Latin *vis* or *virtus,* which in the seventeenth century meant force, virtue, movement as virtuality (in Aristotle *dynamis* as power is realized in *energeia,* the action), the power of action, language's faculty to represent the dynamics of thought and perception. It is paired in book 3 of Aristotle's *Rhetoric* with the term *enargeia,* "clarity and evidence."[21] Metaphors, Aristotle points out, make the object present to the imagination, show events as they happen; figurative speech infuses representation with life and movement. Both meanings are present in Richelet's definition of *energy* in his 1680 dictionary: "A term is energetic when it puts something before our eyes, to portray an action." *Esprit* thus both lends force to discourse and brings to light hidden resemblances and analogies; its influence is deployed in the realm of metaphor and figural speech.

Such influence, as we have seen, was not always perceived as positive. In the *Encyclopédie* article "Esprit," after the obligatory Aristotelian detour, Voltaire, who was more interested in countermodels than in normative ones, went on to describe *faux esprit* in greater detail: "A tiresome search for expressions that are too refined; the affectation of turning into an enigma what others have said more simply; bringing together ideas that seem incompatible; dividing what ought to be united; coming up with false connections; mixing, against propriety, banter with seriousness and smallness with greatness."[22] This allows us to understand not only the nature of the accusations that were launched at the *goût moderne* but also the core of the poetics of modernity. The moderns, Voltaire maintains, tend to bring apparently incompatible objects and images together in a surprising and shocking manner. They operate along two complementary axes. On the one hand, they bring together dissimilar and incongruous ideas and objects, ignoring their differences; on the other, they seem to discern imaginary distinctions in things that are in reality perfectly similar. They separate what should remain whole, and they join what should be left separate; they mix hierarchies and natural species. In their search for surprise they go for the shock value; they ignore distinctions and boundaries and thus alter the natural and social order. Like Marivaux, who, according to the abbé Raynal, "blends the burlesque and the informal," the moderns confuse serious and comic styles, mix high and low, noble and debased, and end up upsetting our view of nature by creating hybrid, even monstrous, creatures. The abbé Le Blanc wrote in a text contemporary with Voltaire's article: "The Greek and Roman authors excite sometimes our admiration for the skill with which they bring together the most distant ideas; those of today try to surprise us by uniting those that are the most contradictory. In writings of all kind, as well as in all types of drawing, there is a tendency today to wed things of antagonistic natures."[23] The same deplorable tendency to bring together incompatible objects in the search for a *discordia concors,* a union of opposites, is detected not only in language but also in the visual arts of the *nouveau goût,* or *style rocaille:*

> Nothing is more monstrous, as Horace observes, than wedding together beings of opposite nature; yet, that is precisely what many artists pride themselves on doing today. They contrast a Cupid with a Dragon, a sea shell with the wing of a bat. They no longer respect any verisimilitude in their productions. They stack confusedly moldings, cornices, pedestals, columns, cascades, branches, and rocks. In one corner of such chaos they will place a frightened Cupid and, to crown it all, a garland of flowers. That is what goes under the name of drawings of a New Taste [*d'un nouveau Goût*].[24]

A similar unrestrained and licentious imagination presided over the creation of neologisms, over the license toward the use of existing terms or the surprising association of words, all aspects that Voltaire, the abbé Desfontaines, and many others saw as the distinctive vices of the *goût moderne.*

Ironically, it was Voltaire's negative assessment of the *faux esprit* that captured the attention of the German writers of the Athenaeum (1798–1800), who took it in a sense quite contrary to its original intent. French theoreticians had presented *esprit* as a purely national phenomenon. The abbé Bouhours had observed that the lack of a good education and worldly refinement unhappily conspired with the Germans' oafish disposition to prevent them from ever becoming *beaux esprit:* "A German *bel esprit* is an odd thing. . . . The *bel esprit* is quite incompatible with the coarse temperament and the massive body of the peoples of the North."[25] Unphased by such a diagnosis, the Germans took to the aesthetics of *esprit* and gave it a new dimension and an extended relevance. The conception of *esprit* that Voltaire rejected eventually found its way into the writings of Jean-Paul Richter and Friedrich Schlegel (and eventually Freud). Spilling out of the realm of conversation, rhetoric, and the aesthetic, *Witz* finds its fullest expression in the written word and, most important—following Kant's reading of Locke and Hobbes—in the discoveries of philosophy and science.[26] That was a departure from the traditional, empiricist stance. Locke had separated wit (the English equivalent of *ingenium*) from judgment and had denied wit any significant role in the process of reason. To him, only judgment offered clear and distinct ideas, whereas wit yielded nothing more than confused representations:

Men who have a great deal of Wit and prompt Memories, have not always the clearest Judgment or deepest Reason. For Wit, lying most in the assemblage of Ideas, and putting those together with quickness and variety, wherein can be found any resemblance or congruity, thereby to make up pleasant Pictures and agreeable visions in the Fancy: Judgment, on the contrary, lies quite on the other side, in separating carefully, one from another, Ideas, wherein can be found the least difference, thereby to avoid being misled by Similitude, and by affinity to take one thing for another. This is a way of proceeding quite contrary to Metaphor and Allusion wherein, for the most part, lies that entertainment and pleasantry of Wit, which strikes so lively on the Fancy.[27]

While Voltaire assimilated the two complementary modes of the understanding, analysis (perceiving fine distinctions) and analogy (revealing hidden resemblances among objects and thoughts), into the broad category *esprit,* Locke separated the two operations and confined each within its proper sphere: analysis belonged to judgment, analogy to rhetorical ornamentation. Wit, like Fancy, assembles and puts together with "quickness and variety," but Judgment "[separates] carefully . . . thereby [avoiding] being misled by Similitude, and by affinity." Wit strives for entertainment and may be misled by superficial similarities. That is what happens with metaphors, which "take one thing for another," with little concern for exactitude toward the nature of phenomena. The scientific spirit, on the contrary, strives to analyze objects and ideas by carefully articulating the real differences that lie beneath the surface of apparently similar phenomena.[28]

In his preface to *De l'esprit des lois* Montesquieu seems to endorse Locke's notion of judgment: "When I have recalled the Antiquity, I have tried to recover its spirit, so as not to consider as similar events which are in reality different, and not to miss the differences of those which appear similar." In this apparently tautological statement Montesquieu insists, from a double perspective, that the historian must avoid falling for superficial similarities and missing the real differences that subtend the apparently seamless texture of the real.[29] The dialectic of treacherous similarities and hidden differences is crucial to Montesquieu. For instance, since laws must be conceived within the context of the structure of government and the human passions that set it in motion (bk. 3, chap. 1), it follows that laws and practices that are apparently similar may in reality have very different effects: there are crucial distinctions that the philosopher must bring into the open. Thus, factions play an important role in the suffrages of the populace and in those of the senate or the aristocracy, but in the former, factions are positive, while in the latter they are dangerous (bk. 2, chap. 2). The customs of the Lacedemonians seem as barbaric and bizarre as those of the mythical Sévarambes,[30] but because virtue was their principle, they contributed to the grandeur of the city rather than to its ruin (bk. 4, chap. 6). Athens always had the same number of soldiers for its defense, but while twenty thousand soldiers were enough to fight against the Persians and the Lacedemonians, they did not suffice to defend the city against Philip of Macedonia at a time when the spirit of virtue no longer prevailed (bk. 2, chap. 3). Frugality was the foundation of the ancient republics, but it would be the ruin of modern monarchies, which are founded upon commerce and consumption (bk. 5, chap. 3). And so on. But Montesquieu also explores the other facet of *esprit,* that is, the discovery of hidden similarities within heterogeneous elements. Underlying regularities in the apparently "infinite diversity of laws and customs" must be accounted for, not by the simple observation of resemblances and metaphorical equivalences, but by inferring from apparently disparate events the existence of principles that are endowed with a general, explanatory power: "I have set down the principles, and I have seen particular cases conform to them as if by themselves, the histories of all nations being but their consequences and each particular law connecting with another law or dependent on a more general one."[31] One might argue, in the spirit of Locke, that the operations of inference, which hypothesize the existence of general rules from the observation of regularities among discrete events, are a far cry from the workings of wit, which simply draws resemblances and "agreeable visions," with no attempt to provide a general, encompassing explanation. However, inferring the existence of general laws and uniformities from the empirical observation of particular cases is not incompatible with the workings of *esprit* or wit: the sudden intuition that leads *esprit* to discover hidden analogies within phenomena is in fact the first step toward the formation of explanatory, general hypotheses. It is important to keep in mind that in *De l'esprit des lois* the linear movement of deduction that characterizes the Cartesian, geometric order (which Montesquieu espouses in the preface) conflicts with the order of *finesse* (which is also operative in his *oeuvre*), that is, with a mode of thinking based on the intuition that order—any order pertaining to the world of human interest (politics and morals)—is constantly shifting and unstable because it must accommodate a wide variety of possible structuring criteria.

The latter order was the one endorsed by the German Romantics. *Witz,* which was depicted as an *ars combinatoria,* as a capacity for detecting both similarities in things that appeared dissimilar (i.e., the operation of *ingenium,* or wit) and dissimilarities in things that appeared alike (i.e., the action of judgment), might actually yield true knowledge and content. The purpose of science, like that of metaphor, is to discover patterns of similarities across categories and boundaries and to detect connections between particularity and universality; *ingenium* is thus coextensive with judgment and is its inseparable ally. According to Kant,

> Intelligence *(ingenium* or *Witz)* unites (assimilates) heterogeneous ideas, which often, according to the law of the imagination (that is, association), lie apart from each other. It is a peculiar faculty of classifying, which belongs to the understanding (as the faculty of recognizing the general) in so far as the understanding attributes objects to a certain class. . . . It is pleasing, generally accepted, and encouraging to find similarities amidst dissimilar objects; and so intelligence provides material for the understanding to make its knowledge more general.[32]

Witz thus denotes a capacity to discover hidden analogies and similarities thanks to agility of mind and to a gift for combining images, for formulating them in a striking and concise manner. It is a step toward the more abstract operations of classification that constitute the understanding, toward rearranging the categories of the world in new patterns of relations.

From that perspective, all the rhetorical operations that Voltaire viewed with suspicion—the sudden joining together of disparate and apparently incongruous objects, which the mind suddenly sees, as in a flash of light, with pleasure and surprise; the drifting *(dérive)* of a mode of thinking given to discontinuity and digression—became, for the German Romantic poets, the essence of creativity. Hence their use of aphorisms and the juxtaposition of fragmented thoughts in an effect of concerted disorder. To them, science might not be divorced from its rhetorical, poetic expression, because it was in the nature of both poetry and science to find some clarity in the cluster of confused analogies that emerge from the perception of the real.

That sudden spark of the understanding—the coming together in a vivid image, which the abbé Bouhours had termed the "brilliance" of style—was the very quality that critics of the *goût moderne* derided under the label of *papillotage* (flicker effect)[33]: "[*Bel esprit*] is a solid body that shines; it is a brilliance that has firmness and body. . . . That is the symbol of *bel esprit* as I see it: it has density and radiance in equal parts. It is, properly speaking, the radiance of reason."[34] In seventeenth-century dictionaries *papillotes* were "éclat des paillettes," scintillating pieces of fabric, and the verb *papilloter* indicated the twinkling shimmer of points of light; in the eighteenth century *papillotage* indicated the rapid blinking of the eyelids, sheltering the eyes from a dazzling light. Common to the denunciation of those visual effects (which were also used metaphorically to describe a type of discursive style) was the mistrust of everything that drew attention to details, away from the whole, which dispersed the focus and shattered the work of art into myriad bright points, each competing for the attention of the recipient, each becoming an end in itself, to the detriment of the unity of composition.[35] More dazzling than enlightening, the diamonds of style radiated a cold light that did not illuminate the mind but tickled the imagination in a purely sensuous, meaningless way. "Nothing is more adverse to the light that must solidify into a body and spread evenly across a written work than those sparks that are produced by striking words against each other, which dazzle us for a moment but then leave us in darkness," wrote Buffon.[36] The spark of *esprit* produced darkness, not light. That notion was not quite novel. Quintilian had already cautioned the writer against the lure of those sparkling fragments of discourse, *lumina* or *sententiae* (points of light, *traits d'esprit*), which emanated *scintillis* (sparks) as through a thick smoke, but no *flammae*, scattered *sententiae*, or *traits d'esprit*,[37] which, if used with too great a frequency, would undermine the impact of the work and turn the body of eloquence into a monstrosity bordering on nonrepresentativeness: "Personally, I think these highlights are in a sense the eyes of eloquence. But I do not want there to be eyes all over the body, lest the other organs lose their function."[38]

Bouhours, however, was careful to emphasize the content value of *bel esprit*, its complementarity with the other operations of the understanding. *Esprit* involved connectedness, the joining of elements gathered from the perception of the particular; it provided the materials that judgment would elaborate into the formulation of universal statements. Discernment, or *bon sens*, emerged, for Bouhours, from the union of *esprit* and judgment: by relying upon both, the mind was able to analyze and elaborate what it had intuitively grasped. Schlegel and Jean Paul too pointed out that the sudden flare of *Witz*, with its discontinuous and digressive character, was peculiarly suited for expressing inchoate states of mind that had not fully emerged to awareness and for shedding some light on the secret workings of consciousness:

> That activity through which consciousness reveals itself most acutely as a fragment is Witz; its essence consists in rivenness and in turn arises from the rivenness and derivativeness of consciousness. Witz is a bolt of lightning from the unconscious world, which for us always exists alongside the

conscious world, and it thus accurately represents the fragmentary state of our consciousness. It is a combination and mixture of the conscious and the unconscious. Without all intention and consciousness something is found that has no connection with what came before it; on the contrary, it always stands, as it were, in stark contradiction to it.[39]

Witz reconciled the aesthetic and the scientific spirit: there was rational value in metaphors and figures of speech and, more fundamentally, in the perception of beauty. Both science and artistic representation relied upon similar operations in the mind: both depended upon the imagination's capacity to take sudden leaps into the realm of hypotheses. As in the *goût moderne* epistemology of *esprit,* in Schlegel's conception rationality could not be divorced from sensuous experience, reason from taste, pleasure from knowledge, vivacity from clarity, the perception of beauty from the understanding of truth. Jean Paul came to similar conclusions when he pointed out that the etymology of *Witz* was related to knowing *(wissen,* therefore *witzigen)* and that *Witz* was a mode of understanding *(Verstand)* that was communicated in correspondences and analogies, in a sensate, tangible form, revealing on the one hand "relations of similitude between incommensurable sizes, i.e., the similarities between corporeal and spiritual worlds . . . , in other words, the equation between oneself and the outer world,"[40] and on the other, the disparate at the heart of the putatively similar: *Witz* ruptures identity and creates disjunction and alienation in "the identical made dissimilar." For Jean Paul, *Witz,* as both knowledge and humor, is able to take minor moments of similarity and turn them into essential relations: the sublime is juxtaposed with the familiar, the ephemeral with the eternal. *Witz*'s unexpected combinations are thus a rebellion against received ideas and their hierarchical positions.[41]

The French philosophes, however, in their efforts to demarcate themselves from the tradition of *galanterie* and from the associations between worldliness, light-heartedness, and *esprit,* took a different path. Perhaps their effort to legitimate and ground scientifically their moral endeavor worked against embracing forms of perception and expression that were associated with *ancien régime* society; their enthusiastic intransigence did not allow them to envision a more integrated conception of the creative enterprise. The philosophes rejected the rhetorical brilliance of *ingenium* and favored a more traditional and strict division of intellectual labor; as Locke had done before, they attributed a rational content to judgment only. In his *Salon of 1767* Diderot followed Edmund Burke's reading of Locke (in Burke's *Introduction on Taste*) by splitting imagination from judgment: "The imagination creates nothing; it imitates; it composes, combines, exaggerates, expands and contracts; it is perpetually occupied with resemblances. The faculty of judgment observes, compares, and seeks only to make distinctions. Judgment is the pre-eminent faculty of the philosopher, and imagination that of the poet."[42] Conversely, *esprit,* defined as a slow and painstaking meandering into irrelevant details, a pointless detour into the realm of the particular, was ejected from the domain of aesthetics and from that of science. In his influential article "Génie," published in the *Encyclopédie,* Diderot's account of the way the mind operated was symptomatic of the expulsion of scientific *esprit* from the aesthetic realm and of its alienation from the activity of genius and poetic imagination. The philosophical (and scientific) spirit of the *géomètre* was deemed incompatible with the disorder and lawlessness of the creative, artistic genius. In his attempt to endow philosophy (i.e., scientific inquiry) with *gravitas* and order, Diderot deprived it of its intuitive, impetuous side. Simultaneity, digression, and multiplicity, need we say it, the very qualities that characterize Diderot's own approach to science and the arts, gave way to systematic and progressive linear thought (the unbroken chain of ideas). *Finesse* was represented simply as attention to detail, as the handmaid of geometry, with its cautious and patient advance. Having begrudged the spark of the poetic imagination to science and philosophy, Diderot's next step was to deem the development of sciences responsible for the decline of poetry:

> In Philosophy, which perhaps requires scrupulous attention, a timid cautiousness, a habit of reflection that does not agree with the warmth of the imagination and even less with the self-confidence of genius . . . one must seek truth ardently but wait for it patiently. [Philosophy] needs men who are able to organize the order and the succession of their ideas: to follow their chain so as to lock it, or to interrupt it if there is any doubt. It needs much searching, discussion, and slowness, qualities to be found neither in the turmoil of the passions nor in the exuberance of the imagination. They belong to a far-reaching and self-possessed mind, which never perceives anything without comparing it with another perception; which seeks what different objects have in common and what distinguishes them; which, in order to bring together distant ideas, traces step by step a long distance; which, in order to grasp the specific, delicate, and fugitive connections between related ideas, as well as their opposition and contrast, is able to sort an object out of the mass of objects of the same, or of a different, species, to lay the microscope upon an imperceptible particle, and to stop observing only after it has observed it for a very long time.[43]

Polymorphous Je ne sais quoi

Esprit is a rhetoric of the sketchy and the unfinished; it is the attempt to catch thought, as it were, in midair, as it takes shape and definition. As such, it is essentially incomplete, always about to add one further touch and a little more definition. Such a process also accounts for the structure of Marivaux's phrase, which to some critics seems to display, as it unravels, the sinuousness of rococo decorative style[44] but is in fact constructed paratactically, with short sentences and few subordinate clauses, out of successive touches, with accretions and additions that show the phases of thought as they happen, discontinuously, detailing the stages of their modifications.[45] Thus, on the one hand, *esprit* is the sudden blaze of light that finds its way into the metaphor or the maxim; the quickness of a condensed form that characterizes the atticist quality of *formes brèves* favored by the moralists; the fulgurating conciseness of *acumen,* sharpening its edge in the *pointe.* On the other hand, it is a flexible and dynamic language that depicts thought in the process of its formation: not only simultaneity but also reiteration and redeployment within discontinuity. Indeed, the relationship between those two modes of *esprit* always posed a problem for Marivaux. The cluster of simultaneous perceptions that constitute *sentiment* or *pensée confuse* are hardly reducible to a clear and distinct representation: "At all times we take action as a consequence of confused ideas that come to us we don't know how, that lead us without any reflection."[46] The bundle of thoughts condensed in the intuition materializes too suddenly and far outpaces linguistic expression; therefore, it cannot be adequately translated into the linear, sequential unfolding of the classical phrase without running the risk of appearing belabored and affected or without making the character who formulates them seem calculating and contrived.[47] In the *Lettre sur les sourds et muets* Diderot showed that he was as intensely aware as Marivaux of the fact that linguistic expression skewed the representation of the affects:

> Our mental state is one thing; our rendition of it—whether to ourselves or to others—is quite another. The complete and instantaneous perception of such a state is one thing; the detailed and continuous effort of attention that we are forced to make in order to analyze it, express it, and explain it to others is quite another. Our soul is a moving scene that we are perpetually copying. We spend a great deal of time in rendering it faithfully, but the original exists as a complete whole, for the mind does not proceed step by step, like expression.[48]

Diderot, however, did not follow Marivaux on the path of linguistic experimentation, twisting and bending the structure of the sentence in the hope of reducing the gap between simultaneity and progressive unfolding.

Such a flexible conception of style as Marivaux's did not sit well with the dictates of neoclassical aesthetics, which demanded that the structure of the written work (a poem, a play, or a novel), like that of the sentence, develop along a continuous, linear progression, each element pulling the next, like the unbroken links of a chain: "[My adventures] hold together neither more nor less than the links of a curb bit," Jacques would say, in his naïve belief that the book of destiny had been written in accordance with the necessity of the sequentially developed Aristotelian fable (a belief that the narrator never fails to challenge).[49] According to the philosophes, the grammar of the fable, like that of the sentence, ought to reflect the temporal and logical structure that rules the natural world: "The progress of any poem must be like that of nature. . . . In nature, ideas, sentiments, movements of the soul are generated according to an order that cannot be reversed without reversing nature itself. . . . In order to be perfect, the texture of fiction must hold entirely to one piece [*il faut qu'elle tienne au-dehors par un seul bout*]," wrote Marmontel,[50] probably under the sway of d'Alembert's *Discours préliminaire* to the *Encyclopédie:* "There scarcely is any science or art . . . whose propositions or rules cannot be reduced to simple notions disposed in such an obvious order that the chain would be absolutely unbroken."[51] In Marivaux's world (as in that of Dufresny, Fontenelle, Montesquieu, Crébillon, and the other representatives of the *goût moderne*), however, no law of linear necessity, no uninterrupted chain of deductions, dictated the progress of thought and narrative, which were always open to the disorder of human caprice, random association, and chance interference and which offered a cluster of confused representations and competing story-lines. For the moderns, no self-evident, overarching order could ever be imposed on the representation of the mind and human affects.

In the second installment of *Le cabinet du philosophe* Marivaux confronted those issues in an elaborate allegory that dramatized the key concepts of the epistemology and the aesthetics of *galanterie* and the *goût moderne*. Since the seventeenth century almost all discussions of *esprit* had relied upon a conveniently vague and ineffable notion that seemed ideally suited for discussing the conceptually intractable phenomena related to confused modes of thought and to aesthetic judgment. That was the *je ne sais quoi* (reminiscent of the Ciceronian *nescio quid*), which Bouhours defined as "the inclination and the instinct of the heart for an object that stirs it."[52] It corresponded to an aesthetics rooted in the passions, which could neither be analyzed too closely nor be reduced to the rationality of well-defined rules. "In fact, it is something so lissome and imperceptible that it escapes the most penetrating intellect. The human mind, which knows that which is most spiritual in the angels and that which is most divine in God, does not know the nature of what is charming in a corporeal object that touches the heart."[53] A polymorphous energy, the *je ne sais quoi* designated the indefinable, the indefinite, and the unachieved in human desire, in the perception of beauty in the work of art and in nature. It was a dynamic drive, always eluding our grasp, hiding its nature or only partially revealing itself. Grace, of which the *je ne sais quoi* was the obscure law, was dynamic, the kind of energy that resided in the harmony and the agreement between the various movements that affected the object, whereas beauty lay in the measurable symmetry between the parts that formed the work of art. Both were seen as necessary to the work of art: the *je ne sais quoi* was the elusive and secret connection *(noeud secret)* that united grace and beauty, much like divine grace united body and spirit, matter and form:

> Beauty is born out of the proportion and symmetry that we encounter among the corporeal and material components of nature. But grace is produced by the uniformity among the inward feelings caused by the affects and the emotions of the soul. . . . And since spiritual beauty is more excellent than corporeal beauty, we almost always prefer a person whose physical beauty is scarce but who has grace to another who has more beauty but no grace. . . . That grace is primarily a movement of the soul is demonstrated by the fact that when we see a beautiful woman, we first evaluate her beauty by the correct relation between all the parts of her body; but we cannot evaluate her grace unless she speaks or laughs or makes some movement. . . . That *je ne sais quoi,* which everybody calls on but which no one can explain, is like a secret link that joins the body and the spirit. . . . For the *je ne sais quoi* is nothing but a divine splendor that is born out of beauty and grace.[54]

Movement, or grace, is essential to the seduction of *je ne sais quoi;* it is the drive that stimulates the mind to explore further the intangible quality of an object that conceals much of itself. Grace consists in the physiognomy and expressiveness that animate facial features, not in their proportion and symmetry. (Marivaux's theatrical heroines are never qualified as beautiful, but always as *aimables,* that is, attractive, desirable.) Grace is a crucial force in an aesthetics that places incompleteness above achievement, imperfection above perfection, suggestiveness over explicitness, and therefore may find attractiveness and charm in ugliness rather than in beauty. Ugliness is a deviation from conventional norms that catches the beholder unawares; by its effect of surprise, it has a more powerful hold over the imagination than beauty because, like the *je ne sais quoi,* it is mobile and intangible and stimulates the imagination to discover the nature of its secret charm. Ugly women, writes Montesquieu, are known to have far more grace than beautiful ones, and they are able to stir the passions in more subtle and insidious ways (a fact consecrated today by the expression *jolie laide*):

> There is sometimes in people or things an invisible charm, a natural grace that cannot be defined and that we have been forced to call the *je ne sais quoi.* It seems to me that it is primarily an effect of surprise. We are stirred by the fact that we like a person more than we thought we would at first; we are pleasantly surprised to see that she has overcome some defects that our eyes still see but our heart no longer believes. That is why ugly women often have grace and beautiful ones rarely do. . . . That is why beautiful women rarely excite intense passion. Passion is almost always reserved for those who have grace.[55]

Admiration for beauty runs along the path of reason, but the sensual appeal of the visually off-kilter is far more powerful because it runs counter to everything we are taught to desire. In other words, it has an element of risk; it embodies a victory for the unknown, as well as for originality and transgression. The troubling seduction of irregular forms foreshadows, albeit in a different key, an aesthetics based on a notion of the sublime as the terrible, the obscure, and the monstrous.[56]

Marivaux's essay on the *je ne sais quoi* is not a treatise like Bouhours's but an allegorical fable that, like the object it describes, suggests rather than demonstrates. In the tradition of the allegorical voyage (like Madeleine de Scudéry's *Carte de tendre*), it presents a spatial fiction in which abstract concepts are illustrated as a trajectory and the discovery of aesthetic pleasure is presented as a process and a journey. The narrator first introduces us to the garden of Beauty, who sits on a throne surrounded by her admirers, who are entirely absorbed in the contemplation of her perfections: "All seemed to be motionless, as if in ecstasy at the view of that woman seated on a throne."[57] Beauty is magnificent and admirable, but she is quite still, silent and expressionless. The admiration she summons in those who contemplate her leaves them still and spellbound. But passive entrancement, no matter how intense, cannot hold their attention for long. As ecstasy fades away after the first effect of surprise, silent admiration gives way to boredom and disgust;

one by one, Beauty's admirers get up and leave.[58] The narrator follows them, only to find that they have all rushed to the garden of the *Je ne sais quoi*. The spectacle there is very different:

> There was nothing special in that place, nothing was prearranged: everything seemed left to chance. Disorder prevailed, but a disorder of the best possible taste. It had a charming effect, but we could not determine nor understand its cause. In other words, we yearned for nothing there; yet, one would have thought that nothing was complete or that something that was supposed to be there was not, since at every moment we saw that something new was being brought in. Despite the fable that counts only three Graces, there was there an infinite number of them, who while moving around were working and touching up everywhere. I say moving around, since they were constantly coming and going. They passed rapidly, succeeded one another, never gave us time to know them well. They were there, but soon they were gone, and others would take their place, only to be replaced in turn, and so on. In a word, they were everywhere, but they stayed nowhere; we never saw one, but one thousand.[59]

Marivaux manages to condense, in a short passage, the essence of his poetics and of the *goût moderne*. Indeed, if it is true that the moderns suffer from the lack of a clearly defined poetics, this text could make up for it, for this is as close as one gets to a true manifesto.

The garden of the *Je ne sais quoi*, unlike that of Beauty, is most definitely not a French garden; there are no symmetric alleyways and no geometrically arranged parterres, only artful negligence and disorder. While Beauty is immobile, the *Je ne sais quoi* is dynamic. Beauty offers herself to contemplation and knowledge, whereas the *Je ne sais quoi* is invisible and ultimately unknowable. Beauty invites sudden enthusiasm; the *Je ne sais quoi* excites curiosity and an ever-renewed desire. Beauty is absorbing, whereas the *Je ne sais quoi* elicits inconstancy and forgetfulness, as new aspects of reality attract the attention of the beholder. Beauty is one; the *Je ne sais quoi*, like the flickering light of *papillotage,* is multiple and diverse. Beauty is unequivocally female, whereas the *Je ne sais quoi,* which in French responds to a male pronoun, is an ambiguously sexed creature whose erotic appeal transcends gender distinctions, or rather, has an androgynous undertone. Beauty resides in absolutist pomp and authority; royal, proud, and commanding, she summons attention and admiration from her devotees. The *Je ne sais quoi* conceals itself and seduces without making any explicit demands on its followers, who remain free to come and go as they please. Beauty embodies the regularity of perfect proportions, symmetry, and balance, while the *Je ne sais quoi* is always incomplete and perfectable: "simple, negligent, irregular."[60] Beauty inhabits a timeless duration, but the *Je ne sais quoi* presents itself as a quick succession of discrete moments, each offering new and unexpected sensations; it inhabits time and history because it unfolds as a series of distinct experiences vying with one another for the beholder's attention.[61]

As a matter of fact, the explorer in the garden of the *Je ne sais quoi* is not purely a beholder: he is an active participant in an experience that transcends visual contemplation and involves the totality of his mental, emotional, and sexual faculties. Rather than being docilely carried away by an intense emotional experience, the explorer in the garden of the *Je ne sais quoi* is always exerted in an effort to grasp something that forever eludes him. *Esprit*, the spark of dynamic intelligence, can only dwell in the realm of imperfection, approximation, and desire that belongs to the *Je ne sais quoi;* it is exiled from the presence of Beauty, whose perfect economy would be troubled by movement and change: "Wishing that *esprit* would come and play on that beautiful face is wishing to see her charm altered," says *Immobile Fierté*, the handmaid of Beauty; "a beautiful face is as achieved as it possibly can be; it can do no better than remain as it is: the movement of *esprit* could only disturb its flawless economy."[62] The *Je ne sais quoi* is the object of a quest involving the totality of the passions that are solicited by the various art forms. From painting to architecture to garden design to decoration and furniture, transcending all hierarchy of arts and genres, what matters is the immersion in a multimedia world of artistic expressions that lure the participants to the spectacle and captivate them with their polymorphous appeal. Indeed, in the garden of the *Je ne sais quoi* artistic experience is freed from all constraints of form and genre; art may be found and enjoyed anywhere, in any manner one wishes, with a freedom that eighteenth-century academic thinking would find quite unacceptable:

"You tell us, here I am, but you do not show yourself." "And yet," he [the *Je ne sais quoi*] replied, "you see nothing but me. In that infinite array of attractions [*grâces*] that incessantly pass before your eyes, coming and going, all different but all equally seductive, some more manly and others more tender, look carefully: I am there. I am always there. In that painting that you love so much, in those objects of all kinds that are so enjoyable to you, in the vastness of the space you inhabit, in everything you perceive that is simple, effortless, perhaps irregular, ornate, or unadorned, I am there to be seen, I am the only source of its charm, I am all around you. Under the guise of the seductive graces, I am the *Je ne sais quoi* that arouses the desire of both sexes;

here I am the *Je ne sais quoi* that delights in the art of painting, there the *Je ne sais quoi* that gives pleasure in architecture, in decoration, in gardening, in everything that may become an object of taste. Do not look for me under one form: I have a thousand, and none is unchanging. That is why I may be seen without being known, without being grasped or defined; people lose sight of me even as they see me, they sense me without comprehending my nature. You will always see me, always seek me out and never find me; that is why you will never grow tired of me."[63]

The contrast between the cold perfection of elegant Beauty and the unfinished irregularity of the *Je ne sais quoi* is a prelude to a post-Longinian conception of the sublime as an aesthetics of excess and energy, an experience of the bizarre that transcends beauty and is more powerful than symmetry and regularity. The aesthetics of the *je ne sais quoi* is grounded in an anthropology of the soul that is based on inconstancy and that responds to an epistemology of confused representation. According to such an epistemology, experience is a succession of minute impressions, infinite in number, that are too small to incite our attention or to be clearly and distinctly defined but that, taken together, reveal the subconscious dynamics underlying sensation. In the preface to the *New Essays on Human Understanding* Leibniz writes:

At every moment there is in us an infinity of perceptions unaccompanied by awareness or reflection; that is, of alterations in the soul itself, of which we are unaware because these impressions are either too minute and too numerous, or else too unvarying, so that they are not sufficiently distinctive on their own. But when they are combined with others, they do nevertheless have their effect and make themselves felt, at least confusedly, within the whole. . . . These minute perceptions, then, are more effective in their results than has been recognized. They constitute that *je ne sais quoi,* those flavours, those images of sensible qualities, vivid in the aggregate but confused as to the parts; those impressions which are made on us by the bodies around us and which involve the infinite; that connection that each being has with all the rest of the universe. It can even be said that by virtue of these minute perceptions the present is big with the future and burdened with the past.[64]

The soul is agitated by a constant movement that escapes the understanding but drives the mind to flee from the awareness of the present moment toward an ever-elusive future that stands in a continuum with the immediate past. Minute perceptions are thus correlative of "minute appetitions" or "minute solicitations" that "determine our behavior without our thinking of it." This description owes much to the Augustinian conception of the passions, which involves something close to a theory of the unconscious, with its belief in the existence of imperceptible ideas. Those minute perceptions account for the dynamics of the soul, which wavers, unaware of its own affects, between sinful temptation and God's grace. Pierre Nicole, the secretary and collaborator of Antoine Arnauld (a correspondent of Leibniz's) and the author of the very popular *Essais de morale,* argued that the soul receives a confused impression of the passions that are conveyed by the fictions and the spectacles that are constantly foisted on it.[65] Because of its limited faculties, the soul is not always clearly and distinctly aware of the imperceptible impressions that drive it to act.[66] Such unawareness is also operative in the realm of taste and aesthetic pleasure, which is ruled by desire. Nicole thus describes the effects of a *je ne sais quoi* that is all the more powerful because it is indistinct:

> We may say that books are collections of ideas and that each book is, as it were, double, because it imprints in the mind two sorts of ideas. It imprints fully formed ideas, conceived and expressed distinctly. But it also imprints another kind of ideas, composed of indistinct thoughts that we feel but are unable to express. As a rule, it is in those stimulating but unformulated thoughts that consists the beauty of writing. . . . The mind yields to an idea by virtue of a principle that it senses only, though it is the foundation of its approval; those principles often include other ideas whose extension is indeterminate, so that should they be clad in words, they would be acknowledged by no one.[67]

The fictional text seduces not only by the clarity of its argument but also through the unconscious inscription of a desire conveyed by the combinatory and associative power of figurative language, a desire that carries both the writer and the reader, despite themselves, beyond the perceptible and definable meaning of the written word. In expanding and possibly deviating comprehension, in completing what has been left unsaid, or in supplementing it, desire composes its own text. (It is worth noting that Diderot's account of Richardson's text's germinating in the reader's mind owes a great deal to Nicole's account of the subliminal, unconscious inscription of textual desire: "Richardson plants in the heart seeds of virtue, which at first remain idle and inactive; they remain hidden until the right moment comes, which shakes them up and brings them to fruition."[68] The difference, of course, is that for Diderot such influence is not malevolent but beneficial.)

The action-oriented drive exercised by confused ideas is rooted in the Augustinian conception of postlapsarian desire, or more precisely, in the notion of a fundamental *inquiétude,* the soul's restless drive toward new objects and goals, its flight from what it already possesses toward something unknown that it yearns to reach. Malebranche grounds the mobility of the ever-desiring soul in the imperfection of our nature, which enables the soul to entertain only a confused knowledge of the ultimate good that would set its will at rest:

> Thus, with the will always parched by a burning thirst, always driven by anxieties and desires for the good it does not possess, it cannot comfortably allow the mind to dwell for any time over abstract truths that do not affect it and that it judges incapable of making it happy. Thus, it continuously urges the mind to consider other objects. . . . But since the emptiness of created things cannot fill the infinite capacity of man's heart, these trifling pleasures, instead of quenching its thirst, only aggravate it and give the soul the vain and foolish hope of being satisfied by the multiplicity of terrestrial pleasures. This leads to a further inconstancy and inconceivable weakness on the part of the mind whose duty it is to find these goods for the soul.[69]

Malebranche portrays *inquiétude* as a painful flight from object to object in which the soul is dragged from one disappointment to the next by a restless will that always hopes to find satisfaction in the object it has yet to possess. But nothing so wrenching ever happens to Marivaux's voyager in the garden of the *Je ne sais quoi*. Though his quest is repeatedly frustrated, he finds no torment in it. "It is true that we enjoy seeking him; though we ardently wish to see him, we are not distressed for not knowing where he is; should we never find him, we are determined always to look for him."[70] The voyager's pleasure comes from a suspension of his desire, from the delayed fulfillment of his search and the expectation of a pleasure to come. For the whole endgame of desire is desire itself. In this recognition of the open-endedness of desire, Marivaux is closer to the abbé Bouhours than to Malebranche. In his account of the *je ne sais quoi,* the former puts a positive spin on the *inquiétude* that spurs the other passions and engenders an anthropology of instability and yearning:

> The *je ne sais quoi* is the object of most of our passions. Besides love and aversion—which set in motion all the movements of our heart—desire and hope, which take up the totality of man's life, have no other foundation. For we always desire, and we always hope. There always will be something ahead of the goal that we have set for us, some uncertain aspiration that we never reach and that becomes the source of our restlessness in the enjoyment of the things that we most ardently wished for.[71]

In a similar mood, rather than attributing uneasiness to the imperfection and the errors of our nature, Leibniz, following Bouhours in his account of minute perceptions, considers *inquiétude,* not as a perverse effect of our fallen condition, but as a quality highly compatible with the realization of happiness in the realm of human interest:

> If you take "uneasiness" or disquiet to be a genuine displeasure, then I do not agree that it is all that spurs us on. What usually drives us are those minute insensible perceptions which could be called sufferings that we cannot become aware of, if the notion of suffering did not involve awareness. These minute impulses consist in our continually overcoming small obstacles—our nature labours at this without our thinking about it. . . . Far from such disquiet being inconsistent with happiness, I find that it is essential to the happiness of created beings; their happiness never consists in a complete attainment, which would make then insensate and stupefied, but in a continual and uninterrupted progress towards greater goods.[72]

Therefore, it does not matter whether the explorer in the garden gets anywhere at all. What matters most is striving toward some goal; as in window-shopping, which was taking hold at that time, the pleasure of wandering through the garden and dividing one's attention among its multiple appeals, being immersed in a total spectacle that "connect[ed] each being with all the rest of the universe," was more enjoyable than the endgame.[73] What the garden offers to the explorer is a narrative with no preordained unity and no ending, a narrative whose fragments may be put together and rearranged by the audience, which is invited to search for any hidden meanings and to reconstitute the narrative's secret chain. In Marivaux's cognitive world there is no drive toward a timeless transcendence that would set the mind at rest, but rather the appreciation of the minute but multiple possibilities offered by the *hic et nunc*, by the manifestations of an ephemeral reality that is loved precisely because of its mortality. The elusiveness of the object represented is as much a function of its dynamic, transformative nature *(vivacité)* as it is a function of reticence, of a capacity to mask itself, of suggesting that its representation is further to be perfected. Desire draws on itself, on the mind's effort to grasp the nature of the unknown: "If a thought or an emotion has too much energy to be adequately expressed, this same thought may be conveyed clearly within the degree of meaning proper to suggest the whole range of its indefinable vivacity."[74]

Thus the aesthetics of *esprit* stimulates the reader's desire and induces him to complete what the author has left unsaid. The audience is not passively carried away by the passions raised by the writer; rather, it is a participant in the search for meaning. "We need a penetrating mind in order to make way into the author's conception: merely understanding his words does not enable us fully to comprehend him. We need to create with him [*il faut composer avec lui*]

and to gather, from what he has not said what he has left unsaid."⁷⁵ Meaning
emerges dynamically as a process, as an open-ended search that is dependent
as much on the *finesse* of the author as on that of the reader: both bring to the
experience an equal share of curiosity, desire, and critical attention. Let us look
at the way Bouhours defines this relationship in the quality of tenuity and agility of thought and expression *(délicatesse),* which belongs to the semantic scope
of *esprit:*

> When you ask me what is a *pensée délicate,* I do not know where to find
> the words to explain it. There are things that are difficult to see all at once
> and so tenuous that they slip away when we think we are holding them. All
> we can do is look closely, again and again, so as to come gradually to know
> them. . . . We need, I believe, to reflect upon the *délicatesse* that pertains
> to works of art by comparison with that which belongs to works of nature.
> The most delicate are those in which Nature took pleasure in working on a
> minute scale, whose barely perceptible substance makes us wonder whether
> she wanted to show or hide her skill, such as a perfectly formed insect, all
> the more admirable as it is less discernible, as Pliny says. Let us say, by anal-
> ogy, that a thought that has *délicatesse* is contained in a few words and that
> its meaning is not discernible nor emphatic. It seems as if it were partially
> concealed so that we might seek it out and guess its nature, as if it peeked
> through so as to allow us the pleasure of discovering it, provided we had
> taste and discernment [*esprit*]. For just as we need magnifying lenses and
> microscopes in order to perceive the masterpieces of Nature, so it belongs
> only to people who are intelligent and enlightened to penetrate the meaning
> of a delicate thought in its entirety. This small mystery is like the soul and
> the *délicatesse* of thought, so that those that have nothing mysterious either
> in their subject matter or in their phrasing, that are plain at first sight, are
> not delicate, though they may be clever. We may therefore conclude that
> *délicatesse* adds a *je ne sais quoi* to the sublime and the pleasurable and that
> thoughts that are only impressive or agreeable resemble those heroines and
> shepherdesses of novels, who wear on their face neither a mask nor a veil:
> their entire beauty leaps into view.⁷⁶

Renouncing all claims of authority over his interlocutor, Philante, Eudoxe
makes a gracious show of his awkwardness in an effort to lend to his treatise the
extemporaneous quality of conversation: "I do not know whether I am making myself clear; I almost do not understand myself, and at all moments I am
afraid of getting lost in my ruminations."⁷⁷ But more important, the speaker's
show of humility invites his interlocutor to come to his aid: clarity of discourse
is not a precondition but rather the end point of a shared quest. "Delicacy" of
thought in matters of the aesthetic imagination is explained by analogy with

the works of nature. The infinitely small invites the scientific mind to sharpen its powers of observation with the help of special instruments of vision, but delicacy of thought is associated less with smallness than with the elusiveness of those objects that do not rise to awareness but are concealed from the curious and penetrating mind. Rhetoric masks meaning so as to stimulate curiosity and intellectual effort, for the understanding goes along with the will, which is fundamentally inconstant. The resistance encountered in the reticent object stimulates the mind, just as the masking of the heroine's face is a powerful erotic stimulant.

Délicatesse is the masking and unmasking of thought, which reveals itself progressively. That is quite different from Diderot's description of philosophical *délicatesse,* which we have encountered above. To Diderot, philosophy required "a scrupulous attention, a timid cautiousness, a habit of reflection that does not agree with the warmth of the imagination."[78] But to Bouhours, intellectual curiosity is not timid and cold, and it is not divorced from the passions. Knowledge is not split from desire and the imagination.

The teasing appeal of masked thought is nowhere more apparent than in the work of Montesquieu, in his rejection of the geometrical and deductive order, of the unbroken chain of demonstrative reasoning, in favor of apparent disorder, discontinuity, and ellipsis. "But one must not always so exhaust a subject that one leaves nothing for the reader to do. It is not a question of making him read but of making him think."[79] In a similar mood, Dufresny had observed that "a thought should never be so complete that it will leave nothing to think about."[80] Montesquieu relies upon the use of reticence: the written words lead to what he has left for the reader to complete and fulfill. In Montesquieu's writing the dynamism of *esprit* reveals its full heuristic potential, and *délicatesse* becomes a regime for liberating the mind from the tyranny of argumentation and from the hold of an authority that relies upon the seamless texture of commonplace. Suggestiveness is pedagogically more effective than explicitness: the reader has to reconstitute the interrupted chain of thought, "a secret, and, as it were, unknown, chain."[81] If frustration should set in, that is the price to pay for his intellectual emancipation, though President Hénault skeptically observed that "the writer gives far too much credit to the reader's intelligence."[82]

Esprit is thus neither in the writer nor in the reader exclusively, but *between* the writer and the reader, as a result of their encounter and their common endeavor. It is not simply the transmission of a clear and distinct message descending from above with philosophical authority, nor is it the experience of an all-consuming emotion. It is a journey in which reaching a destination is less urgent than exploring the circuitous paths that lead to it. The narrator of *Pharsamon,* prefiguring that of *Jacques le fataliste,* suasively invited the reader to follow him on a voyage that could lead them anywhere or nowhere at all. "Follow me, dear reader. To tell you the truth, I do not know where I am going, but let that be the pleasure of the voyage."[83]

6 Between Paris and Rome
Montesquieu's Poetry of History

Montesquieu, a man superior for his ingenious and profound ideas,
glowing with a light that dazzled him, has been unable to discipline his
talent according to the necessary order and method.

—Voltaire

We shall prove . . . that Montesquieu is nothing but a bel esprit.

—Diderot

Genre Bending

When Montesquieu published his inelegantly titled *Considérations sur les causes de la grandeur des Romains et de leur décadence* (Amsterdam, 1734), the republic of letters was not unanimously impressed. Voltaire, always exquisitely attuned to the ebb and flow of the reputation of his rivals (anybody vying for public attention was his rival), welcomed it as a promise of Montesquieu's own decadence: "Have you seen the little and too little book writ by Montesquieu on the decadence of the Empire?" he wrote to Thieriot. "They call it the decadence of Montesquieu. . . . There are many things in it which deserve to be read and that makes me angry with the author for having so lightly treated of so great a matter. This book is full of hints, is less a book than an ingenious *table des matières* writ in an odd style."[1] To Voltaire, who Diderot once said wrote history "as the great sculptors of antiquity created portraits. He enlarges, he exaggerates, he corrects the forms," Montesquieu's own brand of history writing must have seemed disconcerting indeed.[2] In the rapid fire of twenty-three short chapters Montesquieu covered the whole parable of the Roman adventure, from its humble beginnings, when the city was but a few wooden huts on the Tiber, to the waning days of Byzantium, when the empire dwindled to Constantinople and its suburbs. To be sure, conciseness per se was not necessarily seen as a fault. Fénelon, for one, had recommended that the historian avoid "insignificant events" and that he follow "a single, energetic, narrative line."[3] Relying upon the authority of Cicero ("Nothing is more enjoyable in history than a pure and splendid brevity"),[4] Fénelon had absolved the historian from dependence upon too scrupulous a respect for scholarly details or, God forbid, pedantic antiquarianism: "We ought to abandon that superstitious meticulousness to compilers. The main point is to let the reader get immediately to the thick of the matter, to explain the connections and to hasten to the denouement."[5] But Montesquieu had followed that advice too closely: the book was scandalously short. True enough, its author was familiar with myriad ancient historians, canonical and not—from Polybius to Denis of Halicarnassus, Plutarch, Titus-Livius, Sallustius, Suetonius, Tacitus, Frontinus, Flavius Josephus, Dion Cassius, Appian, Florus, Pausanias, Procopius, and others—as well as with an inordinate number of obscure Byzantine chroniclers; the work was packed with references to their *oeuvre,* with quotations and excerpts. However, it also displayed a certain high-handedness toward the fledgling science of archaeology and a tendency to disregard historical accuracy. The most blatant example was Montesquieu's reliance upon the legend of the kings of Rome at a time when the Académie des Inscriptions et Belles Lettres had raised serious doubts about it, with the works of Lévesque de Pouilly and later of Louis de Beaufort.[6]

But it was not for its brevity nor for its eccentric erudition that readers took issue with the essay. The work was perceived as baffling on other grounds. If Fénelon had freed the historian from the strictures of erudition, it was for a reason, namely, so that he could devote all his attention and skill to weaving the events into a *seamless narrative:*

> History must resemble an epic poem. . . . In order to get to this beautiful orderliness, the historian must embrace the totality of the period he is concerned with. He must see it as a whole and at one glance. He must highlight its unity and draw from a single source, so to speak, all the principal events that derive from it. By so doing, he will instruct his reader with profit and interest, he will give him the pleasure of making predictions, and he will put the entire system before his eyes.[7]

The task of the historian was to instruct and enlighten the reader with an inspiring tale invested with a high moral content. The tale had a plot with a beginning, a middle, and an end; like an epic poem, it was a celebration of national pride. History was eloquence: it appealed to the audience's passions, and it induced awe at the grand spectacle of God finally putting human affairs in order. No matter how much toil and struggle nations must endure, history always resulted in an order that was to some a theodicy and to others, such as Voltaire, the triumph of reason and progress. "It is history," wrote Fénelon, "that shows us the great examples, that turns the vices of the bad into instruction for the good, that disentangles the origins and explains the roads that peoples have taken in order to pass from one form of government to another."[8] History was pedagogical and exemplary, intended primarily for the instruction of princes but also for that of ordinary citizens:

> The advantage of history consists in the comparison that a statesman or a citizen may make between foreign laws and customs and his own. That is what induces modern nations to compete in the arts, in commerce, and agriculture. The great mistakes of the past are useful in all respects, and the importance of putting before our eyes the crimes and the misery caused by absurd quarrels cannot be overemphasized. I am confident that by refreshing the memory of those quarrels we may prevent their renewal. . . . Examples have a great effect on the mind of a prince who reads them carefully.[9]

In the same vein, another great orator turned historian, the bishop Jacques-Bénigne Bossuet, the author of a universal history destined for the instruction of the Dauphin, the slow-witted son of Louis XIV, had vaunted, with the tone of an expert puppeteer addressing his fairgrounds audience, the beautiful completeness of the vast spectacle of history that, in the pen of a skillful writer, unfolded for the edification of a riveted audience:

> Such a digest, Monseigneur, offers you a grand spectacle. You may see the past centuries unfold, so to speak, before your eyes: see how the empires succeed one another and how religion, in its different manifestations, holds sway from the beginning of time to our own time. . . . Seeing everything included in an abridged version, discovering its order and progress, is to comprehend everything that is great among men and to hold the thread of all the events in the universe.[10]

But Montesquieu's Roman history did not offer the comfort of a familiar, overarching narrative; events did not unfold like the uninterrupted links in a chain; the reader did not feel that he was given to hold the thread connecting the rise and fall of empires across the ages. Indeed, Montesquieu was suspicious of grand narratives and exemplary tales. "History has been written like tragedy, with a unity of action that readers appreciate because it gives them cheap emotions and because it seems to instruct them without any effort of memory and judgement," he wrote in his notebooks.[11] History writing after his own heart did not turn the reader into the passive recipient of an engrossing spectacle. Unlike tragedy or epics, his own history had no apparent unity of action and no reassuring denouement. It gave the audience plenty of things to mull over, perhaps too many, according to some. His essay on the Romans bypassed many of the traditional vantage points of Roman historiography; it followed unfamiliar pathways and rearranged the events along new axes.

For instance, Montesquieu ignored or underplayed the two major milestones that had been central in virtually all traditional historiography of Rome: the Augustan empire and the emergence of Christianity, which were causally related in most providential accounts of Rome (such as Bossuet's, Rollin's, and Lenain de Tillemont's). The triumph of the true faith had been, of course, the focal point of Bossuet's universal history, but Montesquieu treated the rise of Christianity as just another step in the dissolution of the original Roman spirit and a move toward decadence. The foreign faith, together with the universal right of citizenship, contributed to its alienation: "Rome was no longer mistress of the world, but received laws from the entire universe. . . . That, apart from the secret means God chooses and that he alone knows, did much for the establishment of the Christian religion. For there was no longer anything foreign in the empire, and people were prepared to accept all the customs an emperor might wish to introduce."[12] The Christian emperors, from Constantine to Justinian, showcased disastrous policies, corruption, and tyrannical rule. In contrast, Montesquieu had nothing but praise for Julian the Apostate, who was usually the object of the contempt of the faithful. Absent or given passing mention are the great figures of the *vertu des païens,* the self-sacrificing heroes displayed in all Christian reappropriations of Stoic virtue, as well as the matinée idols of civic republicanism, the two Brutuses (of Brutus the tyrannicide, whom Rousseau venerated, and Pompey we learn only that they "killed themselves with inexcusable precipitation");[13] Coriolanus, Regulus, and Scipio the African, on whom Bossuet duly reports,[14] are all shamefully absent. Even more surprising, the notorious Tarquinius, the last of the kings who, as legend had it, single-handedly discredited the monarchy in the eyes of the Romans, is given a sort of rehabilitation. Montesquieu also devotes much attention to the great men who resisted Rome: Hannibal and Mithridates each get their own chapter, and the Barbarian Attila, who ravaged Rome, is described in a chapter provocatively titled "Attila's Greatness" as "one of the greatest monarchs that history has ever mentioned."[15]

The most glaring gap in the book, and the one that sets it apart from the historiography of Montesquieu's time, is the refusal to pay homage to, or even simply to acknowledge, Roman culture, the extraordinary flourishing of letters and manners that reached its apex during the reign of Augustus. No previous French account of Rome, from Guez de Balzac to Saint-Evremond to Bossuet to Voltaire, had failed to glorify it. Montesquieu refuses to indulge in the myth of a cultural *translatio imperii,* which had seduced all the apologists of *le Grand Siècle,* all the writers who had equated the cultural achievements of the age of Augustus with those of the age of Louis XIV.[16] He is silent on the culture of *urbanitas,* the founding myth of French sociability, and the pivotal axis of Guez de Balzac's attempt to transplant the flower of Roman eloquence to the soil of French absolutist, polite society. In his letters and discourses Guez de Balzac had lovingly polished the image of a refined and sociable Rome, in which military virtues were not incompatible with a taste for the arts and Roman generals were so dashing that they would have cut a nice figure in contemporary French salons:

> The Senate and the military campaigns, the civil and the martial affairs had their season; conversation, theater, and poetry had theirs. The pleasures of good taste were never enjoyed more, and the same hand that had won a war and signed the destiny of nations would write a comedy or applaud those who played them. Every day did not bring with it a Hannibal to defeat or an Africa to subjugate. Anthony and Pompey's sons only died once. After that came that general quietness during which the most agitated became idle and everybody yielded to a government that was as serene as a family.[17]

But Montesquieu is deeply distrustful of the Pax Romana, the "general quietness" that oversaw the flourishing of *urbanitas.* His disapproval of Augustus's soft despotism ("Augustus, a scheming tyrant, conducted [the Romans] gently to servitude")[18] is matched only by his contempt for Louis XIV, whom Voltaire had hailed—together with Augustus—as one of the representatives of the "four happy ages" of history, "those in which the arts have been perfected and which, serving as the epitome of the grandeur of the human spirit, are an example to posterity."[19] By contrast, Montesquieu finds little to admire in Louis le Grand and in the imperial dream that fostered his policies: "He seemed to have power only for ostentation: everything was empty swaggering with him, even his politics. . . . In a century and a part of the world in which heroism had become impossible Louis XIV had the foible to pursue it."[20] Both reigns were characterized by a despotism that concealed its grip under the veil of an all-pervading ideology conveyed by a strictly controlled propaganda: "Augustus (this is the name flattery gave Octavius) established order—that is, a durable servitude. For in a free state in which sovereignty has just been usurped, whatever can establish the unlimited authority of one man is called good order, and whatever can maintain the honest liberty of the subjects is called commotion, dissension, or bad government."[21]

Rather than lingering on the cultural achievements of Roman writers and orators (with whom Montesquieu nonetheless was intimately familiar and whom he ardently admired, as is apparent everywhere in his notebooks), Montesquieu represents Romans as a rough and crude people ideally equipped for predation and dominion. The book is more an essay on the anthropology of power than a satisfied look at one's roots, at our-ancestors-the-Romans (unsurprising, perhaps, for an admirer of Boulainvilliers). Montesquieu gives the much-celebrated "sublime and eloquent" simplicity of the ancients, highly prized by writers from Fénelon to Voltaire, an entirely new spin that prefigures Nietzsche's account of master morality: "Simplicity (and scarce culture of the mind) is good for victory; witness the early Romans, the Tartars, the Arabs."[22] The citizens of the Roman republic, he suggests, were drawn to action because of the simplicity, the narrowness, and the unreflectiveness of their moral motivations, which led them toward a single goal instead of, as in the case of the moderns, a multiplicity of small, conflicting goals. Their "virtue" was an action-oriented passion endowed with "force" and directness and hence with strong creativity.[23] Montesquieu was apparently drawn to the Romans for reasons similar to those that drew Rousseau: both argued that the ancients embodied the ideal of a society in which sovereignty was achieved effortlessly and unselfconsciously. Both saw in the classical *polis* an organic and harmonious community with no division of functions and labor, in which *moeurs* and customs had the same efficacy as laws, the political order reflected the ethical order of personal conduct, and the duties of public life merged harmoniously with those of the private sphere, with no conflict and no division within the self.

Unlike Rousseau, however, Montesquieu's *Considerations* do not hide his revulsion at the Romans' cruelty, untrustworthiness, greed, and predatory impulses. In the *Considerations* virtue comes the closest to the etymological root of *virtus,* that is, sheer force, drive, energy: "Each Roman, more robust and belligerent than his opponent, always relied on himself. Courage—the virtue which is the consciousness of one's own strength—came to him naturally."[24] The Romans are able to master themselves and to weed out all the impulses that are not necessary to their survival and to their continuous, limitless growth. Their organic, synthetic society is composed of a few cohesive parts and does not allow for the free growth of complex individuals; their terrible simplicity of purpose is achieved thanks to a history in which they had to struggle against forces that threatened their survival: "But, always striving and always meeting obstacles, Rome made its power felt without being able to extend it, and, within a very small orbit, practiced the virtues which were to be so fatal to the universe."[25] Despite several portraits of strong individuals, such as Cato, Caesar, and Sylla, one is struck by the intent to represent the Romans as a single, collective body composed of many simple elements devoid of an inner life and of the peculiarities of individual character.[26] That is so crucial to Montesquieu that for him the decline of the Roman state coincides precisely with the dissolution of the public spirit resulting from the incorporation of new, foreign elements into the city, which fragmented the original unity of its collective *génie:* "After this, Rome was no longer a city whose people had but a single spirit, a single love of liberty, a single hatred of tyranny. . . . Once the peoples of Italy became its citizens, each city brought to Rome its genius, its particular interests. . . . The city, torn apart, no longer formed a complete whole. . . . The people no longer saw Rome with the same eyes, no longer had the same love of the *Patrie,* and Roman sentiments were no more."[27]

Elsewhere, and particularly in *De l'esprit des lois,* Montesquieu emphasizes virtue's sacrificial component as an aspect of the Christianized heroic ideal that was fostered upon young pupils by education in the Jesuit and Oratorian colleges. According to that portrayal, virtue presents some similarities not only with Corneille's representation of glory but also with Augustinian charity. Virtue is a selfless investment of energy in an object that overrides any narrow self-interest: "In order to be a good man, one must have the intention of being one and love the state less for oneself than for itself."[28] That is not so in the *Considerations,* where virtue is described in a very unchristian and unheroic way. There the strength of Roman virtue lies in the absence, not of selfish drives, but of any incompatibility between the selfish drives (the calculation of utility) and devotion to public welfare. In other words, the early Romans did not differentiate between their personal, individual interest and that of their nation, because they did not perceive themselves as separate beings, independent of the community. Indeed, the Romans were just as selfish and greedy as the moderns, in fact even more so, but the civil and military organization of the republic was such that it was able to integrate those vices and put them in the service of the public. Moral life was continuous with economic and political life, and the good of the individual merged into that of the state. (That admirable integration collapsed under the empire, when corruption and greed disintegrated Roman society and institutions.) Qualities like heroism, courage, and endurance were coextensive with the material conditions of survival and economic growth: the apparent sacrifice of self-love, family affections, and private feelings to the state was in reality a way to preserve those affections, because without the survival of the state there would have been no family and no private life at all. The Roman republic demonstrates how powerful the passions can be when they are directed toward a unique goal: "There is nothing so powerful as a republic in which the laws are observed not through fear, not through reason, but through passion—which was the case with Rome and Lacedaemon; for then, to the wisdom of a good government is joined all the strength a faction could have."[29] The fearsome discipline of the Roman armies was the result of their utter lack of an independent spirit (we would say individualism), something the barbarians, who had a regrettable tendency to switch loyalties in the midst of battle, had in plenty.[30]

It was noted by Montesquieu's contemporaries that the *Considerations* aimed at debunking the Roman myth and scaling it down. Mathieu Marais wrote to President Bouhier, "People say that . . . the Romans are very badly treated and that he [Montesquieu] portrays those ancient rulers of the universe as scoundrels without virtue."[31] If that were true, it would hardly have been original. Many had trodden on that path before Montesquieu, from the chevalier de Méré, who saw in Roman majesty nothing but "the avarice of conceited bourgeois," to Saint-Evremond, who reduced awe-inspiring republican virtue to the more familiar, far less heroic terms of modern *amour-propre,* to Voltaire, who debunked Roman patriotism in his *Essai sur les moeurs:* "That love of country consisted, for more than four hundred years, in bringing back to the communal booty whatever had been plundered from other nations: it was the virtue of bandits."[32] What is more, both Saint-Evremond and Voltaire showed a desire to weed out the ancient myths and fables and to unearth the facts that lay buried beneath age-old layers of prejudice, ideology, and fantastic story-telling.[33] "I hate that admiration founded upon fables and established through the errors of false judgement," declared Saint-Evremond; "there are so many authentic things to admire among the Romans that we spoil them when we fall for tall tales. To purge them of that sterile wonder is to honor them."[34] As for Voltaire, he had little patience with vestal virgins and the Capitol's watchful geese.[35]

But Montesquieu's Roman history is not simply a debunking of myths; such a skeptical, enlightened project is undoubtedly present in this work, but it is not foremost. It is true that its methodology may be described as a product of the Enlightenment: Montesquieu wishes to set things straight, to establish the validity of evidence culled from multiple sources and documents, to examine the facts in light of conflicting interpretations, to balance carefully considerations about the political culture of the Romans with military, economic, and legal evidence. He sets one historian against another with little regard for the pieties of established tradition. Much of Montesquieu's writing in the *Considerations* is aglow with underlying polemics with other historians, who, he suggests, use uncritically a language imbued with an ideology that must be exposed and analyzed. It is also well known that this essay is Montesquieu's first systematic attempt to come up with a theory of historical causality that would place the apparent randomness of particular events in the wider context of cultural and political evolution—a kind of *longue durée*. The focus on this double logic of causation, which allowed Montesquieu to distinguish between general causes *(causes générales* or *causes éloignées)* and particular events *(accidents particuliers* or *causes occasionnelles),* did earn him the approval of nineteenth-century positivists, who praised him for producing a "philosophy of history," or a work in which "the historian focuses on what is truly general in history: the chain of probable causes and probable effects."[36] In a similar vein, d'Alembert had written approvingly that Montesquieu "might have entitled his book *A Roman History Intended for Statesmen and Philosophes.*"[37]

Nothing, however, could be further removed from Montesquieu's sensitivity than such a depersonalized, disengaged assessment of historical causality. D'Alembert would have been more correct had he suggested that this strange and genre-bending book be named *A Roman History Intended for Poets.* For what Montesquieu pursues here is not simply a critical reflection on Roman historiography from the Latin sources to his own time. What he strives to achieve is a definition of the role and the significance of "antiquity" for the moderns: how to define the kernel of that elusive, fascinating, and notoriously controversial ideal that was very much alive in the Enlightenment, in the ongoing quarrel between the ancients and the moderns.

Montesquieu, the quintessentially modern author of the *Persian Letters,* the *bel esprit* whom his friend Mme de Tencin used to call "my little Roman," was drawn to the wonder of a world larger than life that he grew up admiring. A student of the Oratorian College of Juilly, he was steeped in the knowledge of antiquity, in Greek and Latin; the first manuscript we have by his hand is a *Historia romana,* a rhetorical exercise in Latin, written in his early teens, that records the boy's wonder at the cruelty of the dictator Sylla. "The history of the Roman Empire is what deserves our attention the most," wrote Voltaire in the *Encyclopédie,* "because the Romans have been our masters and our legislators."[38] More fundamentally, Montesquieu shows that it was through awareness of the ancients that the moderns had constructed an identity for themselves; it was antiquity that had revealed modernity to itself: "As soon as we started reading the ancients and we spent one century commenting and translating them, . . . we saw the moderns emerge."[39]

In the *Considerations* Montesquieu confronts the ancients on their own ground, as a civilization, as a myth very much alive in the modern world, and above all as an aesthetics and a body of literature. The *Considerations* represent a tour de force insofar as they manage to combine a variety of modes and genres that would otherwise seem incompatible. They are a reflection on historical causality; they take a critical, enlightened approach toward historiographical myths and stereotypes; they are the celebration of political liberty, both ancient and modern; and finally, they are the rewriting or appropriation, in a modern language and style, of a vast body of historical literature in Latin and Greek. Each chapter is based on the work of one or more ancient historians, which Montesquieu sometimes transcribes, at other times reformulates in his own terms.

Such rewriting involves far more than simply putting one's sources to scholarly use. The *Considerations* are a mosaic assembling the many vestiges and ruins transmitted by antiquity, integrating them into a unique style that was distinctive enough to deserve blame for being "peculiar" and "original" (a description that was not intended as complimentary) and thoroughly *modern.* Indeed, this work is an example of that rich, erudite palimpsest literature that alternated literary homage and lampooning of ancient models, a literature in search of itself, which could invent itself only through critical confrontation with previous discourses. Montesquieu's work, however, is neither adaptation (like La Motte's) nor parodical rewriting, but appropriation. His intent is to recreate the passion, the movement, and the energy of the ancient texts (much as Diderot was hoping to do) and through them to recapture the movement of the Roman adventure in all the awe and horror it inspires. In so doing, he turns historical analysis into a kind of poetry. But he does not espouse the classicist tendency to rework the fragments of antiquity into a new totality glorifying the French monarchy or its culture. Montesquieu refuses to produce a continuous narrative endowed with the completeness of a divine, or state-inspired, teleology. Rather, he reworks those texts so as to disassemble previous narratives and question the tenets of contemporary historians and theoreticians of absolutism. His own history—provocative, fragmentary, and disconcerting—sets the stage for a radical questioning of the meaning of ancient and modern liberty and for a confrontation between the ancient sublime and the taste of the moderns, the much-reviled *goût moderne.*

Sublime Saillies

Montesquieu's contemporaries, however, accustomed as they were to a different historiographical style, were for the most part bewildered by what they saw as a dangerous contamination of eloquence by a misuse of *esprit,* which had its place in the literature of *petit-goût* and in *galanterie* but not in history writing, which demanded a dignified and stately pace. Upon the publication of the *Considerations* one reader commented typically:

> People find his ideas obscure; that may be an effect of the discontinuous style [*style coupé*] that he affects. There are many *a capite,* and at every step we may say, borrowing Quintilian's expression, that it is *soluta oratio, et e singulis non membris sed frustis conlata.* That lack of connections is taxing to the mind. Such a style may be appropriate to maxims, to meditations, or to *histoires galantes.* But a book that reasons and argues, that embraces a system and requires the laying out of principles, cannot accommodate such fits and starts. What it needs is something more cushioned [*moelleux*].[40]

Indeed, there was very little *moelleux* in the *Considerations,* and readers felt that something had hit them very hard. They found little to caress the ear and coddle the understanding into that happy "discovery of connections" that Fénelon and Bossuet had made the hallmark of good historical writing; there was none of the continuous, harmonious, and gradual development of an unbroken train of ideas that to Buffon revealed in a discourse the same texture as in the works of nature.[41] Instead of finding connections, they complained of interruptions, gaps, and obscurity in the fast-paced sentences and chapters.

The accusation of indulging in *esprit* was to accompany Montesquieu throughout his career and thereafter. Toward the end of the century Louis-Sébastien Mercier would thus preface his play *Montesquieu à Marseille,* in which he did his best to cleanse his hero of all traces of *bel esprit:* "The physiognomy of Montesquieu considered as a writer has something peculiar [*singulier*] and hard to pin down: precision, agility, depth—he covers all that with a veil of enigma; his thought is far-reaching and his phrase short, discontinuous even. Momentous ideas are presented as epigrams; he is solid, yet he constantly sharpens his style as if he were nothing but a *bel esprit.*"[42] In Antoine-Léonard Thomas's inaugural address to the French Academy in 1767 his Ubuesque eulogy of the historical writings of his predecessor, Jacques Hardion, the author of a twenty-volume universal history, was a barely disguised censure of Montesquieu. No one could miss the many allusions: energy, rapidity, lack of transitions, reticence, subtlety, and an insightfulness "painful" to the mind were the peculiar defects of Montesquieu's style. Thomas found Hardion's honorable mediocrity profoundly endearing:

> [Hardion's] style was as modest as himself. He succeeded in avoiding the kind of forcefulness that too often shades into excess; the rapidity that, compressing objects, jumbles them; the subtlety [*finesse*] that suppresses too many transitions in order to suggest others; the painful insightfulness that affects to enclose into one idea the seed of twenty others. Most important, he rose above that luxury of *esprit,* which enjoys its riches only when it can parade them.[43]

Voltaire's early negative judgment on Montesquieu's style would never waver. He found in *The Spirit of the Laws* the same defects that were heralded by the *Considerations:*

> A book on the law needs . . . no witticisms [*saillies d'esprit*] and no digressions unrelated to the subject. . . . I was looking for a thread in that labyrinth, but the thread would break at almost every chapter. I have been deceived: I have found the spirit of the author, who has a great deal of it, and seldom that of the laws. He does not walk but he hops [*sautille*]; he entertains more than he enlightens; he sometimes satirizes more than he forms an opinion. One wishes that such a remarkable mind had tried to instruct rather than astonish.[44]

Sautillement connoted the effeminate and foppish demeanor of *petits-maîtres* and *persifleurs* and the interrupted style of conversation that was satirized by Crébillon, Diderot, and Duclos. Obscurity, digression, and fragmentation characterized, in Diderot's *Indiscreet Jewels* "the fashion of the scoffers [*persifleurs*]," people who "used to begin a conversation with one person, then pirouette and continue it with another, and finish with a third, for whom it was half unintelligible, half impertinent."[45] *Saillies,* hyperbolic exaggeration, and a desire to astonish were traits typical of worldly conversation, according to Duclos: "It was not one of those speeches in which there is only common sense; it was a torrent of *saillies;* everybody would ask questions and no one would answer right; people understood each other perfectly or they did not, which amounted to the same for those who were clever. Exaggeration was the ultimate, fashionable figure: with no spirited sentiments and no important activity in mind, people always spoke its language."[46] In Claude Dupin's caustic critique of *De l'esprit des lois,* Montesquieu's writing, like conversation, was marred by "those odd expressions made to astonish; those antitheses that sound so pleasant; those fiery figures of speech generously sprinkled here and there."[47]

Such improper abundance of rhetorical figures opposes *briller* to *éclairer, éblouissement* to *lumières,* surprise to persuasion. Voltaire, Diderot, and Rousseau all oppose admiration to persuasion, or *frapper* to *toucher:* "Nothing salient, nothing remarkable; neither the words, nor the turns, nor the sentences, are memorable; there is nothing in it to admire or to be struck by. And yet one feels the soul melt; one feels moved without knowing why. The strength of the sentiment may not strike us, but its truth affects us."[48] In the eighteenth century, those whom the purists and the neoclassicists deemed likely to sink into the pitfalls of verbal excess and ornament (such as hyperbole and *saillie,* affectation and *esprit*) were the *mondains,* those who practiced worldliness. But that had not always been the case. We are struck by a sense of déjà vu when we look back at early-seventeenth-century debates, for we realize that the very same quarrel had been played out against quite a different political background in the world of letters. At that time the debate had pitted the grand eloquence of the scholarly and the *savants* against the simplicity of the worldly writers; the partisans of the *latinisant* and erudite Guez de Balzac against those of the worldly and atticist Voiture. The former, like François Ogier, would claim that "extraordinary things expressed in magnificent language not only persuade but also astonish the audience."[49] The latter would rebut, quoting Boileau, that "it is truly a principle of Longinus that 'elevated and grand thoughts provoke admiration and surprise, but no belief in the soul.' . . . Extraordinary and lofty expressions enchant the mind without taking hold of the will; those of Monsieur de Balzac overwhelm the imagination without moving the heart and without leading the mind where intended."[50]

In the eighteenth century, by a significant reversal, rhetorical *enflure* and bad taste were attributed to the *petit goût* of the worldly, while sublime simplicity graced the work of the writers and scientists who adhered to the *grand goût,* those who claimed to find their inspiration in the writings of the ancients. The criticism the prose of Montesquieu suffered from was not always distinguished by rigorous coherence; it presented, however, one persistent thesis, namely, that the author's immoderate desire to astonish and impress the audience won out over all concern for clarity, persuasion, and truth. Such astonishment resulted from the obscurity of his broken and disjointed sentences *(style coupé),* the staccato rhythm, or the abuse of *traits saillants* (flashing rhetorical figures improperly). Both indiscretions were reprehended by Voltaire in his *Lettre sur l'esprit:* "Those amusements of the imagination, those subtleties, those turns of phrase, those surprising expressions [*traits saillants*], those jokes, those short and discontinuous sentences [*petites sentences coupées*], those ingenious liberties that are so common today, are suited only to minor works made for entertainment."[51] Voltaire was not referring here to anyone in particular, but that judgment was consistent with his lifelong critique of Montesquieu. But this time Montesquieu would find an unlikely ally. In a review of Voltaire's *Lettre sur l'esprit* (1744) the abbé Desfontaines scoffed: "That may be true in general. But why should the discontinuous sentences [*sentences coupées*] be inappropriate to the most dignified style? They sometimes constitute the sublime, as in the words: God said, let there be light, and there was light. Is it not the case that M. de Voltaire himself sometimes presents in his tragedies some examples of those discontinuous sentences and those surprising expressions [*traits saillants*]?"[52] For once the satirical abbé, well served by his desire to nag Voltaire, had hit the nail on the head.

But what was the precise meaning of the contested term *saillie* (sally)? In the *Dictionnaire de l'Académie, saillie* means primarily a sudden and unexpected leap forward, or a movement by fits and starts, like intermittent spurts issuing forth from a fountain, a *jet d'eau;* a sudden shift, a jibe or a swing. Rhetorically it denotes all those figures of speech—"dazzling and surprising *traits d'esprit*"—that stand out in a discourse and seem to spring forth spontaneously. On that point all the successive editions of the *Dictionnaire* are in agreement. But when it comes to defining the discursive context in which such figures may occur, things change significantly. In the first edition, of 1694, we read that those *traits d'esprit* may appear "in a work of eloquence, of poetry, in conversation. [One says:] a lively, noble, clever and pleasing *saillie.* That orator, that poet, have striking *saillies.*" *Saillie* is unequivocally positive; it is characteristic not only of conversation but also of high style *(une saillie noble),* of eloquence and poetry. It is consistent with the sublime brevity of atticist style in the Bible ("God said, let there be light, and there was light") or in Corneille's *Horace* ("Qu'il mourût," which was universally praised as the ultimate example of sublime energy). That is no longer the case in the fifth edition of the *Dictionnaire* (1798), which greatly narrows the spectrum of *saillie* by confining it strictly within conversational witticism. Gone is all reference to poetry and eloquence and to the written word; instead, we are told that a man who frequently resorts to *saillie* is superficial and lacks coherence in his thinking: "*Saillie* denotes dazzling and surprising witticisms that seem to emerge naturally in a written work and in conversation. . . . One says of a man who indulges in *saillies* that his mind is all in *saillies* but that he lacks depth and coherence." Few examples could be more indicative of the shift that took place in the later part of the eighteenth century, which delegitimized the very idea of the figural power of discourse by narrowing its scope to oral expression and to the undervalued, fatuous worldliness of *petit goût.*

In the seventeenth century there had been no clear-cut distinction between the use of figures in conversation and their use in the high eloquence of poetry and the written word. *Saillie* and *esprit* traced their origins all the way back to the source of eloquence, that is, to the works of Quintilian *(sententiae)* and to Longinus's notion of the sublime, namely, that brevity and surprise were not necessarily the result of affectation but an effect of pathos. In the eighteenth century, however, a new desire for respectability—and an unfortunate alliance between pathos and melodrama—established boundaries and interdictions, broke connections between levels of discourse and experience, and reinforced the hierarchy of styles. Writers rejected the kinship between art and the aesthetics of worldliness that had been vital to the seventeenth century: "Now that our language is being denatured and degraded," d'Alembert declared, "great writers will find [the true language] by barring from their works the ephemeral twitter of our coteries."[53] Voltaire, Diderot, and Rousseau were no longer capable of discriminating between "the magnificence of figures," which might or might not be fatuous or grandiloquent, and "the force of the emotions," which belonged to the authentic sublime. Desfontaines was therefore right to remind that *sentences coupées* and *traits saillants* were truly the legacy of the Longinian sublime and that Voltaire himself relied upon them whenever he wished his language to wield the maximum impact.

Montesquieu's originality consists in the fact that going against the grain of the neoclassical spirit, he never refrained from experimenting with stylistic boundaries. There was plenty of genre-bending irreverence not only in the *Persian Letters,* where the pathos of belief coexisted with irony, but also in his scholarly works. Montesquieu always welded registers of style and genre in personal and daring ways. "A writer [*un homme d'esprit*]," he wrote in his notebooks, "is in his works creator of idioms, turns of phrase, and conceptions; he dresses his thought as he pleases, molds and creates it thanks to a style that is different from the current one but that does not aim at seeming so. A man who writes well does not write like others, but like himself; often it is by speaking incorrectly that he speaks well."[54] In his writings, and particularly in the *Considerations*, the aesthetics of admiration and energy that was associated with the sublime of the ancients came to be joined with the principle of surprise, which was quintessentially modern, that is, compatible with the *goût moderne*. Indeed, admiration, energy, and surprise were to him fundamental passions and emotions that invested with equal force the political and the aesthetic realms: Rome was admirable both as a political model and as an object to be considered aesthetically. "Good prose is like a majestic river that rolls its waters; good verses are like a fountain that gushes forth under pressure: out of this upheaval of poetry emerges something that gives us pleasure."[55] However, in the staccato rhythm of phrases bursting forth, in the sudden leaps of thought, in the bypassing of explicit logical connections, in the dazzling images, the writing of the *Considerations* is closer to poetry than to the ebb tide of the Ciceronian *copia* and the Longinian *plèthos,* the majestic river of prose rolling its waves (Longinus compares it to a spreading fire or a flood).[56] The prose of the *Considerations* approaches a poetic form that Montesquieu finds more congenial for expressing the cluster of conflicting passions and contrarieties that Rome embodies for him: Rome cannot simply be narrated and analyzed, it must be considered in wonder.[57]

A few years before he wrote the *Considerations,* or perhaps in conjunction with them, about 1728, Montesquieu started to jot down ideas for an essay on the notion of taste, but he never finished it.[58] It was revised over the years and published posthumously in the *Encyclopédie* in 1757, a late offering to the great enterprise of the Enlightenment. But the *Essai sur le goût* was not exactly illustrative of Enlightenment aesthetics. It was the work of a previous generation, the product of the *goût moderne.* And yet it was armed with a modern aesthetics and epistemology that Montesquieu set down to confront that awe-inspiring monster, the epitome of the ancient spirit, Rome. The result was a striking synthesis, Montesquieu's double paean to Rome and to the modern age.

Of Ancient and Modern Desire

In the *Histoire universelle* Bossuet had opened his remarks on Rome with fanfare and loud brass: "We have finally come to that great empire that has swallowed all the empires of the universe, whence have emerged all the greatest kingdoms of the world we presently inhabit and whose laws we still observe."[59] By contrast, Montesquieu opens his first chapter with a negative clause, sweeping away all previous grandiosity: "We should not form the same impression of the city of Rome in its beginnings as we get from the cities we see today, except perhaps those of the Crimea, which were built to hold booty, cattle, and the fruits of the field. . . . The City did not even have streets. . . . The houses were located without any particular order and were very small."[60] And yet, we would be mistaken to assume that from the onset Montesquieu intended simply to demythify Rome and scale it down. In the revised edition published in 1748 this paragraph was added: "But the greatness of Rome soon appeared in its public edifices. The works which conveyed and today still convey the strongest impression of its power were produced under the kings. Already the Romans were beginning to build the Eternal City."[61] The purpose is to present Rome in the starkest contrast, as a scene of contrarieties, as a shabby settlement *and* a monument to timeless power. That requires simultaneously embracing the myth and dispelling its illusions.

The sublime that Montesquieu pursues rejects all grandiloquence in favor of a conception of energy in style that aims less at producing rapture *(ravissement)* and enthusiasm, which would lull the reader into passivity ("the sublime . . . overwhelms and carries away . . ."), than at stimulating his curiosity and his understanding by modulating moments of surprise ("and produces in us an admiration blended with astonishment and surprise").[62] Indeed, *étonnement,* admiration, and surprise are key concepts in the contest between ancient and modern aesthetics. To Montesquieu, admiration is the fundamental passion raised by antiquity, and one that modernity, mired in the *badinage* of *petit goût,* seems to have cast aside: "We may hardly believe the extent of the decay of admiration in our century."[63] In French, *admiration* is a term that conflates two meanings that English distinguishes: admiration (respect, esteem, awe) and wonder (astonishment or surprise). The former involves an ethical judgment, while the latter is a complex aesthetic and intellectual response to an object that overwhelms our habits and defies the range of familiar concepts. The latter is the meaning that Descartes emphasized in his *Traité des passions de l'âme:* "Wonder [*admiration*] is a sudden surprise of the soul which causes it to apply itself to consider with attention the objects which seem to it rare and extraordinary."[64] Wonder is a passion that jolts the mind into a sudden shock, an initial suspension of its faculties, but subsequently predisposes it to form creative ideas: "Although it is good to be born with some inclination to this passion, because it is conducive to science, we must at the same time afterwards try to free ourselves from it as much as possible."[65] Descartes warns us against surrendering to *admiration* for fear of falling into *étonnement,* or astonishment, by which he means a kind of paralysis, a short-circuiting of thought (as in being *stunned*). Significantly, in his own account of the sublime Burke will note the central role played by astonishment and the paralysis it produces in the mind: "The passions caused by the great and sublime in nature, when those causes operate most powerfully, is astonishment; and astonishment is that state of the soul, in which all its motions are suspended, with some degree of horror. In this case, the mind is so entirely filled with its object, that it cannot entertain any other, nor by consequence reason on that object which employs it."[66]

But Montesquieu's own treatment of the Roman myth aims less at stunning us into passive reverence than at jolting us into thought-provoking surprise. His own text prevents the reader from becoming absorbed into a story of wonder and fury by scattering everywhere stop signs, interruptions and sudden changes of pace and tone; by alternating hot and cold moods: "This calls for reflection," he typically warns the audience, "otherwise we would see events without understanding them, and, by not being aware of the difference in situations, would believe that the men we read about in ancient history are of another breed than ourselves."[67]

In the *Considerations* Montesquieu has found a language capable of expressing the same ethos of energy that shapes the Roman experience. Following the Aristotelian principle that one must show the very movement of things as they are happening, Montesquieu brings all the powers of rhetoric to bear on a work that ought to strike the reader—by the abruptness of contrasts (parallels, antithesis, and chiasmus), the use of hyperboles, metaphorical expressions, the artful editing of events and reflections—with the same visual and dynamic impact as tragedy. Montesquieu, a great admirer of Corneille and Crébillon the elder, was convinced that modern tragedy was the only genre capable of withstanding comparison with the literature of the ancients: "That kind of writing is, by its very nature, the epitome of movement. Everything is, so to speak, on fire. Narrative and historical account need no ornament. One does not hear, but one sees, everything"; "strength is to be found in sensory images."[68] In the *Considerations* Montesquieu wants to bring the representation back to its Homeric, mythical sources, to the primitive ideal of a purely dynamic poetic language that would not say but show (the endgame of the sublime being silent monstration). Roman history is presented as action and spectacle: "When we carefully examine the multitude of obstacles confronting Hannibal . . . , we have before us the finest spectacle presented by antiquity"; "Pompey, in a rapid succession of victories . . . served the spectacle of Roman magnificence more than its true power"; "This is the place to set before ourselves the spectacle of things human."[69] Spectacles were, of course, a political tool in ancient Rome, a powerful means of raising and manipulating the passions of the crowd: "The people do not follow the orator's reasoning; they may be impressed by images and by figures of eloquence, but nothing moves them more than spectacles. . . . All great upheavals have been caused by the sight of some unexpected action. The death of Lucretia, . . . the action of Brutus, . . . the sight of Virginia killed by her father, . . . Caesar's blood-spattered tunic."[70] But in French tragedy, as in Montesquieu's text, the visual spectacle is effected by language, and it takes place in the mind's eye, in keeping with a rhetoric that emphasizes the visual impact of figural language *(hypotyposis, enargeia, phantasia,* or *evidentia)*, which lends discourse its hallucinatory power to captivate an audience (Quintilian) and to drive a mob to violent action (Longinus).[71] In the *Considerations,* spectacles are staged so as to respond to the soul's desire to embrace at once as many objects as possible, thus answering an essentially modern desire:

> It is therefore the pleasure that we receive from one object that drives us to another; that is why the soul is always looking for new things and finds no repose. That is why one will always be sure that by showing it a great deal of things, more than it had expected, one will always please it. . . . Since we like to see a considerable number of objects, we would like to extend our vision, inhabit several places at once, and cross more space; in other words, our soul does not accept boundaries and would like to extend the sphere of its presence. Its great pleasure is to expand its vision far and wide.[72]

The desire to bypass the sequential chain of cause and effect so as to enjoy a simultaneous view of things responds to the epistemology of the *homme d'esprit,* whose intuitive vision reaches further than that of most men.[73] But above all, it responds to the avid curiosity that results from the anthropology of *inquiétude,* the restless desire for an ever-changing reality that characterizes the modern experience. "Our soul does not accept boundaries"; its pleasure comes from the ever-renewed experience of a wide range of perceptions, and its inexhaustible curiosity fosters a continuous quest. Montesquieu's aesthetics seemed to fit his own nature; a letter addressed to him by his friend Mme de Lambert testifies to his restlessness: "As for you, it seems to me that you are not fond of lingering, not even on what you like; and whatever you like, it is not for long. Your happiness, therefore, is in the interval; restlessness, to you, is bliss; you have a quarrel with repose."[74] The law of the modern individual, like that of the Romans, is dynamism and protean adaptability: "A talented man [*un homme d'esprit*] . . . creates himself, so to speak, at every moment, according to the needs of the moment; he knows and feels the exact relation in which he stands to the world."[75] Modern energy consists in the increased diversification and renewal of desire through as many experiences as possible. In that sense Montesquieu's work on the Romans is a celebration of the passions of the modern age.

In the *Considerations,* therefore, Montesquieu favors a style that relies less on sequential connections than on an unexpected swerve: from ancient to modern times, from Rome to modern France; from economic to military to moral considerations; balancing the account of one historian with that of another; mixing tones and registers of language. As if looking on from a distance, the historian is able to embrace, by way of contrast, many diverse objects, to condense moments that stand far apart in time: "In the abyss in which he found himself, [Mithridates] devised a scheme for carrying the war to Italy and going to Rome with the same nations that subdued it some centuries later, and by the same route."[76] The narration undergoes sudden changes of rhythm, quickening its pace and compressing time: "The Romans had hardly subdued the Carthaginians when they attacked new peoples and appeared everywhere on earth to invade every country"; "They found them in those places where Mastery of the World was contested three times over."[77] Rapidity involves suggestion rather than explicitness: "In order to write well, one must skip transitional ideas: enough, as to avoid being tedious, not too much, for fear of being misunderstood. It is those felicitous suppressions that drive M. Nicole to say that all good books are double"; that is, they are written once over by the reader's desire.[78] In the *Essai sur le goût* Montesquieu praises the Roman historian Florus for condensing, into one powerful and unexpected *pointe,* what otherwise would have been a lengthy analysis. Dazzling brevity becomes a condition for the spectacle of *evidentia* to have its impact:

> A thought is great when by saying something it suggests a great deal more and when we discover at one glance things that we could have gathered only after much reading. Florus portrays in a few words all of Hannibal's faults: "When he was able to profit from victory, he preferred to enjoy it": *cum victoria posset uti, frui maluit.* He gives us a complete idea of the whole Macedonian war by saying, "Starting it was winning it": *introisse victoria fuit.* He paints the complete spectacle of Scipio's life when he writes of his youth, "This will be Scipio, who grows for the destruction of Africa": *hic erit Scipio, qui in exitium Africae crescit.* You think you see a child who grows and is raised like a giant.[79]

In that sense, brevity and *saillie* in Montesquieu's writing reflect the dictates of the Longinian sublime, which aims at erasing all connecting tissue, leaving only a pared-down, fragmented, but highly dramatic expressiveness: "By evening out and leveling everything with transitions, . . . you will descend into a language that has no edge [*pointe*] and no spur [*aiguillon*]; the force of your discourse will be smothered."[80] Hence the frequent use, in the *Considerations*, of chiasmic contrasts and sharp-edged endings: "After the reduction of the Carthaginians, Rome had almost nothing but small wars and great victories, whereas before it had had small victories and great wars"; "In Naples today there are fifty thousand men who live on herbs alone, and have as their sole possession only half a cotton garment. These people, the most unhappy on earth, fall into frightful despondency at the slightest smoke from Vesuvius. They are foolish enough to fear becoming unhappy."[81]

The need to shake the audience from indifference and ennui leads Montesquieu to emphasize the role of emotion; indeed, his prose does not conceal the historian's passions behind a veil of objectivity but artfully modulates them by alternating between seeming indifference and a sudden blaze of anger, between reticence and an unexpected outburst. His style offers a study in contrast. Montesquieu approves of Suetonius for alternating between sang-froid and anger and for suddenly intruding upon a seemingly objective narrative: "Suetonius describes Nero's crimes with startling coolness, making us believe that he does not feel the horror of what he is describing. He suddenly switches and says that the universe, which for fourteen years suffered this monster, finally abandoned him. . . . This produces different kinds of surprise."[82] In chapter 15 of the *Considerations* Montesquieu interrupts the steady flow of his narrative to intervene with a series of harried exclamations that culminate in a rhetorical question: "How many wars do we see undertaken in the history of Rome, how much blood shed, how many peoples destroyed, how many great actions, how many triumphs, how much statecraft, how much sobriety, prudence, constancy, and courage! But how did this project for invading all nations end—a project so well planned, carried out and completed—except by satiating the happiness of five or six monsters?" And he ends with a theatrical flourish worthy of the tragic stage: "What! This senate had brought about the extinction of so many kings only to fall into the meanest enslavement to some of its most contemptible citizens, and to exterminate itself by its own decrees? We build our power only to see it the better overturned?"[83]

With its emphasis on variety, contrast, rapidity, and surprise, this style reflects what Montesquieu finds fascinating in the ethos of the Romans, namely, the promptness of their action, the energy they deploy in their relentless advance. "Consuls waged war with great impetuosity. They went straight for the enemy, and strength decided matters immediately."[84] "They were able to embark upon those swift and rapid marches that we may admire but may not imitate, and they never appeared more suddenly than after a defeat. . . . Nothing brings more terror to the mind . . . than an enemy materializing when he is the least expected. . . ."[85] Rome is a body constantly thrust forward in a flight that cannot be checked; it is a conquering nation that collapses under the weight of its own success. Rome can prosper only as long as it keeps growing, but the very principle that keeps it alive and struggling is the one that will bring its death. Rome is bent on survival, and its enduring life comes from its willingness constantly to confront and defy death. At the beginning of the republic its energy feeds on the resistance it encounters: "Rome was therefore in an endless and constantly violent war. . . . All the peoples of Italy . . . opposed to it an unbelievable resistance and Rome learned its obstinacy from them."[86] However, as the Roman Empire grows beyond all bounds to cover the surface of the globe, a death wish takes over, and the city turns murderous against itself. The struggle for absolute power thus unleashes a desire for death.

Montesquieu is fascinated by the prodigious anomaly of such an organism, which he describes as a bloated political aberration, a multitude of bodies capped by a single, monstrous head: "Thus Rome was really neither a monarchy nor a republic, but the head of a body formed by all the peoples of the world."[87] Emphasizing the excess of such an experience, Montesquieu frequently uses hyperboles and chthonian metaphors; the Roman adventure can find adequate expression only in cosmic revolutions and the catastrophies that emerge from the bowels of the earth: "In this war, Philip was swept along by the Romans as by a torrent" (chap. 5, p. 62); "When they made war on some prince, they overwhelmed him, so to speak, with the weight of the entire universe" (chap. 6, p. 75); "While Rome conquered the universe, a secret war was going on within its walls. Its fires were like those of volcanoes which burst forth whenever some matter comes along to increase its ferment" (chap. 8, p. 83); "As a river slowly and silently undermines the dikes erected against it, and finally overthrows them in a moment, flooding the countryside they protected, so in the same way the sovereign power that acted insensibly under Augustus overthrew things violently under Tiberius" (chap. 14, p. 129); "By the most extraordinary circumstance of the world, Rome had so completely annihilated all peoples that, when Rome itself was conquered, it seemed that the earth had given birth to new peoples to destroy it" (chap. 15, p. 153).

Anticipating Burke's definition of the sublime as an effect of fear and horror, Montesquieu's admiration shades into revulsion. Even the virtue of the Romans, which he celebrates in his notebooks and in *The Spirit of the Laws,* is portrayed here as monstrous, because it overrides the whole range and variety of more moderate passions: "It was an overpowering love for the Patrie which—taking leave of the ordinary rules for crimes and virtues—hearkened only to itself and saw neither citizen, friend, benefactor, nor father. Virtue seemed to forget itself in order to surpass itself, and it made men admire as divine an action that at first could not be approved because it was atrocious."[88] Indeed, Montesquieu is wary of virtue. Virtue is a drive to unity and an unlimited expenditure of force, and Montesquieu believes that such unrestricted force is a danger. Though he is sensitive to the beauty embodied in the heroic ideal of social cohesiveness and passionate belief that will later seduce Rousseau and the Jacobins, he also finds it pointless and destructive.[89]

Montesquieu's conception of happiness and moral excellence is the very antithesis of the virtuous ideal. For Montesquieu, happiness consists, not in a search for moral excellence and the weeding out of the passions in favor of a select few, but in the careful balancing and harmonization of all the passions that are natural to social beings. A society may be conducive to happiness, not when its members experience no inner conflict, but when society is able to accommodate the greatest variety of goals and values; not when all its members work toward the same purpose, but when all the different forces within society, including potentially destructive but natural instincts such as *inquiétude,* anxiety, ambition, emulation, and jealousy, are carefully balanced against each other. Because of his commitment to pluralism and moderation, Montesquieu sees nothing but trouble in virtue's unlimited drive to self-affirmation: "Only those people who are extremely vicious and extremely virtuous have a certain strength; as it goes too far in the former, it may not be checked in the latter."[90] "It has eternally been observed," he writes in *The Spirit of the Laws,* "that any man who has power is led to abuse it; he continues until he finds limits. Who would think! Even virtue has need of limits."[91] Even the passion for goodness may degenerate when unaware of its own drive to power and when unchecked by a counterbalancing force. Virtue and viciousness converge from the two extremes of the moral spectrum.

Montesquieu experiences a tension between, on the one hand, a model of society based on a creative, single-minded drive toward unity, passionate faith, and metarational devotion to the collectivity and, on the other, a pluralistic, unstable, and desacralized model of society, one in which conflicts among various desires have constantly to be negotiated, boundaries and alliances redrawn. This latter model is inherently heterogenous and imperfect; its reason is nothing but a capacity to accommodate the "prodigious diversity" of local customs and idiosyncratic practices. Diversity is usually better than uniformity, which is the pet peeve of "small minds," easily fascinated by the idea of perfection and symmetry.[92] Nothing could be more remote from the unlimited drive of virtuous and revolutionary energy than Montesquieu's praise of the slow, staggering pace of passion-free institutional habits. He goes so far as to place quite a bit of faith in the cooling effects of custom-sanctioned legal procedure, in their "tempering, modification, accommodation, terms, alternatives, negotiations, remonstrances," because they are the last bulwark against the energy of reckless political will and the evils of best intentions gone awry: "What would have become of the finest monarchy in the world if the magistrates, by their slowness, their complaints, and their prayers, had not checked the course of even the virtues of its kings. . . ?"[93] Unlike late Enlightenment thinkers such as Condorcet, Montesquieu places very little faith in the universality of rational law and in the possibility of streamlining all human institutions according to a universal, rational model based on science.[94] To him, such universalism may lead to despotism. A despotic government tries to be simple and expedient because it follows a voluntaristic model—the will of a single man, or that of the "general will"—hence it always starts out by eliminating the procedural forms that stand as an obstacle between itself and the realization of its will. A moderate government, by contrast, is a complex machine that follows the Newtonian model of a balance achieved through the interplay of opposite forces and passions, which neutralize each other.[95]

And yet it is precisely such a model of government that seduces Montesquieu in a Roman history that to his eyes embodies far more than a parable of monstrous hubris. The Roman republic was admirable not so much because it was virtuous (i.e., cohesive) but because it was a flexible system that was able to accommodate internal dissension and strife. Montesquieu's Rome was endowed with essentially "modern" institutions, because it was founded upon the ultimately modern idea that a system can achieve stability, not when its forces are perfectly ordered and working toward the same goal, but when the system can withstand controlled chaos and internal pull toward opposite directions. To Montesquieu, in the modern world order emerges from a precarious balance among imperfect elements. (The same is true for Marivaux, who conceives the individual's inner life as a decentralized coexistence of various passions that neutralize one another in a system of controlled disorder.)[96]

In that sense all the characters of the modern spirit that the *Essai sur le goût* had emphasized—individual curiosity, restlessness, ambition, desire—are shown to be present in the Roman spirit. Indeed, the most significant difference between Montesquieu's description of Rome and that of his contemporaries revolves around the issue of liberty and strife. "You may see the causes of the divisions, and eventually the fall, of the republic in the rivalry of its citizens and their love of liberty pushed to an excessive and intolerable scrupulousness," intoned Bossuet. Rome, he said, had been ruined by "the perpetual envy of the people against the Senate," and those "divisions threaten to ruin the state."[97] "At the beginning of the republic, citizens were possessed with a frenzy for freedom," chimed in Saint-Evremond.[98] Not so to Montesquieu (who follows here Machiavelli's classic account of Roman contentiousness).[99] The *Considerations* formulate for the first time an important idea that was to find a prominent place in *The Spirit of the Laws,*[100] namely, that imperfection and desire are not only characteristic of modern existence but the essential precondition to liberty:

> We hear in the authors only of the dissensions that ruined Rome, without seeing that those dissensions were necessary to it, that they had always been there and always had to be. . . . What is called union in a body politic is a very equivocal thing. The true kind is a union of harmony, whereby all the parts, however opposed they may appear, cooperate for the general good of society—as dissonance in music cooperates in producing overall concord. In a state where we seem to see nothing but commotion there can be union—that is, a harmony resulting in happiness, which alone is true peace. It is as with the parts of the universe, eternally linked together by the action of some and the reaction of others. But, in the accord of Asiatic despotism—that is, of all government which is not moderate—there is always real dissension. The worker, the soldier, the merchant, the magistrate, the noble are joined only inasmuch as some oppress the others without resistance. And, if we see any union there, it is not citizens who are united, but dead bodies buried one next to the other.[101]

The final *pointe* crowns this extraordinary defense of the struggles implicit within political and civil liberty: happiness does not consist in the tranquility imposed by a comprehensive order nor in the inner peace experienced by an individual who is never at odds with himself, but, paradoxically, in the freedom to engage in a painful struggle that results from the innate *inquiétude* and contentiousness of human nature.[102] Montesquieu's brand of liberalism is a philosophy that embraces imperfection as a condition for social life.[103] A good government is not only agitated; it is also a balancing act. It is an institution capable of setting limits to its power by dividing sovereignty among its constituents: "The laws of Rome had wisely divided public power among a large number of magistracies, which supported, checked and tempered each other. Since they all had only limited power, every citizen was qualified for them."[104] Lest we think that Montesquieu limits the applicability of this kind of combative liberty to the republic, and to the civic sphere of politics, one should consider a passage from his notebooks addressed to his son, in which Montesquieu broadens the spectrum of such *inquiétude* by making an analogy between the drive to social mobility etched within every modern, monarchical subject and the physical laws of the universe (the Newtonian model of a balance between opposite forces). Competitiveness and *inquiétude* are also dominant motifs in the civil sphere of social relations, in which an individual is not content with being confined within his or her own circle but constantly desires to be elsewhere or to be like someone else, a condition that is innate, and not simply a product of modern decadence:

> As the physical world subsists only because each particle of matter tends to distance itself from the center, so the political world is sustained by each person's inner and restless desire [*désir intérieur et inquiet*] to expand out of the sphere in which he has been placed. An austere morality labors in vain to erase the traits that the greatest of craftsmen has imprinted in our souls. An ethics that seeks to operate on the heart of man ought to regulate those sentiments, not destroy them.[105]

According to the Rousseauian-Jacobinic myth, antiquity was a powerful tool to brandish against the alleged decadence of modern times. The discourse of civic virtue opposed dramatically, on the one hand, the modern, self-centered, feminized, subject of commercial and polite society, who was characterized negatively by a capacity to entertain and transmit desires that were satisfied through her investment in objects of pleasure and who recognized herself in the self-indulgent works of *petit-goût,* and on the other, the citizen of the virtuous republic, an unequivocally male subject, who was defined by his unconditional attachment to his civic duties in the public sphere, at the expense of the enjoyment of private life and social relations in civil society, by frugality and a disposition to give himself entirely to the community.[106] One sentence would sum up those two very different human types: "In a good republic people say *Us,* and in a good monarchy they say *Me.*"[107] That was the lesson relentlessly upheld by the works of art of the *grand goût,* by an exemplary history, and by the advocates of a return to the "sublime simplicity" of the ancients. But Montesquieu never entirely surrendered to the lure of archaic virtue. Ultimately, what attracted him to antiquity was not the sublime ideal of unity that subordinated the individual to a glorified conception of the State. What he admired in antiquity was the expression of liberty, the same restless desire, curiosity, and richly diversified experience that were the qualities of the modern age.

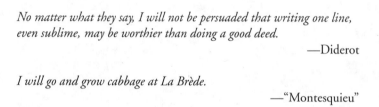

Montesquieu for the Masses, or Implanting False Memory

No matter what they say, I will not be persuaded that writing one line, even sublime, may be worthier than doing a good deed.

—Diderot

I will go and grow cabbage at La Brède.

—"Montesquieu"

Electrifying the Social Sphere

Twenty years after the death of Montesquieu, in May 1775 the *Mercure de France* published a story signed by an obscure Mingard that purported to reveal a touching act of generosity performed by Montesquieu while he was visiting Marseilles. On a tour of the harbor the *président* had requested the services of a boatman, from whom he heard a sad tale. The young man was trying to put together enough money to pay for the ransom of his father, a merchant who on his way to Smyrna had been taken prisoner by pirates and was now held as a slave in Tetouan (northern Morocco). Moved to pity but wishing to remain incognito, Montesquieu gave the young man a purse full of louis d'or, and later he secretly arranged to have the ransom paid. To the author of the article, the anecdote had much to teach about family values and the philosopher's role in society:

> Sweet, precious, soothing philosophy . . . when those who enlighten and improve their fellow beings are the first to offer the example of virtue! What

a touching tableau for those who know him . . . is the life of the author of *De l'esprit des lois!* It was a life entirely sacrificed to compassion and good deeds; letters and pleasure were only accessory to it. How happy he was to see that the wife he adored, a wife worthy of him, disdained the courtship paid to grace and beauty in order to devote herself to helping the needy.[1]

We might find such rhetoric dismaying; very likely Montesquieu would have too. After all, he wrote nothing about the sentimental effusions of charity (rather, he saw it as a matter of justice that the state ensure its citizens the right to work and a sufficient living);[2] his marriage was not quite the stuff of romance; he would have been surprised to learn that his entire life had been dedicated to good deeds rather than to writing and even more surprised to hear about the whole affair, which, to the best of our knowledge, never happened.

Contemporaries, however, found it deeply appealing and the anecdote quickly became very popular. It circulated widely in eulogies and memoirs; in 1777 Mme de Montesson turned it into a play for her private theater; Mme Roland mentioned it in her *Mémoires;* Jean-Paul Marat gushed over it in his *Eloge de Montesquieu,* which he presented to the Academy of Bordeaux in 1785; and the story ended where it was fated to end, as a *drame* on the public stage. One Joseph Pihles, a lawyer from Tarascon-en-Foix, managed to have his *Bien-fait anonyme* performed at the Théâtre-Français in 1783. Although his play was translated into German[3] and even captured Hegel's attention,[4] it had a harder time in Paris. It enjoyed one night of vibrant success, however, when the actors invited M. le baron de Secondat, Montesquieu's son, to attend the performance. "His presence worked marvels on the actors and the audience," we may read in Bachaumont's *Mémoires secrets,* "they played with exceptional fervor, and the audience's enthusiasm was brought to paroxysm. That little charade sanctioned the success of the play, and in that moment of effervescence it may go quite far."[5] Indeed, that night at the Théâtre-Français must have been quite a fête. With only a little planning by the actors, the performance offered a moment of near-spontaneous effervescence, of all-out enthusiasm during which the parterre joined the actors in the exalted sense of their own goodness. It was for such moments that Louis-Sébastien Mercier lived and toiled the thankless life of the playwright. Perhaps he was present at the performance; at any rate, he referred to the happening obliquely in his *Tableaux:* "It is the parterre who pays back the nation's debt [to its writers]; . . . it applauds a victorious general and the son of Montesquieu. The people feel and understand merit and are moved as if by an electric commotion."[6]

In Mercier's view, the theater was the medium best suited to the production and transmission of intense civic and patriotic emotion. Conveyed by the theater, emotions would spread like electricity through the audience and across the nation, carrying powerful currents of change. To Mercier and many others, much was amiss in the nation, and it was up to the philosophe and the playwright to set things right. Mercier said it very forcefully in a provocative essay on the theater published in 1772: "The fastest and most effective method of arming the forces of human reason and unloosening at once upon the people a great mass of light would surely be the theater."[7] Mercier formulated a comprehensive theory of drama that included a poetics and a political approach. (He also challenged vigorously the monopoly that actors exercised upon theatrical works and the monarchical system of theatrical privilege. Later he brought that challenge to the public in several *mémoires judiciaires,* which goes a long way toward explaining his protracted marginalization.)[8] His ideas about the public role of the patriotic writer and dramatic art were indebted to those of Diderot, d'Alembert, and Léonard-Antoine Thomas, who had been an early mentor. In the wake of the reforms they had envisioned, Mercier imagined a new pact between the enlightened playwright and theatrical audiences.

It would be difficult to overstate the extent and the significance of the changes that had taken place in the relationship between the writer and the public since the 1740s. In 1730, in his influential manifesto *Le philosophe,* César Chesneau Dumarsais had argued that the philosophe was an *honnête homme.*[9] What he meant, of course, was that a freethinker was not necessarily a scoundrel and that one did not need to accept the Church's teachings in order to love one's fellow beings. But he also meant that the philosophe was a sociable member of civil society, someone who enjoyed "sociable exchange among *honnêtes gens.*" Dumarsais ended his essay recommending that the philosophe shed his prejudices and devote his attention not only to science but also to the study of sociability: "If they have worked on the mind, let them remember that they still have much work to do on what we may call the heart and on the science of manners [*la science des égards*]."[10] The latter expression is reminiscent of La Motte and Marivaux's "science of society" (la science du monde) and "the science of the human heart," which was the province of "those great geniuses called . . . *beaux esprits,*" a science, in other words, that consisted in the belief that human beings were situated beings, shaped by complex webs of imperceptible and unacknowledged social rules.[11] The more vital and essential those rules, Marivaux argued, the more invisible they were, and the easier it was to dismiss them as irrelevant to philosophical analysis and to literary and artistic representation. "Let us imagine a science of so important an application that every man, whoever he is, must know it early in his life if he wants to be admitted to that junction of interests, relations, and reciprocal needs that bind us to one another."[12] Its very familiarity and ordinariness placed such a science below the threshold of analysis. Marivaux felt keenly the need for a language capable of delving below the apparent banality of the real and accounting for the "nothings" that constitute the texture of experience. In 1749, however, when he delivered that lecture to the French Academy, Marivaux had little hope of seeing his program realized: writers, *beaux esprits,* who explored "the science of manners" were becoming increasingly obsolete. The province of women and applied savoir-faire, the observation of the social was now seen as a practical kind of art and not as a form of knowledge. Only salonnieres, not artists, need be concerned with it.[13]

Indeed, from approximately the second half of the century on, many writers had risen to stake for themselves a different ground. Rousseau's portentous critique of sociability was by no means exceptional. Not only was sociability no longer the worthy object of a fledgling anthropological science, it was also not a desirable object of artistic representation. In the eyes of Duclos, Thomas, d'Alembert, and Diderot, the public was corrupt; its manners were effeminate and affected; its taste was decadent, and all the arts were suffering a general decline. Nothing admirable could come out of a close acquaintance with, and examination of, the sociable sphere. Educated people's language, manners, and clothing were deemed degrading and inappropriate to artistic representation: "Something else that's no less shocking: the minor customs of civilized people. The rituals of courtesy, so attractive, so pleasant, and admirable in the polite world, are disagreeable in the arts of imitation. . . . The arts of imitation require something that is savage, crude, striking, enormous. . . . To the platitude of our curtsies and bows, add that of our clothing; . . . I defy painters and sculptors of even the greatest genius to turn this paltry system to advantage."[14]

If the artist and the philosophe could not entirely avoid company, they should at least limit their dealings with conversational circles as much as they could, since neither the scientist nor the artist could draw any inspiration from *le monde:* "What would be the use to a philosopher of our frivolous conversations? Only to narrow his mind, to rob him of the excellent ideas he might acquire through reading and meditation. It was not at the Hôtel de Rambouillet that Descartes discovered the application of algebra to geometry," argued d'Alembert in 1753. It is true, he added, that fiction writers—or *beaux esprits*—must frequent society in order to know and understand their fellow beings, but they ought to be spectators to, not participants in, such a distasteful comedy: "I wish, at least, that they were simple spectators to that insincere gathering, attentive enough not to have to come back too often to a comedy that is not always good to watch. Let them observe the play in the same way that a parterre judges the actors, who do not dare to offend it. In other words, let them go there in the same spirit in which Apollonius of Tyana went to Rome in Nero's time: to see, he said, what kind of a beast a tyrant was."[15] It is not quite clear who in d'Alembert's mind might fit Nero's shoes; at any rate, such a parallel between Nero's court and the eighteenth-century salon from the pen of a friend, a regular guest, and a beneficiary of Mme du Deffand, Mlle de Lespinasse, Mme Geoffrin, and Mme Necker may come as a surprise. In fact, it was precisely at a time when the salon had become a forum for the practice and the dissemination of philosophy, when hostesses had deferred to the interests of their guests and had become the mediators and facilitators of their careers and their intellectual exchange, that the writings of the philosophes reflected little or no acknowledgment of their utility.[16] There was scarcely any effort to credit worldliness with any diversity; on the contrary, social venues and practices as varied as the court, the salon, and the private academy were treated as if they were one and the same thing, and in the writings of the philosophes they were often held in equal dislike.

Following Duclos, Diderot, d'Alembert, and Rousseau, Mercier expressed a similar distaste for the language and the ethos of society:

> Why is this writer's work nice and tidy but cold and lifeless? Why does it have no enthusiasm? Why is its style halfhearted and awkward? It is because the author frequents some circles where *esprit* always takes the place of emotion, where everything is subjected to the fussiest discussion, where people argue ceaselessly about nothing. His soul dries up and is perverted by the clash of those different opinions. The sacred fire dies out; *esprit* replaces everything; the vigorous traits that distinguish genius are lost. . . . The expressions that appear in a book are modeled after those of conversation: they become timid, cautious, polite, and arcane. The art of writing becomes a trade, and every morning the writer churns out his assignment without any emotion or excitement.[17]

Much like La Bruyère a century earlier, Mercier deplores the professionalism of the worldly, who turn art into a trade, but this time it is not for the sake of preserving language's purity but for that of enthusiasm, deemed incompatible with argumentative reason and discussion, that he turns against conversational *esprit*. Léonard-Antoine Thomas, for his part, deplores the fact that the people who frequent society "must always strive to tone down, to assassinate, so to speak, language and inventiveness [*esprit*]."[18] Ironically, it is to antiphilosophical satire that we must turn if we wish to find any trace of the close interaction that existed between philosophy and worldliness. Thus, Palissot (in the manner of Molière) evoked the calamitous effects that philosophy had on formerly frivolous hostesses, who, under its influence, had turned their salons into pretentious *bureaux d'esprit*.[19]

In the writings of the philosophes, while sociability and love of the public good were extolled in their ideal, theoretical form, they fared poorly when it came to their actual, embodied manifestations, of which worldliness was a major one. There was a dark side to the exultant proselytizing of an Helvétius and a d'Holbach in favor of a civil society conceived, in the wake of thinkers of the Scottish Enlightenment such as David Hume, William Robertson, and Adam Ferguson, as the harmonization of individual self-interests and the self-regulating environment for the flourishing of moderate passions.[20] Religion and natural law may well have converged to sacralize the *idea* of society and man's natural sociability, but that did not prevent many of the same thinkers who paid an enthusiastic tribute to the cult of society from being profoundly dissatisfied with its tangible physiognomy in the contemporary world.[21] Following Shaftesbury, Diderot saw civil society as a well-wrought mechanism conducive to the happiness of the individual, but his disaffection with the public at large, and not only with France's political institutions, was deep and far reaching. Society as he knew it offered no inspiration to the creative genius. Rather, the consumerist public and the private marketplace were such that they hindered any outburst of enthusiasm and innovation: "In the present century and under the present reign the impoverished nation has framed not a single great enterprise, no great works, nothing that might nourish the spirit and exalt the soul. At present great artists don't develop at all, or are compelled to endure humiliation to avoid dying of hunger. At present there are a hundred easel paintings for every large composition, a thousand portraits for every history painting; mediocre artists proliferate and the nation is flooded with them."[22] The nobility of art, Diderot argued, was debased by a public that was neither knowledgeable about works of art nor an inspiring model for the artist. The public demanded and consumed works composed on a small scale, of doubtful execution and uninspired or lewd content, works that reflected the public's own lack of values, its narrow range of experience, and its *petit goût*.

Even though the public targeted by Diderot was construed as an unholy alliance of the luxury of the *fermiers-généraux,* the seductiveness of royal mistresses, actresses, and *petites-maîtresses,* and the vile complacency of the artists that flattered their depravity, one cannot help suspecting that Diderot's contention was not with a specific portion of the public but with the elite bourgeois public as a whole. The true menace lurking in the alleged corruption of the contemporary world was modern life itself, the very ordinariness of life in a civilized society. The philosophe, whether he was a scientist, a writer, a novelist, or an art critic—and Diderot was all those things—looked at the reality of the modern world, at its comfort, its peaceful ways, and its subdued complexity, and found it stifling and small. In the absence of overwhelming spectacles of war and cosmic violence, how was the poet supposed to nourish his inspiration? Diderot drew a causal connection between the flourishing of art and the experience of historical trauma that did not quite agree with the mainstream praise of the golden age as a product of Augustus's and Louis's peaceful rule; on the contrary, it seemed to construe those epochs of artistic outburst as the direct offspring of devastating civil war (the wars that led to the collapse of the Roman republic and the sixteenth-century French wars of religion):

> Poetry requires something enormous, barbaric, and savage. When the fury of civil war or fanaticism puts a knife in man's hand, when blood flows in streams upon the earth, then Apollo's laurels flourish. They want to be irrigated. In times of peace and leisure they wither. The golden age might have produced a song, perhaps, or an elegy. Epic and dramatic poetry require other manners. When shall we see the birth of poets? It will be after a time of disaster and great misfortune, when the beleaguered people will draw a breath. Then the imagination, shaken by terrible spectacles, will depict things unknown to those who have not seen them. . . . Talent is of all times; but the men who have it languish unless extraordinary events heat up the masses and bring it forth. . . . What will the poet resort to when the people's manners are weak, trivial, and affected; when the faithful imitation of conversations yields nothing but a string of phony, trifling, senseless expressions; when there no longer is any frankness nor candor; when a father calls his son "Monsieur" and a mother calls her daughter "Mademoiselle"; when public ceremonies lack all dignity, domestic life lacks warmth and honesty, and solemn acts truthfulness? He will try to embellish them; he will choose the circumstances that best respond to his intent; he will neglect the others and venture to invent some.[23]

Artistic expression would not emerge from the sedate and comfortable existence of modern cities. The French nation was at peace, and no one was asked to die for the homeland or for anything that the philosophes deemed worthwhile. Social climbing was the only exertion that the nation knew well; it was a devouring obsession, but it was devoid of grandeur. A culture of politeness had dulled human relations for aristocratic and bourgeois families alike; it had taken the edge off conflicts and dampened the passions. Artists were eager for the expression of basic and primitive human conflicts, for issues of life and death, for the simple language of the struggle to survive—all aspects of existence that artists, together with the rest of the public, were prevented from experiencing firsthand.

But what could be done to counteract all that? The tragedies of *le Grand Siècle,* those dark flowers of the nation's wars, were embalmed in splendor and no longer a source of inspiration. In vain had Crébillon the elder upped the ante with his truculent and blood-thirsty Atreuses and Catilinas. Voltaire had exploited the genre for all it was worth, and he had only succeeded in showing how difficult it was to bring it back to life. The new theatrical dramas and visual representations that Diderot, Greuze, Beaumarchais, and Sedaine strove to propose were replete with situations borrowed from ancient tragedy, not from modern life: fathers cursing their sons, sobbing daughters, grieving friends, repentant spouses, despairing widows, violated maidens, and suicidal philosophers. The writers of *drames* tried to extract as much dramatic value as they could from the conflicts of bourgeois family life, but for all their efforts, it seemed as if they were beating a dead horse. As for the lower classes, their calamities had not yet crossed the boundaries of the burlesque and libertine genres, in which they had been confined from time immemorial, and they were still awaiting their eulogist. The Sadean sublime had yet to make an appearance before the large public. Diderot and Rousseau dreamed of baptizing art in rivers of blood. They yearned confusedly for the revitalizing powers of civil wars, for the sacrifices of fanaticism and the holocaust of the battlefield, and subsequent events demonstrated that those yearnings may not have been entirely misplaced. Of course, such discontent was not incompatible with a widespread appreciation of the moral and social enlightenment of the modern age; it subtended the trumpeting of progress, as a basso continuo subtends the intricacies of melody in the upper register.[24]

The philosophes were relentless in telling the public that it was no longer capable of experiencing any passions:

> If a people has frivolous and superficial habits; if instead of that profound sensitivity that focuses the mind and concentrates it on certain objects, it experiences only a restless activity that extends to everything but focuses on nothing; if *by being too sociable it becomes every day less sensitive;* . . . if it no longer dares to love, hate, admire, or be irate from the heart; if everybody

feels obliged to be elegant, polite, and cool; if women lose every day their true ascendancy; if that ardent and generous emotion that they have a right to expect is replaced by a base and cowardly sentiment; if fortunate and unfortunate events are nothing but an object of conversation and never of emotion; if the lack of noble aspirations constrains the soul and accustoms it to prize small things: what will become of the eloquence of such a people? . . . Our age is generally turned toward a spirit of discussion; that kind of spirit, endlessly bent on comparing ideas, must necessarily undermine the energy of our emotions.[25]

The picture they painted was dire indeed. *Sociabilité* was the antithesis of *sensibilité*. A frivolous, conventional, hedonistic, and amoral society had grown incapable of experiencing strong emotions, of expressing empathy and compassion; the people were afraid to show their feelings or were not even aware they had any. A feminized society was apparently subservient to women but had made men unable to love women as women supposedly wished to be loved.[26] Conversation, discussion, and the circulation of ideas, which the salonnieres had done so much to foster, had the unforeseen effect of stupefying the public into insensitivity. People were confronted with too wide a range of trends and ideas; as a consequence, they were unable to care for any of them. They consumed ideas in the same manner as they followed fads and whims, and they were willing to cast both off with equal casualness. Another leitmotif of philosophical discontent, one that neither Montesquieu nor Marivaux would have endorsed, was that in modern society emotions were too diversified and varied to take any hold; a multitude of petty interests and pursuits prevented the emergence of a single, all-consuming passion: "The sentiment of glory demands the removal of ordinary passions. Either it does not exist or it pervades the entire soul. You will seldom find it in a nation dedicated to what we call the enjoyment of society; in such a nation the multitude of pleasures spoils the passions."[27] *Petit goût* was the death of the soul; it was *apatheia*.

Something had to be done to shake the people out of their complacency, their deadening conventionality, and their emotional slumber. The responsibility belonged to the eloquent writer, to the philosophe, the artist, and the playwright, to grab the public by the throat and shake some life into it. Writers must rescue the nation from itself, much as the ancient orators had rescued the homeland during times of war and turmoil. Only this time the *patrie* had to be saved not from the distress of war but from the comforts of civilization and the impending threat of mediocrity. "No, the republican orator is not . . . the plaything of a coterie or a circle," thundered Thomas, "he is a man to whom nature has given an inescapable preeminence: he is the protector of the nation, its sovereign, its king."[28] If the people were no longer able to experience any strong passions, it was the task of art to educate and transform them. But how? The philosophes thought that the passions were unwelcome in the conversational circle, that they were incompatible with a democratic discussion and exchange of ideas; conversation and society were antithetical to anything elevated and noble. Passions seethed and burned in solitude. Writers were therefore pictured in the seclusion of their *cabinet de travail*, surrounded with the effigies of a public abstracted from its actual, embodied existence and transformed into a ghostly, allegorical version of itself: "I like to portray to myself the generous citizen meditating alone in his cabinet. The *patrie* stands by his side. Justice and humanity are in front of him. The ghosts of the wretched surround him; pity moves him, tears pour from his eyes."[29]

But passions were also kindled in the encounter between an eloquent individual and a large multitude assembled in one place and drawn to the oratorical spectacle of one talking to many. In the absence of a national tribune such an event could only take place in the theater. The images used to describe the relationship between the (implicitly oratorical) theatrical spectacle and the public were significant: "It is there that, like the sound of the trumpet that one day will awaken the dead, a simple and luminous eloquence will rouse in one moment a slumbering nation. It is there that the magnificent thought of one man will set every soul on fire by an electric commotion," wrote Mercier.[30] Invariably, the public was represented as an inert and lifeless mass, an unresponsive audience suddenly jolted into life, Frankenstein-like, by the massive injection of the electric energy of the poet's eloquence. Mme Necker had evoked in her memoirs the electricity that animated worldly conversation, the healing effects that the participants to the conversational exchange had upon one another: "It is a way of acting upon one another, of giving each other pleasure reciprocally and with vivacity . . . , of making one's *esprit* manifest by all the nuances of accent, gesture, glance; of producing at will a kind of electricity that emits sparks, relieves some of their excessive vivacity, and awakens others from a distressing apathy."[31] That reciprocity, which Mme Necker had appreciated as the precondition for the transmission of conversational energy, was no longer valued. For Mercier, electricity flows downward from a single source, the powerful *sentiment* transmitted by the writer: "It is [in the theater] that a man whom reason has misled is brought to the tribunal of nature and often . . . may discover truth thanks to the electric shock of sentiment."[32] Thomas similarly invites the reader to imagine a universe without life, sensation, and motion that the power of eloquence infuses with a capacity to feel: "Imagine nature without movement: everything is dead; no communication; the universe is an assortment of isolated masses and motionless bodies, eternally still. It is the same for souls. Sentiment is what animates and moves them; it circulates like motion; like the clash of bodies, it has its own laws. Therefore, you ought to depict with energy everything that you wish to inspire me."[33]

Teaching sentiment and feeling to an insentient mass demanded new forms of spectacle and a new language. In their desire to shock the audience into *sensibilité* Diderot and Mercier called for a theater of cruelty that would take the Aristotelian principle of terror and pity to new lengths, or rather, would bring back the violence that had characterized the theater of the ancients and that French *bienséance* had banished from the stage:

> Then, we would quiver with dread when going to a spectacle, and yet we could not help ourselves; then, instead of those small, fleeting emotions, that cool applause, those occasional tears that poets have to be content with, [the enlightened playwright] would take our breath away and bring awe and terror to our soul. We would see those phenomena of ancient tragedy, so real, yet so little understood, being revived among us.[34]

Mercier was opposed to the convention of the happy ending—vice punished and virtue rewarded—which had traditionally distinguished fiction from history and had made fiction more "moral" than history: "If we wish to make a profound impression and break the hearts of the spectators by portraying the greatest misfortunes, then the action must be coherent and truthful. Why pull the dagger out once it has pierced the heart? Why dry those flowing tears? No. If a spectacle is an illusion, let that illusion grieve the spectator as much as possible; let it be durable, and let every man agonize until the cause of the public misfortune is gone."[35] In Mercier's view, the theater ought to exercise a form of virtuous terrorism: the audience would be held hostage to a harrowing illusion and forced to feel the pain of those portrayed by the spectacle until that pain, the "public misfortune," was put to an end.

That program was only partially successful. Like tragedy, the new conventions of the *drame* came under the satirical grind of the *petits théâtres,* which produced parodies such as *L'humanité ou le tableau de l'indigence, triste drame par un aveugle Tartare* (1761), *La lacrymomanie ou la manie des drames,* or *La manie des drames sombres* (1777), which mercilessly lampooned the philosophes' abuse of terror and pity for the amusement of audiences who were apparently unmoved by their efforts. In *L'humanité,* for instance, a mother choreographs her son's funeral procession so that it meets with the procession of the father, on his way to the gallows:

> Surrounded by mournful torches, the funeral brings to a halt the procession of the father in chains, flanked by ferocious sentinels; let that father, alerted by Nature, shudder, cover his forehead with his hands injured by shameful shackles, and raise to heaven a heartrending lament. Let his executioners be moved, the spectators dismayed, everybody in fearful expectation; let, from the midst of the multitude, finally rise a cry, a vengeful cry, the expression of Humanity and the scourge of the first monster who will dare violate it.[36]

In *La manie des drames* Prousas, a playwright, declares:

> I favor touching and pathetic plots
> Which antiquity did not know;
> Great crimes followed by stirring remorse;
> Coffins, graves and skulls.
> That's what I like and always will.
> Yes, I like to cry, I sure do![37]

The Ungrateful Benefactor

Mercier, however, did not base his entire dramaturgy on terror and pity alone. He also appealed to another fundamental passion of classical theatrical doctrine, admiration.[38] That passion was particularly suited to a genre that was to become increasingly popular, especially during the Revolution, a genre that might be called "dramatic pantheon," or *le grand homme à la scène*.[39] Those plays offered eloquent tableaux of the lives of great men, among which men of letters figured prominently. They dramatized the genre of the academic eulogy, which had flourished since 1758, when the French Academy had started to award the prize of eloquence to the best eulogies of the nation's great men.[40] Mercier, who was an admirer and a correspondent of Léonard-Antoine Thomas's, the unchallenged master of the genre, had competed for the prize in 1765, with his *Eloge de Descartes,* and had composed several plays featuring the lives of great men, notably a *Molière,* or *La maison de Molière,* a "tableau of the private life of the man of letters," which made much of the playwright's alleged marital problems. The *drame*—with its emphasis on *attendrissement,* on a *pathétique* that transcended the commonplace distinction between tragedy and comedy, on the glorification of private life in its trivial and simple details—was particularly suited to illustrate an ideology that portrayed men of letters as examples of sublime simplicity, benevolence, and selfless devotion to the improvement of the human condition. The *drame* depicted both the heroic dimension of bourgeois life and the bourgeois dimension of national heroes: Mercier praised Shakespeare because "all his heroes are men, and the combination of simplicity and heroism is engrossing."[41] The eulogistic staging of the philosophe's life and character was also the best way to counteract the antiphilosophical propaganda, which, as early as 1720 had exploited the theater as a powerful tool for spreading the image of an egotistical, unpatriotic, and antisocial philosophe.[42] In response to the success of Palissot's satires, such as *Le cercle ou les originaux* (1755) and *Les philosophes* (1760), the theater and the visual arts were flooded with virtuous and moribund Socrates and Catos.[43]

It was perhaps after witnessing that memorable event at the Théâtre-Français, when the parterre had risen to applaud the son of Montesquieu and a mediocre play, that Mercier decided to make his own contribution to the myth by writing *Montesquieu à Marseille* (published in Lausanne in 1784 and, like many of Mercier's plays, never performed). In the preface, Mercier expressed the hope that others would follow in his footsteps and bring to the stage those writers whom the public knew and loved best, "those who belong, so to speak, to our circle, since their names, their works, and their character traits are always present in our intimate conversations" (9). As modern-day audiences feel toward celebrities, people then entertained a cozy sense of familiarity with writers like La Fontaine, Racine, Fénelon, Corneille, and also Voltaire, who had become household names. They kept their busts on the mantelpiece and felt that they knew them intimately—their quirks, their foibles, and their *bons mots:* "Oh! If someone were to put on the stage our good La Fontaine, with his innocence, his simplicity, and his absent-mindedness, everybody would be touched by this charming tableau . . . , which would bring back to us a man whose name alone enchants the soul and seduces reason!" (9). Mercier intends to catch Montesquieu in an intimate moment, not as a great man, but as a sensitive and compassionate man, for "the true man of genius is a good man" (5). Such a play must be able to grasp "the style and the character of its hero," not an easy task with Montesquieu, whose language poses a challenge to Mercier: "The imitation of his vivid, bold, and swift style, of its energy and fine humor, will be the bane of every writer. It would be much easier to imitate Fénelon, Voltaire, and Jean-Jacques Rousseau" (6–7).

Ultimately setting those fears aside, Mercier enacts in his play a peculiar kind of eulogistic ventriloquism whereby he lends his voice to Montesquieu, who returns the favor by uttering some of Mercier's ideas, bestowing upon them the prestige of his own stature. Thus, we should not be surprised to learn that Montesquieu turns out to be, just like Mercier, the advocate of a didactic, philosophical theater: "Nothing improves our morals better than a good play. There is the triumph of public instruction" (act 3, sc. 4, p. 127). He has also become a militant *philosophe*: "The main point is to discover, as you have done," says his friend the abbé Guasco, "what is useful or harmful to human beings, what makes them happy or unhappy. . . . You will be the cause of a new legislation, which will become universal. The new ages will shake off the dregs of error and mirror themselves in a purer light" (act 3, sc. 3, p. 109). Mercier portrays Montesquieu as an antimonarchist—"I distinctly realize what I have not yet said in my works: that at all times and places human nature . . . under the governance of one person has been humiliated and despised" (ibid., p. 110)—and as a cosmopolitan and universalist—"Europe must make one family only," he says. "National characters, already prodigiously altered, must entirely disappear to make way for the love of peace and the feeling of equality. That will encourage peoples to acquire the same customs and the same spirit" (ibid., pp. 118–19). Finally, Mercier allows Montesquieu to confess his shortcomings: "Ah! why is my book done? I said nothing of what I should have said" (ibid., p. 105).

It is, however, in his private life that Montesquieu is reconfigured most significantly. The play acquits him once and for all of any suspicion of ever having been a *bel esprit*. Modestly dressed in black, Montesquieu appears as a self-effacing "melancholic little man" who does not speak much and who does not mind waiting for hours in the anteroom of a banker, sitting on a bench and being snubbed by the servants. "What! That small man dressed in black and with no servants and carriage! . . . But he looks so down-to-earth," says Monsieur de Pérouville, the banker who has arranged for the payment of the ransom (act 1, sc. 6, p. 58). Much of the play revolves around the notion of *reconnaissance* in its double meaning of "recognition" and "gratitude." Montesquieu struggles with both: he does not want to be recognized for who he is, and he does not want to accept the gratitude of the people whom he has helped; he refuses to be admired for his *oeuvre*, and he does not want to be thanked or even acknowledged for his generosity. The play's main action consists, therefore, of Montesquieu's obstinate struggle to frustrate the sense of obligation other people feel toward him and to evade all expression of thankfulness. Throughout the play, even after he has been recognized and unmasked by his beneficiaries, Montesquieu is on the run from their pesky gratitude.

Indeed, if there is much to admire in his character, there is little to like in the way the play portrays him. Mme de Pérouville, the banker's wife, and the only one in the play who has read *De l'esprit des lois,* is his strongest advocate and the embodiment of the public's and Mercier's viewpoint. As if separated by an odd time-lag, she does not see Montesquieu as a person inhabiting the present, but as a living legend. Montesquieu walks around carrying the weight of posterity upon his shoulders; understandably, he seems crushed by it. He is only a shadowy version of himself, enjoying little more than a posthumous existence. In a conversation with her husband, a simple businessman who has no time to read books, Mme de Pérouville tries to force upon him a sense of the importance of Montesquieu's work: "He is the author of *De l'esprit des lois!* . . . You will see the work of a man who shall live through the most remote posterity. . . . That little man, I tell you, will do much good even after he is gone." To which Monsieur de Pérouville sensibly replies: "But now that he is alive he does not look all that cheerful, and his countenance is rather melancholic" (ibid., pp. 58–59). Indeed, all of Montesquieu's virtues are otherworldly, which explains the baffling insensitivity with which he frustrates the most elementary human and social obligations that others feel toward him.

An otherworldly character, however, presents a special challenge. In *Du théâtre,* published in 1772, three years before the *Mercure* article triggered the legend, Mercier had written enthusiastically about the staging of generosity: "We ought to put on the stage a generous man. It would be a great role model, and it would warm this author's soul. What elation he would feel in his work! He would portray that magnanimity that turns a good deed into a work of art and goes so far as to hide the generous hand that distributes its benefits."[44] The *Mercure* anecdote had therefore given Mercier a unique chance to fill a gap, alas a necessary one, in the eulogistic literature. In carrying out such a program, however, Mercier was not only taking on a formidable challenge but also ignoring the sound advice that had been offered by several generations of Christian moralists. Pierre Nicole and Rousseau had both written, a century apart, violent pamphlets against the pernicious influence of the theater on morals, but they were sharp connoisseurs of spectacle, and they knew a good play when they saw one. Both had warned playwrights against the danger of good intentions: "Most Christian virtues are unsuited to the stage," Nicole had written. "Silence, patience, moderation, wisdom, poverty, and penance are not virtues whose representation might interest the spectators. . . . A modest and silent clergyman would make a strange character in a comedy. The theater needs what passes for noble and impressive in men's opinion, which is incompatible with Christian wisdom and *gravitas.*"[45] Rousseau, who had been enlightened not only by Nicole but also by the recent developments of the *drame,* agreed: "Reason is completely useless on the stage. A man with no passions or a man always capable of controlling them would interest no one. It has already been noted that a stoic character would be insufferable in a tragedy."[46] But Mercier did not care for such admonitions. "We ought to prove to the eloquent Rousseau," he replied, "that the staging of a man capable of controlling his passions would be engrossing and that the portrayal of a stoic beaten but unshaken by misfortune would be worthy of the public's attention, all the more so if he were shown on his deathbed."[47]

In fact, modesty, silence, and the repression (or sacrifice) of the selfish passions, no matter how untheatrical, were crucial to the new mythology of the *littérateur,* which singled out the best in the Christian and Stoic traditions of repression and sublimation. Looming behind the shadow of the generous Montesquieu were those of the virtuous and self-sacrificing Socrates, Seneca, and Cato, the epitome of good eloquence and service to the *patrie.* The crux of Montesquieu's legendary act of generosity was his obstinate rejection of all expression of gratitude, which was perceived as both moving and bewildering (in other words, as sublime). The epigraph to Pilhes' *Le bienfait anonyme* was a passage from Seneca's *De beneficiis,* "Quam dulce, quam pretiosum est, si gratias sibi agi non est passus, qui dedit, si dedisse, dum dat, oblitus est!"[48] Seneca's treatise had greatly influenced the conceptualization of the vast, far-reaching, and complex network of patronage and clientage that dominated French society in the *ancien régime* both culturally and economically. Its elaborate casuistry of benefit and gift-giving could not but resonate in a society raised on the aristocratic ethos of honor, service, and reciprocity and in the intense, passionate investment in the binding ties of noncommercial exchange.[49] Diderot himself found Seneca's treatise poignant and inspiring; for him, it evoked an admiration akin to that caused by the kind of theater advocated by Mercier. "I read it three times in a row; at the fourth, I was still wetting its pages with my tears, not the tears we shed for the narrative of a great misfortune, for tragedy, for *Iphigénie* or *Mérope,* which are a combination of pleasure and pain, but those that flow blissfully when the soul is moved by a great action, a delicate sentiment, those that are caused by admiration and that I shed for the heroes of Corneille."[50] Such a parallel between two genres as diverse as a Latin treatise on manners and the French classical theater might seem perplexing, but in fact the theater was considered the genre best able to project the same enthusiasm and admiration for the spectacle of virtue that Seneca's treatise illustrated. What is more, Diderot was well aware that Corneille's theater was steeped in the same culture of reciprocity and honor that Seneca advocated.[51]

To Seneca, reciprocity was indeed an essential aspect of gift-giving; he compared it to a ballgame, in which the players measure their moves according to the capacities of their partners.[52] His treatise is a scrupulous analysis of the exchange of benefits that considers every possible angle and variation. If Seneca reproves those who make explicit demands on the gratitude of their recipients, he also finds much to censure in a situation in which the giver deprives the recipient of his right to express his gratitude and to free himself from the burden of the gift. "In the case of a benefit it is as right to accept a return as it is wrong to demand it." Not accepting a return means not playing a fair game: "Just as if our benefits could be great only when it was impossible to return gratitude to them! It is as if some spiteful player should purposely try to discomfit his fellow-player, to the detriment of the game, which of course can only be carried out in a spirit of cooperation." There is as much art in repaying a benefit as in bestowing one, and the man who has received a benefit looks for ways to make an appropriate return, just as a player awaits the proper moment to leap forth to catch the ball. Seneca makes it clear that giving the recipient the chance to express his gratitude is as vital to a good exchange as the original benefit itself.

In the legendary account of Montesquieu's generous gesture, however, the balance of reciprocity has dramatically collapsed. The inequality in the relationship between the giver and the recipient is a departure from the Stoic model, or, for that matter, from Corneille's consecrated model of noble exchange: "A service that is above all reward / by the excess of its obligation becomes an offense."[53] Indeed, as we shall see, the play's new moral covenant reflects not only the decline of the aristocratic spirit at the dawn of the bourgeois era but also the profound changes that had taken place in the relationship between the philosophe and the public.

In his account of the events, Mercier follows largely the same script as Pilhes and Dalberg. The action, which spans twenty-four hours, occurs seven months after the initial encounter on the boat between Montesquieu and the young Robert, the son of the elder Robert, the unfortunate merchant. In the initial encounter Montesquieu had given the young man a purse containing "fifteen double louis and ten écus," and taking advantage of the young man's surprise, he had promptly vanished, leaving Robert unable to thank his mysterious donor. The play opens with Montesquieu's visit to M. de Pérouville, the banker who has made the payment of "two thousand écus" for the ransom, plus "fifty louis" to benefit the prisoner. The elder Robert is about to return to his family, not knowing, of course, who has paid his ransom. As Montesquieu is leaving, the young Robert (who does not know yet that his father is on his way home) arrives at the banker's house for some business and recognizes the man of the purse. He rushes to him, but again he is rebuffed. The benefactor denies their acquaintance and abruptly rushes out. Mme de Pérouville enters, and Robert turns to her for comfort. He tells her the whole story, and Mme de Pérouville invites him to come back later that evening, when Montesquieu will be there for supper: she will make sure that Robert has a chance to speak to him. Robert promises to make his claims public: "I have seen him, and alas! I have lost him suddenly; but I will find him again, and he will not get away. Should he reject me, I will pour my tears at his feet; he will be obliged to recognize me" (act 2, sc. 7, pp. 87–88). Robert's desire to express his gratitude *(reconnaissance)* is also a desire to be recognized himself, that is, to have his humanity acknowledged by the man who has obliged him but now denies his existence. In the meantime, Robert the father has arrived in Marseilles and is tearfully reunited with his family.

In the third act, the whole Robert family, Monsieur and Mme Robert and the young Robert with Henriette, his fiancée, arrive, full of trepidation, at the salon of the Pérouvilles in order to ambush the philosophe and fall at his knees. By this time, of course, their debt has vastly increased, and their claims of gratitude have grown tenfold. "Madame, I recall your promise, we are all here," cries the young Robert, "we must fall at his knees. . . ; I have brought my father. . . . You must allow it; we are dying of excitement" (act 3, sc. 4, pp. 123–24). The moment is tense; everybody is gathered in the salon, waiting for Montesquieu to appear. When the *président* finally arrives, Robert goes to him: "My voice is shaking. (*Rushing to M. de Montesquieu.*) Man of God! accept to recognize me" (act 3, sc. 6, p. 130). But the plea falls flat. "Not again. . . . Eh! Monsieur, what do you want from me?" is the great man's icy reply. Unshaken by their entreaties, Montesquieu coolly denies having anything to do with any of them: he is a stranger in Marseilles and has never met them before; they ought to pull themselves together and go away. "All this is tiresome to me and no help to you. Collect your reason and go back to your family to recover the tranquillity you seem to be needing" (ibid., p. 132). The family is in shock, and the young Robert is indignant; such a dismissal undermines the value of Montesquieu's charitable act: "What a barbarity for a benefactor! why taint the happiness we owe you? After having been so charitable, will you be so cruel today as to refuse the tribute that we wish to offer you?" (ibid.). But while the audience closes down on the *président,* intoning, "It's him . . . it's him, it's him," Montesquieu, his back to the wall, manages to escape. He flees the room without taking leave, frustrating the audience's expectations and rebuffing his beneficiaries' claim to a shared emotion.

What are the reasons for Montesquieu's strange behavior? Why is a man who is portrayed as a "sensitive man" acting so ungraciously? The play does not allow the spectator any privileged access to his thoughts; he remains distant and opaque, and a few asides give us only a glimpse of what he feels. The practitioner of an austere stoicism, he seems afraid of drawing too much pleasure from his good deed or of sharing with others a solitary *jouissance*.[54] "What pleasure and excitement he causes me. Let us conceal it," he tells himself when he sees Robert (act. 3, sc. 6, p. 131). And a little later: "Run, Montesquieu; run from your own vanity . . . resist the seduction of such enthralling pleasure [*jouissance*]" (ibid.). Such rigorism would not have been disavowed by a La Rochefoucauld, who believed, in true Augustinian spirit, that self-interest always masquerades as virtue. Only two years before the publication of Mercier's play, Choderlos de Laclos had anticipated the fictional Montesquieu's worst fears with his account of Valmont's sly and self-serving act of benevolence. As the story goes, Valmont, who knows he is being watched by a valet of Mme de Tourvel, the pious woman he wants to seduce, sets up a trap: he will make sure he is present at the moment when a destitute family is being evicted and rescue them from homelessness, knowing that his generous act will be duly reported to the "celestial prude." But the rake is surprised to find, in the spectacle of a whole family kneeling in front of him as to a living image of God, an unexpected and involuntary pleasure.[55]

Mercier would have us believe that the virtuous Montesquieu is too respectful of other people's dignity and too scrupulous about his own motivations to want to see anybody kneel in front of him. When Robert throws himself at his feet, Montesquieu recoils: "Get up, Monsieur, get up; I will endure no one in that position in front of me" (act 3, sc. 6, p. 130). But his refusal to acknowledge them is felt as much more humiliating. As Montesquieu quits the room, he says to himself: "Let us run; am I not rewarded enough by all I am feeling!" (ibid., p. 133). The satisfaction of having acted well is enough of a reward. As Seneca puts it, "And what shall I gain, you ask? . . . Only the gain of having done it. . . . The reward of the virtuous acts lies in the acts themselves."[56] But the point here is not that the giver should be rewarded but rather that the recipient should be given a chance to unburden himself; both ought to be able to engage in mutual recognition.[57] In Mercier's play they do not. Montesquieu prefers to ignore his partners in the exchange and to curtail their right to expression rather than jeopardize his narcissistic self-approval. To Seneca, giving involved two partners who had equal rights. In the play this principle is voiced by the elder Robert: "Is it not true that denying the beneficiary the touching and sacred duty of gratitude amounts to *destroying one half of a good deed?*" (act 2, sc. 7, p. 88, emphasis added). Montesquieu's sublime generosity is marred by the lack of reciprocity. Refusing, however, to be trapped into submissive admiration of the sublimity of Montesquieu's gesture, the Robert family rebels against the constraints that are put upon it. But its rebellion is short-lived.

After Montesquieu has fled the room, his friend the abbé Guasco, who has witnessed the scene with the Pérouvilles, tries to comfort the family: "Calm down and prove your gratitude by submitting to his will, otherwise you will hurt him. He is like that . . . he never wanted to hear any thanks; on the contrary, any commotion is a torment to him" (act 3, sc. 6, p. 136). Robert the elder complies; loosening the knot of resentment, he moves the issue onto an entirely new ground: "Let us respect him, my son; we owe him the sacrifice of our best sentiments, since he demands it. Let us be happy with preserving his traits in our heart; let us recall them to our memory and never erase them; may his name forever be blessed among us!" (ibid.). The abbé applauds such feelings, and he offers them a medal with the effigy of Montesquieu: "I have received this medal from the famous Dassier [*sic*], who came from London in order to sculpt this profile, which posterity will hold dear," he declares. The elder Robert accepts the gift and promptly hands it to Henriette, his future daughter-in-law: "Receive this medal and bequeath it to your children so that they will always recall what the man it portrays has done for us " (ibid.).

With Montesquieu back to where he came from, and where he truly belongs, that is, to the netherworld of the memory of national treasures, commemoration replaces the exchange that never took place between the philosophe and his grateful audience. The play is revealed to be truly a eulogy: not a drama in which the living interact with one another but a ritual of death, a bridge between the shadowy Montesquieu, who for a moment has reached onto the stage from the Elysian Fields, and the audience that is yet to come, the audience that is to rise from Henriette's womb, to prosper and multiply in the shadow of the great man, in the new nation that his work and his generosity will help create. Reciprocity between the great man and the public turns out to be all but impossible: there can be no real engagement between an audience whose existence is only virtual and a being whose only existence is in memory.

The Politics of the Sublime

The philosophes were obsessed with creating memory, with implanting memories of themselves—even grossly exaggerated, embellished, or mythical ones—into the public's mind. But the audience their works addressed did not quite respond to any description of a concrete, contemporary French audience. It did not overlap with the audience of the fairgrounds spectacles nor with those who responded to the seduction of modern erotic painting, who took an afternoon walk in the Tuileries, or who put on a touch of rouge before a *souper.* The audience they had in mind was the purer, nobler, virtuous audience that the work of art would engender and that by necessity was always receding further beyond the uncertain horizon of a worthier future. As Diderot had shown in *Le fils naturel,* the theater was a ritual of commemoration in which the present generation communed, by way of a founding myth, with those who were yet to come: "'A play, Father!' 'Yes, my son. But we shall not raise a platform here; rather, we shall consign to memory an event that concerns us and reproduce it exactly as it was. We will renew it ourselves, every year, in this house, in this hall. . . . Your children will do the same, and so their descendants. I will endure beyond my life and will converse, across the ages, with all my grandchildren.'"[58] In future years Dorval and his family will not perform but will reenact the founding crisis that has made them aware of who they are, a family united by the traumatic experience of sublime virtue.

While the future audience projected its towering shadow over the present, the philosophe conceived himself as a creature of the past, sanctified by immortality. Much like the young Sartre in *Les mots,* he was the hero of a long story with a happy ending.[59] In his imagination he enjoyed the privileges of a posthumous existence and saw himself deceased but living gloriously and usefully in the memory of posterity: "The man who projects himself into the future and who *draws an intense pleasure from the memory of himself* will work through the ages as if he were immortal, . . . for his imagination makes him present to posterity," wrote Marmontel in the article "Gloire" for the *Encyclopédie.*[60] In a letter to Falconet, Diderot confessed that he thought he heard the sweet sound of posterity's eulogistic music playing in his ears a flattering concert: "The man who has written a great and wonderful work does not see it as great and wonderful only during his lifetime. He listens to the faraway concert. He sees it as still great and wonderful for the time he will no longer exist."[61] Such a character could not help but being, like the Montesquieu revisited by Mercier, or like Dorval, rather depressed and scarcely conversant:

"Somber and melancholic . . . ; he was sad in his conversation and his manner, unless he talked about virtue or he felt the emotion of those who passionately love it."[62] His eyes are turned to the heavens, he is deeply absorbed in himself, and he prefers to meditate upon the ideals of humanity rather than interact with those around him. Thus, the young Robert recalled that during their first encounter in the boat, at the crucial moment when he made his fateful decision, Montesquieu had suddenly withdrawn into himself and, ceasing all contact with his companion, fallen into ecstasy: "Averting his eyes from me, he fell into a profound meditation. I respected his silence. The sea was calm and the evening serene. He remained immobile in contemplation for a long time, looking at the sky. . . . His gaze was steady and glistening; in this trance he sometimes would smile with delight" (act 1, sc. 5, pp. 52–53).

If the philosophes had elected to inhabit a sort of time-lag, it was a choice bolstered by their familiarity with the Longinian sublime. For Longinus, great orators formed their own community, set apart from ordinary people, one that stretched across the centuries and was ruled by a virtuous emulation: "Those great men that we intend to imitate are present to our imagination, they enlighten us like a torch, they raise our soul almost as high as the conception we have formed of their own genius, all the more so if we keep this thought clearly in mind: if Homer or Demosthenes were hearing me, what would they think of what I am saying, how would they judge me?" stated Boileau's Longinus.[63] The great men of antiquity represented a kind of tribunal that modern writers had internalized; they were the golden rule against which everything that one did and wrote had to be measured and judged. At the same time, the good orator did not write primarily for the present, but for the future. He would still await his true audience: "An even more powerful motive to inspire us is the thought of how the entire posterity will judge our works." Those who failed to do so would produce nothing but "blind and deficient stillborn offspring."[64]

Appreciating the influence of Longinus's work in the eighteenth century is fundamental to understanding the philosophes' conception of themselves and the work of art in the public sphere. Longinus provided the philosophes with a mythology that they found deeply congenial. In other words, the sublime was the dream of the political at a time when the political was out of the immediate reach of the philosophes. It was a relentless, increasingly clamorous plea for their own relevance in the public sphere.[65] In that respect the true readers of Longinus were not Boileau's contemporaries but the late-eighteenth-century philosophes and eventually the orators of the Revolution. Longinus, a writer of the first century of the Roman Empire, had lamented that the age of great orators had passed and that his was a time of decadence, his discontent was exemplary to the philosophes. Why, Longinus asked, were so many orators of his day capable of grace and verve but so few capable of reaching the sublime?

> Is it not what we usually say? That it is a republican government that nurtures and shapes great genius, for after all, until now good orators have flourished and vanished with it. In fact, perhaps nothing ennobles the soul of great men but liberty. . . . As for us, we have been swathed in the customs and manners of monarchy, . . . we have never tasted that energetic and fruitful source of eloquence. . . . No slave will ever be able to become an orator.[66]

To the first-century rhetorician, absolutist rule fostered petty virtues and trivial passions; greed, avarice, luxury, and love of pleasure contributed to smother the fires of eloquence: "As soon as a man, forsaking the cultivation of virtue, admires only frivolous and perishable things . . . he will no longer be able to raise his eyes above himself and express whatever surpasses ordinary experience. . . . Everything that was noble and great in him will wither and decay and attract only contempt."[67] Such discontent about the present was the basis for the nostalgia that drove the writers of the late Enlightenment to the imaginary community of the great men and orators of the past.

But the sublime meant also the dream of the hegemony of art in society, the obliteration of any distinction between politics and art and, more important, between action and representation. While intellectuals were deprived, in reality, of direct participation in political institutions, everything was possible in the philosophical imagination. The philosophes did not tire of repeating that they would much rather produce good deeds than good writing: their prose was intoxicated with good intentions, and they seemed to care for nothing but the warmest engagement with the real. We should not, however, be misled by those claims: in the aesthetics of the sublime good writing *was* good deeds, and language was action; words, if uttered with enough enthusiasm and belief, would immediately burst onto the stage of reality. One gets the impression that rather than subordinate representation to the real, the philosophes wished to merge reality and representation into one unified, utopian totality. Hence the endless fascination with the *fiat lux,* with the creative bolt of lightning that created a world out of a simple utterance.[68] Hence the obsession with the theater, which was the genre that best resurrected the physicality and the sensual violence of the tribune, the communality of shared emotion in the double rebound of enthusiasm from the speaker to the crowd and back.[69]

A large gathering elevates the soul. Emotion travels from the orator to the people and comes back to the orator. Thousands of people whom he affects reach back to him. Besides his tone of voice, his eyes, all his movements, in harmony with the passion that moves him, persuade the audience that this passion is authentic. He strikes the senses, and through them he grabs the soul and shakes it. But for the writer, everything is quiet. We read him in silence; every man with whom he enters into a conversation is isolated; emotion is solitary; the orator himself is absent. . . . We must admit that the effect of such eloquence is more doubtful and its success more uncertain.[70]

Like the tribune, the theater allows discourse to have an unmediated impact: "When I leave the theater, I do not want to come away with words, but with impressions," wrote Diderot. "The excellent poet is the one whose impact will stay with me for a long time. Playwrights! The truest applause you must want to hear is not the sound of hands clapping after a brilliant verse but the deep sigh that relieves the soul after the constraint of a long silence."[71] Over the self-questioning aesthetics of *bel esprit* the philosophes favored a conception of writing that shared much with sacred eloquence and that opposed *pleasure* to *persuasion,* applause to tears, irony to entrancement. Persuasion demanded the complete surrender of the artist, the absolute sacrifice of language to a purified but emaciated conception of itself. Diderot and the other philosophes were thus following in the footsteps not only of Demosthenes but also of Augustine and seventeenth-century Christian rhetoric. The Augustinian conception of the sacred sublime was borrowed, as we saw earlier, by Fénelon, an author adopted by the Enlightenment, who was fond of quoting long passages from Augustine. In one excerpt that Fénelon translated, Augustine explains how he persuaded the people of Mauritania to abandon their custom of internecine fighting:

> The sublime crushes us with its weight and reduces us to silence, to tears even. . . . I had employed, to the full extent of my capabilities, the strongest expressions in order to eradicate from the heart and the customs of those people such a cruel and longstanding practice. I felt I was getting nowhere as long as I heard their applause. But when I saw them cry, I started to hope.[72]

In a similar mood, d'Alembert emphasized the absolute transparency of eloquence to passion and the immediate transmissibility of the emotion conveyed by discourse from the orator to the public:

> Eloquence is the talent to transmit rapidly and impress deeply into the soul of others the powerful emotion that penetrates us. That sublime talent has

its origin in an exceptional sensitivity to greatness and truth. The same disposition of the soul that makes us inclined to feel vigorous and exceptional emotions is sufficient to project their image outward. Therefore, there can be no art to eloquence, as there is none to feeling.[73]

Eloquence was a matter, not of art, but of conviction, character, and morality. Thus, the modesty and self-effacement of the eloquent writer, his sacrifice to his task, were a small price to pay for the extraordinary power his eloquence had over society: "The poet will be a new Demosthenes," Mercier declared, "and we shall never again see the people inattentive. Joining the title of legislator to that of poet (which were once one and the same), he will fill all hearts with a virtuous hatred of tyrants, and he will teach them to recognize the many paths that lead to despotism."[74] What is the greatest applause that a dramatic author and an actor may expect from their audience? asked Mercier; not applause, but silence and tears. "It is when a profound silence fills the theater hall; when the spectator, his heart broken and his eyes filled with tears, has neither the force nor the desire to applaud; when, sunk into an all-pervading illusion, he forgets acting and art; everything has become real and the scene is permanently engraved in his heart."[75]

However, at a time when writers could not emphasize enough how little they cared for the trappings of art or for *bel esprit* and how much their impact on the audience and the improvement of the human condition meant to them, it was somewhat paradoxical that much of what they wrote focused, not on the real, but on the act of writing (or on the oratorical tribune). The eulogies they wrote for one another were often conversion stories modeled after the lives of saints.[76] They relentlessly reflected upon the glorious writers of antiquity and those of the present, upon the function of art and the debt society owed its artists for the sacrifices they endured for art's sake. It was precisely at a time when literature was supposed to defer to the real that literature could not stop talking about itself, celebrating its own powers and the delight it took in its good intentions. It was as if literature had replaced the image of the society that it hoped to create with that of a heavenly republic of letters, bustling with saints and martyrs. "I confess that my work almost killed me; my hair has all turned white," says Mercier's folksy Montesquieu.[77] The play makes much of the persecutions he had to suffer because of his writings. The philosophes undoubtedly encountered an all-too-real opposition from the religious and secular authorities, as illustrated by the censorship and suppression of the *Encyclopédie,* as well as the imprisonment of Diderot, the exile of Voltaire, and the vicissitudes of Rousseau.[78] The image of the philosophe crucified for the sake of the public, however, was an all-too-cherished component of their self-mythologizing, and there was a grain of truth to Palissot's bitter sarcasm: "They would show much indifference for that sublime chimera that is called glory; and all the while, they would write, conspire, and try to make themselves interesting by seeming to be readying themselves for a persecution that never came. But playing at being persecuted or ready to be so is so flattering! One becomes famous while giving up fame."[79]

There was, however, more than a self-serving strategy to the philosophe's attitude. In his article "Eclectisme," published in volume 5 of the *Encyclopédie,* Diderot listed among the reasons for the decline of philosophy and the arts the poverty of the *homme de génie,* the unwisely placed rewards of the state, and the indifference of a government that had abandoned "the men of the nation; those who represent her with dignity among other nations; those to whom she will owe her rank among future generations; those whom she venerates in her bosom and who are the object of admiration in distant lands." A little further on, Diderot added a brief but intense eulogy of Montesquieu:

> I was writing those reflections on February 11, 1755, on my way back from the funeral of one of our greatest men, saddened by the loss that the nation and the world of letters had suffered and profoundly irate at the thought of the persecutions he had endured. My veneration toward his memory engraved this epitaph, which some time earlier I had intended as an inscription to his great work, *De l'esprit des lois:* "Alto quaesivit coelo lucem, ingemuitque reperta." May it pass to posterity, to let it know that troubled by the threats of enemies he feared, and made sensitive to injuries he would have disregarded had they not seemed to carry the seal of authority, the loss of his peace of mind was the miserable reward that that man, *born sensitive,* reaped for the honor he had brought to France and the important benefit he had given the universe![80]

One cannot help realizing that while Montesquieu's fate had not been half as dire as Diderot paints it, Diderot had many reasons to feel that those words fit his own situation very well. Unrewarded, unrecognized, persecuted by the vilest of the *littérateurs,* abandoned by an ungrateful nation—as Dido was abandoned by Aeneas—the man of letters, undaunted and bold, did not cease to labor for the sake of the people. He was the conscience of the nation. What better metaphor for such a sacrifice than the parable of Montesquieu's secret act of generosity? In this idealized projection of himself the philosophe turns the tables on the public and on the whole system of patronage on which he depends. Rather than being the recipient of the humiliating protection of the powerful, rather than begging from the state the recognition that is with-held from him, the *homme de lettres* finds in himself alone, and in his own resources, the source of all that is life-enhancing for the people. He is now their benefactor, and no longer their beneficiary. In its hyperbolic dream of a power achieved through the spectacle of martyrdom, literature casts its protective shadow upon the whole nation in its advance toward a most auspicious future.

8 ¦ *Everlasting Theatricality*

Arlequin and the Untamed Parterre

*Monseigneur the Public . . . I beg you not to disapprove of Polichinelle
if, following the example of large dogs, he were to piss against the wall of
your attention and inundate it with the torrents of his eloquence.*
　　　　　　　　　　　　　　　—Fuzelier, Lesage, and d'Orneval

*What I like in a narrative is not directly its content or even its structure
but rather the abrasions I impose upon the fine surface.*
　　　　　　　　　　　　　　　—Barthes

Many phenomena lead us to think, however, that prerevolutionary audiences
reacted to the aesthetics of the *drame* in ways that the philosophes found profoundly disconcerting and distasteful. Despite the many injunctions against
theatricality (of which Voltaire and Diderot were the most outspoken representatives at midcentury), manifestations of self-conscious, theatrical awareness of form did not decline on the French stage. Even before the expulsion
of the Italian actors in 1697 a variety of unsponsored playhouses (or *comédies
irrégulières,* which offered plays written outside the dictates of classical, Aristotelian rules) had sprung up on the Parisian fairgrounds and, later in the century, on the boulevards. There, audiences from all walks of life flocked to spectacles that illustrated the culture of critique, satire, parodistic rewriting, and
self-reflexive engagement with classical forms that had been the hallmark of
the *goût moderne.* Pushed to the margins of state-sponsored culture, excluded
from the status of academy-worthy high art, the fundamental principles of
the *goût moderne*—reciprocity and engagement with the audience—continued

to thrive; audiences refused to become alienated and disenfranchised, even if such alienation was presented as a prerequisite to virtuous enlightenment. This chapter focuses on those aspects of theatrical culture that are seldom mentioned in current histories of the theater but are crucial because they illustrate the rebellion of *ancien régime* audiences against subjection by means of emotion-laden illusion.

The Reversibility of Spectacle

The relationship between playwrights and Parisian audiences had never been easy. Voltaire, Rousseau, Diderot, and Mercier followed in the footsteps of predecessors such as Boursault, Dufresny, Baron, Donneau de Visé, and many others in deploring the rowdiness, the lack of attention, the unpredictable taste, and the tyrannical leanings of audiences, whom they sometimes compared to Asiatic despots. A few years before the Revolution, Louis-Sébastien Mercier harangued those audiences with Ciceronian severity ("Quo usque tandem abutere, spectatores . . .") from the pages of his *Tableaux:* "Until when will the spectator abuse his privilege to applaud, interrupt foolishly an eloquent verse, and destroy its effect by cutting it short with restless impudence?"[1] If only audiences had limited themselves to applauding too much. Sometimes, if we may trust Mercier, they pilloried authors and subjected them to humiliating practices reminiscent of ritual sacrifice: "When the parterre screams for the author, it is allowed to fill the hall with inarticulate and savage cries. . . . It increases its bawl until the victim is brought to the stage, and then its applause is nothing but abuse."[2] Throughout the century, spectators in the pit (the *parterre,* by general consensus the recognized leader of the rest of the audience)[3] felt free to address the actors, to interrupt the performance, to clamor for another play, or even to invade the stage. From the early years of the eighteenth century, one royal ordinance after another enjoined audiences to refrain from disrupting, interrupting, and invading the space of the performance, their frequency sufficient proof of their ineffectiveness.[4] In the second half of the century, however, it seemed as if Voltaire, Diderot, and Mercier had finally gotten what they wanted, perhaps even more than they had hoped for. In 1751 thirty or so blue-uniformed and heavily armed *gardes-français* had been conspicuously introduced into the parterre, defusing the customary eruptions of violence but often exercising their function with unchecked arrogance.

Less conspicuously, however, other events had occurred that gradually transformed the relationship between the stage and the audience, events that belonged to a different kind of authority. Many of the reforms that philosophes and playwrights had been asking for had finally taken place. In 1759, thanks to Voltaire's efforts, the stage had been cleared of marquis and *petits-maîtres*. In 1782 spectators in the parterre of the Comédie-Française were no longer allowed to stand, but were seated on benches. In the following years the same innovations were brought to the Comédie-Italienne and the Opéra. Changes in costume brought to the stage the historical accuracy that had become habitual in history painting. As Dorat remarked, "A Sarmatian no longer comes on stage to make love wearing a *grand panier*."[5] Tragic declamation became less solemn and hieratic; actors were invited to deliver their speeches facing one another rather than facing the audience. Prologues and direct addresses to the audience, already scarce by 1740, disappeared altogether. All those changes were part of a general trend toward enhancing illusion and separating the space of the stage from that of the audience. Dramatic action, as the abbé d'Aubignac had long before theorized, was meant to create a world of its own, an autonomous space to which the spectator would be irresistibly drawn, but only if he was willing to forfeit all awareness of himself as a spectator. "In a dramatic performance," wrote Diderot, who looked upon *tirades* and rhetorical set pieces as disruptive, "we should deal with the spectator as if he did not exist. Does anything address him directly? The author has abandoned his subject, and the actor has walked out of his role. Both have quit the stage; I see them in the parterre. As long as the *tirade* goes on, the action is suspended and the scene is vacant."[6] *Tirades* were exploits of virtuosity on the part of authors and actors; they were products of *bel esprit;* they stood out from the rest of the play and invited loud applause. For Diderot, as for Mercier, applause upset the fragile balance of dramatic action; it punctured the autonomy of the fictional world and veered toward ostentatious vulgarity, the phony rhetoric that killed all emotion: "If the frenzy to be applauded takes hold of an actor, he will become excessive."[7]

Apparently, Diderot got what he wished for, and more. That he was not entirely satisfied with the result emerges in a letter written a year after the *Entretiens sur Le fils naturel* to the actress-turned-novelist Mme Riccoboni, in which Diderot mourned the passing of a golden age of theatrical life, when audiences were free to misbehave:

> More than fifteen years ago our theaters were tumultuous places. The coolest heads would heat up upon entering there, and men of good sense would share in the excitement of the insane. We would hear from one side, "Hands

off, Monsieur l'abbé"; elsewhere, "Off with your hat"; from all sides, "Hush, hush the cabal." We were turbulent, we tossed each other around, we pushed one another. The soul was beside itself [*l'âme était mise hors d'elle-même*]. I know of no other disposition more favorable to a poet. The play would start with difficulty and be interrupted often, but was there a good passage? It was an incredible clamor. Encores were endlessly called for; people were enthusiastic about the author, the actor, the actress. The thrill would pass from the parterre to the amphitheater to the boxes. Having arrived excited, we would leave inebriated with enthusiasm. Some would go to the brothel, others to visit polite society; it was like a storm slowly dying away, its hum lingered long after it had departed. That was pleasure. Today, we go there cold, we listen coolly, we depart cold, and I don't know where we go afterwards. Those insolent soldiers posted right and left to temper the excess of my admiration, my sensitivity, and my joy, who make our theaters more tranquil and decorous than our churches, irritate me prodigiously.[8]

Diderot blames the indifference and dejection of contemporary audiences on the presence of the French guards. Reality, however, was more complicated. The interaction between the military police and the audience was undoubtedly contentious; people were occasionally brought to the police and arrested at the discretion of the guards, whose judgment was often seen as arbitrary. But that was not the only factor in the perception of increased audience passivity. *Exempts* and guards had been present in the theaters to arrest offenders as early as 1706, under the especially effective (or repressive, depending on one's point of view) administration of Lieutenant General d'Argenson. Police activity had been particularly intense from 1733 to 1738, when arrests for theatrical infractions peaked, and then again from 1747 to 1751, that is, at approximately the time Diderot describes in his letter as free-for-all liberty of expression (which corresponds to his youthful theatergoing days, 1735–48).[9]

But what most strikes us in his nostalgic portrayal of earlier times is the extraordinary emphasis that Diderot places on activities that in his theoretical writings he normally views as troubling the integrity of the spectacle. The noise, the loud and repeated applause, the enthusiasm for the artistry of this or that actress, the tumultuous and insolent exclamations of members of the audience addressing one another with little regard for the actors and the illusion, the audience's intoxicating mirth—all those activities would lead to breaking down the "fourth wall" separating the audience from the stage, a wall that Diderot had long seen as a condition vital to theatrical reception. In the letter to Riccoboni we read nothing of the oft-praised introspective emotion that makes the audience shiver in silence, the quasi-religious, contemplative entrancement that drives the spectator to forget himself and to espouse the passions of the character onstage. A tumultuous pit seems inhospitable to such feelings. "The soul was beside itself": to Diderot, the aim of the theater was to enable the spectator to recover his regenerated self through a salutary process of alienation, an out-of-body experience. The reader familiar with Diderot's writings on theater is surprised to discover that this same effect is achieved, not by means of a silent communion with the spectacle, but by a carnivalesque fête that transgresses all boundaries between the stage and the audience and subverts much of what Diderot had been advocating in his art and theater criticism. In his letter to Riccoboni the communion between the spectators and the performance is subordinated to the interaction among the spectators. The pit appears as an eminently sociable space in which cabals and factions come together and spill out of the theater into other spaces of *le monde,* such as the salon and the brothel (which for him is also a space of sociability). It would seem that Diderot the theoretician and the playwright clashed with Diderot the theater lover. As a passionate spectator, Diderot resented being deprived of the right to be an active participant, something that, as an author and a theoretician, he had promoted.

A similar conflict may be observed in the writings of Mercier. Mercier was not only a playwright, a theoretician, and a would-be reformer of the theater but also a perceptive observer of actual, embodied audiences. His *Tableaux de Paris* reflect (making allowances for the distortions of satire and polemics) the changes that were taking place in audiences of the late eighteenth century. A quarter-century after Diderot's letter to Mme Riccoboni, Mercier too waxed nostalgic about the past, the days when theatergoers were not deprived of their fundamental rights to self-expression, no matter how outrageously they might behave. Occasionally Mercier too attributed the reason for this decline to the presence of soldiers in the pit: "The parterre, if we except some passing fervor, is fearsomely dull. Should it try to make its existence manifest, soldiers are there to grab it by the collar."[10] At other times, however, he observed that such repression had the contrary effect of fueling insubordination and disorder: "I have witnessed days when the audience felt something like a desire to show its independence. . . . I have reason to believe that the threatening image of the police only adds to the restlessness of the public, which is willing to jeopardize its pleasure because it experiences a much stronger one in defying the blue uniforms. Anarchy has its appeal to youths of all ranks, whose boiling effervescence is hard to restrain."[11] Elsewhere still, Mercier saw in the new system of seating the parterre the main reason for its new-found docility:

The parterre of the theater has lost its ancient privileges. It no longer exercises with vigor an authority that has been contested; it has been robbed of it and has become passive. It has been ordered to sit down, and it has fallen into lethargy. Electricity has been interrupted, for benches no longer allow heads to touch and communicate. In the past an incredible enthusiasm animated it, and a general effervescence lent to theatrical productions an interest that they no longer have. Today, calmness, silence, and icy disapproval have replaced the ancient tumult.[12]

Be that as it may, neither Diderot nor Mercier had much of an explanation for such changes. More important, their perception of that change was highly subjective. As Mercier was born in 1740, the time Diderot depicted as the good old days of freedom, we may safely assume that Mercier's own good old days, to which he does not assign a specific time span,[13] coincided with the late 1750s, that is, precisely with Diderot's bad days of repression. Are we to conclude that those anxieties only reflected a kind of spectatorial midlife crisis? That would be too hasty.

In their revealing studies of revolutionary political and representational practices, Marie-Hélène Huet and Paul Friedland describe the process of alienation that transformed the French people in their functions as theatrical audiences and as political agents. Each analyzes the fundamental shift that transformed the *ancien régime*'s corporate entities (such as the Estates Generals) into collections of isolated individuals willing to delegate their political decisions to representative bodies. The Legislative Assembly and the Convention both claimed to represent them abstractly as the "people" and to be speaking in their name while in fact revoking their agency. Huet shows how the Revolution ruled by means of theater. By dint of carefully choreographed spectacles (such as the king's trial, Marat's funeral, the Convention debates) citizens became not actors but spectators alienated from what went on in their name on the political stage: "The Revolution's constant concern with making the people into a public did not necessarily correspond to any form of political liberalism; that this objective was political in nature is beyond doubt, but it was inscribed in a tradition that consists in repressing by means of the spectacle. To make a spectator of the people, while making sure that the possibility of spectator-actor reversibility remains carefully controlled, is to maintain an alienation that is the real form of power."[14]

Paul Friedland confirms Huet's claim about the political use of the revolutionary spectacle from a different angle. He argues that changes in theatrical practices and doctrines at midcentury paved the way for a revolutionary system of political representation that turned the people into passive spectators of the drama of power. In the passage from the Estates General to the Legislative Assembly the revolutionaries abolished the *ancien régime*'s system of the binding mandate *(mandat impératif)*, in which the relationship between the people and their representatives was one of embodiment, and replaced it with one of alienated representation. In the old system, "political representatives were truly beholden to the constituencies that had elected them," since they were allowed to express only the political positions that the people they represented commissioned them to endorse. The new system, on the contrary, freed the representatives from all dependence on their constituents by creating the fiction of a disembodied and unified general will of the nation, to which the representatives claimed they were beholden. "The Revolutionaries [abolished] the binding mandate as an impediment to the representation of the general will. Representatives would, in effect, sever the bond between themselves and their constituents and relegate the latter to the passive role of spectators to a representative process performed on their behalf."[15]

That is not to say that spectacles had not been put to political use well before the Revolution; Jean-Marie Apostolidès has well shown the central role played by spectacle in the enactment of monarchical power in the seventeenth century.[16] But those were not mass spectacles addressing the nation; their intended audience was the court, and any effect on the nation at large was mediated and oblique. What is more, court spectacles and fêtes tended to be interactive and to include the spectators as participants. Both Rousseau's opposition to theater and Diderot's and Mercier's faith in its potential for reform were based on an analogous awareness of the performative nature of power and of the political uses of spectacle. The only difference was that while Rousseau decried the theater's nefarious effects on an audience alienated from the immediacy of experience and inoculated by spectatorial passions against authentic ones, Diderot and Mercier looked for ways to enhance such alienation and to put it to good use. Hence their advocacy of reforms aimed at deepening the impact of the spectacle and the verisimilitude of stage illusion by means of a greater separation between the stage and the audience. The corollary of such reforms, however, on both the political and the fictional stage, was an increased passivity on the part of the public.

But what, in reality, was the extent of such change? Was it truly the case that beginning in the second half of the eighteenth century *ancien régime* audiences were slowly headed toward becoming the uniformly docile and silent mass audiences of modern times, for whom political elections are a remote spectacle and who politely stand in ovation even when they have been bored stiff? That there was from the mid-eighteenth century on a growing fear that theatrical audiences were becoming indifferent and aloof is undoubted. That philosophes and playwrights were worried about the function of the theater both from an esthetic and a political point of view, that they were ambivalent as to the impact of the theatrical reforms they were proposing, is also a fact. But that audiences were becoming submissive in every respect was a fear belied by any close observer of *ancien régime* theatrical life in all its rich diversity. Let us take Mercier. "Since the parterres have been sitting," he wrote in the *Tableaux de Paris,* obviously undaunted by any fears of contradicting himself, "they have become more noisy and more clamoring than ever; they exercise upon the actors a comical sovereignty that wears them out. The obstinate infighting between the actors and the parterre has become a new and curious spectacle that replaces the expected one. The racket lasts for several hours and seems to amuse the assembly. Soldiers have lately become inactive."[17] In fact, as Marie-Hélène Huet forcefully puts it, *ancien régime* audiences were yearning for the possibility of a "transmutation from the role of receiver to that of actor," and there existed in them a "latent and desired reversibility of the position of spectator. . . . To appeal to an audience is to appeal to this possibility of a spectator-actor exchange, and an audience that does not achieve this exchange, this cycle, this transformation, is a mutilated audience—or, one might say, an alienated one."[18]

In spite of the reformers' efforts to the contrary, in spite of the increased police presence in the pit, audiences throughout the eighteenth century, for better and for worse, stubbornly refused to become alienated. It is apparent from Mercier's own observations, as well as from what we know about *ancien régime* theatrical life, that many strategies and practices enabled spectators to engage in what Huet describes as spectator-actor exchange. Well before the revolutionary upheaval, audiences throughout the eighteenth century had been able to cross the barrier of the fourth wall and to engage in a variety of transgressive acts. Some scholars of revolutionary theater have perhaps given the Revolution (with its embrace of new audiences and its carefully planned theatrical insurrections) too much credit for breaking down the frontier between fiction and reality and for undermining the ideology of the fourth wall. In reality, such undermining had been a persistent, unavoidable phenomenon of theatrical life throughout the century, one that for a long time had pitted rebellious audiences against the would-be reformers who hoped to control them by holding them in emotional thrall.[19]

The most obvious way to achieve a spectator-actor reversal was for spectators literally to become actors by performing in one of the countless *théâtres
de société* (or *comédies bourgeoises*),[20] that is, in private playhouses that enabled
amateurs of all classes of society, from the bourgeoisie to the court, from duch-
esses to shoemakers, to be seen rather than simply see: "People play theater
in certain milieus, not because they love it," observed Mercier, "but because
of the rapport established through their roles. Where is the lover who would
refuse to play *Orosmane?* The most timid beauty takes heart for the role of
Nanine."[21] The theater was a space favorable to framing relations among the
participating actor-spectators; playacting would enable a group of separate individuals to come together and turn themselves into a community, to endow
themselves with an identity, whether for the purpose of courtship, for family
bonding, or for politics. That was a fact well understood by Diderot, Rousseau, and the planners of the revolutionary fête. The physiocrat Pierre-Samuel
Dupont de Nemours noted that in the years between the publication of the
Letter on Spectacles and the outbreak of the Revolution the people yearned to
take center stage and to perform in their own name, in order to escape the
deadening effects of alienating, "tyrannical" boredom:

> The spectacles of the people are *fêtes*. Not idle fêtes . . . but fêtes . . . that
> allow them to be actors and not simply spectators. For the position of an in-
> active spectator has something slackening and lifeless; it often turns boring,
> whereas those who have a role to play and applause to merit are never bored.
> . . . That is why there are now emerging in Europe so many private stages
> [*comédies bourgeoises*]: it is much more enjoyable to play than to watch,
> which is why women everywhere prefer dance to theater: better to be seen
> than to see others. . . . Man was made to be active. If we want to offer the
> people spectacles that would trump that cold and cruel tyrant, that spoiler
> of the world that is boredom, let the people themselves offer them.[22]

The issue of audience participation and involved playacting is implicitly
at the heart of Rousseau's and Diderot's reflections on theatricality. It was on
that point that the two were able to meet across the divide of their ideological
polarization about the social function of spectacle. Diderot's major plays were
intended to be performed for an intimate circle, on the private stage of a salon
(even if they were eventually publicly produced by professional actors). *Le fils
naturel* is a case in point. The play had been staged several times in the theater
of the duc d'Ayen, at the Hôtel de Noailles in Saint-Germain, but only once,
on 26 September 1771, at the Théâtre-Français.[23] In the dialogue with Dorval

a great deal of emphasis is placed upon the distinction between the public theater and the private home: "—Me: But this tone would be scandalous on the stage . . . —Dorval: Forget the stage; go back to the drawing-room. . . . It is not in the theater, it is in the drawing-room that my work must be appreciated."[24] In the preamble to the play, entitled "The True Story behind the Play," Lysimond, Dorval's father, invites his entire family, not to simulate, but to reenact the original event that saw them as protagonists.[25] Lysimond pushes his concern for authenticity so far as to preserve the clothes he wore in prison so as to wear them again on the family's stage.

The play breaks down a number of distinctions that were vital to the theater as the French knew it, namely, the distinctions between the original event and its representation; between reality and fiction; between the protagonists and the actors; and, more crucial for our argument, between the actors and the spectators. In so doing, the play transcends all theatrical boundaries and approaches the kind of celebratory fête that Rousseau describes so lyrically at the end of the *Letter on Spectacles. Le fils naturel* in effect does not claim to be the mimetic *reproduction* of an actual event, but the recurring *reenactment* of that event. The actors are not actors in any conventional sense, but celebrants in a ceremony reminiscent of transubstantiation, one that establishes for generations to come a cult of the family. Taking his cue from the Last Supper, Lysimond invites his children to relive and celebrate the original event in his name so as to perpetuate the memory of a moment that, for all its traumatic effects, brought them together and revealed them to themselves. It is that founding event, indefinitely repeated, that will maintain for future generations their existence as a community. In the eyes of Diderot, theater ought to become a ritual of memory playing a foundational role in the nation's identity.

In their desire to draw the spectators emotionally to the stage, Diderot and Rousseau both imagined a spectacle that would overcome the alienation of representation and collapse all separation between actors and spectators. In Rousseau's childhood memory of the fête the women who have been watching from their windows the regiment of Saint-Gervais cavorting in the street are so drawn to the show that they join in. As they do so, the graceful spirals of the dance unravel; the spectacle dissolves, and everybody is inebriated with a disorderly joy: "We no longer knew what we were doing; everyone was giddy with an inebriant sweeter than wine."[26] The people's elated participation in a performance that represents nothing has no purpose other than to establish a binding sense of community: "But what will be the object of such spectacle? What shall we show? Nothing, if you will. . . . Let the spectators become the spectacle; let them turn into actors. Let each one of them see himself and love himself in everyone else so that all will be better united."[27] The utopian dream of new forms of spectacle pulls Diderot and Rousseau, who see the space of modern theater as symbolic of the prison and the oppressive sway of the state, away from the institution of *ancien régime* theater toward the imaginary open spaces of the ancient republican theater.[28] Diderot envisioned a newborn community both within the confines of the family and within the archaic utopia of immense amphitheaters, reminiscent of ancient coliseums: "Let us measure the strength of a huge gathering of spectators by our knowledge of the action that men have upon one another and of the transfer of passions that takes place during a popular insurgency. Forty or fifty thousand people will not restrain themselves for the sake of propriety. If a great man of the republic were to shed a tear, what effect would his emotion have upon the rest of the spectators?"[29] Diderot yearned for the intoxicating effects arising from a turbulent crowd of all-male spectators massed together in close contact. But in his theoretical writings he was unable to conceive those effects in terms other than the physical, nonverbal transmission of emotion among a merely sentient, undifferentiated mass. Diderot understood very well that the theater was conducive to creating bonds among the spectators, but he was reluctant to consider that those bonds might be predicated upon the exercise of critical, subversive reason, not sheer, animal-like emotion, upon laughter rather than tears. Fifty thousand spectators might be held captive by the speech of one godlike orator; they might cry in unison at the shedding of one tear (but how would they be able to see it?); their potential unleashed force could be devastating if it were not held in check by the emotion emanating from the spectacle or by the authority of the (reassuringly omnipotent and male) orator. But a small group of five hundred spectators obey a different dynamic: they do not lose themselves in the mass; they are able to band together, to form factions and parties, to critique the representation, contradict one another, express themselves in an unexpected and irreverent manner.

Improper Encounters, or Meet the Audience

Parisian audiences had long held privileges that the presence of *fusiliers* was not quite able to undercut. They had ways of making their voices heard and of becoming active participants. Indeed, they took it as their inalienable right to engage in subversive forms of reception that could transform the content of any spectacle, potentially sinking any tragedy into farce. In several crucial passages in his *Tableaux de Paris* Mercier draws our attention to one of the least discussed peculiarities of *ancien régime* audiences:

> It is there that a parterre is electrified in a moment and creates allusions relative to current events. He does it with a calculated and insightful mischievousness. Nothing escapes it: everything becomes subject to interpretation. That is how the public sometimes enjoys its revenge: it is attentive only to those verses whose meaning may be hijacked and made applicable to its anathemas. [Royal] censors and actors are taken by surprise; they did not anticipate, they could not anticipate, what would become of such and such a passage. The public, *which is dying to have its voice heard,* makes it manifest in a hemistich by Corneille that for the last one hundred and forty years has presented a perfectly innocent physiognomy. A mediocre play may be applauded with a fifteen-minute ovation for four usurped verses. The poet takes himself for a genius, but no one thinks of him. His dull verses have morphed into energetic sentiments. That goes so far that on special occasions all performances of tragedies must stop because the audience, hunting for allusions, finds unexpected ones and, searching every recess of the work, forces, whether it wants it or not, an old tragedy set in Mauritania to tell the history of the present.[30]

In the text-fetishistic mentality of academic canon builders such behavior seems inexplicable. When it has been noticed at all, it has been portrayed as a symptom of the immaturity of *ancien régime* audiences rather than as the sign of a radically different attitude toward textuality and reception. Indeed, such phenomena have been relegated by and large to the domain of anecdotal curiosity and *petite histoire.* Yet, in what is perhaps the secret reason of authorial humiliation and resentment, and in an instance of theatricality gone wild, audiences held the habit of systematically twisting the content of a play so as to turn it into a signifier of current events, a chronicle of modern times. Far from allowing themselves submissively to be absorbed into the fictional world, the spectators of the parterre subordinated the play to their own situation, knowingly and maliciously altering the meaning of the text, so as to shoot themselves right into the orbit of the fictional universe and to explode its illusory autonomy. No work of art was protected from such a volatile reception; nothing came out unscathed from its encounter with the fires of the parterre. Not only Voltaire, always a favorite target, but also the revered Corneille and Racine were subjected to that treatment. The most sublime verses became vulnerable to deflationary interpretations. Audiences demonstrated a truly diabolical creativity in finding allusions, equivocations, puns, and wordplay in the most innocent passages. Good plays sunk into ridicule, while mediocre plays were applauded beyond their merits for a verse that was the audience's own creation. The applause went to the audience, not to the hapless author, whose place the parterre usurped. Creativity flared across the audience in the form of *mots d'esprit*, collections of which were published.[31] Mercier wished that he could himself write a book of *parterriana:* "There are scarcely any plays, good or bad, that have not produced a *bon mot*, sometimes wittier and more profound than the work that occasioned it. The pride of the audience has always been at odds with the vanity of the author. From such conflict have emerged very funny incidents."[32] The parterre competes with the playwright, as the center of attention is transferred from the stage to the audience, in a game of improvisational virtuosity that is reminiscent both of the verbal brilliance of salon conversation and of the oratorical jousts that took place in the *collèges*.

Perhaps there was more to that attitude than a special attention paid to language and dramatic forms. In the parterre's argumentative passion for nonpolitical issues there might have been a deflected political drive: "The parterre has always been the stage of the most heated cabals and factions. There has been more squabble about the structure of a few hemistiches than about the exportation of grain or the American war."[33] Rather than seeing the theater as a space in which the power of the monarchy plays itself out in its symbols of dominance, Mercier considers the theater to be an area of relative freedom of expression, a convenient outlet for a political combativeness that cannot be expressed in any other venues: "One feels that the parterre needs to give itself free rein in order to regain in the theater the unconstrained voice it has lost elsewhere."[34] Guy Spielmann has emphasized the highly referential content of the comedy of the *fin de règne* and the first decades of the eighteenth century. In the plays of Thomas Corneille, Dancourt, Regnard, and Dufresny conventional intrigues allowed authors to encode references to current events culled from the gazettes and from legal briefs.[35] In reality, this trend toward a coded but narrowly pointed referentiality was a trait that characterized the entirety of the eighteenth century and included all theatrical genres and all types of performance. Self-referentiality, however, was not limited to textuality, but found an outlet in the interpreting activities of parterre audiences.

In the eighteenth century theatrical language was perceived to be flexible and polyvalent, a nightmare for someone like Boileau, whose invectives against the ubiquitous *équivoque* had enlivened his *Satire XII*, but a delight for writers and censors alike, at least those perverse enough to author books such as *Polissoniana ou recueil de turlupinades, quolibets, rébus, jeux de mots, allusions, allégories, pointes, expressions extraordinaires, hyperboles, gasconnades, espèces de bons mots et autres plaisanteries* (Amsterdam, 1722), a collection from the pen of the abbé Claude Chérier,[36] who was holding the lucrative office of *censeur des théâtres*. The abbé, whose delight in obscene *équivoque* made him the ideal man for the job, in 1726 had granted the official approval to the libretto of a *pastorale comique* written by Alexis Piron and set to music by Jean-François Rameau, *Le pucelage ou La rose,* but its performance was nonetheless forbidden. It was finally produced with great success in 1744 by Jean-Louis Monnet's fairgrounds Opéra-Comique under the more allegorically elegant title *Les jardins de l'hymen ou La rose.* The report of the abbé Chérier in his function as royal censor is worth citing at length:

> Monsieur, the comic pastoral entitled *The Rose* represents allegorically a young girl hesitant about the choice of several lovers who finally, inspired by *Hymen,* makes a decision; therefore, the conduct of the play is so standard and proper as to be above criticism. The name and the title *Rose* do not raise in themselves any dirty suggestions. Every day people say in polite circles *to pluck the rose* when they talk about a lover who has enjoyed the first favors of a young girl; therefore, the title cannot be attacked. It is not quite the same for other terms that occur here and there and that may provoke dangerous allusions, such as *Rose, Bush, Shepherd's Crook, Seeing the Wolf.* . . ; *Shepherd's Crook* [*Houlette*] might be interpreted in a dishonest sense, but only if one really tries hard. . . . I do not believe that they ought to be suppressed because of someone's maliciousness; besides, if we suppressed those words or the phrases that feature them, we would have to suppress the entire play. . . . The more I think about it, the more I believe that the play respects theatrical propriety. All the malicious construals that can be made of *Rose* and *Shepherd's Crook* are nothing but interpretations. We must stick to the meaning of words and not bother with the way some twisted minds may torture and abuse it.[37]

The efficacy of Piron's language lies in the deft use of allegory and the skillful exploitation of the vast stock of images and figures of speech that constitute the interpretive repertory of any audience familiar with the codes of dramatic pastoral. Its success depends upon a collaborative effort that combines what the author has left unsaid with what the audience is willing to contribute. The practice of theatrical reception and censorship, therefore, much like that of libertine courtship, consists in a balancing act between the text's potential for erotic suggestiveness and the audience's creativity in the exercise of its own cultural competence for the expression of its desire. The onus here is on the recipient: the more profligate the censor's imagination, the more severely he will want to excise the work. But in his own disingenuous way the abbé was right: it is not possible to establish a foolproof set of rules that would enable the censor to discriminate between what the words actually say and what they imply or connote or the manner in which they will be interpreted. Preempting all possible interpretations of a text remains an unattainable goal, all the more so at a time when a theatrical text can be made to signify just anything. Each text is a Pandora's box of free associations and connotations whose explosion is channeled, but not checked, by cultural conventions. Ultimately, all power rested with the audience. A theatrical text was a *type* of which each performance was a *token:* each of its occurrences yielded a potentially different work. *Application* and allusion sprung inexhaustibly from the wellspring of the audience's rebellion. As Mercier observed, the audience's capacity to rewrite a play in its own image came not only from its alert erotic imagination but from a repressed political drive that censors were unable to quash completely: "How can we on the one hand anticipate all possible allusions and on the other leave newly minted allusions in preexisting verse?" asked Mercier, musing upon the potentially subversive content of Corneille's and Voltaire's plays, replete with conspiracies and regicides.[38]

Such a tendency to carnivalesque subversion helps to explain the extraordinary vogue enjoyed by dramatic parody throughout the eighteenth century. The drive to self-referentiality tended to breed a desire to explore self-reflexivity in critical, parodistic rewritings of the classical repertory. Playing with language led audiences to reflect upon the language of dramatic forms. Because of the parterre's clever games and unpredictable reception, every serious play teetered on the verge of becoming a parody of itself. "Normally the parodist is nothing but an echo of the parterre," wrote the playwright and parodist Louis Fuzelier, "it is from the parterre itself that he borrows the material to entertain it; all he does is give a theatrical form to the general remarks that he has heard."[39] In the tradition of Molière, Fuzelier professes to be nothing but the faithful, and therefore the best, interpreter of public taste. However, there is more than self-advertisement to that claim. Audiences that had just applauded Voltaire's latest tragedy would flock to see it parodied at the Théâtre-Italien or at the fairgrounds, where Oedipus, Mahomet, or *Sémiramis*'s ghost was played by a mask of the commedia dell'arte, usually Arlequin, or by a marionette. The drive that urged dramatic authors to churn out parodies faster than they could print tickets found its origin and justification in the parterre's schizophrenic taste for both serious plays and comic subversions.

We now know that dramatic genres were not neatly divided among social classes, with the cultivated elites frequenting the Comédie-Française, the Théâtre-Italien, and the Opéra and the uncouth crowds favoring fairgrounds farces and *parades*.[40] In reality, cultivated audiences and connoisseurs of tragedies also liked to deride the masterpieces that they had admired; because of their expertise, they were the fairgrounds' best audience. Such versatility was the result of the peculiarities of royal administration. Theatrical life in the *ancien régime* was richly but rigidly diversified thanks to a system of *privilèges,* or royally granted monopolies, that "protected" and therefore ossified the repertories and the acting styles of the various playhouses, official and nonofficial alike, from the Comédie-Française to the Opéra to the Troupe Royale des Pygmées (an opera company with oversized marionettes that had obtained its own letters patent).[41] Following that system, tragedies and comedies of the French repertory could only be played by the Théâtre-Français, while the Théâtre-Italien had to share with minor playhouses of the fairgrounds and the boulevard a mixed repertory of comedies with masks, parodies, vaudevilles, *parades,* ballet, pantomime, and *machines* (special stage effects). Serious and comic theaters were rigidly separated, with scarcely any possibility of exchange and with a premium placed on the exploitation of competitive and antagonistic styles. Hence the drive to compete among the various forms of spectacle and within the confines of each genre. Each theatrical venue had to perform according to its character and style; however, it was not forbidden to make reference to another's repertory, provided it was adapted to one's allotted language and genre. Audiences loved to shuttle back and forth between the official playhouses and the fairgrounds, between the tragic spectacle and its parodistic reformulation.

But what is less often emphasized is that within the confines of the strictly regulated tragic stage itself, at the very heart of the Comédie-Française, there were forms of theatricality that tended to challenge and destabilize, by means of bathos (the sudden descent in style and manner from the elevated and the sublime to the commonplace), the purported aims of high tragedy. Tragedy and comedy had always coexisted side by side, not so much in the texts themselves, but in the way those texts were produced on the stage and interpreted by the audience. As we have seen, audiences were willing to subvert the content of any spectacle: "High tragedy, which was supposed to draw tears, has degenerated into a clownish farce that excites universal laughter."[42] But there were other, less adversarial manifestations of the coexistence of comic and tragic theatricality. At the Comédie-Française, for instance, it was customary to perform a one-act comedy or farce *(la petite pièce)* in conjunction with a tragedy.[43] Moreover, at the margins of the classical theater a number of minor figures and ancient, customary practices emerged from the shadows of the backstage and, somewhat unassumingly, fulfilled their humble functions in ways that helped to keep alive the kind of mutinous theatricality that reformers such as Voltaire and Diderot were anxious to suppress.

One of those figures was the servant who extinguished the candles after the performance *(moucheur de chandelles)*, or *paillasse,* the heir of the Italian *pagliaccio* and a variant on the *zanni* Pedrolino (a kind of clown whose name meant literally "chopped straw," and the coarse fabric of his outfit also evoked that used in straw mattresses, or *paillasses*). The *paillasse* disappeared from the Comédie-Française after April 1784, when candles were replaced by a new system of illumination, the Argand burner, but he remained very much alive in the fairgrounds and boulevard theaters, where he filled the traditional function of charlatan and *aboyeur* (literally, "barker," the actor who, standing at the door, advertised as loudly as possible the spectacle inside). At the Comédie-Française the role of the *paillasse* was not limited to kindling and extinguishing the stage lights. The *paillasse* filled the space that separated the stage from the audience. Walking straight through the fourth wall, removing barriers and introducing continuity and connection where there should have been division, he acted as an intermediary between the spectators and the universe of spectacle:

> The leading actor cannot always be on stage; his attitude is always a little stiff. He might, in the long run, incite laughter if the *paillasse* did not come to deflect the audience's attention and distract it and, in so doing, strengthen the gravity of his comrade. Besides, there are in every play intervals during which no one is on stage; the *paillasse* comes in handy and fills the void. He stands in for those who are absent. When once upon a time, at the Comédie-Française, the *moucheur de chandelles* used to serve as *paillasse,* the spectators would cry, "Will he laugh, or will he not laugh?" But when the curtain was lifted, the Greek king of kings, the superb Agamemnon, seemed much more majestic. Those verses became more portentous and roaring: "Oui, c'est Agamemnon, c'est ton roi qui t'éveille;/Viens, reconnais la voix qui frappe ton oreille." Agamemnon would preserve his dignity to the end. Perhaps our modern tragedies are booed because there no longer is a *moucheur de chandelles.* The gravest things would become comical if the *paillasse* were not there to function as the butt of the public's mockery.[44]

The *paillasse,* a marginal character with no specific, explicit role, is nonetheless an institution in the theater. He belongs to the stage more than anyone else because, thanks to his capacity to turn even a trivial, everyday action into spectacle, he is the living embodiment of theatricality.[45] Like Arlequin, he is a jack-of-all-trades, a figure without a fixed *emploi* yet capable of playing any role. The *paillasse* is essentially a go-between, an intermediary who both disrupts the mood of the spectacle and makes it possible. By virtue of his insignificance, he is the only one who is allowed to communicate with the audience: "'How can we perform a play without a *paillasse?*' would cry the worried impresario. 'Who will make the audience laugh? Who will communicate with the public? Someone must communicate with it.'"[46] Like the prompter *(souffleur)*, another interloper on the tragic stage, the *paillasse,* who is always on the verge of becoming a nuisance yet absolutely necessary, functions as a foil to the tragic actor; he tames the beast of the parterre and redirects the laughter that always risks disrupting the performance. Perhaps, Mercier suggests, modern tragedies flop because the *paillasse* is no longer there to act as a lightning rod, to direct toward himself the mockeries of the parterre. The majestic Agamemnon and the crude *paillasse* are joined at the hip: the latter enables the former to come forth and deliver his overblown verses.[47] Comedy, rather than upsetting tragedy, is what makes tragedy possible; in other words, theatricality and illusion, rather than excluding each other, may well coexist as two correlated and fully integrated aspects of the spectacle.

In "Le trou du souffleur" (The Prompter's Box) Mercier deplores the intrusive presence of an individual who, rather than making himself invisible, acts as if he were the axis of the spectacle. Oblivious of his subordinate state, the *souffleur* is imbued with a sense of his own importance. It is as if, obeying a desire to revolt, the backstage were always about to flip over and expose itself to the audience, eclipsing the stage. "Like the northern star, which from its fixed point watches everything move around it," the prompter destroys all illusion. "We see the prompter's head bobbing up and down all the time. . . . During a comedy we may see the prompter roll with laughter about a double entendre, drop his score or the manuscript, and be the first to burst out loud, as if the performance were especially for him, just because he happens to be the closest to it."[48]

Before the reforms aimed at enhancing the illusion of verisimilitude were fully implemented, the classical stage allowed for great latitude in the interaction between the *scène* and the *salle*. Both spaces were generically inflected: any reference to the *salle* was comic, while the stage was the space where serious theatrical emotion could vibrate. An unexpected encounter between those two spaces might result in a clash and a bout of improvised comedy. But unless some stunning incident were to cause the play to flop (and the annals of theater are replete with them),[49] spectators could glide easily back and forth between the two. In other words, extemporaneous theatricality did not necessarily dislocate or undermine the spectacle. Comedy always accompanied drama as if its shadow, in the same way that the space of the *salle* always contaminated, or was in a relationship of complicity with, that of the *scène.* David Trott has noted that in spite of the official disdain for the "irregularity" of spectacles, *ancien régime* audiences were always able to enjoy their effect of illusion by means other than those familiar to modern audiences. "Codes functioned by metonymy or synecdoche rather than mimesis; signs stood for the object represented, and the part stood for the whole," as contemporary costume and stage directions indicate.[50]

At the Comédie-Italienne, the juxtaposition of incongruous elements was part of a repertory that normally brought together the leading men and ladies *(premiers amoureux),* who expressed themselves in lofty, sentimental language, and the masks of the commedia dell'arte, who expressed themselves in comic pantomimes *(lazzi)* and grotesque jargon, a structural feature that inspired Marivaux. Bathos was therefore an openly acknowledged comic device of Italian theatricality.[51] But at the Comédie-Française bathos came from the chance encounter between the stage and the audience. Before the spectators were removed from it, the stage was a carnivalesque world that mixed high and low, antiquity and the present, tragedy and farce; where mythical characters tripped on the moccasin of a marquis before drawing their last breath, and Phèdre and Monime were publicly exposed to all sorts of indignities from spectators who were drunk, obnoxious, or both. The serendipitous show imposed by stage spectators onto the rest of the audience had become a staple of satire, the most notorious example being Molière's portrayal of the fop who had caused such a disturbance on the stage with his late arrival in *Les fâcheux.*

In 1759, when the stage was cleared of the marquis, observers like Charles Collé and Edmond Barbier reported in their journals that everybody was thankful that theatrical illusion had been restored to its wholeness. The *Mercure de France* and the *Année littéraire* joined in to celebrate the fact that the tumultuous mingling of actors with spectators had been brought to an end. "French frivolity will no longer stand in ridiculous contrast to Roman gravity. The Marquis de *** will no longer elbow Cato," reported the *Année littéraire.*[52] "Theatrical illusion is now whole. One no longer sees Cesar wiping the powder off the wig of a spectator sitting in the first row, nor Mithridate expiring in the midst of people of our acquaintance; nor the ghost of Ninus bumping into a farmer-general; nor Camille falling dead in the wings onto Marivaux and Saint-Foix, who must shift here and there, to be a party to the assassination, and dodge the blood which spurts on them," wrote Collé.[53] The eviction of spectators was unanimously seen as a victory of antiquity over French modernity, of Roman gravity over modern levity, of order over offensive commingling. It was a victory for Voltaire's project on tragedy and for the authors' desire to preserve the autonomy and the dignity of the fictional world. The inappropriate encounters that had been taking place on the stage were precisely the kind that d'Alembert had condemned in such works as Fontenelle's *Dialogues des morts* (in which Socrates conversed with the courtesan Phryné, and Cato with Ninon de l'Enclos), Marivaux's youthful desecration of Fénelon and Homer, and Marivaux's mixture of popular (low) language and the upper register of sentimental discourse.[54] Stage impropriety mirrored the textual impropriety of parody and the satirical rewriting of the ancient canon that the moderns had been practicing for a long time.

This chorus of approval from the literary establishment notwithstanding, the removal of spectators from the stage did not put an end to the public's desire to undermine the integrity of an illusion that, by and large, was identified with the world of high tragedy, with antiquity, and with the acting style of the Comédie-Française. The parterre went on demonstrating its customary restlessness. And at the Comédie-Italienne, on the fairgrounds, at the boulevard theaters, and at the Opéra-Comique (where the same stage reforms took place in the following years), Cesar and Mithridate kept bumping into Arlequin and Smeraldine, while pages, bourgeois, soldiers, *petits marquis,* students, and theater-lovers in general continued to intrude into the performance in a variety of boisterous and troublesome ways.

In the next section, we will look more closely at one successful fairgrounds play in which parody, bathos, a self-referentiality critical of theatrical genres, and audience participation all coalesced in a memorable production that defied the authority of the theatrical institution.

Arlequin-Deucalion, *or Who Gets the Last Word?*

Besides being the age of enlightenment, the eighteenth century was also the age of parody. Of the twelve thousand plays he inventoried between 1700 and the Revolution, Clarence Brenner did not specify which were parodies or plays referencing preexisting works.[55] A few examples will give an idea of the vastness of the phenomenon. Voltaire's *Mariamne,* performed at the Comédie-Française on 6 March 1724, flopped. While Voltaire was busy writing a new version

(*Hérode et Mariamne,* performed by the Comédie-Française on 10 April 1725) the Comédie-Française produced a version by Nadal entitled *Mariamne* on 15 February 1725. Louis Fuzelier took advantage of the event to produce a parody entitled *Les quatre Mariamne* at the Foire Saint-Germain on 1 March 1725; the title evoked Voltaire's first version, that of Nadal, and two more by other authors. Riding on that wave, on 2 April Piron anticipated the launching of Voltaire's new version with his own parody, performed at the Théâtre-Italien, *Les huit Mariamne,* the title alluded to the four tragedies plus the four *Mariamne*s of Fuzelier's parody. Perhaps the most famous parody of the century was *Agnès de Chaillot,* by Pierre-François Biancolelli, which opened on 24 July 1723 at the Théâtre-Italien on the heels of the success enjoyed by La Motte's *Inès de Castro,* performed on 6 April. *Agnès* had a run of 125 performances, an exceptional number, during the first half of the century and had the distinction of acquiring a life of its own, emancipated from its hypotext. It often happened that a performance launched a cascade of parodies that drew upon one another: from the focal point of the Comédie-Française, parodies would reach the outer circles of the fairgrounds theaters. Thus, La Motte's *Romulus,* performed at the Théâtre-Français on 8 January 1722, was parodied at the Théâtre-Italien on 18 February with *Arlequin Romulus,* by Pierre-Françoise Biancolelli (known as Dominique). It was soon followed by Lesage and Fuzelier's marionettes play *Pierrot Romulus ou le ravisseur poli,* performed by Delaplace and Dolet's Marionnettes Etrangères at the Foire Saint-Germain in 1722. Close to the end of the century, Beaumarchais's *Le mariage de Figaro* sparked an explosion of parodies, all of them produced in 1784: *Les cartes parlantes ou le mariage du valet de carreau,* by Destival de Brabant, at the Théâtre des Grands-Danseurs on 19 June; *Le repentir de Figaro,* by Pariseau, at the Théâtre de l'Ambigü-Comique, on 28 June; *La folle soirée,* by Bonnefoy, at the Comédie-Italienne on 14 July; *La folle nuit,* by an anonymous author, at the Ambigü-Comique on 26 August; *Les amours de Chérubin,* by Desfontaines, at the Comédie-Italienne on 4 November; and *Le mariage par comédie,* by Dorvigny, at the Ambigü-Comique on 9 November or 20 December. Beaumarchais's case was not at all unusual; earlier in the century *opéras lyriques* had frequently generated multiple parodies (*Persée, Phaeton,* and *Roland* each had seven).[56]

As we have seen, the extraordinary vitality and longevity of the parodistic pandemic were undoubtedly owing to the peculiarities of the *ancien régime* policies on theaters, that is, to the rigid stratification of genres and venues. As repertories and acting styles were protected by parlement-enforced monopolies, theaters were prevented from performing certain genres, and each was limited to a specific kind of spectacle and manner. While the heaviest prohibitions were laid by the parlements upon the minor playhouses (the so-called *petits théâtres,* or *spectacles irréguliers*), which were not allowed to perform plays from the classical repertory and often were even forbidden to produce anything endowed with unity of action and dialogue, proscriptions cut both ways. When, in a desperate attempt to lure spectators away from the fairs, the Comédie-Française ventured, a couple of times in the first decades of the eighteenth century, to produce parodies of its own repertory, the parlement remained silent, but Parisian spectators mutinied, and the experiment ended amidst catcalls and universal scorn.[57]

But there were reasons other than legal and economic ones for the public's hunger for works that endlessly reworked, disfigured, and tore apart canonical works. It mattered little whether the hypotext (tragedy, comedy, or opera) had been successful or had flopped. The more visible an author made himself on the literary scene, the more famous or infamous his work became, the more eager audiences were to see it migrate from the center to the periphery of the theatrical world. There, they would enjoy seeing the work picked apart or simply performed in a different style and with a different medium—with puppets, pantomime, or the masks of the Italian *commedia.* Perhaps unique in the history of the European theater, French audiences of the eighteenth century, because of their continuous exposure to endless variations on the same theme, were able to develop a heightened critical sense of stylistic specificity and an appreciation for the diversity and range of acting styles, which were lost once the Revolution abolished the monopoly and introduced freedom of the theaters. It must be noted that the culture of parody could be subversive, but it could also be compatible with a conservative conception of the separation of genres and the preservation of the Aristotelian theatrical rules. Once the performance was over, carnivalesque reversals did not prevent society from returning to its previous, orderly hierarchy nor the Comédie-Française from going on declaiming its tragedies as it had always done. The commingling of genres often aimed less at reversing hierarchies than at chastising any departure from the norm.[58] There would be much to say about the role that parody played both in favor of and against the evolution of dramatic genres. For the purpose of the present argument, however, I will limit myself to discussing one relevant feature in this extraordinarily rich and still largely unexplored theatrical ethos: that the culture of parody was an extension of parterre culture. The same creative and improvisational drive that engaged the audience in a competition with the author resurfaces in parodistic reworkings; the same attention to linguistic detail and the same playfulness grounded in a mastery of codes and forms are operational here. What is more, the spectatorial practices allowed in the fairgrounds theaters enabled the audience to participate in the spectacle in ways that were far more direct and empowering than those that were tolerated in the official theaters.

I will take as an example one of the most remarkable plays written for the fairgrounds theaters, Alexis Piron's *Arlequin-Deucalion,* performed by the troupe of Francisque at the Foire Saint-Laurent on 25 February 1722. Always on the margins of literary respectability, despite several tragedies and a success-ful comedy (*La métromanie,* 1738, which spoofed Voltaire) performed by the Comédie-Française, Alexis Piron (1689–1773) never made it into the French Academy (his youthful *Ode à Priape* was brought up as an obstacle), and he was compelled to spend much of his life doing what perhaps he liked best, that is, haunting parodistic circles, writing satirical works, parodies, and libret-tos for the fairgrounds *opéra-comique.*[59] His talent as a satirist and formidable conversationalist (Grimm said that he was much better than Voltaire) won him protection and a pension from the marquis de Livry, the king's first *maître d'hôtel.* Livry hosted the meetings of the Régiment de la Calotte; Piron was also a member of the Societé du Caveau, founded by Crébillon the younger in order to write parodies of his father's works.[60]

Arlequin-Deucalion enjoyed an exceptionally successful run of thirty per-formances to packed theaters. Piron's play stands out among the repertory of the commedia dell'arte introduced in France by the Italian companies (which the fairgrounds pilfered freely after the exile of the Italians from 1697 to 1716) because it is a fully written work with little room for improvisation on the part of the performers; as such, it is better suited to canonical transmission than most traditional plays of the Théâtre-Italien. Yet, the historical context of the performance is paramount to our appreciation of this work. Embedded in the play are traces of the legal status of the *forains* and of their relationship with the audience; indeed, the dramatic drive that propels the play lies in its challenge to an authority that would muzzle the work. The troubles of the fairgrounds theater dated from the *fin de siècle* and continued, on and off, through the second half of the eighteenth century. In 1690, under the police administra-tion of La Reynie, the Comédiens-Français, who were undergoing a period of decline, had the theater of one Alexandre Bertrand, puppeteer, demolished. Bertrand had replaced his marionettes with live actors and had dared to per-form a complete comedy without permission. In the following years the *forains* tried to circumvent the prohibitions against dialogue and unity of action (an

Aristotelian rule, and as such the birthright of the Comédiens-Français) by devising a variety of creative experiments. They would perform detached scenes; mix dialogue with song (which eventually gave birth to the *opéra-comique*); mix actors with puppets; perform monologues only; combine monologue and pantomime; have actors enter the stage whenever they had to reply to one another and then exit; or have the audience sing couplets in response to the actors onstage. All of those strategies became wildly popular. Audiences flocked to the fairs in hopes of seeing the latest ploy invented to dodge the prohibitions. Police officers would be among the audience; the new stunt would be reported to the authorities; a decree would be promulgated against it; it would spur the invention of a new theatrical device; and the cycle would go on.[61] This repressive system encouraged complicity between the actors and the audience. Both came in order to engage in a ritual of transgression against the representatives of royal authority that involved collaborating with each other, testing the limits of the game and those of law enforcement. The report of a police officer dated 16 February 1712 is enlightening. The officer reports having seen a three-act comedy at the theater of Octave;[62] however, "we have noticed that no actor spoke during the play, but they used placards [*écriteaux*] instead of speech; thanks to them the dialogue was unbroken and the scenes were continuous until the end of the play, with that particularity that the parterre turned to acting: prompted by the orchestra, it lent its singing and its speech to the actors onstage."[63]

By 1721 the theater of Francisque had performed (by permission of the Royal Academy of Music) many successful *opéras-comiques*. The permission, however, was suddenly revoked, and after a period of relative laxity the prohibitions against dialogue came back into force. Lesage, Fuzelier, and d'Orneval, the principal suppliers of *opéras-comiques,* defected in frustration to Delaplace and Dolet's marionette theater, where the curtain showed a Polichinelle with the motto "J'en valons bien d'autres!" (We are no worse than them!). Piron was said to have composed *Arlequin-Deucalion* in a couple of days.[64] It was a tour de force, the response to a crisis and a challenge to the authority of the police as well as to the dictates of theatrical canon. Merging classical mythology with the masks associated with popular culture for a mixed audience familiar with the symbols of high and low theater, the play is an apparently freewheeling improvisation with scarcely any plot. Arlequin embodied Deucalion, the son of Prometheus and the only human who escaped the punitive flood that Zeus had let loose on the whole human race.

When the curtain opens, Arlequin has landed, astride a wine barrel, upon

Mount Parnassus, the residence of the Muses and the only dry spot in a thoroughly soaked world. In fact, he has landed right in the middle of a *Parnasse satirique,* that is, in the contentious space of the Parisian world of letters. In the course of his rambling monologue Arlequin interacts with a number of mythological figures, all emblematic of theatrical institutions: Melpomène, the muse of tragedy; Thalie, the muse of comedy; Apollo; Pegasus, the winged horse of poetic fancy; and Momus, the god of criticism and satire, embodied in the puppet Polichenelle. None of those characters are able to preserve any dignity or grandiosity, but according to the dictates of mock-heroic and burlesque rewriting, all are reduced to the scale of Arlequin's carnivalesque world of basic appetites and insubordination. Of all the masks [*tipi fissi*] of the commedia dell'arte, Arlequin is the most proteiform. Within the loose constraints of his type (gluttony, childish greed, sexual appetite, scatological tendencies, a disposition to deceit coupled with the greatest naïveté), he is like a crutch on which any character can be hung: king *(Arlequin roi par hasard),* emperor *(Arlequin empereur dans la lune),* mythological hero *(Arlequin Jason),* demigod *(Arlequin-Phaëton),* or even animal *(Arlequin cochon par amour).* He is pure dramatic potentiality, the embodiment of theatricality. With his black mask, always recognizable to the spectator but not to the other characters on stage, Arlequin subverts by his presence any illusion of verisimilitude.[65]

The dramatic engine of the play may be located not only in the content of Arlequin's speech but especially in his speech act. By engaging with a variety of characters, Arlequin challenges the Théâtre-Français and the parliamentary decree that forbids fairgrounds actors to engage in dialogue with one another. In a burlesque reversal, Arlequin settles his scores by turning a situation in which he alone was barred from verbal exchange into one in which he is the only speaking character in a world that has turned silent and deserted. A Pyrrhic victory, to be sure, for Arlequin no longer has an audience (a reference to the scarce attendance at opening night). "Here I am, forlorn! I am alone in this world. No one is here to answer me! No matter, I will keep on speaking, if only to preserve the habit. Ah! we are going to have a magnificent soliloquy" (act 1, sc. 1, p. 492).[66] Originally barred from speech by royal authority, Arlequin now has the last word. He is the last man and by default the one and only king. The only voices that are heard besides Arlequin's are those of Polichinelle, who, as a puppet, is allowed to engage in dialogue, and a parrot, whose repeated cries of "Hail to the king! hail to the king!" are answered by Arlequin with a "Many thanks, I am the only king here now" (act 1, sc. 2, p. 495). The parrot is the burlesque incarnation of the dove that in the Bible signaled to Noah the end of the flood, as well as the emblem of a world of letters constantly parroting itself.

Just when Arlequin has resigned himself, after the loss of his wife, Pyrrha, to limit his appetites to mere gluttony, a lady walks onto the stage. Dressed in "Roman" costume (the classical garb of the actors of the Théâtre-Français) and holding a dagger in one hand and a trumpet in the other (the attributes of tragedy and epics), she strides majestically, making faces, gesturing wildly, and uttering "Ah!" "Alas," and "Great Lord!" in the manner of tragic actresses. Wasting no time, Arlequin proposes to her. "She is scary and pathetic. Has she put on fancy rags! What gestures! what expressions! From head to toe she is nothing but convulsion. She might make me laugh every now and then. Let us approach her and cajole her into marrying us" (act 1, sc. 3, p. 496). But the muse of tragedy is unimpressed by a marriage with Arlequin's low farce. Unlike her counterparts at the Théâtre-Français, she is silent, and Arlequin is able to settle his score with the theater that has muzzled him. A loud whistle, the weapon of choice of dissatisfied audiences, is blown right into her ear: "Say something, my priggish lady! You have no reason to act so stiff. Do you realize who it is that you are rejecting? Am I not at the moment the greatest catch in the whole universe, heaven included?" (ibid., p. 498). But Melpomène remains silent. She drags her robes across the stage and exits, lugging with her a few pages ripped from the fifth act of La Motte's tragedy *Romulus,* which was then playing at the Théâtre-Français. Tragedy is a solemn fool with nothing to say. She is immediately followed by Thalie, who enters dancing and prancing, singing light airs. Unlike her predecessor, Thalie appears quite hysterical; she opens her mouth very wide and is about to speak. That is the moment everybody was expecting: "Hell! here is a tough one. Monsieur the officer, beware. I decline my responsibility. God help us with the fine!" cries Arlequin (act 1, sc. 4, pp. 498–99).

Will she or will she not speak? Will the play break the injunction against dialogue and allow the police officer to halt the spectacle and arrest the offenders? Arlequin manages to gag Thalie by placing a hand over her mouth, but the play's entire monologue is a conceit aimed at the very real presence of the representative of royal authority among the audience. Flirting with disaster, the comedy plays at teasing his power. Indeed, the play may be see as an elaborate persiflage that involves three characters: Arlequin, the embodiment of the subordinate theaters; the audience, who is his accomplice; and the victim, as it were, the royal *exempt*.[67] There are times when dialogue seems about to break but is stopped at the last moment by an ostensibly panicked Arlequin, or when Arlequin's interlocutor turns out, unexpectedly, to be legitimate (as with Polichinelle-Momus, who, being made of wood, poses no threat to the Comédiens-Français). In reality, the play's main purpose is to create situations that challenge and neutralize the power of the *exempt*.[68]

But the brunt of the satire is not aimed at the police only. It is also directed against those forms that were closely identified with a state-sponsored culture that in the eyes of many had ossified into the direst conformism. Piron, Diderot (notably in *Paradoxe sur le comedien*), and, at the end of the century, Mercier all railed against the "mannequin," the "tragic monster," the bloated "French Melpomène," who was nothing but a corpse. To Mercier, it was unfortunate that aspiring authors neglected better goals in order to turn into morticians: "To go and unearth a Greek or a Roman cadaver; to color its ashen cheeks, dress its cold limbs, raise it on its wobbly feet, and impress on those pasty eyes, on that frozen tongue, on those stiff arms, the look, the language, the mimicry that are customary on our stage—what a misuse of the mannequin!"[69] The same image of bodily decay may be found in Nicolas Racot de Grandval's *Discours préliminaire* to his *Le pot de chambre cassé* [The Broken Chamberpot] (1749). Grandval (1676–1753), who was a former actor turned satirist, saw tragedy as a swollen body ready to be punctured, as a genre that had degenerated into epic bombast and grandiloquence. "It is not possible that the sales [of the Comédie-Française] will hold for long with those cold plays that are tragedies only in name, that make us neither laugh nor cry, that impress us only with their old rags and their fake diamonds, that are a bulge swelling out of the epic poem, plays that, like dropsy, would be best taken care of with a good perforation."[70]

In *Arlequin-Deucalion* the wrongdoings of the theater have unleashed Zeus's flood. Tragedy's epic swagger has turned to muteness: "What we used to call tragedy was nothing but a mass of fifteen hundred or eighteen hundred *epidramatic* verses" (act 1, sc. 3, p. 496);[71] comedy, were it given a chance to speak, would be a grating blabberer. Much of Piron's play is a lively dramatization of the form of criticism that subtends parody. The shadowy characters that Arlequin encounters are symbols of the official theater culled from the repertory of classical emblems of high culture. The play strikes at a variety of targets. There are paraphrases of verses taken from Marivaux's *La mort d'Annibal,* Voltaire's *Artémire,* La Motte's *Issé* and *Romulus.* But it is against high theater as a whole that Arlequin unleashes his sedition. In the second act, Apollo makes an appearance as an effeminate *petit-maître* who tries to seduce Arlequin's wife, Pyrrha (who has miraculously resurfaced and is, of course, mute). Apollo plays the flute, sings vaudevilles, and leans too close to her. In a typical reversal, it is Apollo, once the symbol of the Sun King, who gets the thrashing that traditionally falls upon Arlequin's rear end. "I am the only male here. Apollo is effeminate and a fop. He has been with those nine girls for centuries, and they are still virgins" (act 2, sc. 3, p. 501). Pyrrha has descended onto the stage riding Pegasus, the winged horse, the symbol of poetic enthusiasm and Pindaric flight. But the wondrous creature has donkey's ears and the wings of a turkey; it is all covered with placards of unsuccessful plays produced by the Théâtre-Français. When Arlequin mounts it, uttering tragic verses, the horse wobbles under the weight of a particularly heavy quotation from *Artémire* and then collapses (a reminder that Voltaire's play had flopped after a few performances). Finally, Pegasus takes off thanks to the help of a hatful of water and the recital of some satirical verses by Jean-Baptiste Rousseau (act 2, sc. 4, p. 501).

But the emblems of classical theater are inseparable from the social order that nurtures them. Inevitably, Arlequin's satire widens to include the totality of the *ancien régime* hierarchical structure. In the third act, Arlequin opens the casket to discover, much to his disappointment, that it contains, not wine, but the jetsam and flotsam of a society swept away by the flood: a book of heraldry; the transcript of a lawsuit between partisans of the ancients and the moderns; a gun, which Arlequin throws into the sea; a lawsuit against the plaintiff's entire family; a bag of money; and finally a Polichinelle puppet. Only the puppet makes himself useful by revealing to Arlequin the meaning of the mysterious prophecy received by Deucalion. According to the myth, in order to recreate the human race, Deucalion and his wife will have to pick up the bones of their grandmother and throw them behind them: their grandmother, Polichinelle explains, is the earth, and stones represent her bones.

Arlequin and Pyrrha comply, but in their doing so the play demonstrates the limits of carnival. The five children who spring up, fully grown, from the earth are nothing but the representatives of the three orders of French society: a farmer and an artisan; a military man and a *robin,* or magistrate; a grotesquely dressed member of the clergy. Each one of them is welcomed differently by an Arlequin turned patriarch; each receives praise or a reprimand, according to his deserts. The soldier has his hat knocked off to punish his insolence: "Doesn't he fancy he is made of a stone more precious than the others! My lord, a little more humility" (act 3, sc. 6, p. 515). The *robin* should never have been born: "He has something wily, flaccid, and arrogant that repels; . . . I wish that when I threw that damn stone I had hurled it deep into the sea or I had got a cramp" (ibid.). The priest will reproduce himself with no need of a woman, and there will always be too many of his kind. Only the farmer and the artisan are declared useful and good. But each child will fulfill his destiny and reproduce the same social order that the flood wiped out. Arlequin seems quite resigned to seeing things resume their normal course; indeed, it does not even occur to him that they might do otherwise. (From the stones thrown by Pyrrha, four women emerge, but being female, presumably they have no rank worth mentioning, and indeed, they are not mentioned.)

Like much of the literature of the moderns, the fairgrounds spectacles were pointed critiques of the existing aesthetic and social order, but they had no utopian vision to propose, no radical departure from the status quo, no drive to reform. The critique they presented, daring as it often was, was split between the bold undermining of the symbols of monarchical culture and the resigned acceptance of the way things were, including the cherished rules of Aristotelian doctrine, the *spectacles réguliers* of the privileged theaters, and the inescapable superiority of the Comédie-Française. We might even ask to what extent the existence of a culture of parody contributed to maintaining tragedy as it was and to ensuring that it preserved its position of prestige. Comic theatricality, such as that embodied in the *paillasse,* kept alive the connection between the audience and the space of representation; it forced the fictional world to open itself up and to engage with the reality of the *salle.* But by keeping that contact on the margins, it provided the spectacle of classical tragedy with a kind of alibi, a convenient means of escaping more stringent demands. When Lesage and d'Orneval published a ten-volume collection of the best plays of the fairgrounds theater, *Théâtre de la foire ou l'Opéra Comique* (1721–37), they prefaced it with a bitter acknowledgment of their subordinate status and a good dose of persiflage:

> It is not with the intent to challenge the immortal masterpieces that ensure the superiority of the Théâtre-Français above all the other theaters of the world that we publish this collection today. We do not even wish to be compared to the two other authorized theaters, even though they too do not always follow Aristotelian principles. It is in order to transmit to posterity a memorial testifying to the different forms taken by the fairgrounds theater. "A wasted effort," will say those who judge of a work by the site of its performance. "Why publish those wretched poems? Is it so as to remind the public of the shameful taste it had for them? The mere title fairgrounds theater implies something low and vulgar that will disgrace the book." . . . Some manufacturers of tragedies and lyric poems will say, seeing the simplicity of our subjects, that they must have taken little effort. They ought to be more cautious. It is not easy to find a middle ground between high and low, to fly

low to the ground without touching it. The sublime is no more difficult to capture than the art of teasing the mind with humor.[72]

Mixing authorial pride with humility, Lesage, d'Orneval, and Piron knew that there was no prestige and no status to be gained for writers of second-tier theaters, regardless of the quality of their spectacles, and that even if the king himself had occasionally hosted marionette shows at court, comedy, let alone farce, was always going to be held as inferior to tragedy. Unlike Voltaire, his lifelong rival, Piron was never elected to the Academy, but remained a minor author despite having written tragedies for the Comédie-Française and successful *comédies regulières.* The epitaph Piron wrote for himself was representative of a whole class of talented authors who by choice or by necessity remained on the margins:

> Here lies . . . Who? By God, a nonentity, a zero.
> Someone who was neither a lackey nor a master;
> Neither a judge, nor an artisan nor a tradesman;
> Nor a farmer, a soldier, a magistrate, a priest;
> Nor a Freemason. He chose to be nothing.
>
> Here lies Piron, who was nothing at all;
> Not even a member of the Academy.[73]

Marivaux, who in his youth had practiced a genre that was typical of low literature, that is, the mock-heroic satire of high epics, and who regularly attended the fairgrounds spectacles, denied the paternity of his early works and never acknowledged being the author of plays like the wonderfully unconventional *Le triomphe de Plutus* (performed by Dominique at the Théâtre-Italien in 1728), very likely inspired by an *opéra-comique* by Dupuy performed at the Foire Saint-Germain on 15 July 1721 by the company of Lalauze, Pierre Alard, and Mlle d'Aigremont. Diderot, who wrote a sketch for an *opéra-comique* set among the fairgrounds stalls,[74] nonetheless despised the culture of the *petits théâtres* because it was commercial and successful. In his writings on the Salons he all but called the actress and *opéra-comique* singer Mme Favart a prostitute. He never mentioned that the pantomime he nostalgically associated with the Greeks was alive and flourishing on the lowly *tréteaux* of the fairgrounds.[75] Even though the uncanny mimic abilities of Rameau's nephew can be better understood in light of the careers of the gifted actors and mimes of the fairs (such as Nicolas Vienne, also known as Beauvisage, the founder of the Théâtre des Associés),[76] the memory of those artists did not deserve being transmitted to posterity; but then again, the nephew was immersed in a satirical subculture that Diderot had portrayed as repugnant and corrupt. To Diderot, the divide between the *grand goût* and the *petit goût* corresponded, to a great extent, to that between *grands* and *petits spectacles,* between sublime entrancement and an inferior, commercially oriented comedy that grew as a parasitical tumor out of the dignified endeavors of the official theaters. In his eyes, salvation for the theater was to come not from below, that is, not from the "irregular" spectacles that the public loved, nor from the unruly activities of the parterre, but from above, from a more enlightened involvement of the state in cultural affairs and from renewed state patronage. Diderot envisioned vast, national amphitheaters, not a multitude of private, independent ventures. That wish was partially realized in the revolutionary reform of the theaters. But when freedom from the constraints of privilege and monopoly finally came in January 1791, it was at the price of stringent regulation and control of the content of spectacles. The Terror finally succeeded in purging, at least for a while, the boulevards and the *opéra-comique* of all vestiges of undignified, impious laughter.[77]

Epilogue: The Costume
of Modernity

We must speak about modern things in the antique manner.

—Diderot

The lively theatrical culture that was reflected in the activities of the parterre was a sign that insubordinate forms of theatricality were being enacted throughout the eighteenth century, despite the playwrights' (and the authorities') attempts to channel and control the audience's response. I have defined such theatricality as the effect of a heightened awareness of forms, as the knowledge that those forms were rooted in the monarchy's (and the authors') appropriation of the culture of antiquity for purposes of self-representation, legitimation, and enhancement; hence the desire to deflect them through parodistic reformulations and reappropriations. A symbiotic relationship developed between the cultural categories of classicism, with its rationalization of forms and its cult of antiquity, and the subversions and parodies of the *goût moderne*.[1]

The philosophes' antitheatrical, neoclassical stance made them wary of such attempts, which they saw as decadent manifestations of a subculture mired in commercialism, mannerism, and inauthenticity. They could not detect in the ferment of the parterres and in the ventures of the fairgrounds playhouses an echo of their own yearnings for change and renewal. While on the one hand the philosophes were suspicious of the disorderly stylistic experimentation that was manifest in parterre activities, on the other they were themselves concerned with breaking loose from the shackles of classical forms as they knew them and with inventing a new language for the arts. Reform was their mantra and their passion. Whereas Voltaire devoted much of his life to reworking the tragedy from within—tinkering here and there, rewriting *Oedipus,* competing now with Corneille, now with Sophocles, in a struggle that he saw as titanic but one that only gained him, as a playwright, a truncated immortality—Diderot attacked the problem from without. In the *Entretiens sur Le fils naturel* he not only invented a new genre that transcended the distinction between comedy and tragedy but also proposed radical reforms of the role of language and visualization on the stage. In a visionary stroke he imagined the birth of what was to become romantic opera and ballet. The theater and the visual arts had been Diderot's (and the philosophes') favorite ground for experimentation and reform. Since the mid-seventeenth century the theater had been held up as not only the highest form of poetic expression, as the most prestigious career for a writer, but also as the best and most effective way to reach a wide audience in real time, hitting it with the irresistible force of ancient oratory. In the theater, the philosophes argued, words became action and tears; rhetoric shaded into drama and good intentions aroused authentic emotion. But in their search for a universal language of the emotions that would overcome dissension and apathy, they cast a disapproving eye toward the medley of idioms, the fragmentation of languages, that fermented in the struggling theaters the audiences loved.

The philosophes were chronically dissatisfied with themselves, even as they cherished dreams of unprecedented relevance to society, and with the rationalizing powers of philosophy, which they (with the exception of Condorcet) saw as antithetical to the arts.[2] Voltaire (who was less happy than he would seem to Barthes) was largely responsible for inventing the myth of *le Grand Siècle,* as well as that of the decadence of his own age.[3] Highly civilized people, Diderot lamented, no longer created; they were too self-conscious. They wrote poetics, criticism, methodologies, and grammars.[4] And indeed, write criticism and dream about poetics they did. Voltaire, d'Alembert, Marmontel, Thomas, and Mercier wrote extensively about grammar, stylistics, the social role of the writer, and the function of art. Voltaire perhaps devoted more energy to his work as a critic than to the rest of his numerous activities. Diderot spent much time mulling over a reform of the arts. While only a couple of his plays became public, he dedicated himself to imagining countless others, which he sketched in his notebooks; he also liked to compose in his imagination large canvases, which he would lovingly describe in his *Salons,* and which he would propose as subjects to the painters he befriended.[5] The sketch, or *esquisse,* was the genre that he favored above all others because it promised much to the imagination;

it suggested everything, while it remained preserved from the curse of labor and manner and from the descent into form. It would be accurate to describe *Jacques le fataliste* as a vast canvas composed entirely of sketches.[6] The art of the philosophes was one of the *esquisse*. It thrived on potentiality; it was an art to come. The arts and the public would engender each other: the arts had to take a vanguard role in creating the ideal public, which alone could appreciate the new productions that would be made for it.[7] Art professed a commitment to reality and to service in the public sphere, but it did not reproduce reality; rather, it was devoted to reinventing it. While the philosophes did not generate great poetry, they became the poets of their unimpeachable ambitions; they reinvented themselves in their function as writers, patriots, intellectuals, republican orators. Like Mme de Merteuil, they engendered themselves and became their own creation.

The sublime they invoked sought to eliminate all mediation so that their eloquent art would become pure engagement with the real, but it was a poetic reality shaped by the literary memories of their *collège* days. The philosophes were caught between two kinds of greatness, both of which they thought were out of their reach: that of past masters, and that of the future generations that philosophy would engender. They had to be content with acting as midwives. Eloquence would make the real happen; it would recreate the world to the size of the artist's soul, which must be vast, ardent, and pure enough to raise the public to the level of his imagination. Artistic excellence was conflated with the cult of ancient virtue, and the artist was called upon to embody in the eyes of the public the civic and moral values that inspired the greatness of ancient art and civilization.[8] In the ideology of the sublime, the artist must personify the qualities that he represents in his art: he cannot represent great men without being one himself.[9] That is a belief that Diderot puts forth in his eulogy on Richardson and that he never quite abandons, despite his sojourn in the hell of *Rameau's Nephew.*

All renewal had to be a return to the origins, to the rejuvenating sources of Sophocles, Homer, Virgil, Demosthenes. Diderot did not refrain from engaging in a bit of deception now and then, ventriloquizing Sophocles, making Philoctetes sound very much like a dutiful father in a *drame bourgeois.* Yet the cult of antiquity pervades his work; the "simplicity" and "naïveté" of the ancient text remained a constant, if elusive, reference. In the pages of the *Salons* Diderot upbraided rococo artists for neglecting to acquaint themselves with the spirit of the classical texts on which their paintings were based; his reprimands were all the more stern as they were prevented from reaching their targets.

The aversion Diderot felt for the modern French ethos was symptomatic of the late Enlightenment process of abstraction, through which artists sought to reach the basic and elemental sources of beauty. That process, which led *drame* playwrights and painters to favor the representation of basic and primordial conflicts—death, sacrifice, violence, revenge—made any reconciliation with the ephemeral, mundane, and mortal quality of reality very problematic. "If our painters and sculptors were henceforth to be obliged to draw their subjects from the history of modern France . . . then painting and sculpture would soon fall into decadence."[10] The modern was by definition unrepresentable; unrepresentability and Frenchness were one and the same. A prejudice of exoticism would draw Diderot to compare the contemporary French costume with that of peoples of the Orient, whom he saw as happily uncontaminated by modernity:

> What's shabbier, more barbarous, more tasteless than French garments, than the dresses of our women? Tell me, what beauty could possibly result if trussed-up dolls like that were introduced into a composition? What a fine effect that would produce, especially in tragic subjects! How to confer upon them even a hint of nobility, of grandeur? In contrast to the dress of Orientals, Asians, Greeks, and Romans, it reveals the talent of the skillful painter and highlights the limits of the mediocre one.[11]

We might assume that for Diderot everything held together and that the main reason why he despised the modern costume was that he saw it as the outer layer of an inner, moral disintegration. However, we cannot but suspect that occasionally it was the clothes that made the man and that giving Caesar a marquis's outfit would have been enough to diminish his character, to turn him into a fairgrounds puppet.[12] Indeed, much in the spirit of a fairgrounds parodist, Diderot sometimes imagines burlesque cross-dressing scenarios: "Deck out Caesar, Alexander, Cato with our hats and wigs, and you'll split your sides laughing." Conversely, putting the most depraved of French kings in a toga would do wonders for his dignity: "If you dress Louis XV in Greek or Roman dress, you won't laugh at all."[13] At times, seeming to forget his own lessons about the uses of antiquity as an artistic ideal, Diderot lets himself fall into outright kitsch, that is, into a sentimentalized aesthetics made of parts pieced together, of fragments detached from their original context and stuck haphazardly onto something foreign to them. His commentary on Noël Hallé's *Minerve conduisant la paix à l'Hôtel de Ville* illustrates that tendency. Diderot utterly despises this painting, as he does most allegorical paintings exposed at the Salon. "One has the impression that Monsieur the Provost of the Trade

Guilds is inviting Minerva and Peace to take chocolate." Yet, he suggests, there might be a way to rescue it from the contempt it richly deserves:

> This picture is laughable; it's an assemblage of overscale doctors and apothecaries perfect for a production of *Le medecin malgré lui*. But move the scene from Paris to Rome, from the city hall to the senate; for these damn red and black sacks crowned with wigs, with their silk stockings diligently secured above the knee, their fancy collars, and their heeled shoes, substitute grave figures with long beards, their heads, arms, and legs unadorned, their chests exposed, wearing long, flowing, ample consular robes; assign the same subject to the same utterly mediocre painter, and you'll see what an interesting, satisfying thing he could make of it.[14]

Antiquity is a formula that can be easily applied, the result almost guaranteed. All one needs is a few touches: removing high heels and stockings, adding a beard, baring a chest. If a few such corrections here and there may morph a mediocre painter into a competent one, and a bad picture into a moving scene, then the modern world, no matter how mediocre and despoiled, may be dressed in ancient drag and rescued from its pit of depravity. Thus, not unlike the Goncourt brothers, who recommended cultivating an *artistic* manner, Diderot recommends cultivating an *antique* one. A touch of superstitious idolatry toward the customs and ceremonies of antiquity—the same that will inspire the revolutionaries to dunk contemporary France into the republican fountain of youth[15]—leads him to associate a certain aesthetics of manners with the sublime and to invest the ancient costume with socially therapeutic powers:

> One rarely becomes a great writer, a great man of letters, a man of reformed taste [*grand goût*] without making a close study of the ancients. There is a simplicity in Homer and Moses about which one would perhaps have to say what Cicero said of Regulus's return to Carthage: "Laus temporum, non hominis": it is more the result of contemporary morals than of individual genius. Peoples with these practices, these robes, these ceremonies, these laws, these customs *could not have another tone*. But it existed, this tone that cannot be invented; that's precisely where we should look, in view of transporting it to our own time, which, while very corrupt or very mannered, is still enamored of simplicity. *We must speak about modern things in the antique manner* [*il faut parler des choses modernes à l'antique*].[16]

Laws, practices, and customs are coextensive with robes and ceremonies, for there is a correlation between politics, manners, publicly displayed symbols, and taste. The same reaction that makes Diderot recoil at the representation of the modern body, both in outfit and manner, draws him, with a touching faith, to the costume of antiquity: if only its appearance, its tone, its baffling simplicity could be transported to his own time, perhaps some radical change might follow. This fetishistic cult of ancient taste prefigures the *anticomanie* of the revolutionaries, who in November 1793 decided to replace the "royalist" images on playing cards with icons of republicanism. Thus the kings were replaced with Brutus, Cato, Solon, and Rousseau (dressed in a toga); the queens with four virtues (Prudence, Unity, Justice, and Fortitude); and the valets with four Roman heroes (Hannibal, Mucius Scaevola, Horace, and Decius Mus). (As we know, it is not one of the minor paradoxes of the Revolution that the event that is credited with the birth of modern democracy should have been steeped in the iconography of antiquity, or, even further removed in time, that of myth.)

The artistic sensitivities of the late Enlightenment were not turned toward the pursuit of the time-driven, contingent appeal of *je ne sais quoi,* but rather toward the cultivation of an ideal beauty abstracted from its environment and made absolute. Diderot's conception of mimesis is revealing. Although, as some critics have noted, his discussion of the *modèle idéal* seems to come close to a Platonist ideal of perfection, in fact his conception of art is willing to embrace imperfection and deformity, but only on the condition that the artist be able to reveal the underlying, essential logic that produced them. Beneath the multitude of apparently random and haphazard malformations, the law of nature works in secret but permanent ways: "Nature does nothing that is not correct. Every form, whether beautiful or ugly, has its cause, and of all extant beings there isn't a single one that is not just as it should be"; that is equally true of a blind woman or of the twisted body of a hunchback.[17] It is up to the artist to decipher and reveal their occult law. A process of abstraction, a reduction of complexity in favor of strongly outlined conflicts, must inform all representation of evanescent, chance-driven reality so as to bring its timeless, universal dimension to the fore. The one thing that Diderot truly cannot abide, the one feature that would condemn all representation to insignificance and triviality, is the incorporation into the artwork of the fleeting, ephemeral moment: "A laughing portrait is without nobility, lacking in character, sometimes even devoid of truth, and consequently quite silly. Laughter is fleeting. One laughs at something specific, but susceptibility to laughter is not an essential character trait."[18] It is significant that the aspect that Diderot singles out as emblematic of things ephemeral is laughter, which he sees not only as a fleeting mood but as the theatrical awareness of the spectator's presence in the picture and as a manifestation of mincing mannerism (like the "smile" that floats on Diderot's lips in his 1767 portrait by Van Loo). In its transient quality, laughter, like clothing, is the emblem of a modernity that speaks to the senses but not to the soul, that gives fleeting pleasure but no true emotion, that is made of composite and indefinite elements rather than starkly dramatic ones. The reference to antiquity, in contrast, has become the foundation for a kind of beauty that rests upon the expression of boldly stated passions. It is a guarantor of universality and permanence akin to the immutability of nature's order and conducible to the quest for the elusive *modèle idéal*. Of course, neither the antique nor the modern was a known quantity; the former was supposed to ground the latter, but both were uncertain and ideal, their language yet to be (re)discovered.

It was not until Baudelaire's own Salon writings that it became possible to imagine an encounter between, on the one hand, a universal, abstract beauty emancipated from the constraints of mimesis and normative references to nature and, on the other hand, a newly rediscovered, modern, emotionally and narratively complex aesthetics of the transitory and the contingent. "He makes it his business to extract from fashion whatever element it may contain of poetry within history, to distil the eternal from the transitory."[19] To Baudelaire, who no longer shared the linear narrative of the cyclical rise and fall of civilizations, modernity (the word was still a neologism in his time)[20] was a concept relative to the situation of the beholder; in fact, modernity was not unique but multiple and indefinitely recurrent:

> Every old master has had his own modernity; the great majority of fine portraits that have come down to us from former generations are clothed in the costume of their own period. They are perfectly harmonious, because everything—from costume and coiffure down to gesture, glance and smile (for each age has a deportment, a glance, a smile of its own)—everything, I say, combines to form a completely vibrant whole. This transitory, fugitive element, whose metamorphoses are so rapid, must on no account be despised or dispensed with. By neglecting it, you cannot fail to tumble into the abyss of an abstract and indeterminate beauty, like that of the first woman before the fall of man.[21]

Baudelaire's embrace of modern costume rested upon the belief (shared by Diderot) that there was an organic, necessary relation between the fashion, the manners, and the spirit of a particular time. But while Baudelaire celebrated the metamorphosis of the fugitive as being vital to the creative process, Diderot recoiled from it. Because he too was convinced that the costume of the modern age reflected its manners and values, his disgust for contemporary fashion was the symptom of an intense, visceral rebellion against contemporary civilization, a comprehensive, all-embracing aversion. Diderot did not look at his time as a poet or as an artist: he looked through it, as a utopian and a visionary. The price to pay for that attitude, as Baudelaire would have it, was an art deprived of sensuality, imperfection, and mortality, an art that was angelic and insipid, like Eve before she sinned.

If we have become inured to the radical oddity of such an attitude, it is because for a long time we have envisioned the Revolution, not as the result of a political crisis and the outcome of a specific political culture, but as the ultimate outburst of a crisis of civilization—a civilization so decadent and servile, as one Salon pamphleteer put it, that it did not deserve having its portrait taken. (Incidentally, the pamphleteer in question was also a court portraitist and a reputed *bel esprit*.)[22] But what if such a crisis of civilization were nothing but an indictment a posteriori, or the effect of a political discourse emerging from certain tendencies within the Enlightenment? As Keith Baker has shown, the notion of crisis, together with organic metaphors of vigor and weakness, health and sickness, was central to the discourse of classical republicanism in its French form; in the ideology of crisis, the life of the republic was always hanging in the balance, always dependent for its salvation on an effort of political will.[23] Debates about the decadent state of culture and the arts in the late Enlightenment must be seen as by-products of that political consciousness. When Diderot writes that the fate of the nation's taste and morals is poised on the edge of the abyss, when he fantasizes that salvation that may come in the form of a violent rediscovery of barbarity, we tend to view his assessment as a reaction to a factual situation of crisis. Instead we should see it for what it actually is: the expression of passionate, if not quite lucid, participation to the pervasive discourse of republicanism, which by that time had become the politically correct jargon among the intellectuals.

The paradox of the *goût moderne* consisted of course in the fact that it soon came to be seen as anything but modern. Instead, the true moderns seemed to be those new intellectuals—the philosophes—who were willing radically to rethink the task of the writer along morally and socially messianic ways. While they borrowed their rallying cries from the language of classical republicanism and their self-image from archaic conceptions of the artist as republican orator, the philosophes were modern insofar as they believed that their work would contribute to refashioning society, to giving birth to a new, enlightened, and engaged public, and in a general, if rather fuzzy, way to making things better and more equitable. In this protracted battle between the ancients and the out-moded *modernes,* the latter seemed to have been left behind; the Revolution drew its symbols and its inspiration largely from the ancients of the *nouvelle vague.*

Yet, the untimely *modernes* of the 1720s and 1730s were moderns too, and in a way that may seem more congenial to us. True, they had lingered on the wrong side of history; they had been "blown away by the powerful gust of philosophy," as Grimm put it; they had outlived their reputation, as Diderot declared. However, in the resistance their work opposed to the new creed and style, in their imperviousness to all utopias, they were, as Antoine Compagnon has said of postrevolutionary and twentieth-century *antimod-ernes* (countermoderns), the true moderns, because they lived on the edge of uncertainty; in their skepticism and wariness, they were not the dupes of modern doctrines and dogmas.[24] Of course, the boundaries were not clearly drawn between the two factions of moderns; there was much intermingling, trespassing, misunderstanding, and being at cross-purposes. The Enlighten-ment, far from being a coherent and unified doctrine, was the result of such tensions and strains.

While someone like Marivaux opposed a tenacious resistance to the new trends, passing for outmoded and idiosyncratic, Montesquieu could be easily co-opted by the ancients of the *nouvelle vague* and even by revolutionary dis-course (now and then fragments of his lines and echoes of his turns of phrase pop up in Robespierre's speeches). Yet Montesquieu, in tune with the ethos of the belated *modernes,* would have remained fundamentally a dissenter (and he probably would have emigrated). He was a skeptic who harbored no illusions about the innate goodness of human nature. He may have been fascinated by republican virtue, but he never dreamed that it could be resuscitated within the contemporary *polis.* The man who had put much effort into devising ways for setting limits and boundaries to the exercise of political will would have been appalled by the idea of a government based upon the exercise of unfet-tered general will. Indeed, Montesquieu's awareness that a shadowy area within the self would forever remain resistant to the light of reason made him espe-cially wary of angelic political plans. As we know, he placed little faith in vir-tue and much trust in articulated political institutions and division of power. Hence this prophetic warning:

> By a misfortune attached to the human condition, great men who are mod-erate are rare; and, as it is always easier to follow one's strength than to check it, perhaps, in the class of superior people, it is easier to find extremely

virtuous people than extremely wise men. The soul takes such delight in dominating other souls; even those who love the good love themselves so much that there is no one fortunate enough not to have to distrust his good intentions; and, in truth, our actions depend on so many things that it is a thousand times easier to do good than to do it well.[25]

A similarly disenchanted belief lies at the core of Marivaux's profound skepticism concerning those virtues that would be extolled by Rousseau and by the Revolution: transparency, sincerity, moral rigorism, and clarity. Nothing in Marivaux's world is ever endowed with absolute moral or political clarity, for he considered absoluteness inhuman, hypocritical, foolish, or a combination thereof. In his utopian comedy *L'île des esclaves* (1725), masters and servants are compelled, by the will of Trivelin turned legislator, to switch places and to play each other's roles, but such playacting, which at the hands of a Delisle de la Drevetière, a Mercier, or a Marmontel would have been the occasion for many an earnest speech about equality and justice for all, has quite a different purpose here.[26] If the masters-turned-slaves must be enlightened about the vices that belong to their privileged condition, conversely the servants-turned-masters have to be purged of the resentment and the yearning for revenge that is part and parcel of their subordinate status. In the end, even though both sides have been healed of their dependence on each other, the world they return to has not been radically transformed; evil and inequality have not been eradicated. In *La double inconstance* (1723) the "sincere" (but comically self-deceived) Arlequin cannot resist the temptation to deliver a few pointed aphorisms in his incarnation as a naïve and good "savage," but he is also quite willing to shed that role in order to become the prince's favorite and marry a scheming courtier. In Marivaux's novels, social prejudice and the bigotry of rank weigh most heavily, not in the minds of the nobles, but in those of the petit bourgeois: his churchwardens, stewards, and petty officials already prefigure the fatuous obtuseness of a M. Homais. As for Diderot, when he was not perched on his pontifical soapbox, he would write like a *moderne* of the first hour, in a skeptical, self-reflexive, ironic, fragmented, discontinuous, and digressive mode, a problematic style unreconcilable with sublime pathos and earnest advocacy. Like Voltaire, who consigned to eternity his extemporaneous, epistolary self, Diderot lovingly crafted and preserved his correspondence with Sophie Volland, the minute, intimate chronicle of his states of mind and fleeting fervors. The emblem of the age was not the talented Rameau but his nephew: the artist bereft of an artwork, who vented his resentment and despair through parody and satire. Diderot himself could never decide whether he wanted to be Socrates, who rejected the law of the state for the sake of moral law and died, or Aristippe, who bowed to the authority of bad laws for the sake of public order and lived happily ever after.[27] He settled for Seneca, who tried being both. As for Voltaire's style, in such texts as the *Lettres philosophiques* and the *Contes* it was propelled, not by a desire for the monumental and the eternal, but by the provocation of *esprit* and *saillie*. It was made up, "like a conversation, of discontinuous witty shafts that erode a position without confronting it directly, and indicate one without defining it."[28]

For the Enlightenment *modernes* did not believe in the revolutionary possibility of establishing a radically new *civitas terrena*. They were antitheoretical and wary of systems; they tinkered around the edges; they were restless and uncomfortable with all doctrines, defining themselves only in light of what they repudiated; they had no plan. Such a mind-set would be swept away by history, but they had literature on their side.

Notes

Introduction

Epigraphs: Charles Pinot Duclos, *Considérations sur les moeurs de ce siècle* (1751), ed. Carole Dornier (Paris: Champion, 2000), 106; Denis Diderot, *The Salon of 1767,* vol. 2 of *Diderot on Art,* trans. John Goodman (New Haven, CT: Yale University Press, 1995), 170, translation modified. Unless otherwise noted, all translations are mine.

1. Robert Darnton, "Philosophers Trim the Tree of Knowledge: The Epistemological Strategy of the Encyclopédie," in *The Great Cat Massacre and Other Episodes in French Cultural History* (New York: Basic Books, 1984; New York: Vintage Books, 1985), 191–213; Darrin M. McMahon, *Enemies of the Enlightenment: The French Counter-Enlightenment and the Making of Modernity* (Oxford: Oxford University Press, 2001).

2. Marcel Proust, *À l'ombre des jeunes filles en fleur (In the Shadow of Young Girls in Flower),* trans. James Grieve (London: Allen Lane, 2002), 48.

3. Louis-Sébastien Mercier, *Du théâtre, ou nouvel essai sur l'art dramatique,* in Mercier, *Mon bonnet de nuit, suivi de Du théâtre* (1784–85), ed. Jean-Claude Bonnet and Pierre Frantz (Paris: Mercure de France, 1999), 1212, emphasis in the original.

4. Jean Le Rond d'Alembert, *Eloge de Marivaux* (1785), in Pierre Carlet de Chamblain de Marivaux, *Théâtre complet,* ed. Jacques Scherer and Bernard Dort (Paris: Seuil, 1964), 22.

5. See Diderot's commentary on Boucher in Denis Diderot, *Salon de 1761,* in *Essais sur la peinture: Salons de 1759, 1761, 1763* (Paris: Hermann, 1984), 120. See also his *Eloge de Richardson* (1762), in *Oeuvres esthétiques,* ed. Paul Vernière (Paris: Garnier, 1968).

6. "A kind of metaphysics of the heart has taken hold of our theaters," wrote Jean Le Rond d'Alembert in his *Discours préliminaire* to *Encyclopédie, ou dictionnaire raisonné des sciences, des arts et des métiers,* ed. Denis Diderot and Jean Le Rond d'Alembert, 32 vols. (Paris, 1751–77), 1 (1751): xxxi. By *metaphysics* he meant pretentious nonsense.

7. On the onslaught against the amateur in midcentury and the decline of the aesthetic values of the early eighteenth century see René Démoris, "Le comte de Caylus et la peinture: Pour une théorie de l'inachevé," *Revue de l'art,* no. 142 (2003): 31–43.

8. Remy G. Saisselin, "Diderot from Outside the Research Machine: Recontextualizing Diderot," *Studies on Eighteenth-Century Culture* 16 (1986): 241–50.

9. Voltaire, *Questions sur l'Encyclopédie* (1771), s.v. "Beau," in *Oeuvres complètes de Voltaire*, ed. Louis Moland, 52 vols. (Paris: Garnier, 1877–85), 18:24.

10. See Thomas Crow, *Painters and Public Life in Eighteenth-Century Paris* (New Haven, CT: Yale University Press, 1985), 39–40.

11. Pierre Carlet de Chamblain de Marivaux, in his one-act comedy *Le triomphe de Plutus*, performed at the Théâtre-Français on 22 April 1728, published in Marivaux, *Théâtre complet*, ed. Henri Coulet and Michel Gilot, 2 vols. (Paris: Gallimard, 1993), 1:575–601.

12. Duclos, *Considérations sur les moeurs de ce siècle*, 178.

13. Voltaire, *Le temple du goût*, ed. Elie Carcassonne (Geneva: Droz, 1938), 67.

14. Ibid., 64.

15. La Font de Saint-Yenne, *Réflexions sur quelques causes de l'état présent de la peinture en France, avec un examen des principaux ouvrages exposés au Louvre le mois d'août 1746* (1747; Geneva: Slatkine Reprints, 1970), 44–45. On La Font see René Démoris and Florence Ferran, *La peinture en procès: L'invention de la critique d'art au siècle des Lumières* (Paris: Presses de la Sorbonne Nouvelle, 2001). The king's artworks were first publicly exhibited in 1750 at the Louvre.

16. Diderot, *Salon of 1767*, 8. In the *Encyclopédie* article "Gens de lettres" Voltaire argued that Louis XIV's patronage had intellectually emancipated writers of small means, freeing them from humiliating dependence on the grandees. See Diderot and d'Alembert, *Encyclopédie*, 7 (1757): 599.

17. Diderot, *Salon of 1767*, 252.

18. "'Little rascal, whom will you imbue with grandeur, solemnity, and majesty if not Religion, Justice and Truth?' 'But,' the artist responds, 'these virtues will serve as overdoors for an administrator in the Department of Finance.'" Ibid., 47. "Vien paints nothing but overdoors. Boucher paints garbage for the boudoir of a grandee. . . . There are pictures lined up from Versailles all the way to the bottom of the faubourg Saint-Marceau, but not a single good painting." Denis Diderot, "Du luxe," in *Mélanges pour Catherine II*, in *Oeuvres*, ed. Laurent Versini, vol. 3, *Politique* (Paris: Robert Laffont, 1995), 295. Joseph-Marie Vien's painting *Saint Denis prêchant la foi en France* (Saint Denis Preaching the Faith in France), of 1767, in the style of *grand goût*, had been praised by Diderot for its "harmony" but blamed by him for its lack of interest, imagination, and "ideal." See Diderot, *Salon of 1767*, 28–39.

19. Diderot, *Salon of 1767*, 6–9. On the role of amateurs and art collectors in the eighteenth century see Rémy G. Saisselin, "Neo-Classicism: Images of Public Virtue and Realities of Private Luxury," *Art History* 4, no. 1 (1981): 14–36.

20. Neoclassicism was in reality nurtured among the financial elites close to Louis XV. It was the powerful financiers Lenormand de Tournehem and the Marquis de Marigny, respectively the natural father and the brother of Mme de Pompadour—both directors of the *bâtiments du roi*, of which the Academy of Painting

and Sculpture was a part—who moved the Academy in the direction of the *grand goût* and classicist narratives. On the other hand, the circle of Mme de Pompadour also favored rococo style and Boucher.

21. Jürgen Habermas, *The Structural Transformation of the Public Sphere: An Inquiry into a Category of Bourgeois Society* (Cambridge, MA: MIT Press, 1989).

22. Voltaire, "Gens de lettres." See Roger Chartier, "The Man of Letters," in *Enlightenment Portraits*, ed. Michel Vovelle, trans. Lydia G. Cochrane (Chicago: University of Chicago Press, 1997), 142–89.

23. "The anti-Rococo program itself was, in its rejection of the sensual, abundant, and worldly, as much a denial of popular impulses and pleasures as it was of the private tastes of the rich and the court." Crow, *Painters and Public Life,* 130–31.

24. Jean-François Marmontel, speech delivered to the French Academy on 20 June 1776, www.academie-francaise.fr/immortels/discours_reponses/marmontel .html. In the *Encyclopédie* article "Parterre" Marmontel notes approvingly that the lack of cultural pretentiousness of theatrical audiences in the pit exposes them to being manipulated by enlightened intellectuals: "They follow the impulsion that is given to them, and they form one mind and one soul with those who, being more enlightened, make them feel and think." *Supplément à l'Encyclopédie* (Amsterdam, 1776), 4:241.

25. Jean Le Rond d'Alembert, *Essai sur la société des gens de lettres et des grands, sur la réputation, sur les Mecènes, et sur les récompenses littéraires* (1753; 2nd ed., 1764), in *Oeuvres de d'Alembert,* vol. 4 (Paris: A. Belin/Bossange Frères, 1822), 374.

26. Duclos, *Considérations sur les moeurs de ce siècle,* 194–95.

27. Duclos wrote: "They become amateurs of *bel esprit,* they advertise their taste; it is their shop sign; they look for things to read, they meddle, they offer support and advice without being asked and without having any right to do so." Ibid., 195. On Louis-Petit de Bachaumont and Anne-Claude Philippe de Tubières, comte de Caylus, see Crow, *Painters and Public Life,* chap. 4.

28. Jean de La Bruyère, "De la société et de la conversation," sec. 75, in *Les caractères* (1688; reprint, Paris: Classiques Garnier, 1990), 175–76.

29. Charles Pinot Duclos, *Acajou et Zirphile* (1744), ed. Jean Dagen (Paris: Desjonquières, 1993). The one-act vaudeville *Acajou et Zirphile* was performed on 28 September 1744 at the Foire Saint-Laurent and eventually was made into a three-act opera by Charles-Simon Favart.

30. Throughout the eighteenth century primarily aristocratic behavioral ideals shaped the identity of the *homme de lettres:* "Rather than looking forward to more modern ideas of social prominence based on property and ownership, eighteenth-century men [and women] of letters looked backward in time, adopting Renaissance strategies of self-fashioning to define themselves as socially prominent and therefore as authorized to speak publicly." Gregory S. Brown, *A Field of Honor:*

Writers, Culture, and Public Theater in French Literary Life from Racine to the Revolution (New York: Columbia University Press, 2002), 24, www.gutenberg-e.org. On the patriotic writer, see ibid., chap. 3.

31. "We may consider that false love of *bel esprit*, which protects ignorance and prides itself on it and which will sooner or later spread it far and wide, as one of the major causes pushing us headlong into barbarism. That will be the result and the endpoint of bad taste. . . . It is to the obsession for *bel esprit* and to the abuse of philosophy that we must attribute our present sluggishness and the decadence of good taste." D'Alembert, *Discours préliminaire*, xxxii–xxxiv.

32. Gita May, "Neoclassical, Rococo, or Preromantic? Diderot's Esthetic Quest," in *Diderot, Digression, and Dispersion,* ed. Jack Undank and Herbert Josephs (Lexington, KY: French Forum, 1984), 180–92. More recently, see the *Washington Post* review of the exhibit The Age of Watteau, Chardin, and Fragonard: Masterpieces of French Genre Painting, at the National Gallery: "France was at its Frenchest. Much of what's on view in the gallery's West Building is off-color and frivolous, as soft as a powder-puff, and as luscious as whipped cream." Paul Richard, "The Frills of France: At the National Gallery, Extravagances That Brought On a Revolution," *Washington Post,* 11 October 2003, C01, www.washingtonpost.com.

33. Edmond de Goncourt and Jules de Goncourt, *L'art du XVIIIe siècle* (1859–75; reprint, Paris: Hermann, 1967), 94.

34. "You belonged to the good old days of pannier gowns, / Of lapdogs, of furry muffs, of abbés and rocaille, / Of harlots and marquis, and suppers and orgies. // White-powdered sheep, salon poets, / Old porcelain and bisque, charming old junk, / Chubby cherubs, pompoms and bright ribbons, / Rosewood furniture and tortoiseshell extravagance. // The people, in their righteous fury, have shattered all that. . . ." Charles Baudelaire, *À Mme du Barry,* in *Poésies diverses, vers retrouvés,* in *Oeuvres complètes,* ed. Claude Pichois and Jean Ziegler, 2 vols. (Paris, Gallimard, 1975–76), 1:219, emphasis in the original. Originally published in *L'artiste* on 1 December 1844, the poem has also been attributed to Privat and Nerval.

35. Jay Caplan, *In the King's Wake: Post-Absolutist Culture in France* (Chicago: University of Chicago Press, 1999), 6.

36. Joan DeJean, *Ancients against Moderns: Culture Wars and the Making of a Fin de Siècle* (Chicago: University of Chicago Press, 1997).

37. Ibid., x, xi.

38. Ibid., 75.

39. A public, it is true, purged of its elements of the *bas peuple:* "Not only does the public judge of a work of art in a disinterested and impartial manner but it does so in the required way, that is, by way of taste and intuition [*sentiment*] and according to the impression that the poem or the painting makes on it. . . . Now, taste tells us much better whether the work of art touches us as it should than any learned dissertation composed by critics in order to account for its merits, to calculate its accomplishments and defects. . . . The word *public* denotes here only those who have enlightened themselves either through reading or through worldly

interaction." Abbé Jean-Baptiste du Bos, *Réflexions critiques sur la poésie et sur la peinture* (1719), 7th ed. in 3 pts. (1770; Geneva: Slatkine Reprints, 1982), pt. 2, chap. 22, pp. 339–51, tellingly entitled "That the public judges well of poems and paintings; of the taste that is required in order to appreciate the merits of those works."

40. Jean-Jacques Rousseau, *Lettre à d'Alembert sur les spectacles* (1758; reprint, Paris: Garnier-Flammarion, 2003), 158.

41. "Taste is often separate from genius. Genius is purely a gift from nature . . . taste is the result of study and time; it relies upon the knowledge of a multitude of established or hypothetical rules; it leads to the production of conventional beauty." Denis Diderot, "Génie," in Diderot and d'Alembert, *Encyclopédie,* 7 (1757): 582. Diderot's assessment of the faculty of *goût* for the artist was more nuanced in *The Salon of 1767.*

42. Diderot, *Salon de 1761,* 120.

43. DeJean, *Ancients against Moderns,* 76.

44. "Speaking of which, did you know that I have a right to be vain! We have here Mme Necker, a beautiful woman and a *bel esprit,* who is crazy about me; she pursues me, insisting that I visit her. Suard courts her with . . . perseverance." Denis Diderot, *Lettres à Sophie Volland* (1774), ed. A. Babelon (Paris: Gallimard, 1950), 2:64. On the role of salonnieres in the system of patronage, see André Morellet, *Portrait de Mme Geoffrin,* in *Eloges de Mme Geoffrin, par MM. Morellet, Thomas et d'Alembert,* ed. André Morellet (Paris: H. Nicolle, 1812); Dena Goodman, *The Republic of Letters: A Cultural History of the French Enlightenment* (Ithaca, NY: Cornell University Press, 1994); and Antoine Lilti, *Le monde des salons: La sociabilité mondaine à Paris au XVIIIe siècle* (Paris: Fayard, 2005).

45. Mercier, *Du théâtre,* 1212. On Diderot's position see below, chapter 7.

46. Denis Diderot, *Paradoxe sur le comédien* (1770), in *Oeuvres esthétiques,* 314.

47. See Voltaire, *Commentaire sur Corneille* (1761–65). Among many other texts of his see *Lettre sur l'esprit* (1744, postface to *Mérope*), *Essai sur la poésie épique* (1727), his articles on *goût* in the *Dictionnaire philosophique* (1752), and of course *Le temple du goût* (1732) and his satirical epic poem *La pucelle d'Orléans* (1730).

48. As in Diderot's extraordinary *Paradoxe sur le comédien,* which has been generally misunderstood; see below, chapter 4.

49. Saisselin, "Diderot from Outside the Research Machine," 243–44. In the *Critique of Judgment* (1790) Kant distinguishes between beautiful and pleasant art: the latter is directed merely at enjoyment, such as conversation, telling stories in an entertaining way, games, music (all his examples relate to worldly activities); the former is purposive for itself. J. H. Bernard, ed., *Kant's Critique of Judgement* (London: Macmillan, 1914), 169–73. See Kant's *Observations on the Feeling of the Beautiful and the Sublime* (1763) for a distinction between the beautiful (feminine wit) and the sublime (manly profundity).

50. "The Enlightenment's Socrates is an ambivalent figure, a strange Janus whose double face is the emblem of an era divided between the drive to shatter the

idols and the need to found new, positive values." Jean-Claude Bonnet, *Naissance du Panthéon: Essai sur le culte des grands hommes* (Paris: Fayard, 1998), 137.

51. See David A. Bell, *The Cult of the Nation in France: Inventing Nationalism, 1680–1800* (Cambridge, MA: Harvard University Press, 2001); and Paul Bénichou, *Le sacre de l'écrivain* (Paris: Gallimard, 1948).

52. Thomas Kavanagh, *The Aesthetics of the Moment: Literature and Art in the French Enlightenment* (Philadelphia: University of Pennsylvania Press, 1996), 12.

53. See Voltaire's *La pucelle d'Orléans* (1730), in *Oeuvres complètes de Voltaire/Complete Works of Voltaire,* ed. Ulla Kölvig et al. (Geneva: Institut et Musée Voltaire; Toronto: University of Toronto Press, 1968–), 7:251–588; and Jennifer Tsien's excellent analysis in *Voltaire and the Temple of Bad Taste: A Study of La Pucelle d'Orléans,* Studies on Voltaire and the Eighteenth Century, 5 (Oxford: Voltaire Foundation, 2003).

54. In the wake of Michael Fried's influential book *Absorption and Theatricality: Painting and the Beholder in the Age of Diderot* (Chicago: University of Chicago Press, 1980) other scholars, such as Marian Hobson, in *The Object of Art: The Theory of Illusion in Eighteenth-Century France* (Cambridge: Cambridge University Press, 1982), have attenuated the rigidity of his description of the shift in the conceptualization of the reception of the artwork that took place in the mid-eighteenth century.

Prologue. Boudoir and Tribune

Epigraphs: Denis Diderot, *The Salon of 1767,* vol. 2 of *Diderot on Art,* trans. John Goodman (New Haven, CT: Yale University Press, 1995), 164, translation modified; Louis-Sébastien Mercier, *Du théâtre, ou nouvel essai sur l'art dramatique,* in Mercier, *Mon bonnet de nuit, suivi de Du théâtre* (1784–85), ed. Jean-Claude Bonnet and Pierre Frantz (Paris: Mercure de France, 1999), 1314; Charles Baudelaire, *De l'essence du rire (On the Essence of Laughter)* (1855), in Baudelaire, *The Painter of Modern Life and Other Essays,* trans. Jonathan Mayne (London: Phaidon, 1964), 149.

1. Lamoignon de Malesherbes, speech to the French Academy, 16 February 1775, www.academie-francaise.fr/immortels/index.html.

2. Lekain [Henri Louis Cain], *Mémoires de Lekain, précédés de réflexions sur cet acteur et sur l'art théâtral par F. Talma* (Paris: Ponthieu, 1825), 430–31.

3. Cicero, *De officiis,* trans. Walter Miller, Loeb Classical Library (Cambridge, MA: Harvard University Press, 1975), 2.14.48, p. 217. Cicero argues that the "debating power" of eloquence *(contentio)* "counts far more toward the attainment of glory" but that "it is not easy to say how far an affable and courteous manner in conversation [*comitas affabilitasque sermo*] may go toward winning the affections" of the audience, in war and in political debate.

4. See Marc Fumaroli, *La diplomatie de l'esprit* (Paris: Hermann, 1994), 289.

5. On the vicissitudes of Guez de Balzac's literary and political ambitions see Christian Jouhaud, *Les pouvoirs de la littérature* (Paris: Gallimard, 2000).

6. Guez de Balzac takes inspiration from the *Nichomachean Ethics,* 1126b–1128b, in which Aristotle develops the three virtues of *comitas, veritas,* and *urbanitas.*

7. Jean-Louis Guez de Balzac, *Oeuvres diverses* (1644), ed. Roger Zuber (Paris: Champion, 1995), 80.

8. The process of "curialization" is by no means as stark as Norbert Elias would have us believe. *The Court Society* (1969), trans. Edmund Jephcott (Oxford: Blackwell, 1983), esp. chap. 6. The aristocracy of the salons were quite capable of playing several roles and juggling military activities and sociability, the battlefield or the dueling ground and the courtly ritual. They managed all those functions simultaneously down to the end of the *ancien régime.* See David A. Bell, *The First Total War* (Boston: Houghton Mifflin, forthcoming).

9. In his *Dialogue des héros de roman* (1664) Nicolas Boileau accuses Madeleine de Scudéry of perverting history and disrespecting ancient heroes by portraying them as modern *galants.* Boileau, *Oeuvres,* 2 vols. (Paris: Garnier-Flammarion, 1969), 2:195–219.

10. Jean-Louis Guez de Balzac, "Discours 2: Suite d'un entretien," in *Oeuvres diverses,* 82–83.

11. See Marc Fumaroli "Rhétorique d'école et rhétorique adulte: La réception européenne du *Traité du sublime* aux XVIe et XVIIe siècles," *Revue d'histoire littéraire de la France* 1 (1986): 33–51, reprinted in Fumaroli, *Héros et orateurs: Rhétorique et dramaturgie cornéliennes,* 2nd ed. (Geneva: Droz, 1996), 377–98.

12. Voltaire, "Éloquence," in *Encyclopédie, ou dictionnaire raisonné des sciences, des arts et des métiers,* ed. Denis Diderot and Jean Le Rond d'Alembert, 32 vols. (Paris, 1751–77), 5 (1756): 529.

13. Cicero, *Orator,* trans. H. M. Hubbell, Loeb Classical Library (Cambridge, MA: Harvard University Press, 1971), 37.128, pp. 401–2.

14. See Anne Richardot, "Un philosophe au purgatoire des Lumières: Démocrite," *Dix-huitième siècle* 32 (2000).

15. From Jacques-Bénigne Bossuet, *Maximes et réflexions sur la comédie* (1694). The aphorism struck Baudelaire, who commented extensively on it in *De l'essence du rire.*

16. Denis Diderot, in *Le neveu de Rameau,* ed. Jean-Claude Bonnet (Paris: Garnier-Flammarion, 1983), 158–59. The piece was prompted by the indignation ignited by the success of Palissot's mean-spirited satire *Les philosophes;* given the polemical circumstances, Diderot emphasized his position.

17. Rétif de la Bretonne, *Les nuits de Paris,* ed. Patrice Boussel (Paris: Editions 10/18, 1963), 96.

18. Quoted in Dominique Quéro, *Momus philosophe: Recherches sur une figure littéraire du XVIIIe siècle* (Paris: Champion, 1995), 461.

19. Denis Diderot, *Est-il bon, est-il méchant?* act 3, sc. 9, in *Oeuvres,* ed. Laurent Versini, vol. 4, *Esthétique: Théâtre* (Paris: Robert Laffont, 1996), 1472.

20. Denis Diderot, *Entretiens sur Le fils naturel,* in *Oeuvres esthétiques,* ed. Paul Vernière (Paris: Garnier, 1968), 114.

21. Diderot, *Le neveu de Rameau,* 55–56.

22. Denis Diderot to Étienne-Maurice Falconet, 4 December 1765, in Diderot and Falconet, *Le pour et le contre: Correspondance polémique sur le respect de la postérité, Pline et les anciens,* ed. Yves Benot (Paris: Editeurs Réunis, 1958), 48–49.

23. Denis Diderot, *Eloge de Richardson* (1762), in *Oeuvres esthétiques,* ed. Paul Vernière (Paris: Garnier, 1968), 39–40.

24. Ibid., 31.

25. Ibid., 30.

26. Ibid., 40.

27. The type of response elicited by Richardson's novels will find a striking echo in the readers' enthusiastic response to Rousseau, especially to *La nouvelle Héloïse,* which was experienced as a religious conversion. As Robert Darnton puts it, "Ordinary readers from all ranks of society were swept off their feet. They wept, they suffocated, they raved, they looked deep into their lives and resolved to live better. . . . Rousseau's own reading showed the influence of the intense, personal religiosity of his Calvinist heritage. His public probably applied an old style of religious reading to new material, notably the novel, which had previously seemed incompatible with it." Darnton, "Readers Respond to Rousseau," in *The Great Cat Massacre and Other Episodes in French Cultural History* (New York: Basic Books, 1984; New York: Vintage Books, 1985), 242, 251.

28. Diderot to Sophie Volland, 17 September 1761, quoted in Diderot, *Eloge de Richardson,* 44. In the *Eloge* Diderot reverses the roles: Diderot is the intruder, and his friend is the enthusiast (44). In the *préface-annexe* to *La religieuse* Grimm (or Diderot) recalls once more the same scene: d'Alainville intrudes upon a tearful Diderot intent on writing Suzanne's letters. See Diderot, *La religieuse,* ed. Roland Desné (Paris: Garnier-Flammarion, 1968), 211.

29. "Illusion," in Diderot and d'Alembert, *Encyclopédie,* 8 (1765): 557.

30. David A. Bell, *The Cult of the Nation in France: Inventing Nationalism, 1680–1800* (Cambridge, MA: Harvard University Press, 2001).

31. See France Marchal-Ninosque, *Images du sacrifice, 1670–1840* (Paris: Champion, 2005).

32. Marc Fumaroli, *L'age de l'éloquence: Rhétorique et "res literaria" de la Révolution au seuil de l'époque classique* (Geneva: Droz, 1980; Paris: Albin Michel, 1994); Paul Bénichou, *Morales du grand siècle* (Paris: Gallimard, 1948); David A. Bell, *Lawyers and Citizens: The Making of a Political Elite in Old Regime France* (Oxford: Oxford University Press, 1994).

33. See André Zysberg, *La monarchie des Lumières, 1715–1786* (Paris: Seuil, 2002), esp. chap. 5.

34. Bell, *Lawyers and Citizens,* 63–66.

35. Ibid., 131–37.

36. Bell, *Cult of the Nation,* 126.

37. "The critics who were most assertive in advocating a moralistic classicism and most severe in their judgment of Rococo tendencies were almost all associated with the Doublet-Bachaumont circle." Thomas Crow, *Painters and Public Life in Eighteenth-Century Paris* (New Haven, CT: Yale University Press, 1985), 123.

38. The *Mémoires secrets* were started by Bachaumont and continued by Pidansat de Mairobert and others, until they reached thirty-six volumes (1777–89).

39. La Font de Saint-Yenne, *Sentiments sur quelques ouvrages de peinture, sculpture et gravure, écrits à un particulier en province* (1754), quoted in Crow, *Painters and Public Life,* 120.

40. Diderot, *Salon of 1767,* 166.

41. See Keith Michael Baker, "Transformations of Classical Republicanism in Eighteenth-Century France," *Journal of Modern History* 73, no. 1 (2001): 32–53.

42. Katie Scott, *The Rococo Interior* (New Haven, CT: Yale University Press, 1995), 262–63; Melissa Hyde, *Making Up the Rococo: François Boucher and His Critics* (Los Angeles: Getty Research Institute, 2006).

43. Alain Génetiot, *Poétique du loisir mondain, de Voiture à La Fontaine* (Paris: Champion, 1997), 67–78. Inspired by the mythological parodies illustrated by Italian poets such as Berni and Tassoni, the genre was explored earlier by Saint-Amant and du Bellay. In 1644 Scarron published *Typhon ou la gigantomachie,* dedicated to Mazarin; Brébeuf wrote a *Lucain travesti* in 1650; Charles Coypeau D'Assoucy, *L'Ovide en belle humeur* in 1653; and Jean-François Sarasin composed in 1654 *Dulot vaincu ou la défaite des bouts-rimés,* his last work.

44. Voltaire, *Discours à l'Académie,* in *Mélanges* (Paris: Gallimard, 1961), 248. For a study of Voltaire's critique of the mixture of genre, class, and identity as monstrosity in the epic poem, see Jennifer Tsien, *Voltaire and the Temple of Bad Taste: A Study of La Pucelle d'Orléans,* Studies on Voltaire and the Eighteenth Century, 5 (Oxford: Voltaire Foundation, 2003).

45. Bernard Le Bouvier de Fontenelle, *Entretiens sur la pluralité des mondes* (1686; reprint, Paris: Didier, 1966), 4.

46. Jean Le Rond d'Alembert, *Réflexions sur les éloges académiques,* in *Oeuvres de d'Alembert,* vol. 2 (Paris: A. Belin / Bossange Frères, 1822), 152.

47. Jean-Baptiste Rousseau, in an epigram published as an appendix to Desfontaines' *Dictionnaire néologique* in the *Pantalo-Phoebana,* quoted in *Marivaux et le marivaudage: Une préciosité nouvelle,* by Frédéric Deloffre, 2nd ed. (Paris: Colin, 1967), 17n6.

48. Voltaire, *Questions sur l'Encyclopédie* (1771), s.v. "Style," in *Oeuvres complètes de Voltaire,* ed. Louis Moland, 52 vols. (Paris: Garnier, 1877–85), 20:436–44. Vincent Voiture was a poet in Mme de Rambouillet's salon, and Mlle Paulet, the daughter of a financier, was a celebrated beauty of the same circle.

49. Jean Le Rond d'Alembert, *Discours préliminaire* to Diderot and d'Alembert, *Encyclopédie,* 1 (1751): xxx–xxxi. For the changing conception of the relationship

between science, worldliness, and society from Fontenelle to d'Alembert and Condorcet see Keith Michael Baker, *Condorcet: From Natural Philosophy to Social Mathematics* (Chicago: University of Chicago Press, 1975), esp. chap. 1.

50. Jean-François de La Harpe, *Lycée ou cours de littérature ancienne et moderne,* 16 vols. (Paris: H. Agasse, 1799), vol. 2, pt. 3, bk. 1, chap. 5, p. 5046, www.lib .uchicago.edu/efts/ARTFL/databases/bibliopolis/cli/.

51. Nicolas Le Camus de Mezières, *Le génie de l'architecture* (1780; reprint, Geneva: Minkoff, 1972), 53.

52. André Pierre Le Gayde Prémonval, *L'esprit de Fontenelle* (1744), quoted in Pierre-François Guyot Desfontaines, *Jugements sur quelques ouvrages nouveaux,* 11 vols. (Avignon: Pierre Giroux, 1744–46; Geneva: Slatkine Reprints, 1967), 1:29.

53. Louis-Sébastien Mercier, "Tréteaux des boulevards," in *Tableaux de Paris,* ed. Jean-Claude Bonnet, 2 vols. (Paris: Mercure de France, 1994), 2:284.

54. See Francis Bar, *Le genre burlesque en France au XVIIe siècle* (Paris: d'Artrey, 1960); Alain Génetiot, *Les genres lyriques mondains* (Geneva: Droz, 1990); Roger Lathuillère, *La préciosité: Étude historique et linguistique* (Geneva: Droz, 1966), 250; and Dominique Bertrand, ed., *Poétiques du burlesque* (Paris: Champion, 1998).

55. César Chesneau Dumarsais, *Traité des tropes* (1729), republished with a commentary by Pierre Fontanier in 1818 (reprint, Geneva: Slatkine Reprints, 1984), 517–18.

56. David Trott, *Théâtre du dix-huitième siècle: Jeux, écritures, regards* (Montpellier: Editions Espaces 34, 2000).

57. See Georges Forestier's introduction to his edition of Racine's theater, *Oeuvres complètes,* 2 vols. (Paris: Gallimard, 1999), 1:xi–lvii.

58. The change was brought about by the concerted efforts of Voltaire, the actor Lekain, and the comte de Lauraguais on 23 April 1759.

59. Mercier, *Du théâtre,* 1353–54.

60. Ibid., 1132.

61. Marian Hobson described this fundamental epistemological and representational shift very well in *The Object of Art: The Theory of Illusion in Eighteenth-Century France* (Cambridge: Cambridge University Press, 1982).

62. Charles Palissot de Montenoy, *Oeuvres complètes de M. Palissot,* vol. 1 (Paris: L. Collin, 1809), 270. On the rich culture of persiflage see the captivating account of Elisabeth Bourguinat in *Le siècle du persiflage, 1734–1789* (Paris: Presses Universitaires de France, 1998). In *Le neveu de Rameau* Diderot lends the voice of the *neveu* to the antiphilosophes: "We shall give a good thrashing to all those little Catos like you, who despise us out of envy; whose modesty is a cover for pride and whose sobriety is the law of necessity" (74).

63. A. C. Cailleau responded to Palissot with his *Philosophes manqués,* performed on 15 May 1760, and on 17 July he presented *Les originaux ou les fourbes punis.* See Valleria Belt-Grannis, *Dramatic Parody in Eighteenth-Century France* (New York: Institute of French Studies, 1931), 162–66.

64. See Alain Viala's introduction to *L'esthétique galante,* ed. Alain Viala et al.

(Toulouse: Société des Littératures Classiques, 1989); and Gérard Defaux, *Molière ou les métamorphoses du comique* (Paris: Klincksieck, 1992), 246.

65. André Félibien, *Description du château de Versailles* (1696), quoted in Quéro, *Momus philosophe,* 254.

66. Nicolas Boileau, *L'art poétique,* canto 3, lines 391–400, in *Oeuvres,* 2 vols. (Paris: Garnier-Flammarion, 1969), 2:108.

67. Voltaire, *Questions sur l'Encyclopédie* (1771), s.v. "Bouffon," in *Oeuvres complètes de Voltaire,* ed. Moland, 18:25.

68. Voltaire to Everard Falkener, n.d., published as a preface to *Zaire,* in *Oeuvres complètes de Voltaire,* ed. Moland, 2:547: "The same audience who applauded him goes to see him become the butt of ridicule at the Théâtre-Italien and at the fairs, drawing from his humiliation a greater pleasure than [the writer] ever drew from his long nights of work."

69. Voltaire to Nicolas-Claude Thieriot, 3 January 1723 (Best. 142), in *Voltaire's Correspondence,* ed. Theodore Besterman, 107 vols. (Geneva: Institut et Musée Voltaire, 1953–65), 1:188.

70. Paul Pellisson, *Discours sur les oeuvres de Monsieur Sarasin* (1655), quoted in Viala et al., *L'esthétique galante,* 57.

71. Alain Viala, "Le dialogue 'à la française' et les modèles italiens: Affirmations et dénégations d'une esthétique," in *Estetica e arte: La concezione dei "moderni,"* ed. Stefano Benassi (Bologna: Nuova Alfia Editoriale, 1991), 45–58; idem, "Le palmarès de la querelle," *D'un siècle à l'autre: Anciens et modernes,* ed. Louise Godard de Donville and Roger Duchêne, 16e colloque du CMR 17, January 1986, Centre National des Lettres (Marseilles: CMR 17, 1987), 171–78.

72. Nicolas Boileau, *L'art poétique,* canto 4, lines 153–54, in *Oeuvres,* 2:113.

73. See Denis Diderot, "Génie," in Diderot and d'Alembert, *Encyclopédie,* 7 (1757): 582–84.

74. See the epilogue notes.

75. Alain Viala, "'Qui t'a fait minor?' Galanterie et classicisme," *Littératures classiques,* no. 31 (1997): 115–33. In the polarization between *galanterie* and classicism the first is *endogène,* the second *exogène.* See also idem, "La littérature galante: Histoire et problématique," in *Quaderni del seicento francese,* ed. Giovanni Dotoli (Bari: Adriatica; Paris, Nizet, 1944), 101–13.

76. Viala, "Qui t'a fait minor?" 126. "Air" refers to a way of being, a manner, or a tone. See Madeleine de Scudéry, *"De l'air galant" et autres conversations (1653–1684): Pour une étude de l'archive galante,* ed. Delphine Denis (Paris: Champion, 1998).

77. Alain Viala, *Naissance de l'écrivain* (Paris: Minuit, 1985).

78. Pellisson, *Discours sur les oeuvres de Monsieur Sarasin,* quoted in Viala et al., *L'esthétique galante,* 65. See also Marc Fumaroli, "L'empire des femmes, ou l'esprit de joie," in *La diplomatie de l'esprit.*

79. Pellisson, *Discours sur les oeuvres de Monsieur Sarasin,* quoted in Viala et al., *L'esthétique galante,* 55.

80. Ibid., 63.

81. Ibid., 64.

82. Scudéry, *"De l'air galant" et autres conversations,* 72.

83. Jean de La Bruyère, "De la société et de la conversation," sec. 77, in *Les caractères* (1688; reprint, Paris: Classiques Garnier, 1990), 177.

84. The language of Corneille provides a good example of such convergence between burlesque *bassesse,* the verbal virtuosity of rhetorical amplification, and a fascination for the materiality of words. In *L'illusion comique,* when Matamore boasts that his sword will spark a fire that will destroy the house of his beloved, the art of masonry never looked so good in *alexandrins* (3.5.747–57).

85. Charles Perrault, *Parallèle des anciens et des modernes* (Paris: Jean-Baptiste Coignard, 1690), 3, 296.

86. Gabriel Naudé, *Mascurat (Jugement de tout ce qui a esté imprimé contre le cardinal Mazarin, depuis le sixiéme janvier, iusques à la declaration du premier avril mil six cens quarante-neuf)* (1650), quoted in Clément Marot, *Oeuvres poétiques complètes,* ed. Gérard Defaux, 2 vols. (Paris: Bordas, 1990), 1:468.

87. Boileau, *L'art poétique,* canto 1, lines 96–97, in *Oeuvres,* 2:89.

88. "Burlesque," in Diderot and d'Alembert, *Encyclopédie,* 2 (1751): 467. The article endorses Boileau's censure of the burlesque.

89. Diderot, *Entretiens sur Le fils naturel,* 155–57.

90. That is Rica's distinctive voice in letter 63. Charles de Secondat, baron de Montesquieu, *The Persian Letters,* trans. George R. Healy (Indianapolis: Hackett, 1964), 106.

91. See Génetiot, *Les genres lyriques mondains,* 132; and Jean Weisgerber, *Les masques fragiles: Esthétique et formes de la littérature rococo* (Lausanne: L'Age d'Homme, 1991), 109.

92. Something similar happens in the visual arts in the early eighteenth century. See Scott, *Rococo Interior,* 263–64.

93. Scudéry, *"De l'air galant" et autres conversations,* 72, emphasis added.

94. The transformation of the role of the salonniere may be an effect of this evolution. See Elena Russo, "From *Précieuse* to Mother Figure: Sentiment, Authority, and the Eighteenth-Century Salonniere," *Studies on Voltaire and the Eighteenth Century* 12 (2001): 199–218.

95. Abbé de Saint Pierre to Voltaire, 2 October 1739, quoted in Jean-Claude Bonnet, *Naissance du Panthéon: Essai sur le culte des grands hommes* (Paris: Fayard, 1998), 36.

96. Voltaire, *Le temple du goût,* ed. Elie Carcassonne (Geneva: Droz, 1938), 83.

97. Voltaire, "Gens de lettres," in Diderot and d'Alembert, *Encyclopédie,* 7 (1757): 599.

98. Pierre Carlet de Chamblain de Marivaux, *Le spectateur français,* in Marivaux, *Journaux et oeuvres diverses,* ed. Frédéric Deloffre and Michel Gilot (Paris: Garnier, 1988), 146.

99. Élie-Catherine Fréron, *Lettres sur quelques écrits de ce temps* (1749–54), vol. 3 (1750), 46–47, quoted in Raymond Naves, *Le goût de Voltaire* (1938; reprint, Geneva: Slatkine Reprints, 1967), 421. Toward the end of the century, *bel esprit* has become a generic slur directed against the philosophes, who are now being branded with the same term they previously had used against the *modernes*.

100. Jean-Jacques Rousseau, *Discours sur les sciences et les arts*, in *Oeuvres complètes*, ed. Bernard Gagnebin and Marcel Raymond, vol. 3 (Paris: Gallimard, 1964), 21.

101. See Jacqueline Lichtenstein, *The Eloquence of Color: Rhetoric and Painting in the French Classical Age* (Berkeley and Los Angeles: University of California Press, 1993). By virtue of the *ut pictura poesis* commonplace, an echo of the wars between Rubénistes and Poussinistes at the Academy of Painting and Sculpture was still lingering in the eighteenth century, in the critique of the *bel esprit*'s verbal virtuosity. Lichtenstein shows how, from the classical times, rhetorical ornament has been associated with the painted body of the prostitute or the effeminate male.

102. Charles de Secondat, baron de Montesquieu, *Mes pensées*, no. 1062, in *Pensées/Le spicilège*, ed. Louis Desgraves (Paris: Robert Laffont, 1991), 389. Louis-Sébastien Mercier, in the wake of Rousseau, deplored women's corrupting influence on the theater: "Nowadays it is the childishness of our fashionable women that appears on the stage; when he has reproduced their tone, a writer fancies himself a true painter, and the poet seems proud of having given a voice to those futile beings who deserve a lesson in being ignored. Instead, they are erected a throne, and this ridiculous fanaticism is consecrated in a nation that is sapped by women of all strong, courageous, and lofty ideals." Mercier, *Du théâtre*, 1211–12.

103. Diderot, *Salon of 1767*, 19–20. See also his dislike of Rousseau's portrait by La Tour: "I search there for the literary censor, the Cato and Brutus of our age, I expect to see an Epictetus, his clothes rumpled, his wig tousled, with a severity frightening to writers, fashionable people, and the powerful, and I see only the author of the *Village Fortune-Teller*, well-dressed, well groomed, well powdered, ridiculously seated on a cane-back chair." *Notes on Painting* (1765), in *Diderot on Art*, trans. John Goodman, vol. 1, *The Salon of 1765 and Notes on Painting* (New Haven, CT: Yale University Press, 1995), 210.

Chapter 1   A Faded Coquette

Epigraphs: Maximilien François Marie Isidor de Robespierre, *Sur les principes de morale politique qui doivent guider la Convention nationale dans l'administration intérieure de la République*, discourse presented at the convention, 5 February 1794; Charles Baudelaire, *Quelques caricaturistes français (Some French Caricaturists)* (1857) in Baudelaire, *The Painter of Modern Life and Other Essays*, trans. Jonathan Mayne (London: Phaidon, 1964), 182.

1. P. M. Conlon provides a concise account of Voltaire's persistent efforts from 1731 to 1746 to be elected to an institution he claimed to despise in *Voltaire's Liter-*

ary Career from 1728 to 1750, Studies on Voltaire and the Eighteenth Century, 14 (Geneva: Institut et Musée Voltaire, 1961).

2. Voltaire to Nicolas-Claude Thieriot, 6 March 1736 (Best. 993), in *Voltaire's Correspondence,* ed. Theodore Besterman, 107 vols. (Geneva: Institut et Musée Voltaire, 1953–65), 5:80.

3. On the relationship between Marivaux and Voltaire see Christophe Cave, "Marivaux revu par Voltaire: L'image de Marivaux dans la *Correspondance* de Voltaire," in *Marivaux et les Lumières: L'homme de théâtre et son temps,* ed. Geneviève Goubier (Aix-en-Provence: Publications de l'Université de Provence, 1996), 195–208.

4. For a description of Marivaux's familial and social background and the difficult life of Nicolas Carlet as director of the Royal Mint of Riom, see Michel Gilot, *Les journaux de Marivaux: Itinéraire moral et accomplissement esthétique,* 2 vols. (Paris: Champion, 1975), vol. 1, chap. 1.

5. Ibid., 1:76.

6. Voltaire, "Gens de lettres," in *Encyclopédie, ou dictionnaire raisonné des sciences, des arts et des métiers,* ed. Denis Diderot and Jean Le Rond d'Alembert, 32 vols. (Paris, 1751–77), 7 (1757): 599–600.

7. On Voltaire's construction of a nobility of authorship see Jay Caplan, *In the King's Wake: Post-Absolutist Culture in France* (Chicago: University of Chicago Press, 1999), chap. 2.

8. Pierre Carlet de Chamblain de Marivaux, *L'indigent philosophe,* in Marivaux, *Journaux et oeuvres diverses,* ed. Frédéric Deloffre and Michel Gilot (Paris: Garnier, 1988), 314–15, hereafter cited as *JOD.*

9. Even though none of Marivaux's plays ever knew the booming success of a play like Destouches's *Le philosophe marié,* which attracted 23,500 spectators between 15 February and 29 March 1727, with an average of 1,200 spectators at each performance, most of them enjoyed a moderate but steady success and many revivals lasting well into midcentury.

10. Denis Diderot, *Le neveu de Rameau,* ed. Jean-Claude Bonnet (Paris: Garnier-Flammarion, 1983), 47–48.

11. Charles Collé, quoted in *Marivaux: Un humanisme expérimental,* by Henri Coulet and Michel Gilot (Paris: Larousse, 1973), 28.

12. Friedrich Melchior von Grimm, Denis Diderot, Jacques-Henri Meister, and Abbé François Raynal, *Correspondance littéraire, philosophique et critique (1751–1793),* ed. Maurice Tourneux (Paris: Garnier Frères, 1877–82), 15 February 1763, 5:236.

13. Quoted in Pierre Carlet de Chamblain de Marivaux, *Théâtre complet,* ed. Jacques Scherer and Bernard Dort (Paris: Seuil, 1964), cxli. See also Coulet and Gilot, *Marivaux: Un humanisme expérimental,* 28.

14. One of the last texts written by d'Alembert, the *Eloge de Marivaux* was read by Jean-Sylvain Bailly in 1785, after d'Alembert's death in 1783.

15. Jean Le Rond d'Alembert, *Eloge de Marivaux* (1785), in Marivaux, *Théâtre complet,* 22.

16. Ibid., 36. The only tragedy written by Marivaux, *Annibal* was performed, with limited success, at the Théâtre-Français in 1720.

17. Marquis d'Argenson, *Notices sur les oeuvres de théâtre,* ed. Henri Lagrave, Studies on Voltaire and the Eighteenth Century, 43 (Oxford: Voltaire Foundation, 1966). Fréron's pronouncement appeared in the *Année littéraire* 1 (1782): 107; it is quoted in G. Larroumet, *Marivaux, sa vie et ses oeuvres* (Paris: Hachette, 1894), 3n1.

18. See Quintilian *Institutio Oratoria* 8.3.6.

19. *JOD,* 701.

20. "*Phébus* is a flower of rhetoric, an ornament, but also an obscure and enigmatic turn of phrase, both too polished and too brief. . . . It means both sharp witticism [*pointe*] and figural excess." Roger Zuber, "Le style Nervèze," in *Les emerveillements de la raison* (Paris: Klincksieck, 1997), 91–92.

21. Louis-Sébastien Mercier, *Mon bonnet de nuit, suivi de Du théâtre* (1784–85), ed. Jean-Claude Bonnet and Pierre Frantz (Paris: Mercure de France, 1999), 750–52.

22. *JOD,* 728.

23. On Trublet see Jean Jacquart, *L'abbé Trublet, critique et moraliste* (Paris: Auguste Picard, 1926), 326–28.

24. Voltaire's verdict on Trublet was couched in an epigram: "He compiled, he compiled, he compiled!" Voltaire, *Le pauvre diable* (1760), in *Oeuvres complètes de Voltaire,* ed. Louis Moland, 52 vols. (Paris: Garnier, 1877–85), 10:107–8.

25. Trublet's project gave rise to a short "Quarrel of Montaigne," fought in the pages of the *Mercure,* between Trublet on the one hand and Marivaux and Prévost on the other. See Sarah Benharrech, "*Lecteur que vous êtes bigearre!* Marivaux et la 'Querelle de Montaigne,'" *Modern Language Notes* 120, no. 4 (2005): 925–49.

26. *JOD,* 728–29.

27. Ibid., 729.

28. See Roger Marchal, *Mme de Lambert et son milieu,* Studies on Voltaire and the Eighteenth Century, 289 (Oxford: Voltaire Foundation, 1991), 248. The seven sages were Fontenelle, La Motte, Mairan, Marivaux, Montesquieu, Duclos, and Marmontel.

29. *JOD,* 729.

30. Pierre Carlet de Chamblain de Marivaux, *Le spectateur français,* in *JOD,* 143.

31. Ibid., 248.

32. Charles Sorel, *Histoire comique de Francion* (1623), Romaciers du XVIIe siècle (Paris: Gallimard, 1958), 410, 413. Amadis was a popular epic hero in the Middle Ages and the inspiration for Don Quixote.

33. Ibid., 126. The *ruelle* was the space between the bed and the wall. In the seventeenth century, when the ceremonial bedroom was considered a public area, women used to receive guests seated on a stately bed.

34. Nicolas de Malebranche, *The Search after Truth* (1674), trans. Thomas M.

Lennon and Paul J. Olscamp (Columbus: Ohio State University Press, 1980), bk. 4, pt. 1, chap. 8, p. 299.

35. Ibid., 299–300.

36. Père Desmolets, *Continuation des mémoires de littérature et d'histoire* (1727), quoted in *JOD*, 703.

37. Pierre-François Guyot Desfontaines, *La relation de ce qui s'est passé au sujet de la réception de Messire Christophle Mathanasius à l'Académie française* (1727), quoted in *JOD*, 702.

38. D'Alembert, *Eloge de Marivaux*, 34.

39. Voltaire to the abbé Trublet, 27 April 1761 (Best. 8974), in *Voltaire's Correspondence*, 45:312–13. The formula seemed to please Voltaire a great deal: see his letters to Formont (29 April 1732) and Moncrif (10 April 1733), quoted in Cave, "Marivaux revu par Voltaire."

40. Jean-François Marmontel, *Mémoires*, ed. Jean-Pierre Guicciardi and Gilles Thierriat (Paris: Mercure de France, 1999), 199.

41. Quoted in *JOD*, 709.

42. "He is condemned to love only himself and his own works." Diderot on Boucher, in *Salon de 1763*, in *Oeuvres esthétiques*, ed. Paul Vernière (Paris: Garnier, 1968), 452.

43. *JOD*, 323.

44. Jay Caplan suggests that psychology is just an illusion Marivaux's theatrical characters live by. Relations among them are structured in symmetrical patterns "as if to underscore the resemblance of the players to pieces on a game board and to undermine the self-deceptively psychological terms in which the characters interpret their destiny." *In the King's Wake*, 109. But psychology at the time was, indeed, rigidly codified in a way not unlike the rules of a chess game.

45. Pierre Carlet de Chamblain de Marivaux, *Réflexions sur l'esprit humain à l'occasion de Corneille et de Racine* (1749), in *JOD*, 472.

46. Marivaux, *Le spectateur français*, in *JOD*, 232. See Marcel Proust, *Journées de pélerinage*, in *Pastiches et mélanges* (Paris: Gallimard, 1971), 71–72: "For no one is original, and luckily for sympathy and understanding, which are such great pleasures in life, our individualities are cut from a universal fabric. If we were able to analyze the soul as we do matter, we would see that below the apparent diversity of minds, as well as below that of things, there are only a few simple bodies and irreducible elements and that in the composition of what we take to be our personality enter very ordinary substances that may be found everywhere in the universe."

Chapter 2   Fakes, Impostors, and Beaux Esprits

Epigraphs: Nicolas de Malebranche, *Traité de morale* (Cologne: Balthasar d'Egmont, 1683), 1.12.18; Louis-Sébastien Mercier, "Coulisses," in *Tableaux de Paris*, ed. Jean-Claude Bonnet, 2 vols. (Paris: Mercure de France, 1994), 2:481.

1. For the purpose of this discussion, I focus on circumscribed aspects of the rich semantic baggage of the word *esprit*. It may mean "mind" as a faculty of reasoning or the faculties peculiar to a person. In his *Dictionnaire universel* (Rotterdam, 1690) Antoine Furetière writes, "*Esprit* denotes reasoning, the functions of the soul which act by its different organs: judgement, imagination, and memory. . . . *Esprit* may also mean the special qualities that characterize a person, the talents he applies to one thing or another. . . . *Esprit* also indicates the meaning, the intent, the motivation of something."

2. Pierre-François Guyot Desfontaines, *Lettres de M. l'abbé *** à M. l'abbé Houtteville au sujet du livre de la Religion chrétienne prouvée par les faits,* in Pierre Carlet de Chamblain de Marivaux, *Journaux et oeuvres diverses,* ed. Frédéric Deloffre and Michel Gilot (Paris: Garnier, 1988), 690–91, hereafter cited as *JOD*.

3. *JOD*, 717, emphasis added.

4. Alexis Piron to the abbé Dumay, 12 may 1755, in *Alexis Piron épistolier,* ed. Gunnar Von Proschwitz (Göteborg, Sweden: Acta Universitatis Gothoburgensis, 1982), 160.

5. Montaigne used the term occasionally, as in *Essais* 3.5: "The activities of *beaux esprits* enhance the value of language."

6. Pierre Corneille, *La place royale* (1637), act 5, sc. 1.

7. See Molière, *L'école des femmes* (1663), 3.3.817–25: "Every simple woman is docile to our lesson; . . . But a clever one is quite another animal. . . . Her *bel esprit* helps her to make sport of our principles, and to turn her vices into virtues." With Rousseau, Arnolphe is redux: "But I would much rather deal with a simple and uneducated girl than with a *savante* and a *bel esprit,* who would preside over a literary academy in my own house. A woman *bel esprit* is the scourge of her husband, her children, her friends, her servants, everybody." Jean-Jacques Rousseau, *Emile,* bk. 5, in *Oeuvres complètes,* ed. Bernard Gagnebin and Marcel Raymond, vol. 4 (Paris: Gallimard, 1969), 768.

8. Alain Viala, *Naissance de l'écrivain* (Paris: Minuit, 1985), 149.

9. In Molière's *Les précieuses ridicules,* act 1, Mascarille poses as a *bel esprit.*

10. Charles Pinot Duclos, "Sur la manie du bel esprit," in *Considérations sur les moeurs de ce siècle* (1751), ed. Carole Dornier (Paris: Champion, 2000), 194–204.

11. Père François Garasse, *Doctrine curieuse des beaux esprits de ce temps* (Paris: S. Chappelet, 1623), bk. 1, sec. 10, p. 63.

12. Malebranche, *Traité de morale,* 1.12.15.

13. For instance, when the Italian Jesuit Daniello Bartoli's highly successful *Dell'huomo di lettere difeso ed emendato,* first published in Rome in 1645, was translated in into French in 1654, it bore the title *Le guide des beaux-esprits.* In 1769 it underwent another translation and was renamed *L'homme de lettres.* Bartoli's book enjoyed wide success, with nineteen Italian editions and translations into English, German, and Castilian. Significantly, the 1769 French translation stressed the dignity and the absolute disinterestedness of intellectual activity. See Roger Char-

tier, "The Man of Letters," in *Enlightenment Portraits,* ed. Michel Vovelle, trans. Lydia G. Cochrane (Chicago: University of Chicago Press, 1997), 169–70.

14. Alain Niderst, "Le bel esprit," in *L'esprit en France au 17e siècle,* ed. François Lagarde (Tübingen: Biblio 17, 1998), 75–84. For a contemporary understanding of the concept see Père Dominique Bouhours, *Les entretiens d'Ariste et d'Eugène* (1671), ed. Bernard Beugnot and Gilles Declercq (Paris: Champion, 2003); Madeleine de Scudéry, *"De l'air galant" et autres conversations (1653–1684): Pour une étude de l'archive galante,* ed. Delphine Denis (Paris: Champion, 1998); François de la Rochefoucauld, *Réflexions diverses* (1731), in *Oeuvres complètes,* ed. L. Martin-Chauffier and Jean Marchand (Paris: Gallimard, 1964), 499–541; and Jean de La Bruyère, *Les caractères* (1688; reprint, Paris: Classiques Garnier, 1990), esp. "De la société et de la conversation" and "Des jugements." Among scholarly studies see Viala, *Naissance de l'écrivain,* esp. 147–51; Linda Timmermans, *L'accès des femmes à la culture (1598–1715): Un débat d'idées de Saint François de Sales à la Marquise de Lambert* (Paris: Champion, 1992), 111ff. and chap. 2; Marc Fumaroli, *L'âge de l'éloquence: Rhétorique et "res literaria" de la Révolution au seuil de l'époque classique* (Geneva: Droz, 1980; Paris: Albin Michel, 1994), 674; idem, *La diplomatie de l'esprit* (Paris: Hermann, 1994); Roger Lathuillère, *La préciosité: Étude historique et linguistique* (Geneva: Droz, 1966); Mercedes Blanco, *Les rhétoriques de la pointe: Baltasar Gracián et le conceptisme en Europe* (Paris: Champion, 1992); and idem, "Esprit," in *Dictionnaire raisonné de la politesse et du savoir-vivre,* ed. Alain Montandon (Paris: Seuil, 1995), 329–58.

15. Pierre Carlet de Chamblain de Marivaux, *Oeuvres de jeunesse,* ed. Frédéric Deloffre and Claude Rigault (Paris: Gallimard, 1972), 320.

16. *JOD,* 471.

17. Corneille had come under fire in the prefaces that Voltaire wrote for his edition of Corneille's work, and both Corneille and Racine were indicted for the crimes of *esprit* and *papillotage* in Diderot's *Les bijoux indiscrets.*

18. *JOD,* 473.

19. Jean Le Rond d'Alembert, *Eloge de Marivaux,* in Pierre Carlet de Chamblain de Marivaux, *Théâtre complet,* ed. Jacques Scherer and Bernard Dort (Paris: Seuil, 1964), 29, emphasis in the original.

20. For the salonniere's role as cultural mediator, brokering the relationship between artists and patrons, see André Morellet, *Portrait de Mme Geoffrin,* in *Eloges de Mme Geoffrin, par MM. Morellet, Thomas et d'Alembert,* ed. André Morellet (Paris: H. Nicolle, 1812), esp. 56–59.

21. Voltaire, "Gens de lettres," in *Encyclopédie, ou dictionnaire raisonné des sciences, des arts et des métiers,* ed. Denis Diderot and Jean Le Rond d'Alembert, 32 vols. (Paris, 1751–77), 7 (1757): 599.

22. Ibid.

23. Antoine Gombauld, chevalier de Méré, *De la conversation,* in *Oeuvres complètes du Chevalier de Méré* (1668), ed. Charles-Henri Boudhors, 3 vols. (Paris: Fernand Roches, 1930), 2:119.

24. La Bruyère, "Des jugements," sec. 18, 353–54.

25. Charles de Secondat, baron de Montesquieu, *Histoire véritable,* in *Oeuvres complètes,* ed. Roger Caillois, 2 vols. (Paris: Gallimard, 1949), 1:451.

26. Molière, *La critique de L'école des femmes,* sc. 3, in *Oeuvres complètes,* ed. Robert Jouanny, 2 vols. (Paris: Garnier, 1962), 1:484. Montesquieu was wary of the possible mortifications looming over the after-dinner *bel esprit:* "In conversation and at the table I was delighted if I could find a man who was willing to be brilliant; a man like that is always exposed, while all the others are shielded by him." Charles de Secondat, baron de Montesquieu, *Mes pensées,* no. 213, in *Pensées/Le spicilège,* ed. Louis Desgraves (Paris: Robert Laffont, 1991), 246–47.

27. Bouhours, *Les entretiens d'Ariste et d'Eugène,* 238–39, emphasis added.

28. Voltaire, "Esprit," in Diderot and d'Alembert, *Encyclopédie,* 7 (1757): 599. See also Duclos, *Considérations sur les moeurs de ce siècle,* 195: "We see men who have no status other than idleness; they turn themselves into amateurs of *bel esprit;* they display their taste, it becomes their advertisement [*affiche*]."

29. Charles Pinot Duclos, *Acajou et Zirphile* (1744), ed. Jean Dagen (Paris: Desjonquières, 1993), 47.

30. La Bruyère, "De la société et de la conversation," sec. 75, 175–76.

31. See Dinah Ribard, "Philosophe ou écrivain?" *Annales: Histoire et sciences sociales* 55, no. 2 (2000): 355–88.

32. In *bouts-rimés,* or set rimes, players must compose on the spot at least two lines of verse around the riming words they are given.

33. The source may be found in Pierre de L'Estoile's *Journal des règnes de Henri III et Henri IV,* 25 November 1583. The journal was published in 1741, and Diderot recounts the episode in a note to "Des lettres de Sénèque," bk. 2 of *Essai sur les règnes de Claude et de Néron,* sec. 10, in *Oeuvres,* ed. Laurent Versini, vol. 1, *Philosophie* (Paris: Robert Laffont, 1994), 1127.

34. Charles de Secondat, baron de Montesquieu, *The Persian Letters,* George R. Healy (Indianapolis: Hackett, 1964), letter 54, pp. 91–93.

35. See Elizabeth Goldsmith, *Exclusive Conversations* (Philadelphia: University of Pennsylvania Press, 1988).

36. Madeleine de Scudéry, "De la conversation," in *"De l'air galant" et autres conversations,* 73.

37. Montesquieu, *Mes pensées,* no. 1740, in *Pensées/Le spicilège,* 547.

38. See esp. Montesquieu, *Mes pensées,* nos. 1003 and 1005, in ibid., 379–81.

39. Jean-François Marmontel, *Mémoires,* ed. Jean-Pierre Guicciardi and Gilles Thierriat (Paris: Mercure de France, 1999), 135–36.

40. Tallemant des Réaux thus "unmasked" the poet Vincent Voiture: "He pretended to compose on the spot. That may have happened a few times, but he often brought with him pieces he had composed at home." *Historiettes,* ed. Antoine Adam, 2 vols. (Paris: Gallimard, 1960–61), 1:489. See also Alain Génetiot, *Poétique du loisir mondain, de Voiture à La Fontaine* (Paris: Champion, 1997), 415–29.

41. See Marc Fumaroli, "L'art de la conversation ou le forum du royaume," in *La diplomatie de l'esprit,* 298–301.

42. See Antoine Lilti, "Sociabilité et mondanité: Les hommes de lettres dans les salons parisiens au XVIIIe siècle," *French Historical Studies* 28, no. 3 (June 2005): 415–45.

43. Louis-Sébastien Mercier, "Du Style," in *Tableaux de Paris,* 2:298.

44. Voltaire to Berger, 2 February 1736 (Best. 967), in *Voltaire's Correspondance,* ed. Theodore Besterman, 107 vols. (Geneva: Institut et Musée Voltaire, 1953–65), 5:37. On this letter see Christophe Cave, "Marivaux revu par Voltaire: L'image de Marivaux dans la *Correspondance* de Voltaire," in *Marivaux et les Lumières: L'homme de théâtre et son temps,* ed. Geneviève Goubier (Aix-en-Provence: Publications de l'Université de Provence, 1996), 195–208. D'Alembert included the letter in his *Eloge de Marivaux.*

45. Reported by d'Alembert in *Eloge de Marivaux,* 20. That judgment about the Italians was corroborated by Diderot: "In the Italian theater, our Italian actors play with more freedom than our French actors; they pay less attention to the audience. Very often it is entirely forgotten. There is in their action something original and effortless that I like." Denis Diderot, *De la poésie dramatique,* chap. 21, in *Oeuvres esthétiques,* ed. Paul Vernière (Paris: Garnier, 1968), 268. Molière had mocked those actors who played for the parterre. In Molière's *Les précieuses ridicules,* sc. 9, Mascarille asks: "How are we supposed to recognize a good line if the actor does not pause, so as to warn us that we have to start a brouhaha?" Mercier also complained about the actor's unfortunate tendency to overact at the expense of the integrity of the play: "His exuberance dooms the play; the author is ridiculed by the excesses of the actor. . . . Don't we often see the fire, the eloquence of the character, destroyed by an actor who preferred to put himself [*son esprit*] ahead of the author?" Louis-Sébastien Mercier, *Du théâtre, ou nouvel essai sur l'art dramatique,* in Mercier, *Mon bonnet de nuit, suivi de Du théâtre* (1784–85), ed. Jean-Claude Bonnet and Pierre Frantz (Paris: Mercure de France, 1999), 1476–77.

46. Voltaire, *Lettre sur l'esprit* (1744, postface to *Mérope*) in *Oeuvres complètes de Voltaire,* ed. Louis Moland, 52 vols. (Paris: Garnier, 1877–85), 19:3–9.

47. See Emmanuelle Hénin, "Poétique de l'illusion scénique: Des poétiques italiennes de la Renaissance à la doctrine classique," *Littératures classiques,* no. 44 (2002): 15–34, and her masterful *Ut pictura theatrum: Théâtre et peinture de la Renaissance italienne au classicisme français* (Geneva: Droz, 2003).

48. Jean Chapelain, *Préface à l'Adonis du Chevalier Marin,* in *Opuscules critiques,* ed. A. C. Hunter (Paris: Droz, 1936), 85. See also idem, *Lettre sur la règle des vingt-quatre heures* (1630), in ibid., 115: "I postulate as a foundation that imitation in dramatic poetry must be so perfect that there should be no perception of difference between the original and the imitation, since the latter aims at presenting things as if they were real and present to the mind, in order to purge it of its passions."

49. Denis Diderot, *The Indiscreet Jewels,* trans. Sophie Hawkes (New York: Marsilio, 1993), 165–66. Corneille, however, was well aware that in the theater

rhetoric was subservient to action: "One of the differences between the dramatic poet and the orator is that the latter is free to display his art and make it remarkable, whereas the former must carefully conceal it, since he is not the one to speak, and those who do speak are not orators." Pierre Corneille, *Discours de l'utilité et des parties du poème dramatique* (1660), in *Oeuvres complètes*, ed. Georges Couton, 3 vols. (Paris: Gallimard, 1980–87), 3:134.

50. Louis-Sébastien Mercier, "Rime," in *Tableaux de Paris*, 2:452, emphasis added. *Epic*, of course, is the unfortunate intrusion of epic bombast into drama.

51. Pierre Carlet de Chamblain de Marivaux, *La voiture embourbée*, in *Oeuvres de jeunesse*, 313–14, emphasis in the original.

52. Christian Jouhaud, "Histoire et histoire littéraire: Naissance de l'écrivain," *Annales: Economie, société, civilisations* 43, no. 4 (1988): 859.

53. Günter Berger, ed., *Pour et contre le roman: Anthologie du discours théorique sur la fiction narrative en prose du XVIIe siècle*, Papers on French Seventeenth-Century Literature, 92 (Tübingen: Biblio 17, 1996), 181–82.

54. For Furetière, in his *Dictionnaire*, illusion is "false appearance, artifice intended to show something that does not exist or to show it differently than it actually is. Optics displays a thousand agreeable illusions through polyedric or faceted lenses and through magic lanterns. . . . It is also said of the artifice of the Demon, who makes visible what does not exist."

55. François Hédelin, abbé d'Aubignac, *La pratique du théâtre*, ed. Hélène Baby (Paris: Champion, 2001), bk. 1, chap. 6, pp. 81–82. The pictorial and optical roots of theatrical illusion in France may be found in the Italian Renaissance, a time when stage decorations were inspired by the theories of perspective held by Brunelleschi, Vasari, Alberti, and Peruzzi. See Hénin, "Poétique de l'illusion scénique," 19–20. On the innovations of the early-seventeenth-century French stage see also Jean Rousset, *L'intérieur et l'extérieur: Essais sur la poésie et sur le théâtre au XVIIe siècle* (Paris: Corti, 1968), 165–82; and Georges Forestier, *Le théâtre dans le théâtre sur la scène française du XVIIe siècle*, 2nd ed. (Geneva: Droz, 1996).

56. See Molière's *L'impromptu de Versailles* (1663) for a critique of bad theatricality and the emphatic mannerisms of the actors of the Hôtel de Bourgogne.

57. Pierre Carlet de Chamblain de Marivaux, foreword to *La vie de Marianne*, ed. Frédéric Deloffre (Paris: Garnier, 1957), 5. Claude Crébillon's satire of Marivaux's language in the novel, in chap. 25 of *L'écumoire ou Tanzaï et Néadarné* (1734), is notorious. Tanzaï rebukes Néadarné, who admires this style: "'What beautiful reflections,' said Néadarné. 'Were it true that they are as beautiful as you say,' Tanzaï replied, 'I still would not like them. I find them lengthy and inappropriate, and nothing is more ridiculous than a display of *esprit* where it is not needed. . . . If by chance an event invites a reflection, let that be short.'" Crébillon, *Oeuvres*, ed. Ernest Sturm (Paris: François Bourin, 1992), 296.

58. Blaise Pascal, *Pensées*, ed. Léon Brunschvicg (Paris: Garnier-Flammarion, 1976), nos. 147, 150, p. 93.

59. La Bruyère, *Les caractères*, preface, 61–62.

60. *JOD*, 117.

61. Ibid., 118.

62. François de Salignac de la Mothe-Fénelon, *Les aventures de Télémaque*, ed. Jacques Le Brun (Paris: Gallimard Folio, 1995), bk. 17, p. 376.

63. Pierre Carlet de Chamblain de Marivaux, *Le spectateur français*, in *JOD*, 118.

64. Baldassarre Castiglione, *Le livre du courtisan*, trans. Alain Pons after the 1580 translation by Alain Chappuis (Paris: Gérard Lebovici, 1987), 55–56.

65. "Artistic or artful self-expression in poetry, as in society, is partly a matter of self-concealment as well as concealing one's art or artifice." Jeffrey Barnouw, "The Beginnings of Aesthetics and the Leibnizian Conception of Sensation," in *Eighteenth-Century Aesthetics and the Reconstruction of Art*, ed. Paul Mattick Jr. (Cambridge: Cambridge University Press, 1993), 58.

66. Mercier, "Coulisses," 482–83.

67. In *Manon Lescaut*, for instance, the gambler and trickster Des Grieux styles himself a "chevalier d'industrie."

68. "Essai sur l'origine et les progrès des connoissances humaines," *Mercure de France*, September 1753, 53, quoted in Jean Weisgerber, *Les masques fragiles: Esthétique et formes de la littérature rococo* (Lausanne: L'Age d'Homme, 1991), 82.

69. See La Rochefoucauld, *Oeuvres complètes*, 486–87, *Maxime supprimée 563*.

70. *JOD*, 314–15.

Chapter 3   The Sly and the Coy Mistress

Epigraphs: Jean-Louis Guez de Balzac, *Paraphrase, ou de la grande éloquence (à M. Costar)*, discourse 6, in *Oeuvres diverses* (1644), ed. Roger Zuber (Paris: Champion, 1995), 163; Denis Diderot, *The Salon of 1767*, vol. 2 of *Diderot on Art*, trans. John Goodman (New Haven, CT: Yale University Press, 1995), 267; Marcel Proust, *John Ruskin*, in *Contre Sainte-Beuve, précédé de Pastiches et Mélanges*, ed. Pierre Clarac and Yves Sandre (Paris: Gallimard, 1971), 128 (the reference is to Buffon's *Discours sur le style*, his inaugural speech to the French Academy, delivered on 25 August 1753.

1. "What goes for intelligence [*esprit*] goes for taste and philosophy: nothing is more rare than having it, more impossible than acquiring it, and more common than believing one has it." Jean Le Rond d'Alembert, *Essai sur la société des gens de lettres et des grands, sur la réputation, sur les Mecènes, et sur les récompenses littéraires* (1753; 2nd ed. 1764), in *Oeuvres de d'Alembert*, vol. 4 (Paris: A. Belin / Bossange Frères, 1822), 346.

2. Père Dominique Bouhours, *Le bel esprit*, in *Les entretiens d'Ariste et d'Eugène* (1671), ed. Bernard Beugnot and Gilles Declercq (Paris: Champion, 2003), 249.

3. See Marian Hobson, *The Object of Art: The Theory of Illusion in Eighteenth-Century France* (Cambridge: Cambridge University Press, 1982), 47–48.

4. On the influence and the legend of Fénelon throughout the eighteenth century and the Revolution see Jean-Claude Bonnet, *Naissance du Panthéon: Essai sur le culte des grands hommes* (Paris: Fayard, 1998), 41–49.

5. Part of the success of *Les aventures de Télémaque* was due to the fact that it was read as a satire of Louis XIV. See also Fénelon's famous *Lettre à Louis XIV,* December 1693, published in the eighteenth century by d'Alembert, reprinted in François de Salignac de la Mothe-Fénelon, *Oeuvres,* ed. Jacques Le Brun, 2 vols. (Paris: Gallimard, 1983), 1:543–51. The letter, which circulated clandestinely, anticipates the critique of absolutism formulated in *Télémaque* and subsequently in the *Tables de Chaulnes* (1711), a detailed program of government for the Duke of Burgundy. The idea was to counteract the power of the king with that of the aristocracy and the Estates General.

6. François de Salignac de la Mothe-Fénelon, *Lettre à l'Académie* (1714), ed. Ernesta Calderini (Geneva: Droz, 1970), 40.

7. Ibid., 48–49.

8. François de Salignac de la Mothe-Fénelon, *Discours à l'Académie française,* in *Oeuvres,* 1:535–36.

9. Fénelon, *Lettre à l'Académie,* 51.

10. Ibid., 57. That parallel was a staple of rhetorical literature from Quintilian to Longinus. See Longinus, *Traité du sublime,* trans. Nicolas Boileau (1674), ed. Francis Goyet (Paris: Le Livre de Poche, 1995), 12.4, p. 93; see also Fénelon's "Cicéron et Démosthène," in *Dialogues des morts,* in *Oeuvres,* 1:369–76. Montesquieu emphasizes the orator's character: "Cicero always thought of himself first, Cato always forgot about himself. The latter wanted to save the republic for its own sake, the former in order to boast of it." Charles de Secondat, baron de Montesquieu, *Considérations sur les causes de la grandeur des Romains et de leur décadence* (1734; 2nd ed., 1748), trans. David Lowenthal as *Considerations on the Causes of the Greatness of the Romans and Their Decline* (New York: Free Press, 1965), chap. 12, p. 116. On Demosthenes's linguistic sobriety see also Guez de Balzac, *Paraphrase,* 165; and Charles Perrault, *Parallele des anciens et des modernes* (Paris: Jean-Baptiste Coignard, 1690), 163.

11. François de Salignac de la Mothe-Fénelon, *Dialogues sur l'éloquence* (1718), in *Oeuvres,* 1:35.

12. See Blaise Pascal, *Lettre à sa soeur Mme Périer, sur la mort de leur père,* 17 October 1651, in *Oeuvres complètes,* ed. Jacques Chevalier (Paris: Gallimard, 1954), 496.

13. François de Salignac de la Mothe-Fénelon, *Explication des maximes des saints,* in *Oeuvres,* 1:1011.

14. Donatien-Alphonse-François de Sade, *Justine ou les infortunes de la vertu,* 1778 (Paris: Garnier-Flammarion, 1969).

15. The political implications of Fénelon's spiritualism did not escape the scrutiny of the court. His doctrine of *pur amour* incurred the combined disapproval of his one-time protector Mme de Maintenon and Bossuet. Fénelon was disgraced,

deprived of his preceptorship, and exiled; twenty-three propositions from his *Explications* were condemned by Pope Innocent XII in 1699, at about the time Fénelon's friend and spiritual leader Mme Guyon, the founder of quietism, was imprisoned in the Bastille.

16. François de Salignac de la Mothe-Fénelon, *Les aventures de Télémaque,* ed. Jacques Le Brun (Paris: Gallimard Folio, 1995), 321, 400.

17. Fénelon, *Dialogues sur l'éloquence,* in *Oeuvres,* 1:37, emphasis added.

18. Georges Forestier, "Imitation parfaite et vraisemblance absolue: Réflexions sur un paradoxe classique," *Poétique,* no. 82 (1990): 187–202.

19. Fénelon, *Lettre à l'Académie,* 83.

20. Marc Fumaroli, "Illusion et dramaturgie dans *L'illusion comique,*" *XVIIe siècle,* nos. 80–81 (1968): 107–32, reprinted in Fumaroli, *Héros et orateurs: Rhétorique et dramaturgie cornéliennes,* 2nd ed. (Geneva: Droz, 1996), 271. For a comparison of natural and artificial signs in poetry and painting see Abbé Jean-Baptiste du Bos, *Réflexions critiques sur la poésie et sur la peinture* (1719), pt. 2, chap. 40. See also François Hédelin, abbé d'Aubignac, *La pratique du théâtre,* ed. Hélène Baby (Paris: Champion, 2001), bk. 1, chap. 6, p. 87.

21. Diderot, *Salon of 1767,* 206 (on Hubert Robert's *Port of Rome*), emphasis added.

22. Fénelon, *Lettre à l'Académie,* 57.

23. Fénelon, *Explication des maximes des saints,* in *Oeuvres,* 1:1074–75.

24. Longinus *Traité du sublime* 15.1. The visual aspect of hypotyposis must be taken as a metaphor for the emotion created by the image: "We are the spectators of a theater without visuals but not without spectacle. Words raise a virtual scene, a theater of the emotions, a communication among souls. The illusion of presence relies upon the actual communion between the poet-rhetorician and his audience." Francis Goyet, "De la rhétorique à la création: Hypotypose, type, pathos," in *La rhétorique: Enjeux de ses resurgences,* ed. Jean Gayon, Jacques Porier, and Jean-Claude Gens (Brussels: Editions Ousia, 1998), 61.

25. "Besides many other properties, images have that of enlivening and rousing emotion in a speech. So that when they are joined to other evidence, they not only persuade but conquer, so to speak; they dominate the audience." Longinus *Traité du sublime* 15.9.

26. Ibid.

27. "Hypotyposis is a Greek word that means *image, tableau.* It occurs in those descriptions in which events are depicted as if they were before our eyes; in which what is narrated is displayed; in which the original is given instead of the copy, and pictures are replaced by the objects themselves." César Chesneau Dumarsais, *Traité des tropes* (1729), republished with a commentary by Pierre Fontanier in 1818 (reprint, Geneva: Slatkine Reprints, 1984), 151.

28. Denis Diderot, *Pensées détachées sur la peinture* (1781), in *Oeuvres esthétiques,* ed. Paul Vernière (Paris: Garnier, 1968), 824.

29. Longinus *Traité du sublime* 17.2. "The interest and the charm of Richardson's

work is such that it conceals its artistry even to those who are most capable of perceiving it." Denis Diderot, *Eloge de Richardson* (1762), in *Oeuvres esthétiques*, 40.

30. Fénelon, *Lettre à l'Académie*, 78–79.

31. Abbé Marc-Antoine Laugier, *De la manière de bien juger les ouvrages de peinture* (1771), 84, quoted in Hobson, *Object of Art*, 62. Laugier was the author of the neoclassical *Essai sur l'architecture* (1753).

32. In the *Republic*, bk. 10, Plato opposes *eikastikê*, which reproduces the object while preserving its exact proportions, to *phantastikê*, which seeks to reproduce it for the eye by means of tricks based on color and drawing, not geometrical calculations. The latter was akin to sophistry. See Emmanuelle Hénin, *Ut pictura theatrum: Théâtre et peinture de la Renaissance italienne au classicisme français* (Geneva: Droz, 2003), 27.

33. Aristotle, *The Poetics*, trans. G. M. A. Grube (Indianapolis: Bobbs-Merrill, 1958), 4.48b, pp. 7–8.

34. Denis Diderot, *Salon de 1763*, in Diderot, *Essais sur la peinture: Salons de 1759, 1761, 1763* (Paris: Hermann, 1984), 220. Jean-Baptiste-Marie Pierre (1713–89), admitted to the Academy in 1742 and the successor of Boucher as first painter to the king in 1770, was an appreciated history painter. Diderot admired his compositions but found his drawing style cold and dry (Diderot, *Salon of 1767*, 299).

35. When confronting the impact of landscape painting by Vernet, Diderot declares: "Their character is such that the spectator who had remained unmoved and serene at the seashore is astonished by [its representation on] the canvas." *Salon of 1767*, 121.

36. On theories of illusion in eighteenth-century painting see Eveline Manna, "Discours contre la peinture et mise en question de la perception au tournant du XVIII siècle," in *Ecrire la peinture entre XVIIIe et XIXe siècles*, ed. Pascale Auraix-Jonchière (Clermont-Ferrand: Presses Universitaires Blaise Pascal, 2003), 57–74; and Sylvain Menant, "Les fins de la peinture selon l'abbé Du Bos," in *Les fins de la peinture*, ed. René Démoris (Paris: Desjonquières, 1990), 157–62.

37. Fénelon, *Dialogues sur l'éloquence*, in *Oeuvres*, 1:4.

38. Malebranche too saw style as belonging to the realm of worldly desire *(concupiscence)* and the materiality of the body and its passions: "All the various styles ordinarily please us only because of the secret corruption of our heart. . . . It we wish to reflect upon . . . what happens in ourselves when we are reading some well-written piece . . . we would find that this relish we take in the delicacies of effeminate discourse has no other source than a secret inclination for softness and voluptuousness. In a word, it is a certain attraction to what affects the senses, not awareness of the truth, that causes us to be charmed by certain authors and to be carried away by them almost in spite of ourselves." Nicolas Malebranche, *The Search after Truth* (1674), trans. Thomas M. Lennon and Paul J. Olscamp (Columbus: Ohio State University Press, 1980), bk. 2, pt. 3, chap. 5, p. 185.

39. Antoine Arnauld and Pierre Nicole, *La logique ou l'art de penser* (1662; reprint, Paris: Flammarion, 1970), pt. 2, chap. 20, p. 339, emphasis added. On this

passage see Louis Marin, *La critique du discours* (Paris: Minuit, 1975), 67–74. On the association between color and rhetoric see Jacqueline Lichtenstein, *The Eloquence of Color: Rhetoric and Painting in the French Classical Age* (Berkeley and Los Angeles: University of California Press, 1993).

40. Review of André Pierre Le Gayde Prémonval, *L'esprit de Fontenelle* (1744), a collection of anas, in Pierre-François Guyot Desfontaines, *Jugements sur quelques ouvrages nouveaux,* 11 vols. (Avignon: Pierre Giroux, 1744–46; Geneva: Slatkine Reprints, 1967), 1:38.

41. Fénelon, *Lettre à l'Académie,* 93. Racine's text had been the object of a debate between La Motte and Boileau on the nature of the sublime and the role of metaphors. See Nicolas Boileau's *Réflexions critiques sur quelques passages du rhéteur Longin,* reflection 11, in *Oeuvres complètes* (Paris: Gallimard, 1966), 560.

42. Corneille's "Qu'il mourût" from *Horace* (3, 6, 1022) and "Moi, dis-je, et c'est assez" from *Medea* (1, 5, 321).

43. Nicolas Boileau, preface to Longinus, *Traité du sublime,* trans. Boileau, ed. Goyet, 70.

44. Augustine *De doctrina Christiana* 4.24.53, quoted in Fénelon, *Lettre à l'Académie,* chap. 4, "Projet de rhétorique."

45. Denis Diderot, *Entretiens sur Le fils naturel* (1757), in *Oeuvres esthétiques,* 101–2.

46. Paraphrasing Longinus (*Traité du sublime* 9.2) and prefiguring Diderot's *Entretiens sur Le fils naturel,* the abbé Bouhours gives as an example of nonverbal, sublime expressiveness Ajax's silence, powerfully set off by Ulysses' insincere verbosity: "We admire him for his silence, which signifies all the nobility of his soul. . . . Ulysses cajoles Ajax, who does not even condescend to reply, and this silence has a *je ne sais quoi* that is greater than anything he might have said." Père Dominique Bouhours, *De la manière de bien penser dans les ouvrages d'esprit* (1687; reprint, ed. Suzanne Gellouz, Toulouse: Atelier de l'Université de Toulouse-Le-Mirail, 1988), 168.

47. Denis Diderot, *Lettre sur les sourds et muets,* in *Lettre sur les aveugles, Lettre sur les sourds et muets,* ed. Marian Hobson and Simon Harvey (Paris: Garnier-Flammarion, 2000), 124–25. Those verses from *Phaedra* had launched a "Quarrel of Racine" that pitted La Motte's *Discours sur la poésie* against Boileau's *Réflexions critiques sur quelques passages du rhéteur Longin,* reflection 11, published posthumously in 1713. The quarrel rebounded in the eighteenth century, opposing another Jesuit professor of Louis le Grand, the abbé d'Olivet (*Remarques de grammaire sur Racine,* 1738) to the abbé Desfontaines (*Racine vengé,* 1739). In *Questions sur l'Encyclopédie* (1771), s.v. "Amplification," Voltaire asked, "Was it appropriate for the man who has Mentor ramble on and on to shut Théramène's mouth?" *Oeuvres complètes de Voltaire,* ed. Louis Moland, 52 vols. (Paris: Garnier, 1877–85), 17:183–93. Leo Spitzer resurrects La Motte's and Fénelon's arguments in "L'effet de sourdine dans le style classique: Racine," in *Études de style* (Paris: Gallimard, 1970), 262–68.

48. *Aposiopesis*, which means stopping abruptly in the middle of a sentence because of an excess of emotion, comes from the Greek *aposiopao*, "to be silent after speaking, to observe a deliberate silence." See Quintilian *Institutio Oratoria* 9.2.54–55.

49. Diderot, *Salon of 1767*, 117.

50. Diderot, *Lettre sur les sourds et muets*, 116–17. See also idem, *Salon of 1767* (on Renou's *Christ at the Age of Twelve Debating the Law with the Doctors*), 278–85.

51. Diderot, *Salon of 1767*, 106.

52. See Francis Goyet's introduction to Boileau's translation of Longinus, *Traité du sublime*, 5–60.

53. Jean-Louis Carra, *M. de Calonne tout entier* (Brussels, 1788), vii–viii, quoted in Thomas Crow, *Painters and Public Life in Eighteenth-Century Paris* (New Haven, CT: Yale University Press, 1985), 222.

54. Sophia Rosenfeld, *A Revolution in Language: The Problem of Signs in Late Eighteenth-Century France* (Stanford, CA: Stanford University Press, 2001), 138.

55. Ibid., 165–66.

56. As we know, both Marianne and Jacob often find themselves in trial-like situations, thus becoming eloquent advocates of their own situations.

57. Pierre Carlet de Chamblain de Marivaux, *Le cabinet du philosophe*, "Du style" (1734), in Marivaux, *Journaux et oeuvres diverses*, ed. Frédéric Deloffre and Michel Gilot (Paris: Garnier, 1988), 384, hereafter cited as *JOD*.

58. Pierre Carlet de Chamblain de Marivaux, *Lettre sur les habitants de Paris*, in *JOD*, 35.

59. Marivaux, "Du style," in *JOD*, 386.

60. Ibid., 387.

61. Ibid., 383. Marivaux's justification of neology as an effect of intellectual progress and increased clarity prefigures Condorcet's, who stated that "men, in becoming enlightened, acquire more ideas; the nuances distinguishing objects become finer and more precise. Languages must therefore be perfected and enriched, for their true richness does not consist in the number of words but in the abundance of those that express clear ideas with precision." "Des avantages et des progrès des sciences," inaugural speech to the French Academy, 21 February 1782, www.academie-francaise.fr/immortels/index.html.

62. Marivaux, "Du style," in *JOD*, 386, 383.

63. Pierre Carlet de Chamblain de Marivaux, *Le spectateur français*, in *JOD*, 148.

64. Georges-Louis Leclerc de Buffon, "Discours sur le style," inaugural speech to the French Academy, 25 August 1753, www.academie-francaise.fr/immortels/index.html.

65. Thus the *Encyclopédie* article on style upholds the traditional distinction between simple, middle, and sublime style: the first for letters, fables, and "informal conversation"; the third for "noble and elevated subjects"; the second for

everything in between (whatever that may be). Chevalier de Jaucourt, "Style," in *Encyclopédie, ou dictionnaire raisonné des sciences, des arts et des métiers,* ed. Denis Diderot and Jean Le Rond d'Alembert, 32 vols. (Paris, 1751–77), 15 (1765): 551. See also Voltaire, *Questions sur l'Encyclopédie* (1771), s.v. "Style," in *Oeuvres complètes de Voltaire,* ed. Moland, 20:436–44; and idem, "Genre de style," in Diderot and d'Alembert, *Encyclopédie,* 7 (1757): 594.

66. Jean Le Rond d'Alembert, "Elocution," in *Oeuvres de d'Alembert,* 4:617.

67. Jean Le Rond d'Alembert, *Discours préliminaire* to Diderot and d'Alembert, *Encyclopédie,* 1 (1751): xxxi.

68. Boileau noted that in the world of poetry, farm animals were not all created equal. Thus, while the pig *(truie, cochon)* or the calf *(veau)* could never gain admittance, the cow was welcome, provided that she was a *génisse* and not a *vache;* the sheep too, provided that she was a *brebis* and not a *mouton.* Boileau, *Réflexions critiques sur quelques passages du rhéteur Longin,* 532.

69. Voltaire, *Lettre sur l'esprit* (1744, postface to *Mérope*), in *Oeuvres complètes de Voltaire,* ed. Moland, 19:3–9.

70. *Manner,* of course, is not quite a synonym of *style.* in the tradition of Giovanni Bellori and Giorgio Vasari, Diderot often uses it in the sense of "mannerism," a work inspired by academic models and not by nature. See his article "Manière" in Diderot and d'Alembert, *Encyclopédie,* 10 (1765): 34–35. For a discussion of manner and mannerism in painting see Erwin Panofsky, *Idea: A Concept in Art Theory,* trans. Joseph J. S. Peake (Columbia: University of South Carolina Press, 1968).

71. See Diderot, *Salon of 1767,* 252–54 (on Lépicié's *Painting of a Family*); and idem, *Paradoxe sur le comédien* (1770), in *Oeuvres esthétiques,* 310: "Great poets, great actors, and perhaps great imitators of nature in general, whoever they are, are endowed with a great imagination, great judgment, fine tact [*tact fin*], and an unfailing sense of taste [*goût très sûr*]."

72. See Diderot's discussion of the *modèle idéal* in the *Salon of 1767* and in *Essais sur la peinture,* chap. 1.

73. Diderot, *Salon of 1767,* 119–20, translation modified.

74. Ibid., 121. "O Chardin, it is not white, red, and black that you are blending on the pallet, it is the very substance of things; it is air and light that you are holding at the tip of your brush and are laying on the canvas." Diderot, *Salon de 1763,* 218.

75. "One has only to walk about the Salon and listen to the various judgments proposed there to become convinced that, in this genre, as in literature, success, the greatest success, is a sure thing for mediocrity; that happy mediocrity which puts the average spectator and artist on the same level." Diderot, *Salon of 1767,* 253.

76. Appendix 3 to Denis Diderot, *Salon III: Ruines et paysages* (Paris: Hermann, 1995), 516.

77. Denis Diderot, "On Mannerism," in Diderot, *Salon of 1767,* 321.

78. Diderot, *Salon of 1767,* 155. "What a clamor of disparate objects! We feel its

utter absurdity; and yet, we are unable to avert our eyes from this painting" (ibid.). On Boucher's pastorals and landscapes see Diderot, *Salon de 1761,* and Diderot, *Essais sur la peinture,* 120.

79. The cyclical nature of such evolution is confirmed by the reference to Seneca, the undisputed embodiment of late imperial mannerism. Of course, a few years later Diderot will go out of his way to rescue his hero from such accusations in *Essai sur les règnes de Claude et de Néron.* See below, chapter 5. See also Voltaire: "Like an artist who gradually shapes his taste, so a nation shapes hers. For centuries she stagnates into barbarism, then rises a fragile dawn; finally, the daylight sets in, followed by a long and sad twilight. We have all agreed for quite some time that despite François I's efforts to encourage in France the emergence of taste in the arts, good taste did not set in until the century of Louis XIV; and we now lament the fact that the present age is degenerating." *Questions sur l'Encyclopédie* (1771), s.v. "Goût," in *Oeuvres complètes de Voltaire,* ed. Moland, 19:270–84.

80. Diderot, *Salon of 1767,* 118.

81. Jean-Jacques Rousseau, *Discours sur l'origine de l'inégalité,* in *Oeuvres complètes,* ed. Bernard Gagnebin and Marcel Raymond, vol. 3 (Paris: Gallimard, 1964), 169–70.

82. Diderot, "On Mannerism," 323.

83. Denis Diderot, *Notes on Painting* (1765), in *Diderot on Art,* trans. John Goodman, vol. 1, *The Salon of 1765 and Notes on Painting* (New Haven, CT: Yale University Press, 1995), 193.

84. Ibid., 214, translation modified.

85. Denis Diderot, *Regrets sur ma vieille robe de chambre* (1772).

86. Diderot, *Pensées détachées sur la peinture,* 825.

87. Diderot, *Salon of 1767,* 50. Referring to Boucher's *Angélique et Médor,* Diderot writes: "That man takes up the brush only to show me tits and bums. I am happy to see them; but I do not want them to be displayed." Denis Diderot, *The Salon of 1765,* in *Diderot on Art,* 1:26, translations modified.

88. See Michael Fried, *Absorption and Theatricality: Painting and the Beholder in the Age of Diderot* (Chicago: University of Chicago Press, 1980).

89. Diderot, *Notes on Painting,* 212.

90. Diderot, *Salon of 1767,* 50. Diderot compares his impression of the *Suzanne* by Giuseppe Cesari, cavalier d'Arpino (1568–1640), to that of Lagrenée.

91. I borrow Elisabeth Ladenson's terms from her book *Proust's Lesbianism* (Ithaca, NY: Cornell University Press, 1999), 66.

92. René Démoris, "Peinture et cruauté chez Diderot," *Colloque international Diderot,* ed. Anne-Marie Chouillet (Paris: Aux Amateurs de Livres, 1985), 299–307.

93. Diderot, *Pensées détachées sur la peinture,* 767.

94. Ibid., 792.

95. See esp. Diderot, *Salon de 1761,* 120. See also Edmond de Goncourt and Jules de Goncourt, *L'art du XVIIIe siècle* (1859–75; reprint, Paris: Hermann, 1967), 95.

96. See France Marchal-Ninosque, *Images du sacrifice, 1670–1840* (Paris: Champion, 2005), 263.

97. See, e.g., Diderot, *Entretiens sur Le fils naturel,* 168–72; idem, *Eloge de Richardson;* the commentary on Fragonard's *Corésus and Callirhoé* in Diderot, *Salon of 1765,* 141–48; and the remarks on the elder Lagrenée's *Sacrifice of Jephta* in ibid., 40. Carle Van Loo had painted a *Sacrifice d'Iphigénie* in 1757, the same year that Guimond de la Touche's *Iphigénie en Tauride* was performed triumphantly at the Comédie-Française.

98. Démoris, "Peinture et cruauté chez Diderot," 302–3.

99. Diderot, *Notes on Painting,* 211.

Chapter 4   Capturing Fireside Conversation

Epigraphs: Louis-Sébastien Mercier, *Du théâtre, ou nouvel essai sur l'art dramatique,* in Mercier, *Mon bonnet de nuit, suivi de Du théâtre* (1784–85), ed. Jean-Claude Bonnet and Pierre Frantz (Paris: Mercure de France, 1999), 1316; Denis Diderot, *Essai sur les règnes de Claude et de Néron,* in *Oeuvres,* ed. Laurent Versini, vol. 1, *Philosophie* (Paris: Robert Laffont, 1994), 972.

1. Denis Diderot, *Eloge de Richardson* (1762), in *Oeuvres esthétiques,* ed. Paul Vernière (Paris: Garnier, 1968), 30.

2. Mercier, *Du théâtre,* 1147.

3. Ibid.

4. Jean-Jacques Rousseau, *Emile,* bk. 5, in *Oeuvres complètes,* ed. Bernard Gagnebin and Marcel Raymond, vol. 4 (Paris: Gallimard, 1969), 762–63.

5. Pierre Carlet de Chamblain de Marivaux, *Télémaque travesti,* in *Oeuvres de jeunesse,* ed. Frédéric Deloffre and Claude Rigault (Paris: Gallimard, 1972), 724–25.

6. Pierre Carlet de Chamblain de Marivaux, *Le paysan parvenu,* ed. Frédéric Deloffre (Paris: Garnier, 1959), 73. Both Marianne and Jacob are able to *conceive* who they are; in that respect they anticipate the self-determination of the libertine persona, who is able to subordinate his character to his will, with the sole reservation that for Marivaux such a will is subconscious. See André Malraux, *Le triangle noir: Laclos, Goya, Saint-Just* (Paris: Gallimard, 1970), 34.

7. Jean Rousset, "Marivaux et la structure du double registre," in *Forme et signification: Essai sur les structures littéraires de Corneille à Claudel* (Paris: Corti, 1964), 45–64.

8. Denis Diderot, *Entretiens sur Le fils naturel* (1757), in *Oeuvres esthétiques,* 81.

9. Pierre Carlet de Chamblain de Marivaux, *La vie de Marianne,* ed. Frédéric Deloffre (Paris: Garnier, 1957), 9.

10. In *Jacques le fataliste* Diderot too reflected on the paradoxical nature of the opposition between narrative verisimilitude and historical truth. Seventeenth-century baroque novelists, in Aristotelian fashion, believed that historical truth,

unlike poetic truth, need not be plausible *(vraisemblable);* the search for verisimilitude was proof of the novel's moral superiority over history writing.

11. The choice of location is not irrelevant; a *pont-neuf* was a vaudeville song, a composition inspired by current events, often parodistic and obscene. See Louis-Sébastien Mercier, "Complaintes," in *Tableaux de Paris,* ed. Jean-Claude Bonnet, 2 vols. (Paris: Mercure de France, 1994), 2:954; and Robert Isherwood, *Farce and Fantasy: Popular Entertainment in Eighteenth-Century Paris* (Oxford: Oxford University Press, 1986), chap. 1.

12. Jean-Pierre Sermain, "Pourquoi riez-vous? La question du *Paysan parvenu,*" *Revue Marivaux,* no. 6 (1997): 209–29.

13. Charles Baudelaire, *De l'essence du rire (On the Essence of Laughter)* (1855), in Baudelaire, *The Painter of Modern Life and Other Essays,* trans. Jonathan Mayne (London: Phaidon, 1964), 164.

14. Ibid., 154.

15. "The only difference [between comedy and tragedy for the Greeks] consists in parabasis, a speech that in the midst of the play was held by the chorus in the name of the poet to the people. Yes, it was a complete interruption and dissolution of the play, during which (just as in the play itself) the greatest licentiousness reigned and the chorus, which had stepped out to the outer limits of the proscenium, said the grossest vulgarities to the people. The name is derived from this stepping out (ekbasis)." *Kritische Friedrich-Schlegel-Ausgabe,* ed. Ernst Beheler et al. (Munich: Ferdinand Schöningh, 1958–), 18:85, fragment 668, English translation by Michel Chaouli in *The Laboratory of Poetry: Chemistry and Poetics in the Work of Friedrich Schlegel* (Baltimore: Johns Hopkins University Press, 2002), 200. See Paul de Man, "The Rhetoric of Temporality," in *Blindness and Insight: Essays in the Rhetoric of Contemporary Criticism,* 2nd ed. (Minneapolis: University of Minnesota Press, 1983), 218.

16. Chaouli, *Laboratory of Poetry,* 200.

17. De Man, "The Rhetoric of Temporality," 222.

18. Pierre Carlet de Chamblain de Marivaux, *Lettres contenant une aventure,* in Marivaux, *Journaux et oeuvres diverses,* ed. Frédéric Deloffre and Michel Gilot (Paris: Garnier, 1988), 86, hereafter cited as *JOD.*

19. David Hume defined the self not as a substance or a substratum but as a "bundle or collection of different perceptions" with no unified core, no identity beyond that which is produced in the imagination by the uninterrupted flow of impressions. See *A Treatise of Human Nature,* ed. P. H. Nidditch (Oxford: Clarendon, 1978), 252. And Rousseau wrote, "I would tell myself that all we do is constantly begin anew; that there is no link to our existence other than a sequence of present moments, the first of which is always the one that is happening here and now. We die and are reborn at every moment of our life." Jean-Jacques Rousseau, *Emile et Sophie, ou les Solitaires* (1762), in *Oeuvres complètes,* 4:905.

20. Pierre Carlet de Chamblain de Marivaux, *Le spectateur français,* in *JOD,* 208.

21. Georges Poulet, *La distance intérieure* (Paris: Plon, 1952), 1–34; Leo Spitzer, "A propos de *La vie de Marianne:* Lettre à M. Georges Poulet," *Romanic Review,* 1953, 102–26, reprinted in Spitzer, *Études de style* (Paris: Gallimard, 1970). See also J. S. Spink, "Marivaux: The 'Mechanism of the Passions' and the 'Metaphysics of Sentiment,'" *Modern Language Review* 73, no. 2 (1978): 278–90.

22. As Thomas Kavanagh beautifully argues in *The Aesthetics of the Moment: Literature and Art in the French Enlightenment* (Philadelphia: University of Pennsylvania Press, 1996), esp. chap. 1.

23. Jean Le Rond d'Alembert, *Eloge de Marivaux* (1785), in Pierre Carlet de Chamblain de Marivaux, *Théâtre complet,* ed. Jacques Scherer and Bernard Dort (Paris: Seuil, 1964), 20.

24. Marivaux, *Le spectateur français,* in *JOD,* 207–8.

25. Marivaux, *Lettres contenant une aventure,* in *JOD,* 99.

26. Marivaux owes to Madeleine de Scudéry an interest in half-conscious states of mind, which are part of Scudéry's phenomenology of love. For both, the rise of true *tendresse* always presupposes unawareness (a *surprise de l'amour*). Surprise is a proof of the genuineness of the emotion. See James S. Munro, "Sensibility and the Subconscious in Marivaux and Mlle de Scudéry," *Romance Studies,* no. 15 (Winter 1989): 89–97.

27. Marivaux, *La vie de Marianne,* 169.

28. Pierre Nicole, *De la charité et de l'amour-propre* (1675), in *Essais de morale,* ed. Laurent Thirouin (Paris: Presses Universitaires de France, 1999), 412.

29. Marivaux, *Le spectateur français,* in *JOD,* 114; idem, *L'indigent philosophe,* in *JOD,* 311; idem, *Le cabinet du philosophe,* in *JOD,* 335.

30. Pierre Carlet de Chamblain de Marivaux, *Pharsamon ou Les nouvelles folies romanesques,* in *Oeuvres de jeunesse,* 603; idem, *La vie de Marianne,* 55–56.

31. See Georges May, *Le dilemme du roman au dix-huitième siècle* (New Haven, CT: Yale University Press, 1963).

32. Marivaux, *L'indigent philosophe,* in *JOD,* 311.

33. Ibid., 276.

34. See Marcel Mauss, *Essai sur le don: Forme et raison de l'échange dans les sociétés archaïques* (1923–24); and Georges Bataille, *La part maudite* (1976), translated into English as *The Accursed Share:* "For I shall always be concerned, however it may seem, with the apparently lost sovereignty to which the beggar can sometimes be as close as the great nobleman, and from which, as a rule, the bourgeois is voluntarily the most far removed." *The Accursed Share,* 2 vols. (New York: Zone Books, 1988–91), 1:197.

35. Marivaux, *L'indigent philosophe,* in *JOD,* 275.

36. Marivaux, *Le cabinet du philosophe,* in *JOD,* 351.

37. Marivaux, *Le spectateur français,* in *JOD,* 114.

38. Marivaux, *Lettre sur les habitants de Paris,* in *JOD,* 8.

39. Ibid., in *JOD,* 149.

40. Marivaux's conception of expressive spontaneity prefigures that of Rousseau: "If I were, like all the others, to produce a work meticulously written, I would not be making a self-portrait, but a made-up likeness. What we have here is a portrait, not a book. I will work, as it were, in a camera obscura. I will need no skill other than that needed for reproducing the traits that I see in there. I have made a decision regarding style as well as subject matter. I will not try to make it smooth; I will change it according to my mood; I will always have the style that comes to me. I will say each thing as I feel and see it, with no elegance or scruple; without bothering about the medley [*bigarrure*]. Abandoning myself both to the memory of the [past] impression and to the present feeling, I will paint a double portrait of my state of mind, at the moment when the event took place and at the moment I will be writing it. My style—uneven and artless, now rapid, now detailed; now sensible, now mad; now grave, now light—will itself be part of my story." Jean-Jacques Rousseau, *Fragments autobiographiques*, sketches for *Les confessions*, in *Oeuvres complètes*, ed. Bernard Gagnebin and Marcel Raymond, vol. 1 (Paris: Gallimard, 1959), 1154.

41. "Corneille and Montaigne were, after Dufresny, the only writers whom Marivaux sometimes consented to approve of. Montaigne even more than Corneille, for the reason that his manner of writing belonged to him more; it was less likely to be copied by the multitude and therefore more likely to receive the approval of a writer who prided himself on resembling no one." D'Alembert, *Eloge de Marivaux*, 35n20.

42. Marivaux, *Le cabinet du philosophe*, in *JOD*, 388.

43. Jean-Louis Guez de Balzac, entretien 18, in *Les entretiens*, ed. Bernard Beugnot (Paris: Société des Textes Français Modernes, 1972), 290. Cicero wrote: "Plainness of style seems easy to imitate at first thought, but when attempted, nothing is more difficult. . . . [The style] should be loose but not rambling; so that it may seem to move freely, but not to wander without restraint. . . . For the short and concise clauses must not be handled carelessly, but there is such a thing even as a careful negligence [*neglegentia diligens*]. Just as some women are said to be handsomer when unadorned—this very lack of ornament becomes them—so this plain style gives pleasure even when unembellished: there is something in both cases which lends greater charm [*venustas*], but without showing itself. Also all noticeable ornament, pearls as it were, will be excluded; not even curling-irons will be used; all cosmetics, artificial white and red, will be rejected; only elegance and neatness will remain." Cicero, *Orator*, trans. H. M. Hubbell, Loeb Classical Library (Cambridge, MA: Harvard University Press, 1971), 23.77–79, pp. 363–64. See also John C. Lapp, *The Esthetics of Negligence* (Cambridge: Cambridge University Press, 1971).

44. Charles de Secondat, baron de Montesquieu, *Essai sur le goût*, in *Oeuvres complètes*, ed. Roger Caillois, 2 vols. (Paris: Gallimard, 1949), 2:1255. See also Paul Pellisson, *Discours sur les oeuvres de Monsieur Sarasin* (1655): "We may say that two things make poetry admirable: the inventiveness, which gives it its name, and ease, which is

absolutely necessary. I do not mean ease in composing, which, though it may sometimes be a gift, should always be held as suspect. I mean the ease that readers enjoy in a composition that has cost its author the greatest pains. One might compare it to those terraced gardens the expense of which is hidden and which, having cost millions, seem nothing but the work of chance and nature." Quoted in *L'esthétique galante,* ed. Alain Viala et al. (Toulouse: Société des Littératures Classiques, 1989), 62.

45. Charles de Secondat, baron de Montesquieu, *Mes pensées,* no. 1971, in *Pensées/Le spicilège,* ed. Louis Desgraves (Paris: Robert Laffont, 1991), 607–8.

46. "Conversation must appear so free that it must seem as if no idea were ever rejected; one should be able to say anything that comes to mind, with no preconceived design to talk about one thing rather than another. . . . That is why I would like you never to know what you must say, though you should know what you are saying." Madeleine de Scudéry, "De la conversation," in *"De l'air galant" et autres conversations (1653–1684): Pour une étude de l'archive galante,* ed. Delphine Denis (Paris: Champion, 1998), 73.

47. Charles de Secondat, baron de Montesquieu, *Essai sur le goût,* ed. Louis Desgraves (Paris: Payot et Rivages, 1993), 38.

48. Marivaux, *Le cabinet du philosophe,* in *JOD,* 335.

49. Voltaire, *Lettre sur l'esprit* (1744, postface to *Mérope*), in *Oeuvres complètes de Voltaire,* ed. Louis Moland, 52 vols. (Paris: Garnier, 1877–85), 19:3–9.

50. After the flop of *La Mort de César* (29 August 1743) and his recent rejection by the Academy (February 1743).

51. Lionel Gossman, "*Ce beau génie qui n'a point compris sa sublime mission:* An Essay on Voltaire," *French Review* 56, no. 1 (1982): 44.

52. But the proponents of the drame will, for the same reasons laid out by Voltaire: "The Parisian . . . will see that verse on the stage is but a fake ornament that corrupts the mind at the very moment it wishes to devote itself to sentiment and image." Louis-Sébastien Mercier, "Rime," in *Tableaux de Paris,* 2:452. At the dawn of the eighteenth century, in his *Discours sur la tragédie,* Antoine Houdar de la Motte had been the first to propose introducing prose into tragedy.

53. That is, the exaggerated praise of something or someone one wishes in fact to satirize. See Elisabeth Bourguinat, *Le siècle du persiflage, 1734–1789* (Paris: Presses Universitaires de France, 1998).

54. Denis Diderot, *Paradoxe sur le comédien,* in *Oeuvres esthétiques,* 357. I have loosely based my translation on Lee Strasberg, *The Paradox of Acting* (New York: Hill & Wang, 1957).

55. Diderot, *Paradoxe sur le comédien,* 314, 358, 358–59, emphasis added.

56. Denis Diderot, *The Indiscreet Jewels,* trans. Sophie Hawkes (New York: Marsilio, 1993), 166.

57. Diderot, *Paradoxe sur le comédien,* 360, 362.

58. Ibid., 315.

59. Diderot, *Indiscreet Jewels,* 167.

60. Jean Le Rond d'Alembert, *Essai sur la société des gens de lettres et des grands,*

sur la réputation, sur les Mecènes, et sur les récompenses littéraires (1753; 2nd ed., 1764), in *Oeuvres de d'Alembert,* vol. 4 (Paris: A. Belin / Bossange Frères, 1822), 361.

61. Louis-Sébastien Mercier, untitled manuscript quoted in Pierre Frantz, "L'usage du peuple," in *Louis-Sébastien Mercier: Un hérétique en littérature,* ed. Jean-Claude Bonnet (Paris: Mercure de France, 1995), 78.

62. Diderot, *Paradoxe sur le comédien,* 362. Diderot follows Fénelon closely in his admiration for Sophocles' *Philoctetes:* both oppose the "sublime simplicity" of Sophocles to the decadence of contemporary theater. See François de Salignac de la Mothe-Fénelon, *Lettre à l'Académie* (1714), ed. Ernesta Calderini (Geneva: Droz, 1970), 93–94. In the *Paradoxe,* under cover of translation, Diderot freely rewrites Philoctetes' address to Neoptolemus as if it were a *drame bourgeois.*

63. Voltaire, *Lettre sur l'esprit,* 3. See also idem, *Commentaire sur Corneille* (1761–65).

64. Denis Diderot, *The Salon of 1767,* vol. 2 of *Diderot on Art,* trans. John Goodman (New Haven, CT: Yale University Press, 1995), 15.

65. Ibid., 188–89.

66. Denis Diderot, *De la poésie dramatique* (1758), in *Oeuvres esthétiques,* 260, 262.

67. Louis-Sébastien Mercier, "Triomphe de Voltaire: Janot," in *Tableaux de Paris,* 2:266. Of course, Mercier is being ironic: five hundred performances would have been a phenomenal number. Janot was the character played by the actor Volange (Maurice-François Rochet) in Dorvigny's immensely popular play *Les battus paient l'amende,* performed at the Variétés-Amusantes in 1778. Despite Mercier's praise, the play's *poissard* language was far from being "realistic" or untouched by crafted conventions; not surprisingly, since it had emerged from the imagination of a handful of aristocrats, writers, and amateurs, members of the Société du Bout du Banc (which counted among its members the comte de Caylus, the abbé de Sade, uncle of the marquis, Maurepas, La Chaussée, and Voisenon), founded in 1735. See Valeria Belt-Grannis, *Dramatic Parody in Eighteenth-Century France* (New York: Institute of French Studies, 1931), 138–39.

68. Pierre Carlet de Chamblain de Marivaux, foreword to *Les serments indiscrets* (1732), in Marivaux, *Théâtre complet,* ed. Henri Coulet and Michel Gilot, 2 vols. (Paris: Gallimard, 1993) 1:663.

69. "That eternal surprise of love, the one and only subject of Marivaux's comedies, was the main criticism that he had to endure concerning the subject matter of his plays." D'Alembert, *Eloge de Marivaux,* 20.

70. Let a screenwriter attempt to cross the boundaries, and language will dissolve into the grunts and groans of the Joel and Ethan Cohen's *Blood Simple* (1984), which is closer to the reality of the action it depicts than a conventionally written thriller. Conversely, what we take for real in "reality shows" is real in the limited sense that it reflects the reality of television formulas, a reality filtered by gauzy and contrived visual and narrative clichés. See Alessandra Stanley, "Blurring Reality with Soap Suds," *New York Times,* 22 February 2003, A-19. Director-screenwrit-

ers such as David Mamet and Eric Rohmer create subtle cognitive dissonance by blurring the line between informal conversation and "written" formality.

71. Voltaire to Jean-Baptiste Nicolas Formont, 18 April 1732 (Best. 464), in *Voltaire's Correspondence,* ed. Theodore Besterman, 107 vols. (Geneva: Institut et Musée Voltaire, 1953–65), 2:303.

72. Marivaux, foreword to *Les serments indiscrets,* 663.

73. See, e.g., Marmontel's *Mémoires* and *Eléments de littérature,* s.v. "Familier"; Crébillon's *L'écumoire;* and Diderot's *Les bijoux indiscrets.*

74. Pierre Corneille, *Discours de la tragédie* (1660), in *Oeuvres complètes,* ed. Georges Couton, 3 vols. (Paris: Gallimard, 1980–87), 3:154–55.

75. Marivaux, *Les serments indiscrets,* act 2, sc. 5; idem, *Les fausses confidences,* act 3, sc. 12; idem, *Le triomphe de l'amour,* act 3, sc. 9; Jean Racine, *Mithridate* 4.5.1382, in *Oeuvres complètes,* ed. Georges Forestier, 2 vols. (Paris: Gallimard, 1999), 1:675.

76. Quoted in d'Alembert, *Eloge de Marivaux.*

77. Jean-Marie Apostolidès, *Le prince sacrifié: Théâtre et politique au temps de Louis XIV* (Paris: Minuit, 1985), 116–17.

78. D'Alembert, *Eloge de Marivaux,* 20.

79. "Speech is action [*Parler c'est agir*]. . . . The entire representation of a tragedy consists in speech. . . . If we examine it carefully, we realize that the action resides in the imagination of the spectator, who, led skillfully by the author, is driven to conceive it as visible; yet, nothing is visible there but speech." François Hédelin, abbé d'Aubignac, *La pratique du théâtre,* ed. Hélène Baby (Paris: Champion, 2001), bk. 4, chap. 2, "Des discours en général," 407–8.

80. Jean-François de La Harpe, *Lycée ou cours de littérature ancienne et moderne,* 16 vols. (Paris: H. Agasse, 1799), vol. 11, pt. 3, bk. 1, chap. 5, p. 5049, www.lib.uchicago.edu/efts/ARTFL/databases/bibliopolis/cli/.

81. On the lower bourgeoisie's taste for seventeenth-century classical artists such as Poussin, Le Sueur, and Le Brun see Thomas Crow, *Painters and Public Life in Eighteenth-Century Paris* (New Haven, CT: Yale University Press, 1985), chap. 1.

82. Ibid., chap. 2.

Chapter 5   Grace and the Epistemology of Confused Perception

Epigraphs: Voltaire, *Lettre à M. D***,* in *Oeuvres complètes de Voltaire,* ed. Louis Moland, 52 vols. (Paris: Garnier, 1877–85), 22:1–11; Roland Barthes, *Le plaisir du texte* (1973; reprint, Paris: Seuil, 2000), 111.

1. Voltaire, "Esprit," in *Encyclopédie, ou dictionnaire raisonné des sciences, des arts et des métiers,* ed. Denis Diderot and Jean Le Rond d'Alembert, 32 vols. (Paris, 1751–77), 5 (1755): 973.

2. Antoine Furetière saw the burlesque and the conceit as forms of verbal excess issuing from the same source: "That genre of writing [burlesque] which came to us from Italy, together with witticism and nonsense, still betrays the libertinism

of its origins." Preface to his *Enéide travestie* (Paris, 1649). See also Jean-Louis Guez de Balzac: "As for that ancient grace that belonged to the writings of the Romans before the plaster and the coloring of the Spanish altered its purity, . . . you may conclude that the Spaniards ruined everything in the world." Quoted in Jean Jehasse, *Guez de Balzac et le génie romain, 1597–1654* (Saint-Etienne: Publications de l'Université de Saint-Etienne, 1977), 46.

3. Voltaire to the abbé Trublet, 27 April 1761 (Best. 8974), in *Voltaire's Correspondence,* ed. Theodore Besterman, 107 vols. (Geneva: Institut et Musée Voltaire, 1953–65), 45:312–13. For a history of the concept of *esprit* see Mercedes Blanco, *Les rhétoriques de la pointe: Baltasar Gracián et le conceptisme en Europe* (Paris: Champion, 1992), introduction. On the identification between Italian poetry and the excess of esprit see Alain Viala, "Le dialogue 'à la française' et les modèles italiens: Affirmations et dénégations d'une esthétique," in *Estetica e arte: Le concezioni dei "moderni,"* ed. Stefano Benassi (Bologna: Nuova Alfia Editoriale, 1991), 45–58; and Cecilia Rizza, "Le clinquant du Tasse," in *La France et l'Italie au temps de Mazarin,* ed. Jean Serroy (Grenoble: Presses Universitaires de Grenoble, 1986), 201–8.

4. Morvan de Bellegarde, *Lettres curieuses de littérature et de morale,* quoted in Bernard Magné, *La crise de la littérature française sous Louis XIV: Humanisme et nationalisme,* 2 vols. (Paris: Champion, 1976), 1:63.

5. Nicolas Boileau, *L'art poétique,* canto 2, lines 105–10, in *Oeuvres,* 2 vols. (Paris: Garnier-Flammarion, 1969), 2:95. Bellegarde's ires were directed against the generation of Voiture and Sarasin; when his text was written, the *goût moderne* was just emerging.

6. *Equivoque* is made to stand for the poetics of *galanterie.* See Nicolas Boileau, *Satire XII,* in *Oeuvres,* 1:33–34.

7. *Turlupinade* (from the stage name of the seventeenth-century actor Henri Legrand, who was Belleville on the tragic stage and Turlupin on the fairgrounds) is one of the many negative terms indicating jokes and wordplay, usually with a sexual or a scatological content.

8. The expressions are from the abbé Raynal in a text from 1748, quoted in Marivaux, *Journaux et oeuvres diverses,* ed. Frédéric Deloffre and Michel Gilot (Paris: Garnier, 1988), 714, hereafter cited as *JOD.*

9. Blaise Pascal, *Pensées,* ed. Léon Brunschvicg (Paris: Garnier-Flammarion, 1976), no. 1.

10. Ibid., 49–50.

11. See Jeffrey Barnouw's excellent synthesis in "The Beginnings of Aesthetics and the Leibnizian Concept of Sensation," in *Eighteenth-Century Aesthetics and the Reconstruction of Art,* ed. Paul Mattick Jr. (Cambridge: Cambridge University Press, 1993), 52–95.

12. Pierre Carlet de Chamblain de Marivaux, *La vie de Marianne,* ed. Frédéric Deloffre (Paris: Garnier, 1957), 166, emphasis added.

13. Ernst Cassirer defines the type of reason that is associated with *délicatesse* as follows: "The concept of 'délicatesse' as used by Bouhours, amounts, as it were,

to a new organ. The aim of this organ is not, as with mathematical thinking, consolidation, stabilization, and fixation of concepts; on the contrary, it is expressed in lightness and flexibility of thought, in the ability to grasp the finest shades and the quickest transitions of meaning." *The Philosophy of the Enlightenment* (Princeton, NJ: Princeton University Press, 1951), 300. See also Annie Becq, *Genèse de l'esthétique française moderne* (Paris: Albin Michel, 1994), esp. 97–114.

14. Pierre Carlet de Chamblain de Marivaux, *Le spectateur français*, in *JOD*, 256.

15. Marivaux, *La vie de Marianne*, 32–33. On sensitivity see Anne Vila, *Enlightenment and Pathology: Sensibility in the Literature and Medicine of Eighteenth-Century France* (Baltimore: Johns Hopkins University Press, 1998), esp. 128–40, for an analysis of *La vie de Marianne*.

16. Pierre Carlet de Chamblain de Marivaux, *Lettre sur les habitants de Paris*, in *JOD*, 34.

17. Pierre Carlet de Chamblain de Marivaux, "Sur la pensée sublime," in *Pensées sur différents sujets*, in *JOD*, 67.

18. Père Dominique Bouhours, *Le bel esprit*, in *Les entretiens d'Ariste et d'Eugène* (1671), ed. Bernard Beugnot and Gilles Declercq (Paris: Champion, 2003), 251.

19. This sense, which goes all the way back to a Galenic conception of the mind-body union, was attested by Antoine Furetière's *Dictionnaire universel* (Rotterdam, 1690), s.v. "Esprit": "*Esprit*, in terms of medicine, indicates those volatile and weightless atoms that are the smallest components of bodies, which give bodies their movement, act as a bridge between the body and the faculties of the soul, and allow the soul to perform all its operations. . . . *Esprit* is a subtle body, always moving, made of blood and vapors, carrier of the mind's faculties and commands by dint of nerves and muscles."

20. Ibid.

21. The Aristotelian text wavers, sometimes confusedly, between *energeia* and *enargeia*. The uncertainty between the two will shape the entire history of rhetoric. See Aristotle *Rhetoric* 3.1410b; and Michel Delon, *L'idée d'énergie au tournant des Lumières, 1770–1820* (Paris: Presses Universitaires de France, 1988), 36.

22. Voltaire, "Esprit," 974–75. See also idem *Lettre sur l'esprit* (1744, postface to *Mérope*), in *Oeuvres complètes de Voltaire*, ed. Moland, 19:3–9: "What we call *esprit* . . . is the art of uniting two distant objects, or dividing two objects that seem joined, or opposing them to each other."

23. Abbé Le Blanc, *Lettres de Monsieur l'abbé Le Blanc: Nouvelle edition de celles qui ont paru sous le titre de Lettres d'un François*, 3 vols. (Amsterdam, 1751) 3:359, quoted in Jean Weisgerber, *Les masques fragiles: Esthétique et formes de la littérature rococo* (Lausanne: L'Age d'Homme, 1991), 104.

24. Ibid., 2:51–52, quoted in Weisgerber, *Les masques fragiles*, 106–7.

25. Bouhours, *Le bel esprit*, 180–81.

26. See Thomas Hobbes, *Human Nature*, written in 1640 and published in 1650, chap. 10, sec. 4, quoted in Barnouw, "Beginnings of Aesthetics," 57: in wit,

or *ingenium,* "quick ranging of mind . . . is joined with curiosity of comparing the things which come into the mind, one with another: in which comparison, a man delighteth himself either with finding unexpected similitude of things, otherwise much unlike, in which men place the excellency of fancy . . . , or else in discerning suddenly dissimilitude in things that otherwise appear the same . . . which is commonly termed by the name of judgment: for to judge is nothing else, but to distinguish and discern: and both fancy and judgment are commonly comprehended under the name of wit, which seemeth to be a tenuity and agility of spirits."

27. John Locke, *An Essay Concerning Human Understanding* (1690), ed. Peter Nidditch (Oxford: Clarendon, 1975), bk. 2, chap. 11, sec. 2, p. 156.

28. The same mistrust of the value of *esprit* for the sciences may be found in Dumarsais: "[The philosopher] is not always able to avoid the vivid turns of phrase that come to mind by a prompt connection of ideas that we may be surprised to see joined. It is this sudden assemblage of ideas that is commonly called *esprit.* But it is also his least favorite, since to this glitter he prefers the painstaking distinction among ideas; he'd rather explore their exact extent and connection so as to avoid being misled and carried away by some random connection of ideas. It is in such discernment that consists what we call judgement and exactitude of mind." César Chesneau Dumarsais, *Le philosophe* (1730), in *Le Philosophe: Texts and Interpretation,* ed. Herbert Dieckmann (Saint Louis: Washington University Studies, 1948), 41.

29. Charles de Secondat, baron de Montesquieu, *The Spirit of the Laws,* ed. and trans. Anne M. Cohler, Basia Carolyn Miller, and Harold Samuel Stone (Cambridge: Cambridge University Press, 1989), xliv. In his early *Essai sur les causes qui peuvent affecter les esprits et les caractères* Montesquieu, like Locke, divides the two operations of the understanding along social and generic lines, but his whole work suggests that he sees those two modes as complementary: "*Esprit* for the worldly consists in bringing together the most distant ideas; *esprit* for the philosopher consists in distinguishing them. To the former, all ideas have some relation, however distant; to the latter, they are so distinct that nothing can join them." Montesquieu, *Oeuvres complètes,* vol. 2 (Paris: Gallimard, 1949), 58.

30. The subject of Denis Vairas's utopian novel, *Histoire des Sévarambes.*

31. Montesquieu, *Spirit of the Laws,* xliii.

32. Immanuel Kant, *Anthropology from a Pragmatic Point of View* (lectures delivered in 1772–73 and published in 1798), trans. Victor Lyle Dowdell (Carbondale: Southern Illinois University Press, 1978), 118–20.

33. Ironically, we find the same language in Diderot's passionate defense of Seneca's style against the numerous detractors who, for centuries, have accused Seneca of excessive subtlety of *esprit* and of a "desire to shine." When he falls in love with Seneca, Diderot switches gears: "Seneca speaks with the warmth of his soul and the nobility of his character. If he has brilliance, it is like a diamond or the stars, whose nature it is to sparkle. Blaming him for an affectation of brilliance is like blaming the swallow for the grace of its flight. Seneca has the tone of *bel esprit*

as someone else would have a tone of conceit, without being aware of it." Denis Diderot, *Essai sur les règnes de Claude et de Néron,* in *Oeuvres,* ed. Laurent Versini, vol. 1, *Philosophie* (Paris: Robert Laffont, 1994), 1130.

34. Bouhours, *Le bel esprit,* 239.

35. As Marian Hobson observes, the *papillotage* of rococo painting is the visual equivalent of the narrative techniques of interruption used by Scarron and Diderot. *The Object of Art: The Theory of Illusion in Eighteenth-Century France* (Cambridge: Cambridge University Press, 1982), 52. See also Diderot: "A prolixity of incidents can impose a flicker effect on the mind that's just as unpleasant as the one inflicted on the eyes by poor distribution of light, and while this flickering light destroys harmony, the flickering of excess incident disperses interest and destroys unity." Denis Diderot, *The Salon of 1767,* vol. 2 of *Diderot on Art,* trans. John Goodman (New Haven, CT: Yale University Press, 1995), 291.

36. Georges-Louis Leclerc de Buffon, "Discours sur le style," inaugural speech to the French Academy, 25 August 1753, \www.academie-francaise.fr/immortels/index.html.

37. "Hence, though these things seem to glitter and to some extent to stand out, their brilliance may be said to resemble not so much a flame as a few sparks emerging from the smoke (indeed they are invisible when the whole speech is bright, just as stars cannot be seen in sunlight." Quintilian, *The Orator's Education,* ed. and trans. Donald A. Russell (Cambridge, MA: Harvard University Press, 2001), 8.5.29, pp. 421–22.

38. Ibid., 8.5.34, pp. 423–24.

39. *Kritische Friedrich-Schlegel-Ausgabe,* ed. Ernst Beheler et al. (Munich: Ferdinand Schöningh, 1958–), 12:392–93, English translation by Michel Chaouli in *The Laboratory of Poetry: Chemistry and Poetics in the Work of Friedrich Schlegel* (Baltimore: Johns Hopkins University Press, 2002), 203–4.

40. Jean Paul, *Werke,* ed. Norbert Miller, 6 vols. (Munich: C. Hanser, 1966–75), vol. 5, *Vorschule der Asthetik,* 171, quotation trans. Paul Fleming in "The Dissonant Whole: Jean Paul's Polyphonic Prose" (PhD diss., Johns Hopkins University, 2002), 27.

41. I rely here upon Paul Fleming's analysis in "The Dissonant Whole," 26–33.

42. Diderot, *Salon of 1767,* 113.

43. Denis Diderot, "Génie," in Diderot and d'Alembert, *Encyclopédie,* 7 (1757): 583.

44. See Patrick Brady, *Rococo Style versus Enlightenment Novel* (Geneva: Slatkine, 1984); and idem, *Structuralist Perspectives in Criticism of Fiction: Essays on "Manon Lescaut" and "La Vie de Marianne"* (Bern: Lang, 1978).

45. "The phrase is deployed by successive touch-ups, by replications and corrections. By using simple procedures, such as reiteration, corrective adjustment, apposition, he creates a phrase that is so flexible that it will not find its equal until Proust, or at least until the Goncourts." Frédéric Deloffre, *Marivaux et le marivaudage: Une préciosité nouvelle,* 2nd ed. (Paris: Colin, 1967), 443.

46. Pierre Carlet de Chamblain de Marivaux, *Le paysan parvenu,* ed. Frédéric Deloffre (Paris: Garnier, 1959), 129–30.

47. "After those short reflections, which in the mind of our admirers occur in one instant, and not consecutively as we describe them here" (Marivaux, *Lettre sur les habitants de Paris,* in *JOD,* 37); "All I do is unravel the chaos of their ideas: I itemize whatever they experience wholesale" (idem, *Le spectateur français,* in *JOD,* 126); "By the way, what came to my mind at that time, though lengthy to say, only took an instant in my thought" (idem, *La vie de Marianne,* 72); "That thought came spontaneously; it may seem contrived, but it isn't: nothing is simpler" (ibid., 37); "Can we say all that we feel? Those who believe that do not feel much, and they probably only see half of what one can see" (idem, *Le paysan parvenu,* 142).

48. Denis Diderot, *Lettre sur les sourds et muets,* in *Lettre sur les aveugles, Lettre sur les sourds et muets,* ed. Marian Hobson and Simon Harvey (Paris: Garnier-Flammarion, 2000), 111.

49. Denis Diderot, *Jacques the Fatalist and His Master,* trans. J. Robert Loy (New York: Collier Books, 1959), 29.

50. Jean-François Marmontel, *Poétique française* (Paris: Lesclapart, 1763). I thank Luc Monnin for bringing this text to my attention.

51. Jean Le Rond d'Alembert, *Discours préliminaire* to Diderot and d'Alembert, *Encyclopédie,* 1 (1751) ix.

52. Père Dominique Bouhours, *Le je ne sais quoi,* in *Les entretiens d'Ariste et d'Eugène,* 281. In France, the earliest formulation of an aesthetics of *je ne sais quoi* is probably by the poet Jean Ogier de Gombauld, "Sur le je ne sais quoi," his inaugural speech to the French Academy in 1635. On the history of the concept see Erich Köler, "*Je ne sais quoi:* Ein Kapitel aus der Begriffgeschichte des Unbegreiflichen," *Romanistisches Jahrbuch* 6 (1953–54): 21–59; Jean-Pierre Dens, *L'honnête homme et la critique du goût* (Lexington, KY: French Forum, 1981), esp. chap. 3; Pierre-Henri Simon, "Le je ne sais quoi devant la raison classique," *Cahiers de l'Association Internationale des Études Françaises* 11 (May 1959): 104–17; and Delon, *L'idée d'énergie au tournant des Lumières,* 65–71. See also Barnouw, "Beginnings of Aesthetics."

53. Bouhours, *Le je ne sais quoi,* 284.

54. André Félibien, entretien 1 in *Entretiens sur les vies et les ouvrages des plus excellents peintres anciens et modernes* (1666), ed. René Démoris (Paris: Les Belles Lettres, 1987), 120–22.

55. Charles de Secondat, baron de Montesquieu, *Essai sur le goût,* in *Oeuvres complètes,* 2:1253–54. For a later formulation see Jules Barbey d'Aurevilly, *La vengeance d'une femme,* in *Les diaboliques* (1874): "There is much less variety than we think in the human countenance, whose traits obey a narrow and inflexible geometry and may be reduced to a few general types. Beauty is one: only ugliness is diverse. . . . God has ordered that physiognomy alone should be infinite, because physiognomy is the immersion of the soul into the perfect or imperfect, pure or tormented, outline of the face." In *Oeuvres romanesques complètes,* ed. Jacques Petit, 2 vols. (Paris: Gallimard, 1964–66), 2:233–34.

56. See Edmund Burke, *A Philosophical Enquiry into the Origin of Our Ideas of the Sublime and the Beautiful* (1757), ed. David Womersley (London: Penguin Books, 1998), pt. 2.

57. Pierre Carlet de Chamblain de Marivaux, *Le cabinet du philosophe,* in *JOD,* 347.

58. For Dominique Bouhours, the ideal of beauty is associated negatively with the pomp and magnificence of the rhetorically inflated noble style (the Ciceronian *genus vehemens* or the swollen sublime), which excites cold admiration but carries no persuasion and does not stir the emotions: "In matters of taste [*esprit*] it is neither the grand nor the [emphatic] sublime that we like: it is an undefinable quality [*je ne sais quoi*] of tenuity and agility [*fin et délicat*]. . . . Beauty itself, when it is so splendid, is overpowering rather than pleasing. Whatever is offered exclusively for admiration quickly becomes tiresome and no longer excites any emotion." There is in those definitions an implicit critique of the monarchical pomp of Versailles. *Pensées ingénieuses des anciens et des modernes* (1689), quoted in Sophie Hache, *La langue du ciel: Le sublime en France au XVIIe siècle* (Paris: Champion, 2000), 93.

59. Marivaux, *Le cabinet du philosophe,* in *JOD,* 349–50.

60. Ibid., 350.

61. The *Je ne sais quoi* presents life, as Thomas Kavanagh puts it, "as an epiphany of unexpected discontinuities rather than as a fulfillment of promised coherencies. The life portrayed . . . is one open far more to the abrupt redefinition of surprise than to the predictable certitudes of the sequence." Kavanagh, *The Aesthetics of the Moment: Literature and Art in the French Enlightenment* (Philadelphia: University of Pennsylvania Press, 1996), 7.

62. Marivaux, *Le cabinet du philosophe,* in *JOD,* 349.

63. Ibid., 350–51.

64. Gottfried Wilhelm Leibniz, *New Essays on Human Understanding,* trans. and ed. Peter Remnant and Jonathan Bennett (Cambridge: Cambridge University Press, 1996), preface, secs. 53, 55. Written in 1703–4, the book was not published until 1765.

65. Unconscious and imperceptible impressions, which are stored in the soul and exercise a covert action, account for the effect of theater on the spectator and of literature on the reader: "The passions that take hold of us are imprinted in our books and then carry this imperceptible imprint right into the soul of those who read them. . . . By reading the books of other human beings, we are imperceptibly filled with their vices." Pierre Nicole, "De la manière d'étudier chrétiennement," from *Essais de morale,* vol. 2, secs. 8 and 9, quoted in Pierre Nicole, *Traité de la comédie et autres pièces d'un procès du théâtre,* ed. Laurent Thirouin (Paris: Champion, 1998), 50n27.

66. Grace acts through imperceptible and unformulated thoughts, which are more powerful determinants to action than linguistically mediated thoughts. The idea of injustice, for instance, "is blended and confused in the mind of men with objects that hold our attention more directly. We know those actions directly, but

we feel their injustice only by virtue of accessory ideas that we do not distinguish clearly and whose effect is felt only through the aversion they give us for those actions." Pierre Nicole, *Traité de la grâce générale,* quoted in Louis Marin, "La critique de la représentation théâtrale classique à Port-Royal: Commentaires sur *Le Traité de la comedie* de Nicole," *Continuum* 2 (1990): 81–105.

67. Pierre Nicole, *Essais de morale,* quoted in ibid., 99.

68. Denis Diderot, *Eloge de Richardson* (1762), in *Oeuvres esthétiques,* ed. Paul Vernière (Paris: Garnier, 1968), 31.

69. Nicolas Malebranche, *The Search after Truth* (1674), trans. Thomas M. Lennon and Paul J. Olscamp (Columbus: Ohio State University Press, 1980), bk. 3, pt. 1, chap. 4, p. 212.

70. Marivaux, *Le cabinet du philosophe,* in *JOD,* 350.

71. Bouhours, *Le je ne sais quoi,* 293.

72. Leibniz, *New Essays on Human Understanding,* II, xxi, sec. 36, pp. 188–90.

73. The quotation is from ibid. On window-shopping and the Saint-Germain fair as shopping theater under Louis XIV's reign see Joan DeJean, *The Essence of Style* (New York: Free Press, 2005), chap. 12.

74. Pierre Carlet de Chamblain de Marivaux, "Pensées sur la clarté du discours," in *Pensées sur différents sujets,* in *JOD,* 53.

75. Louis-Sébastien Mercier, paraphrasing Saint-Evremond in "De la réticence," in *Mon bonnet de nuit, suivi de Du théâtre* (1784–85), ed. Jean-Claude Bonnet and Pierre Frantz (Paris: Mercure de France, 1999), 741. *Il faut composer avec lui* may also be intended as "we need to make a deal with him" or "we need to come to terms with him."

76. Père Dominique Bouhours, *De la manière de bien penser dans les ouvrages d'esprit* (1687; reprint, ed. Suzanne Gellouz, Toulouse: Atelier de l'Université de Toulouse-Le-Mirail, 1988), 158–61.

77. Ibid., 161.

78. Diderot, "Génie," 583.

79. Montesquieu, *Spirit of the Laws,* bk. 11, chap. 20, p. 186.

80. Charles-Rivière Dufresny, *Les amusements sérieux et comiques* (Paris: Claude Barbin, 1699), amusement 1, quoted in *Moralistes du XVIIe siècle,* ed. Jacques Chupeau (Paris: Robert Laffont, 1992), 977.

81. Charles de Secondat, baron de Montesquieu, *Quelques réflexions sur les Lettres persanes,* in *Lettres persanes,* ed. Paul Vernière (Paris: Garnier, 1975), 6.

82. Quoted in Bertrand Binoche, *Introduction à De l'esprit des lois de Montesquieu* (Paris: Presses Universitaires de France, 1998), 12. See also Roger Laufer, *Style rococo, style des Lumières* (Paris: Corti, 1963), 25.

83. Pierre Carlet de Chamblain de Marivaux, *Oeuvres de jeunesse,* ed. Frédéric Deloffre and Claude Rigault (Paris: Gallimard, 1972), 457.

Chapter 6   Between Paris and Rome

Epigraphs: Voltaire, *Idées républicaines par un membre d'un corps* (1765), in *Oeuvres complètes de Voltaire,* ed. Louis Moland, 52 vols. (Paris: Garnier, 1877–85), 24:413–32; Denis Diderot, *Le neveu de Rameau,* ed. Jean-Claude Bonnet (Paris: Garnier-Flammarion, 1983), 74.

1. Voltaire to Nicolas-Claude Thieriot, November(?) 1734 (Best. 780), in *Voltaire's Correspondence,* ed. Theodore Besterman, 107 vols. (Geneva: Institut et Musée Voltaire, 1953–65), 3:326, original letter in English.

2. Denis Diderot, fragment on portraits and history painting in appendix 2 to *Salon III: Ruines et paysages* (Paris: Hermann, 1995), 515.

3. Fénelon, *Lettre à l'Académie,* chap. 8, "Projet d'un traité sur l'histoire," 108–9.

4. "Pura et illustri brevitate dulcius." Cicero *Brutus* 25.262.

5. Fénelon, *Lettre à l'Académie,* 111.

6. See Patrick Andrivet and Catherine Volpilhac-Auger, introduction to Charles de Secondat, baron de Montesquieu, *Considérations sur les causes de la grandeur des Romains et de leur décadence,* in *Oeuvres complètes de Montesquieu,* ed. Françoise Weil and Cecil Courtney, vol. 2 (Oxford: Voltaire Foundation; Naples: Istituto Italiano per gli Studi Filosofici, 2000), 23. Even a few years later, in *The Spirit of the Laws,* ed. and trans. Anne M. Cohler, Basia Carolyn Miller, and Harold Samuel Stone (Cambridge: Cambridge University Press, 1989), bk. 11, chaps. 12–14, Montesquieu does not seem to doubt the existence of the Roman monarchy.

7. Fénelon, *Lettre à L'Académie,* 110.

8. Ibid., 106.

9. Voltaire, "Histoire," in *Encyclopédie, ou dictionnaire raisonné des sciences, des arts et des métiers,* ed. Denis Diderot and Jean Le Rond d'Alembert, 32 vols. (Paris, 1751–77), 8 (1765): 223.

10. Jacques-Bénigne Bossuet, foreword to *Discours sur l'histoire universelle,* ed. Jacques Truchet (Paris: Garnier-Flammarion, 1966), 41. On the rhetorical nature of history in the eighteenth century see Lionel Gossman, "History and Literature: Reproduction or Signification," in *Between History and Literature* (Cambridge, MA: Harvard University Press, 1990), 227–56.

11. Charles de Secondat, baron de Montesquieu, *Mes pensées,* no. 1183, in Montesquieu, *Pensées/Le spicilège,* ed. Louis Desgraves (Paris: Robert Laffont, 1991), 403.

12. Charles de Secondat, baron de Montesquieu, *Considerations on the Causes of the Greatness of the Romans and Their Decline,* trans. David Lowenthal (New York: Free Press, 1965), chap. 16, p. 148. Unless otherwise noted, I refer to the edition revised by Montesquieu in 1748 and published under the title *Grandeur et décadence des Romains,* ed. Jean Ehrard (Paris: Garnier-Flammarion, 1968). Whenever necessary, I have also used the original 1734 edition, published in the *Oeuvres complètes de Montesquieu,* vol. 2. English translations are from Lowenthal's translation, which is based on the 1748 edition, with minor modifications.

13. Ibid., chap. 12, p. 117.

14. "It is undoubtedly great men who constitute the strength of an empire. . . . The Roman state had a temperament . . . most productive of heroes." Bossuet, *Discours sur l'histoire universelle*, pt. 3, chap. 6, pp. 404–5.

15. Montesquieu, *Considerations*, chap. 19, p. 177.

16. See Jean-Marie Apostolidès, *Le roi machine* (Paris: Minuit, 1981), esp. chap. 6.

17. Jean-Louis Guez de Balzac, *Suite d'un entretien de vive voix, ou De la conversation des Romains*, in *Oeuvres diverses* (1644), ed. Roger Zuber (Paris: Champion, 1995), 75.

18. Montesquieu, *Considerations*, chap. 13, p. 123.

19. Voltaire, *Le siècle de Louis XIV*, chap. 1. See also Frederick II's preface to *La Henriade* (1717): "The century of Louis the Great, of which it can be said, without any flattery, that it equals perhaps that of Augustus, gives us the same example of a happy and tranquil reign in the interior of the kingdom." In *La Henriade*, in *Oeuvres complètes de Voltaire/Complete Works of Voltaire*, ed. Ulla Kölvig et al. (Geneva: Institut et Musée Voltaire; Toronto: University of Toronto Press, 1968–), 2:361.

20. Montesquieu, *Mes pensées*, nos. 1302 and 1306, in *Pensées/Le spicilège*, 456, 458.

21. Montesquieu, *Considerations*, chap. 13, p. 121.

22. Montesquieu, *Mes pensées*, no. 1088, in *Pensées/Le spicilège*, 391.

23. "Since corrupt peoples rarely do great things and have established few societies, founded few towns, and given few laws; and since, on the contrary, those with simple and austere mores have made most establishments, recalling men to the old maxims usually returns them to virtue." Montesquieu, *Spirit of the Laws*, bk. 5, chap. 7, p. 49.

24. Montesquieu, *Considerations*, chap. 2, p. 36.

25. Ibid., chap. 1, p. 32.

26. Giuseppa Saccaro Del Buffa, "Le passioni come artificio storiografico nelle *Considerazioni* di Montesquieu," in *Storia e ragione*, ed. Alberto Postigliola (Naples: Liguori Editore, 1987), 220.

27. Montesquieu, *Considerations*, chap. 9, pp. 92–93.

28. Montesquieu, *Spirit of the Laws*, bk. 3, chap. 6, p. 26. See also idem, *Mes pensées*, no. 221, in *Pensées/Le spicilège*, 253: "It is the love of their country that lends Greek and Roman histories that nobility that is unknown to ours. Virtue, beloved by all who have a heart, is the perpetual springwell of all their actions. When one thinks of the meanness of our motives, the inadequacy of our means, the greed with which we pursue contemptible rewards, of our ambition so remote from the love of glory, one is stunned by the diversity of the spectacles. Now that those two peoples are gone, it seems as if men's stature had shrunk a great deal." See also Montesquieu, *Spirit of the Laws*, bk. 4, chap. 4.

29. Montesquieu, *Considerations*, chap. 4, pp. 45–46.

30. "When they were mixed in with the barbarians, they contracted the spirit of independence which marked the character of these nations." Ibid., chap. 18, p. 171. Such spirit is far from negative for Montesquieu: "Each age has its peculiar temperament: a spirit of turmoil and independence rose in Europe with the

Gothic government." Montesquieu, *Mes pensées,* no. 810, in *Pensées/Le spicilège,* 351–52.

31. Jean Bouhier, *Correspondance littéraire du Président Jean Bouhier,* ed. Henri Duranton (Saint-Etienne: Université de Saint-Etienne, 1987), letter 13, p. 144.

32. Antoine Gombauld, chevalier de Méré, *Suite de la vraie honnêteté,* in *Oeuvres complètes du Chevalier de Méré* (1668), ed. Charles-Henri Boudhors, 3 vols. (Paris: Fernand Roches, 1930), 2:92; Charles de Saint-Evremond, *Réflexions sur les divers génies du peuple romain dans les divers temps de la république* (1684), in *Oeuvres en prose,* ed. René Ternois, vol. 2 (Paris: Marcel Didier, 1965), 229; Voltaire, introduction to *Essai sur les moeurs et sur l'esprit des nations,* ed. Réné Pomeau, 2 vols. (Paris: Garnier, 1963), 1:181. Montesquieu is no less severe; see *Considerations,* chap. 6, p. 74.

33. A move that was indebted to Bernard Le Bouvier de Fontenelle's *De l'origine des fables:* "The tales of the Greeks were unlike our novels, which pass as such and not as history: all ancient history was fabulous." Corpus des oeuvres de philosophie en langue française, 3 (Paris: Fayard, 1989), 187.

34. Saint-Evremond, *Réflexions sur les divers génies du peuple romain,* 222.

35. Voltaire turned legend into parody: "The great Romulus, king of a village, is the son of the god Mars and a nun who went searching for water with her jug. He had a god for a father and a whore for a mother. . . . The Gauls from yonder came to plunder Rome. Some say that they were scared away by geese, others, that they took with them a lot of gold and money; more likely, in those times there were in Italy a lot more geese than money. We have ourselves copied the early Roman historians, at least when it comes to their taste for tales. We have our oriflamme carried by an angel and our holy ampulla carried by a pigeon." Voltaire, *De l'histoire* (1764), in *Oeuvres complètes de Voltaire,* ed. Moland, 19:352–56.

36. Emile Faguet, preface to Montesquieu, *Considerations* (Paris: Nelson, n.d.), quoted in Corrado Rosso, "Demiurgia e parabola delle *élites* nelle *Considerations,*" in Postigliola, *Storia e ragione,* 188.

37. Jean Le Rond d'Alembert, *Eloge de M. le Président de Montesquieu,* in Diderot et d'Alembert, *Encyclopédie,* 5 (1755): vii.

38. Voltaire, "Histoire," 223.

39. Montesquieu, *Mes pensées,* no. 120, in *Pensées/Le spicilège,* 216.

40. Pasquale Anfossi, quoted in Françoise Weil's introduction to Montesquieu's *Considerations,* 45–46. The Latin *soluta oratio, et e singulis non membris sed frustis conlata* translates as "This leads as a rule to a broken style, made up not of cola, but of tiny scraps, and devoid of structure." Quintilian, *The Orator's Education,* ed. and trans. Donald A. Russell (Cambridge, MA: Harvard University Press, 2001), 8.5.27, p. 421. On Montesquieu's use of *saillies* throughout his *oeuvre* see Corrado Rosso, "L'ideale letterario di Montesquieu et il problema delle saillies," in *Montesquieu moralista: Dalle leggi al "bonheur"* (Pisa: Libreria Goliardica, 1965), 26–60.

41. See Georges-Louis Leclerc de Buffon, "Discours sur le style," inaugural speech

to the French Academy, 25 August 1753, www.academie-francaise.fr/immortels/index.html.

42. Louis-Sébastien Mercier, preface to *Montesquieu à Marseille* (Lausanne: Heubach, 1784), 6–7.

43. Antoine-Léonard Thomas, "De l'homme de lettres considéré comme citoyen," inaugural speech to the French Academy, 22 January 1767, www.academie-francaise.fr/immortels/discours_reception/thomas1.html.

44. Voltaire, *Idées républicaines par un membre d'un corps.* Voltaire may have borrowed here the critique formulated by the financier Claude Dupin, who had published in 1749 an acerbic pamphlet against *De l'esprit des lois.* Dupin, the author of the widely circulated quip that Montesquieu's treatise was nothing but "de l'esprit sur les lois," had written that the pace of the book was "so uncertain, so rapid, so leaping that we lose our way at every moment; all of a sudden, we are transported, from a familiar country to the most exotic regions." *Réflexions sur quelques parties d'un livre intitulé De l'esprit des loix,* quoted in Corrado Rosso, "Montesquieu et Claude Dupin: Una stroncatura infelice," in Rosso, *Montesquieu moralista,* 252. It might have been the Dupin *coterie* that Diderot had in mind, along with that of Bertin-Hus when he had the Neveu declare, "We shall prove that de Voltaire is no genius; that Buffon, always perched on stilts, is nothing but a pompous haranguer; that Montesquieu is nothing but a *bel esprit.*" Diderot, *Le neveu de Rameau,* 74.

45. Denis Diderot, *The Indiscreet Jewels,* trans. Sophie Hawkes (New York: Marsilio, 1993), 247.

46. Charles Pinot Duclos, *Acajou et Zirphile* (1744), ed. Jean Dagen (Paris: Desjonquières, 1993), 61.

47. Dupin, *Réflexions sur quelques parties d'un livre,* quoted in Rosso, *Montesquieu moralista,* 252. Montesquieu's disclaimer, in the preface to *The Spirit of the Laws,* xliv, forestalls such criticism: "The sallies [*traits saillants*] that seem to characterize present-day works will not be found here. As soon as matters are seen from a certain distance such sallies vanish."

48. Jean-Jacques Rousseau, preface to *Julie or the New Heloise,* trans. Philip Stewart and Jean Vaché, in *The Collected Writings of Rousseau,* ed. Roger D. Masters and Christopher Kelly, vol. 6 (Hanover, NH: University Press of New England, 1997), 10.

49. François Ogier, *Apologie pour Monsieur de Balzac,* ed. Jean Jehasse (Paris: Claude Morlot, 1623; Saint-Etienne: Editions Universitaires de Saint-Etienne, 1977), 72.

50. Pierre Costar, *Suite de la défense des oeuvres de Mr de Voiture, à Monsieur Ménage* (Paris: Augustin Courbé, 1665), 72, quoted in Sophie Hache, *La langue du ciel: Le sublime en France au XVIIe siècle* (Paris: Champion, 2000), 69–70.

51. *Oeuvres complètes de Voltaire,* ed. Moland, 19:3–9.

52. Pierre-François Guyot Desfontaines, *Jugements sur quelques ouvrages nou-*

veaux, II vols. (Avignon: Pierre Giroux, 1744–46; Geneva: Slatkine Reprints, 1967), 1:238.

53. Jean Le Rond d'Alembert, *Essai sur la société des gens de lettres et des grands, sur la réputation, sur les Mécènes, et sur les récompenses littéraires* (1753; 2nd ed., 1764), in *Oeuvres de d'Alembert,* vol. 4 (Paris: A. Belin/Bossange Frères, 1822), 362.

54. Montesquieu, *Mes pensées,* no. 721, in *Pensées/Le spicilège,* 339.

55. Ibid., no. 2101, p. 634.

56. See Longinus, *Traité du sublime,* trans. Nicolas Boileau (1674), ed. Francis Goyet (Paris: Le Livre de Poche, 1995), 12.4, p. 93. A parallel has been drawn between Montesquieu's prose and Tacitus's: "The mechanism of Tacitus's style is original. Ellipsis is very frequent with him. As he leaps from one object to the next, he touches only on the main points; he subtly understates them; he omits transitions; he is a profound soul who seems to have several erogenous zones." Louis-Sébastien Mercier, "Tacite," in *Mon bonnet de nuit, suivi de Du théâtre* (1784–85), ed. Jean-Claude Bonnet and Pierre Frantz (Paris: Mercure de France, 1999), 266. See also Catherine Volpilhac-Auger, *Tacite et Montesquieu,* Studies on Voltaire and the Eighteenth Century, 232 (Oxford: Voltaire Foundation, 1985).

57. For an excellent analysis of the poetic quality of Montesquieu's text see Pierre Rétat, "Images et expression du merveilleux dans les *Considerations,*" in Postigliola, *Storia e ragione,* 207–17.

58. Charles de Secondat, baron de Montesquieu, *Essai sur le goût,* ed. Louis Desgraves (Paris: Payot et Rivages, 1993). Montesquieu started working on the essay about 1726–28, influenced by his reading of the abbé Du Bos's *Réflexions critiques sur la poésie et sur la peinture* (1719); he revised it in 1735 and again toward the end of his life, without completing it.

59. Bossuet, *Discours sur l'histoire universelle,* pt. 3, chap. 6, p. 392.

60. Montesquieu, *Considerations,* chap. 1, pp. 23–24.

61. Ibid., p. 24.

62. Longinus, *Traité du sublime,* trans. Boileau, ed. Goyet, 1.4, p. 74.

63. Montesquieu, *Mes pensées,* no. 1071, in *Pensées/Le spicilège,* 390.

64. René Descartes, *Traité des passions de l'âme,* sec. 70, in *Philosophical Works of Descartes,* trans. E. Haldane and G. R. T. Ross (New York: Dover, 1911), unpaginated.

65. Ibid., sec. 75.

66. Edmund Burke, *A Philosophical Enquiry into the Origin of Our Ideas of the Sublime and the Beautiful* (1757), ed. David Womersley (London: Penguin Books, 1998), pt. 2, sec. 1, p. 101.

67. Montesquieu, *Considerations,* chap. 3, p. 39.

68. Montesquieu, *Mes pensées,* nos. 118 and 1444, in *Pensées/Le spicilège,* 215, 477. On the visual dimension of theatrical narrative see François Hédelin, abbé d'Aubignac, *La pratique du théâtre,* ed. Hélène Baby (Paris: Champion, 2001), bk. 4, chap. 2, pp. 407–8.

69. Montesquieu, *Considerations,* chap. 4, p. 49; chap. 7, p. 81; chap. 15, p. 138.

70. Montesquieu, *Mes pensées*, no. 1507, in *Pensées/Le spicilège*, 486. See also idem, *Spirit of the Laws*, bk. 11, chap. 15, p. 176: "The Roman people, more than any other, were moved by spectacles."

71. Longinus *Traité du sublime* 15.1. See also Quintilian: "Vividness [*enargeia*], or, as some say, 'representation' [*evidentia*], is more than mere clarity of expression, since instead of being merely transparent it somehow shows itself off. It is a great virtue to express our subject clearly, but also in such a way that it seems to be actually seen [*ostendit*]. A speech does not adequately fulfil its purpose or attain the total domination [*plene dominatur*] it should have if it goes no further than the ears, and the judge feels that he is merely being told the story of the matters he has to decide, without their being brought out and displayed to his mind's eye [*oculis mentis ostendit*]." Quintilian, *Orator's Education*, 8.3.61, pp. 375–76.

72. Montesquieu, *Essai sur le goût*, 16–17.

73. Montesquieu, *Mes pensées*, no. 2061, in *Pensées/Le spicilège*, 630: "A great man is someone who sees rapidly, far away, and accurately."

74. Mme de Lambert to Montesquieu, 10 December 1728, quoted in Rosso, *Montesquieu moralista*, 57.

75. Charles de Secondat, baron de Montesquieu, *Essai sur les causes qui peuvent affecter les esprits et les caractères*, in *Oeuvres complètes*, vol. 2 (Paris: Gallimard, 1949), 57.

76. Montesquieu, *Considerations*, chap. 7, p. 81.

77. Ibid., chap. 5, p. 57; chap. 12, p. 117.

78. Montesquieu, *Mes pensées*, no. 1970, in *Pensées/Le spicilège*, 607. On Pierre Nicole's statement see Montesquieu, *Considerations*, chap. 5, p. 32.

79. Montesquieu, *Essai sur le goût*, 17–18.

80. Longinus, *Traité du sublime*, trans. Boileau, ed. Goyet, 20.1–21.1, pp. 106–7.

81. Montesquieu, *Considerations*, chap. 5, p. 56; chap. 14, p. 133.

82. Montesquieu, *Essai sur le goût*, 29.

83. Montesquieu, *Considerations*, chap. 15, p. 138. This is a paraphrase of Claudian's *Rufinum* 1.22–23, "Tolluntur in altum ut lapsu graviore ruant" [They were raised high so as to fall with greater clash], which was to have been the epigraph of the *Considérations*. See Montesquieu, *Mes pensées*, no. 1519, in *Pensées/Le spicilège*, 488.

84. Montesquieu, *Considerations*, chap. 1, p. 27.

85. Ibid., manuscript variation to chap. 2 quoted in Françoise Weil's edition of the *Considérations*, 102.

86. Montesquieu, *Considerations*, chap. 1, pp. 27–29.

87. Ibid., chap. 6, p. 75.

88. Ibid., chap. 11, p. 111. This description of the proximity between the atrocious (or the bestial) and the divine may be indebted to Plutarch's commentary on the first Brutus, the executioner of his children. (Montesquieu had read and appreciated Plutarch's *Life of Brutus*.) We may also note the disjunctive analysis of Brutus's motivations and the historian's suspension of judgment: "It was an act

that cannot be praised or blamed enough, for it was either a superiority of virtue that made his heart impassive or a violent passion that made it insensitive, neither being negligible, but surpassing human nature and touching on the divine or the bestial." Plutarch, *Publicola,* trans. Amyot (1645), quoted in Charles de Saint-Evremond, *Réflexions sur les divers génies du peuple romain dans les divers temps de la république* (1684), in *Oeuvres en prose,* ed. René Ternois, vol. 2 (Paris: Marcel Didier, 1965), 228.

89. "The only talent worthy of Rome is conquering the world and enforcing on it the rule of virtue." Jean-Jacques Rousseau, *Discours sur les sciences et les arts,* in *Oeuvres complètes,* ed. Bernard Gagnebin and Marcel Raymond, vol. 3 (Paris: Gallimard, 1964), 15. "Men conquered with no motive and no utility. They ravaged the earth in order to exercise their virtue and display their excellence. Now that we have been assessing the value of things more fairly, heroes have been covered with ridicule; and those who would defend them, would be a thousand times more ridiculous still." Montesquieu, *Mes pensées,* no. 575, in *Pensées/Le spicilège,* 321.

90. Montesquieu, *Mes pensées,* no. 1935, in *Pensées/Le spicilège,* 589.

91. Montesquieu, *Spirit of the Laws,* bk. 11, chap. 4, p. 155; see also bk. 28, chap. 41, p. 595.

92. Ibid., bk. 29, chap. 18, p. 617. Montesquieu repeatedly criticizes the fascination for uniformity; see ibid., bk. 5, chap. 14, and bk. 6, chap. 2.

93. Ibid., bk. 3, chap. 10, p. 29; bk. 5, chap. 10, p. 57.

94. "A good law must be good for all men, as a true proposition is true for everybody." Marie-Jean-Antoine-Nicolas de Caritat, marquis de Condorcet, *Observations sur le vingt-neuvième livre de "L'esprit des lois"* (1817), quoted in Montesquieu, *De l'esprit des lois,* ed. Robert Derathé, 2 vols. (Paris: Garnier, 1973), 2:548. On Condorcet's objections to Montesquieu's pluralism see Jean Erhard, "L'aune ou le mètre?" in *L'esprit des mots* (Genève: Droz, 1998), 295–306.

95. "In order to put together a moderate government, one must offset powers against each other, fine-tune and regulate them, encourage one so as to enable it to resist another. It is a masterpiece of legislation that chance rarely assembles and that prudence is never allowed to put together." Montesquieu, *Mes pensées,* no. 892, in *Pensées/Le spicilège,* 366–67; see also idem, *Spirit of the Laws,* bk. 5, chap. 14. Montesquieu uses the metaphor of the machine to account not only for the dynamism of political communities but also for the rhetorical organization of *De l'esprit des lois:* "When a work is systematic, one must be sure to embrace the whole system. You see a great machine, made to produce an effect. You see wheels that turn in opposite directions; you may think, at first, that the machine will destroy itself, that the mechanism will fail and the machine will stop. But it keeps going; and all those pieces that seemed to destroy one another work together toward the intended goal." Montesquieu, *Mes pensées,* no. 2092, in *Pensées/Le spicilège,* 633.

96. The stability of the whole is assured by an "inner policing that mediates between the [various] inclinations of the heart and, when it is active, induces them to correct and offset one another, to balance and help one another; according to

the occasion, they are the remedy to the disorder that they sometimes raise in us." Pierre Carlet de Chamblain de Marivaux, *Suite des réflexions sur l'esprit humain*, in Marivaux, *Journaux et oeuvres diverses*, ed. Frédéric Deloffre and Michel Gilot (Paris: Garnier, 1988), 483. See also Sarah Benharrech, "*Lecteur que vous êtes bigearre!* Marivaux et la 'Querelle de Montaigne,'" *Modern Language Notes* 120, no. 4 (2005): 925–49.

97. Bossuet, *Discours sur l'histoire universelle*, pt. 3, chap. 7, p. 423.

98. Saint-Evremond, *Réflexions sur les divers génies du peuple romain*, 231.

99. *Virtù* for Machiavelli is systemic or relational. His account of what it meant to be a citizen in the Roman republic reflects his conception of the conditions of the Florentine republic in the early fifteenth century. There is mutuality between the leaders and the led, with open access to office for all. Directed and used in the right way, internal conflict, aggression, and ambition are sources of strength, health, and growth. See Niccolò Machiavelli, *Discorsi sopra la prima deca di Tito Livio* (1513–17), in *Opere*, ed. Corrado Vivanti (Turin: Einaudi-Gallimard, 1997–), 1:202–12. Machiavelli's and Montesquieu's ideas of popular government stand in stark contrast to the Rousseauian (as well as to the revolutionary) idea of the indivisibility of the general will.

100. See Montesquieu, *Spirit of the Laws*, bk. 19, chap. 27 (the famous chapter on the English constitution), pp. 325–33.

101. Montesquieu, *Considerations*, chap. 9, pp. 93–94. Montesquieu prudently added "Asiatic" to "despotism" in 1748.

102. For a parallel between the harmony of the state and musical harmony see Cicero *De republica* 2.42; and Plutarch *De musica* 25–34.

103. "Liberalism imposes extraordinary ethical difficulties on us: to live with contradictions, unresolvable conflicts, and a balancing between public and private imperatives which are neither opposed nor at one with each other." Judith Shklar, *Ordinary Vices* (Cambridge, MA: Harvard University Press, 1984), 249.

104. Montesquieu, *Considerations*, chap. 11, p. 103. The internal struggles that characterize a free state are not to be equated with civil war; they are the ordinary rivalry, expressed within the confines of the law, between social classes organized as political constituencies (the senate and the plebeians in Rome, the House of Commons and the House of Lords in England). In Rome their degeneration into full-fledged civil wars was not necessary to the system but contingent upon a whole set of other circumstances. It is not within the scope of this chapter to give an account of Montesquieu's complex analysis of the degeneration of Roman liberty.

105. Montesquieu, *Mes pensées*, no. 5, in *Pensées/Le spicilège*, 187–88. In his acceptance of *inquiétude* as essential to human nature, Montesquieu is closer to Leibniz than to Malebranche.

106. See Jean-Jacques Rousseau, *Considérations sur le gouvernement de Pologne*, in *Oeuvres complètes*, ed. Bernard Gagnebin and Marcel Raymond, vol. 3 (Paris: Gallimard, 1964), 966: "Every true republican suckled the love of the *patrie*—that is, of laws and liberty—together with his mother's milk. That love is the founda-

tion of his whole existence; all he sees and all lives for is the patrie; alone, he is nothing; without the *patrie* he no longer exists, and if he is not dead, he is worse than dead." And in idem, *Economie politique,* ibid., 252: "Virtue is the conformity of the individual will to the general will."

107. Montesquieu, *Mes pensées,* no. 1891, in *Pensées / Le spicilège,* 580.

Chapter 7   Montesquieu for the Masses, or Implanting False Memory

Epigraphs: Denis Diderot to Mme d'Epinay, 1767, quoted in Jack Undank, introduction to *Est-il bon, est-il méchant?* ed. Undank, Studies on Voltaire and the Eighteenth Century, 16 (Geneva: Institut et Musée Voltaire, 1961), 104; Louis-Sébastien Mercier, Montesquieu in *Montesquieu à Marseille* (Lausanne: Heubach, 1784), act 3, sc. 3, p. 100.

1. *Le Mercure de France,* May 1775, 204, quoted in Corrado Rosso, *La réception de Montesquieu* (Pisa: Editrice Goliardica, 1989), 13–14.

2. See Charles de Secondat, baron de Montesquieu, *De l'esprit des lois,* ed. Robert Derathé, 2 vols. (Paris: Garnier, 1973), vol. 2, bk. 23, chap. 29.

3. The play was translated by one Von Dalberg, the manager of the National Theater of Mannheim, in 1787.

4. The young Georg Wilhelm Hegel referred to it in an early work, *Der Geist des Christentums und sein Schicksal.* See Rosso, *La réception de Montesquieu,* 47–57.

5. Louis Petit de Bachaumont, *Mémoires secrets pour servir à l'histoire de la république des lettres en France (Mémoires de Bachaumont),* 36 vols. (London: J. Adamson, 1777–89), vol. 26, 17 September 1784. See also Friedrich Melchior von Grimm, Denis Diderot, Jacques-Henri Meister, and Abbé François Raynal, *Correspondance littéraire, philosophique et critique (1751–1793),* ed. Maurice Tourneux (Paris: Garnier Frères, 1877–82), January 1784, 13:474–75, and March 1777, 11:444, for the reception of Montesson's play.

6. Louis-Sébastien Mercier, "Rumeurs théâtrales," in *Tableaux de Paris,* 2:707.

7. Louis-Sébastien Mercier, *Du théâtre ou nouvel essai sur l'art dramatique,* in Mercier, *Mon bonnet de nuit, suivi de Du Théâtre,* ed. Jean-Claude Bonnet and Pierre Frantz (Paris: Mercure de France, 1999), 1131–32.

8. On Mercier's career as a "patriot playwright" and his struggles with the Comédiens-Français see Gregory S. Brown, *A Field of Honor: Writers, Culture, and Public Theater in French Literary Life from Racine to the Revolution* (New York: Columbia University Press, 2002), chap. 3., www.gutenberg-e.org.

9. Composed in 1730, Dumarsais's manifesto was published in 1743 in Amsterdam. It was borrowed and rewritten by Voltaire and published subsequently in the *Encyclopédie.* For a complete history of its diffusion see Herbert Dieckmann, ed., *Le Philosophe: Texts and Interpretation* (Saint Louis: Washington University Studies, 1948).

10. *Egards* means something closer to "thoughtfulness" and "respect."

11. In his eulogy of Valincour, presented to the French Academy on 16 March

1730, Antoine Houdar de La Motte had praised Valincour's mastery of a science of manners that was like the glue that held together the other sciences and made them accessible: "That science of manners [*science du monde*], which is not always known to men of letters, so pleasurable though it is profound, and without which other sciences would be a dry and uninviting exchange, whereas it could, all by itself, subsist without the help of the others." www.academie-francaise.fr/immortels/index.html.

12. Pierre Carlet de Chamblain de Marivaux, *Réflexions sur l'esprit humain à l'occasion de Corneille et de Racine* (1749), in Marivaux, *Journaux et oeuvres diverses,* ed. Frédéric Deloffre and Michel Gilot (Paris: Garnier, 1988), 476, hereafter cited as *JOD.*

13. Intuitive and applied knowledge of the social put to practical uses is confined by Rousseau to women only (to Emile's wife, Sophie), or, more specifically, to the salonniere, as Léonard-Antoine Thomas notes regarding Mme Geoffrin: "No one has been more successful in the art of capturing and understanding character, even in small things. Such an art is necessary to those who want to know human beings, especially in polite society, where civility and fear of ridicule have erased all conspicuous traits. It requires a deft perception, the talent of grasping tenuous relations between manners and morals, between character and tone of voice, between demeanor and the passions one tries to conceal. Every emotion has its expression to an expert eye." Léonard-Antoine Thomas, *A la Mémoire de Mme Geoffrin,* in *Eloges de Mme Geoffrin, par MM. Morellet, Thomas et d'Alembert,* ed. André Morellet (Paris: H. Nicolle, 1812), 87–88.

14. Denis Diderot, *Notes on Painting* (1765), in *Diderot on Art,* trans. John Goodman, vol. 1, *The Salon of 1765 and Notes on Painting* (New Haven, CT: Yale University Press, 1995), 222.

15. Jean Le Rond d'Alembert, *Essai sur la société des gens de lettres et des grands, sur la réputation, sur les Mecènes, et sur les récompenses littéraires* (1753; 2nd ed., 1764), in *Oeuvres de d'Alembert,* vol. 4 (Paris: A. Belin / Bossange Frères, 1822), 361.

16. This holds true for those writings that were intended for publication; private correspondence often presents a different picture. For the relationship between the philosophes and the salon see Dena Goodman, *The Republic of Letters: A Cultural History of the French Enlightenment* (Ithaca, NY: Cornell University Press, 1994); Daniel Gordon, *Citizens without Sovereignty: Equality and Sociability in French Thought, 1670–1789* (Princeton, NJ: Princeton University Press, 1994); and Elena Russo, "From *Précieuse* to Mother Figure: Sentiment, Authority, and the Eighteenth-Century Salonniere," *Studies on Voltaire and the Eighteenth Century* 12 (2001): 199–218.

17. Louis-Sébastien Mercier, "Danger de certaines sociétés pour le poète," in Mercier, *Du théâtre,* 1315–16.

18. Léonard-Antoine Thomas, *Essai sur les éloges* (1773), bk. 2, chap. 28, p. 28, in *Oeuvres complètes,* 7 vols. (Paris: Desessarts, 1802), vol. 4, emphasis added, http://humanities.uchicago.edu/ARTFL/ARTFL.html.

19. See Charles Palissot de Montenoy, *Les philosophes* (1760), act 1, sc. 1, in *Théâtre du dix-huitième siècle,* ed. Jacques Truchet, 2 vols. (Paris: Gallimard, 1972–74), 2:144.

20. Paul-Henri-Dietrich d'Holbach, *Morale universelle ou les devoirs de l'homme fondés sur sa nature* (1776). On sociability and natural law, see Gordon, *Citizens without Sovereignty.*

21. Alongside such dissatisfaction, there were attempts, such as André Morellet's treatise "De la conversation," to confer philosophical utility on worldly conversation. The abbé Galiani's *Dialogues sur le commerce des blés* (1771), much praised by Diderot, is a learned debate on political economy framed within a social gathering. See Antoine Lilti, "Vertus de la conversation: L'abbé Morellet et la sociabilité mondaine," *Littératures classiques,* no. 37 (1999): 213–28. But Morellet's text was published well after the Revolution had swept away a world that he regards nostalgically from afar (see Morellet, *Eloges de Mme Geoffrin*); his perspective is shaped by that distance.

22. Denis Diderot, *The Salon of 1767,* vol. 2 of *Diderot on Art,* trans. John Goodman (New Haven, CT: Yale University Press, 1995), 77.

23. Denis Diderot, *De la poésie dramatique,* chap. 18, in *Oeuvres esthétiques,* ed. Paul Vernière (Paris: Garnier, 1968), 261–62.

24. "As for me," wrote Mercier, "I am convinced of the advantages we enjoy over our ancestors. Our manners are more gentle, and men are less harsh and barbaric. . . . Our vices derive from generalized exchange in our immense society; they derive from a luxury that has brought us new pleasures; but we no longer have the vices that derive from fanaticism, superstition, pride of rank, and capricious haughtiness." Louis-Sébastien Mercier, "Des prôneurs de l'antiquité," in *Mon bonnet de nuit,* 873–74.

25. Thomas, *Essai sur les éloges,* bk. 2, chap. 38, p. 177.

26. On women's influence on the theater Mercier, who had often taken feminist positions and had written in favor of *femmes auteur,* was even more vehement than Rousseau: "Today it is the childishness of our fashionable women that is put on stage; when we have rendered their tone, we fancy we have become true painters, and the poet is proud to have lent a voice to those futile beings that one ought to ignore if one wishes to amend them. Instead, we erect a throne to them and consecrate that ridiculous fanaticism of the nation, which is thus deprived of all noble, energetic, and courageous ideas; that is why it loses every day that discernment that consigns everybody to their proper place." Mercier, *Du théâtre,* 1211–12.

27. Thomas, *Essai sur les éloges,* bk. 1, chap. 1, 3:5–6.

28. Ibid., bk. 2, chap. 28, 4:28.

29. Antoine-Léonard Thomas, "De l'homme de lettres considéré comme citoyen," inaugural speech to the French Academy, 22 January 1767, www.academie-francaise.fr/immortels/ discours_reception/thomas1.html.

30. Mercier, *Du théâtre,* 1131–32.

31. Quoted in Marguerite Glotz and Madeleine Maire, *Les salons du XVIIIe siècle* (Paris: Hachette, 1945), 57.

32. Mercier, *Du théâtre,* 1148.

33. Thomas, *Essai sur les éloges,* bk. 2, chap. 38, 4:175–76.

34. Denis Diderot, *Entretiens sur Le fils naturel* (1757), in *Oeuvres esthétiques,* 115.

35. Mercier, *Du théâtre,* 1365–66.

36. Quoted in Valleria Belt-Grannis, *Dramatic Parody in Eighteenth-Century France* (New York: Institute of French Studies, 1931), 91–92, translation mine.

37. Ibid., 99, translation mine.

38. Pierre Corneille, *Discours de l'utilité et des parties du poème dramatique* (1660), in *Oeuvres complètes,* ed. Georges Couton, 3 vols. (Paris: Gallimard, 1980–87), 3:117–41.

39. The prize had previously been awarded to royal eulogies. See Jean-Claude Bonnet, *Naissance du Panthéon: Essai sur le culte des grands hommes* (Paris: Fayard, 1998), 122–27. During the Revolution, Villemain d'Abancourt performed *La bienfaisance de Voltaire* (1791); Marie-Joseph Chénier, *Jean Calas* in 1791 and *Fénelon ou les religieuses de Cambrai* in 1793; Jean-Nicolas Bouilly, *J. J. Rousseau à ses derniers moments* in 1791 and *René Descartes, trait historique en deux actes et en prose* in 1796; and Andrieux, *L'enfance de J. J. Rousseau* in 1794.

40. Bonnet, *Naissance du Panthéon.*

41. Mercier, *Du théâtre,* 1329.

42. *Le philosophe à la mode,* performed at the Petite Tragédie des Jésuites in May 1720, the work of Jean-Antoine Du Cerceau, 1670–1730, a Jesuit priest who taught humanities at La Flèche, Rouen, and Bourges and later became the preceptor of the Prince de Conti, was the object of a fifty-page article in *Le Mercure* in June 1720 (the editor of the Mercure in June 1720 was the abbé Buchet). The program distributed at the performance declared: "What we mean by the name *Philosophe à la mode* is a species of so-called sage whose philosophy is nothing but an infinite love for himself and a perfect indifference for the rest of humanity. . . . What we intend to show in this play is that this kind of philosophy, which renders a man indifferent to the *patrie,* to his peers, his friends, and everything that does not touch his immediate interest, is the poison and the ruin of civil society." Quoted in Ira O. Wade, *The "Philosophe" in the French Drama of the Eighteenth Century* (Princeton, NJ: Princeton University Press, 1926), translation mine.

43. In 1759 Voltaire published a *Socrate,* but he did not have it performed; Sauvigny had his *La mort de Socrate* performed at the Théâtre-Français in 1763, and Linguet represented his own *Socrate* in 1764. By 1762 the philosophes had won the battle of public opinion, but the satirical onslaught did not subside. Among the various titles we find *L'homme dangereux* (Palissot, 1770) and *Le séducteur* (marquis de Bièvre, 1783). See Wade, *"Philosophe."*

44. Mercier, *Du théâtre,* 1253.

45. Pierre Nicole, *Traité de la comédie* (1667), par. 14, in *Traité de la comédie et autres pièces d'un procès du théâtre,* ed. Laurent Thirouin (Paris: Champion, 1998), 64.

46. Jean-Jacques Rousseau, *Lettre à d'Alembert sur les spectacles* (1758; reprint, Paris: Garnier-Flammarion, 2003), 66–67.

47. Mercier, *Du théâtre,* 1249.

48. "How sweet, how precious is a gift, for which the giver will not suffer us to pay even our thanks, which he forgot that he had given, even while he was giving it!" Seneca, *De Beneficiis (On Benefits),* 2:6.2, in *Moral Essays,* vol. 3, ed. and trans. John W. Basore (Cambridge, MA: Harvard University Press, 1989), 61.

49. Sharon Kettering, "Friendship and Clientage in Early Modern France," *French History* 6 (1992): 139–58; idem, "Gift-Giving and Patronage in Early-Modern France," ibid., 2 (June 1988): 131–51.

50. Denis Diderot, *Essai sur les règnes de Claude et de Néron,* in *Oeuvres,* ed. Laurent Versini, vol. 1, *Philosophie* (Paris: Robert Laffont, 1994), 1179.

51. See Bradley Rubidge, "Rates of Exchange: Reciprocation and Commerce in Seventeenth-Century Heroic Drama" (PhD diss., Stanford University, 1993).

52. Seneca *De Beneficiis* 2.17.3–5.

53. "Un service au dessus de toute récompense / A force d'obliger tient presque lieu d'offense." Pierre Corneille, *Suréna,* 3.1.705–6, in *Oeuvres complètes,* ed. Georges Couton, 3 vols. (Paris: Gallimard, 1980–87), 3:1269.

54. Separating *virtus* and *voluptas,* Montesquieu seems to share with the stoic Seneca the belief that "virtue is not associated with pleasure at all, for virtue despises pleasure, is its enemy, and recoils from it as far as it can, being more acquainted with labour and sorrow." *De Beneficiis* 4.2.4.

55. "I have been surprised at the pleasure we feel in doing a good deed: I would be tempted to believe that those we call virtuous do not have as much merit as we credit them with." Pierre-Ambroise-François Choderlos de Laclos, *Les liaisons dangereuses* (1782; reprint, Paris: Garnier-Flammarion, 1996), letter 21, p. 120.

56. Seneca *De Beneficiis* 4.1.2–3.

57. That aspect was precisely what caught the attention of Hegel in his reading of this play in *Der Geist des Christentums.* See Rosso, *La réception de Montesquieu,* 47–48.

58. Denis Diderot, introduction to *Le fils naturel ou Les épreuves de la vertu* (1757), in Truchet, *Théâtre du dix-huitième siècle,* 2:4.

59. "I would envision my life from the perspective of my death, and all I saw was a foreclosed memory from which nothing could escape." Jean-Paul Sartre, *Les mots* (Paris: Gallimard, 1964), 189.

60. Jean-François Marmontel, "Gloire," in *Encyclopédie, ou dictionnaire raisonné des sciences, des arts et des métiers,* ed. Denis Diderot and Jean Le Rond d'Alembert, 32 vols. (Paris, 1751–77), 7 (1757): 716, emphasis added.

61. Denis Diderot to Étienne-Maurice Falconet, 4 December 1765, in Diderot and Falconet, *Le pour et le contre: Correspondance polémique sur le respect de la postérité, Pline et les anciens,* ed. Yves Benot (Paris: Editeurs Réunis, 1958), 49.

62. Denis Diderot, *Le fils naturel ou Les épreuves de la vertu,* in Truchet, *Théâtre du dix-huitième siècle,* 2:3.

63. Longinus, *Traité du sublime,* trans. Nicolas Boileau (1674), ed. Francis Goyet (Paris: Le Livre de Poche, 1995), 14.1–2, p. 96.

64. Ibid., 14.3, p. 96.

65. "A great revolution of ideas has taken place in the last thirty years. Public opinion nowadays in Europe is an overwhelming force to be reckoned with. . . . The influence of writers is such that today they may reveal their power and no longer disguise the legitimate authority they have over minds." Mercier, "Belles-lettres," in *Tableaux de Paris,* 1:971.

66. Longinus, *Traité du sublime,* trans. Boileau, ed. Goyet, 44.2–4, pp. 136–37.

67. Ibid., 44.8, p. 137.

68. Jules Brody rightly points out that most of Boileau's monosyllabic examples of sublime expression ("Qu'il mourût," "Moi") are drawn from drama, "that literary form in which language most nearly becomes one with action." *Boileau and Longinus* (Geneva: Droz, 1958), 91. Horace's and Medea's sublime utterances are cited, for instance, in Diderot's article "Génie," in vol. 7 of Diderot and d'Alembert's *Encyclopédie.*

69. "Tragedy will be heard and appreciated by citizen of all ranks; it will have an intimate relation with political affairs and, replacing the pulpit and the tribune [*la tribune aux harangues*], it will enlighten the people about their true interests, it will present them under a striking light, it will exalt in their heart an enlightened patriotism, and it will make them cherish their homeland." Mercier, *Du théâtre,* 1176.

70. Thomas, *Essai sur les éloges,* bk. 2, chap. 38, 4:177.

71. Diderot, *De la poésie dramatique,* chap. 3, in *Oeuvres esthétiques,* 197.

72. Augustine *De doctrina Christiana* 4.24.53, quoted in François de Salignac de la Mothe-Fénelon, *Lettre à l'Académie* (1714), ed. Ernesta Calderini (Geneva: Droz, 1970), 44–45. In his *Dialogues des morts,* dialogue 32, Fénelon has Demosthenes rebuff Cicero: "They admired you, while I was forgotten by my audience. You entertained it with your wit, while I would strike, devastate, and terrify with lightning." *Oeuvres,* ed. Jacques Le Brun, 2 vols. (Paris: Gallimard, 1983), 1:371–72.

73. John Le Rond d'Alembert, inaugural speech to the French Academy, 19 December 1754, quoted in *Oeuvres de d'Alembert,* 4:305. See also idem, *Discours préliminaire* to Diderot and d'Alembert, *Encyclopédie,* 1 (1751): xi: "As for those pedantic puerilities that have been honored with the name of rhetoric . . . and stand to oratorical art in the same way as scholasticism stands to true philosophy, they are good only for giving of eloquence a barbaric notion."

74. Mercier, *Du théâtre,* 1181.

75. Louis-Sébastien Mercier, "Battements de mains," in *Tableaux de Paris,* 1:533.

76. Fontenelle's eulogies of the members of the Academy of Sciences were for the most part conversion stories, which endlessly rehearsed a sudden turn to science after some inaugural event, away from the strictures of society and institu-

tional authority. See Dinah Ribard, "Philosophe ou écrivain," *Annales: Histoire et sciences sociales* 55, no. 2 (2000): 378–79.

77. Mercier, *Montesquieu à Marseille,* act 3, sc. 3, p. 102.

78. See Darrin M. McMahon, *Enemies of the Enlightenment: The French Counter-Enlightenment and the Making of Modernity* (Oxford: Oxford University Press, 2001).

79. Charles Palissot de Montenoy, *Petites lettres sur de grands philosophes* (1757), in *Oeuvres complètes de M. Palissot,* vol. 1 (Paris: L. Collin, 1809), 272.

80. In Diderot and d'Alembert, *Encyclopédie,* 5 (1755): 285, emphasis added. The full lines in Latin, from bk. 4, lines 691–92, of Virgil's *Aeneid,* on the death of Dido, read: "Oculisque errantibus alto / Quaesivit coelo lucem, ingemuitque reperta" [Her eyes drifting to the heavens / she seeks the light and grieves upon having found it].

Chapter 8   Everlasting Theatricality

Epigraphs: Louis Fuzelier, Alain-René Lesage, and Jacques-Philippe d'Orneval, "Harangue de Polichinelle au public," in *La grand'mère amoureuse,* parody in three acts of *Atys* performed with puppets on 10 March 1726, quoted in Charles Magnin, *Histoire des marionnettes en Europe* (1862; Geneva: Slatkine Reprints, 1981) 160; Roland Barthes, *The Pleasure of the Text,* trans. Richard Miller (New York: Hill & Wang, 1975), 11–12.

1. Louis Sébastien Mercier, "Battements de mains," in *Tableaux de Paris,* ed. Jean-Claude Bonnet, 2 vols. (Paris: Mercure de France, 1994), 1:532.

2. Louis Sébastien Mercier, "L'auteur! L'auteur!" ibid., 1:1133. Acknowledging the applause from the pit was considered undignified for authors. Gregory S. Brown notes that "there are no recorded incidents of playwrights actually taking the stage." *A Field of Honor: Writers, Culture, and Public Theater in French Literary Life from Racine to the Revolution* (New York: Columbia University Press, 2002), 85, www.gutenberg-e.org.

3. "We call *parterre* the group of spectators who have their places in the pit [*parterre*]; they are the ones who decide the merit of plays; we say: the judgement, the cabal, the applause, the booing of the parterre." "Parterre," in *Encyclopédie, ou dictionnaire raisonné des sciences, des arts et des métiers,* ed. Denis Diderot and Jean Le Rond d'Alembert, 32 vols. (Paris, 1751–77), 12 (1765): 87. See also Jean-François Marmontel, "Parterre," in *Supplément à l'Encyclopédie* (Amsterdam, 1776), 4:241–42.

4. Ordinances were issued on 12 January 1685 ("Ordinance forbidding anyone from creating disorder in the playhouse"), 16 November 1691, 19 January 1701, 18 May 1716 (for the Comédie-Italienne), 10 April 1720, and 7 December 1728. See Adolphe Jullien, *La comédie et la galanterie au 18e siècle* (Paris: Edouard Rouveyre, 1879), 76–77; and Emile Campardon, *Les comédiens du roi de la troupe italienne*

(Paris: Berger-Levrault, 1880), 238. For a complete history of the activities and the policing of the parterre see Jeffrey Ravel's illuminating book *The Contested Parterre: Public Theater and French Political Culture, 1680–1791* (Ithaca, NY: Cornell University Press, 1999).

5. A pannier gown. Claude-Joseph Dorat, *La déclamation theâtrale, poème didactique en trois chants, précédé d'un discours* (Paris, 1766), quoted in Angelica Goodden, *Actio and Persuasion: Dramatic Performance in Eighteenth-Century France* (Oxford: Clarendon, 1986), 74.

6. Denis Diderot, *Entretiens sur Le fils naturel* (1757), in *Oeuvres esthétiques,* ed. Paul Vernière (Paris: Gallimard, 1968), 102.

7. Ibid., 103.

8. Denis Diderot to Mme Riccoboni, 15 November 1758, in Diderot, *Oeuvres complètes,* vol. 10, ed. Jacques Chouillet and Anne-Marie Chouillet (Paris: Hermann, 1980), 441–42.

9. Ravel, *Contested Parterre,* chap. 4.

10. Louis Sébastien Mercier, "Fusiliers au spectacle," in *Tableaux de Paris,* 1:483.

11. Louis Sébastien Mercier, "Rumeurs théâtrales," ibid., 2:705.

12. Louis Sébastien Mercier, "Théâtre national," ibid., 2:88.

13. Mercier refers both to the practices of ancient audiences in Greek and Latin theaters and to those of the theater he knew during his youth, at an unspecified "earlier" time.

14. Marie-Hélène Huet, *Rehearsing the Revolution: The Staging of Marat's Death, 1793–1797,* trans. Robert Hurley (Berkeley and Los Angeles: University of California Press, 1982), 35.

15. Paul Friedland, *Political Actors: Representative Bodies and Theatricality in the Age of the French Revolution* (Ithaca, NY: Cornell University Press, 2002), 71.

16. See Jean-Marie Apostolidès, *Le roi-machine: Spectacle et politique au temps de Louis XIV* (Paris: Minuit, 1981); and idem, *Le prince sacrifié: Théâtre et politique au temps de Louis XIV* (Paris: Minuit, 1985).

17. Louis Sébastien Mercier, in "Parterres assis," in *Tableaux de Paris,* 2:1470. We must acknowledge that in Mercier's portrayal of the actors as victims of the parterre there was a good deal of wishful thinking.

18. Huet, *Rehearsing the Revolution,* 33–34.

19. See, e.g., Pierre Frantz, "Naissance d'un public," *Europe* 703–4 (1987): 26–32; Judith Schlanger, "Théâtre révolutionnaire et représentation du bien," *Poétique* 22 (1975); Susan Maslan, *Representations and Theatricality in French Revolutionary Acts: Theater, Democracy, and the French Revolution* (Baltimore: Johns Hopkins University Press, 2005).

20. Martine de Rougemont, *La vie théâtrale en France au XVIIIe siècle* (Paris: Champion, 1988), chap. 13, "Les théâtres d'amateurs"; David Trott, *Théâtre du dix-huitième siècle: Jeux, écritures, regards* (Montpellier: Editions Espaces 34, 2000), 165–82. The *Mercure* of April 1732 estimates the number of theaters in Paris to be 50; in the 1748 issue 20 of the *Correspondance littéraire* Grimm writes that there are

at least 160. Trott, *Théâtre du dix-huitième siècle,* 167. In *Farce and Fantasy: Popular Entertainment in Eighteenth-Century Paris* (Oxford: Oxford University Press, 1986), Robert Isherwood has evoked the elite's taste for erotic parades, a genre that migrated from the fairgrounds to the private stages.

21. Louis Sébastien Mercier, "Théâtres bourgeois," in *Tableaux de Paris,* 1:534.

22. Pierre-Samuel Dupont de Nemours to the Margrave Carl Friedrich of Baden, 31 December 1772, in *Carl Friedrichs Von Baden brieflicher Verkehr mit Mirabeau und Du Pont,* ed. Carl Knies, 2 vols. (Heidelberg, 1892), 2:17–18.

23. See Jacques Trouillet's introduction to Diderot's *Le fils naturel* in *Théâtre du dix-huitième siècle,* ed. Jacques Truchet, 2 vols. (Paris: Gallimard, 1974), vol. 2.

24. Diderot, *Entretiens sur Le fils naturel,* 85–86.

25. Diderot, *Le fils naturel,* in Truchet, *Théâtre du dix-huitième siècle,* 2:4.

26. Jean-Jacques Rousseau, *Lettre à d'Alembert sur les spectacles* (1758; reprint, Paris: Garnier-Flammarion, 2003), 192–93.

27. Ibid., 168.

28. "But let us not adopt those exclusionist spectacles that miserably confine a small number of people in a dark chamber; that hold them fearful and immobile in silence and inaction; that offer to the eye nothing but walls, spikes, soldiers, and wretched images of servitude and inequality." Ibid.

29. Diderot, *Entretiens sur Le fils naturel,* 122.

30. Louis Sébastien Mercier, "Tragédistes," in *Tableaux de Paris,* 2:750–51, emphasis added.

31. A relevant collection is the abbé Jean-Barthélémy de La Porte and Jean-Marie-Bernard Clément's *Anecdotes dramatiques* (Paris: Veuve Duchesne, 1775) and the journal edited by La Porte, *Les spectacles de Paris* (1751–89). A frequently cited incident is that in which the actor Jean Mauduit de Larive abandoned the Comédie-Française after the parterre heckled him with loud applause when he uttered this verse from Racine's *Iphigénie:* "*La rive* au loin gémit," or "The distant shore laments." See Mercier, "L'auteur! L'auteur!" 2:1132.

32. Louis Sébastien Mercier, "Cabale," in *Tableaux de Paris,* 2:154. Martine de Rougemont is one of the very few to have appreciated this aspect of theatrical reception beyond its dimension of anecdotal amusement: "That intellectual game is developed to a point that seems incredible today. It involves an improvised rewriting and, above all, an appropriation of the play. The exuberance of the reactions is indicative of the extraordinary attention that spectators pay to each word uttered by the actors and by the parterre itself." *La vie théâtrale en France au XVIIIe siècle,* 230.

33. Mercier, "Cabale," 2:154.

34. Mercier, "L'auteur! L'auteur!" 2:1134.

35. Guy Spielmann, *Le jeu de l'ordre et du chaos: Comédie et pouvoirs à la fin de règne, 1673–1715* (Paris: Champion, 2002), 201–37. See also Jeffrey Ravel, "Certitudes comiques et doutes judiciaires: Le procès La Pivardière (1697–1699)," in *Représentations du procès: Droit, théâtre, littérature, cinéma,* ed. Christian Biet and Laurence Schifano (Paris: Université Paris X-Nanterre, 2003), 437–43.

36. Try as we may, the English language simply does not have as many words as French to indicate mischievous wordplay. *Turlupinade* (see above, chapter 5), *polissonnerie, quolibet,* and *gasconnade* (Gascons had quite a reputation) all meant "whimsicality" with a sexual or a scatological twist. Chérier's collection also promises much in the way of wordplay, set rhymes, puns, allusions, equivocations, allegories, witticism, hyperboles, and uncommon expressions.

37. Abbé Claude Chérier, in Claude Parfaict and François Parfaict, *Dictionnaire des théâtres* (Paris, 1767), 3:116, quoted in Emile Campardon, *Les spectacles de la foire,* 2 vols. (Paris: Berger-Levrault, 1877), 2:197–98. In 1744 Piron remarked in a letter to Maurepas, who as a fellow member of the *poissarde* Société du Bout du Banc was well versed in such issues: "I have read *The Rose* in a circle in which there were two bishops in their sixties and some ladies who had reached the age of piety. The work was graciously received by them. They only read in it what I had meant to say. True, they found the words *Rose, Rosier, Houlette,* and *Jardin* suggestive of a few little things, but they all agreed (I asked them explicitly) that the veil of allegory was so tightly woven that there was not the smallest crack to expose nudity." Quoted in Pascale Verèb, *Alexis Piron, poete (1689–1773): La difficile condition d'auteur sous Louis XV* (Oxford: Voltaire Foundation, 1997), 107. Needless to say, allegory was precisely the problem.

38. Mercier, "Théâtre national," 2:86.

39. Louis Fuzelier, *Discours sur les parodies,* in *Parodies du nouveau théâtre italien,* 4 vols. (Paris: Briasson, 1738; Geneva: Slatkine Reprints, 1970).

40. See Henri Lagrave, *Le théâtre et le public à Paris, de 1715 à 1750* (Paris: Klincksieck, 1972), chap. 3; Ravel, *Contested Parterre;* Spielmann, *Le jeu de l'Ordre et du chaos;* Trott, *Théâtre du dix-huitième siècle;* and Michèle Root-Bernstein, *Boulevard Theatre and Revolution in Eighteenth-Century Paris* (Ann Arbor, MI: UMI Research Press, 1984). In the prologue to Lesage's *Turcaret* (1709) Don Cléofas and the devil Asmodée observe the audience at the Comédie-Française: "—Don Cléofas: What an elegant gathering! How many ladies! —Asmodée: There would be even more of them were it not for the fairgrounds spectacles: most women are crazy about them. I am glad to see that they have the same taste as their lackeys and their coachmen." In Truchet, *Théâtre du dix-huitième siècle,* 1:89. More to the point, most fairgrounds and boulevard playhouses had private loges. While the prices for a parterre ticket were much lower at the fairs than at the Comédie-Française (1 livre compared with 5 sous), those for the first loges were comparable (4 livres and 6 livres). For lists of prices see Lagrave, *Le théâtre et le public,* 234–36; and Verèb, *Alexis Piron,* 94.

41. Louis XIV granted Dominique de Normandin letters patent registered with the Parlement of Paris in 1675 allowing him the exclusive privilege to exploit his spectacle. See Campardon, *Les spectacles de la foire,* 2:286. Toward the end of the seventeenth century, at the time of the solidification of the classical doctrine, the king stopped granting privileges to the minor spectacles, trying instead to consolidate monopolies to fewer venues. Privilege was the "Power accorded to a Person

or a Commonality to do or enjoy something to some advantage to the exclusion of others." Joseph-Nicolas Guyot, *Le grand vocabulaire françois,* vol. 23 (Paris, 1772), 313. See also Root-Bernstein, *Boulevard Theatre and Revolution.*

42. Mercier, "Rumeurs théâtrales," 2:705.

43. The practice had been introduced by Molière and resumed by La Motte in 1722, when his tragedy *Romulus* was followed by *Le mariage forcé.* See Lagrave, *Le théâtre et le public,* 350–59; and Charles Varlet de la Grange's report on Molière's first performance for Louis XIV, on 24 October 1658, quoted in Virginia Scott, *Molière: A Theatrical Life* (Cambridge: Cambridge University Press, 2000), 91–92.

44. Louis Sébastien Mercier, "Paillasse," in *Tableaux de Paris,* 2:429. Agamemnon's lines, from Racine, *Iphigénie,* 1.1.1–2, in *Oeuvres complètes,* ed. Georges Forestier, 2 vols. (Paris: Gallimard, 1999), 1:703, translate as, "Yes, it is Agamemnon, your king, who is waking you up. / Come, recognize the voice that strikes your ear."

45. In Fatouville's *Arlequin-Protée* (1683), Arlequin, who impersonates an actor in a play within the play, boasts to Columbine that he plays the main character, "who always puts an end to the play." "Then you must be the *moucheur de chandelles,* who always ends the play [*che finisce sempre gli atti*]," Columbine replies. *Théâtre du XVIIe siècle,* vol. 3, ed. Jacques Truchet and André Le Blanc (Paris: Gallimard, 1992), 253.

46. Mercier, "Paillasse," 2:431.

47. The two verses quoted here, drawn from Racine's *Iphigénie,* had become the target of Diderot's, Voltaire's, and Mercier's criticism, standing for all that they found exaggerated in classical elocution. See Diderot's *Paradoxe sur le comédien,* Voltaire's *Discours sur la tragédie,* and Mercier's *Du théâtre, ou nouvel essai sur l'art dramatique.*

48. Louis Sébastien Mercier, "Le trou du souffleur," in *Tableaux de Paris,* 2:1332–35.

49. See the description and analysis of one such incident in Jeffrey Ravel's "*La reine boit!* Print, Performance, and Theater Publics in France, 1724–1725," *Eighteenth-Century Studies* 29 (Summer 1996): 391–411.

50. Trott, *Théâtre du dix-huitième siècle,* 190.

51. See Ferdinando Taviani and Mirella Schino, *Il segreto della commedia dell'arte* (Florence: Casa Usher, 1982); and Spielmann, *Le jeu de l'ordre et du chaos,* 323–24: "It is the disjunction between the serious and the parodistic that triggers the comical effect, not parody alone."

52. *L'année littéraire,* 3 May 1559, quoted in Barbara Mittman, *Spectators on the Paris Stage in the Seventeenth and Eighteenth Centuries* (Ann Arbor, MI: UMI Research Press, 1984), 98.

53. Charles Collé, *Journal et mémoires de Charles Collé sur les hommes de lettres, les ouvrages dramatiques, et les événements les plus mémorables du règne de Louis XV (1748–1772),* 3 vols. (Paris: Firmin Didot, 1868), 2:172, quoted in Mittman, *Spectators on the Paris Stage,* 98.

54. D'Alembert had deplored the mixture of high and low in Marivaux's novels: "We must acknowledge that Marivaux, by wanting to put too much truth in

his low-life tableaux, has indulged in some sordid details that are at odds with the refinement of his other portrayals. That refinement, however, justifies our indulgence for—if I am allowed here a technical term—those *bambochades.* The painter of the human heart fortunately makes us forget the painter of the populace." Jean Le Rond d'Alembert, *Eloge de Marivaux* (1785), in Pierre Carlet de Chamblain de Marivaux, *Théâtre complet,* ed. Jacques Scherer and Bernard Dort (Paris: Seuil, 1964), 22. The term *bambochade* (low farce) was usually applied depreciatively to genre scenes in Flemish painting. In the *Dictionnaire de l'Académie,* 4th ed. (1762), it is defined as "the name that we give to certain grotesque paintings. Composition of low-life subjects [*sujets populaires*] of a low nature."

55. Clarence D. A. Brenner, *Bibliographical List of Plays in the French Language, 1700–1789* (1947; reprint, New York: AMS Press, 1979).

56. See Evaristo Gherardi, *Le théâtre italien, ou le recueil général de toutes les comédies et scènes françaises jouées par les comédiens italiens du roi,* 6 vols. (Paris: J. B. Cusson et P. Witte, 1700); *Parodies du nouveau théâtre italien,* 4 vols. (Paris: Briasson, 1738); and Alain-René Lesage and Jacques-Philippe d'Orneval, *Le théâtre de la foire ou l'opéra-comique, contenant les meilleures pièces qui ont été représentées aux Foires Saint-Germain et Saint-Laurent,* 10 vols. (Paris: Ganeau, 1721–37). Several modern anthologies are more readily available: see Marcello Spaziani, ed., *Il teatro della "foire": Dieci commedie di Alard, Fuzelier, Lesage, D'Orneval, La Font, Piron* (Rome: Ateneo, 1965); Derek Connon and George Evans, eds., *Anthologie de pièces du théâtre de la foire* (Egham, Surrey: Runnymede Books, 1996), with the complete scores of the vaudevilles; and Dominique Triaire, ed., *Parades extraites du théâtre des boulevards* (Montpellier: Editions Espaces 34, 2000). See also Valleria Belt-Grannis, *Dramatic Parody in Eighteenth-Century France* (New York: Institute of French Studies, 1931); Frank Whiteman Lindsay, *Dramatic Parody by Marionnettes in Eighteenth-Century Paris* (New York: King's Crown Press, 1946); David Trott, "Pour une typologie des séries parodiques dans le théâtre du XVIIIe siècle," paper delivered at the international colloquium "Parodie et série dans la littérature française du XVIIIe siècle," Université de Paris IV-Sorbonne, 14 November 1998, in *Séries parodiques au siècle des Lumières,* ed. Sylvain Menant and Dominique Quéro (Paris: Presses de l'Université Paris-Sorbonne, 2005).

57. See Ravel, *Contested Parterre,* 127.

58. In *Marotte ou l'enfant trouvé,* a parody of Voltaire's *Mérope* (1743) by members of the Société du Caveau (Pannard, Gallet, Laffichard, and Boizeau de Ponteau), when Marotte is about to kill the presumed murderer of her son, his guardian hastens to stop her: "*Dans quel désordre vous seriez/Par votre injuste haine,/Contre les règles vous auriez/Ensanglanté la scène.* (What a mess you were about to make! Because of your unjust hatred, you would have spilled blood on the stage and broken all the rules.)" Belt-Grannis, *Dramatic Parody,* 315. A similar parterre rebellion against the infringement of theatrical bienséance (one could not show a murder onstage) caused the failure of Voltaire's first *Mariamne.* See Ravel, "*La reine boit!*"

59. Piron had been accepted by the academicians in 1754, but the abbé Jean-François Boyer, preceptor to the dauphin (and an ally of Jean-Pierre de Bougainville, the Academy's other candidate), felt obliged to warn Louis XV about the pornographic poem. The king, who knew it, pretended he did not and gave himself the pleasure of having the abbé read it to him in full. But at that point Piron's election was no longer a possibility.

60. The Régiment de la Calotte was an imaginary militia founded in 1702 by royal officers and courtiers that took aim at the pompous language of contemporary tragedy and at the antiquarian *gravitas* of the parlements; they specialized in composing dramatic parodies and satirical eulogies. See Antoine de Baecque, *Les éclats du rire: La culture des rieurs au 18e siècle* (Paris: Calmann-Levy, 2000); and Léon Hennet, *Le régiment de la Calotte* (Paris, 1886). On the Société du Caveau see Brigitte Level, *Le Caveau: Société bachique et chantante* (Paris: Presses Universitaires de la Sorbonne, 1988); and Marie-Véronique Gauthier, *Chanson, sociabilité, et grivoiserie au 19e siècle* (Paris: Aubier, 1992).

61. See Emile Campardon, "Procès des comédiens français et des comédiens forains," in Campardon, *Les spectacles de la foire*, 2:250–85.

62. Jean-Baptiste Costantini, a former actor at the old Comédie-Italienne, which had been shut down in 1697; he had since become an impresario on the fairgrounds.

63. Quoted in Campardon, *Les spectacles de la foire*, 2:187. The same procedure is explained thoroughly in the prologue to *La forêt de Dodone*, performed by Francisque in 1721. A countess, a chevalier, and a marquis discuss the merits of the placards: "At the time of the placards we could see two children dressed as Cupid [carrying the placards swinging in the air and being pulled up and down. . . . That was a spectacle in itself. . . . As the children switched the placards all the time, they would offer us a changing tableau. . . . The spectators would become actors themselves. As soon as a placard was rolled out, the orchestra gave the cue, and we would immediately hear the most discordant chorus one could ever imagine." Dominique Lurcel, ed., *Le théâtre de la foire au XVIIIe siècle* (Paris: Union Générale d'Editions, 1983), 175–76.

64. For two analyses of the play see Pierre Gobin, "L'Arlequin-Deucalion de Piron: Pertinence de l'impertinence," *Studies on Voltaire and the Eighteenth Century* 192 (1980): 1478–86; and Walter Rex, "Inversions and Subversions in the *Théâtre de la Foire*, or, the End of Piron's *Arlequin-Deucalion*," in *The Attraction of the Contrary: Essays on the Literature of the French Enlightenment* (Cambridge: Cambridge University Press, 1987), 49–72.

65. Spielmann, *Le jeu de l'ordre et du chaos*, 341–42.

66. I use Jacques Truchet's edition, based upon the revised edition published in vol. 3 of Piron's *Oeuvres* (1776), in Truchet, *Théâtre du dix-huitième siècle*, 1:491–516.

67. "Persiflage," writes Mercier, "is a continuous mockery under the false appearance of approval. We use it to lead the victim into all the ambushes that

are laid out for it. We entertain a whole assembly at the expense of the victim, who, deceived by the appearance of ordinary politeness, is unaware of being ridiculed." Louis Sébastien Mercier, "Persiflage," in *Tableaux de Paris,* 1:384. See Elisabeth Bourguinat, *Le siècle du persiflage, 1734–1789* (Paris: Presses Universitaires de France, 1998).

68. A similar game occurred during the performance of d'Orneval's *opéra-comique Arlequin Traitant,* performed at the Foire Saint-Germain on 22 March 1716, on the heels of the March 1716 edict establishing a chamber of justice to prosecute the tax collectors suspected of malfeasance. D'Orneval inserted in the play portraits of well-known *gens d'affaires.* In the second act, Arlequin is in hell; he points his finger toward a spectator in the audience, who gets up angrily, goes onto the stage, and slaps Arlequin with his glove. The police are ready to intervene, and the audience expects all hell to break loose. But the offended individual was an actor; the butt of the joke were the *exempt* and his men.

69. Louis Sébastien Mercier, "Tragédies modernes," in *Tableaux de Paris,* 2:892. A reminder, perhaps, of Diderot's "grands mannequins d'osier," mentioned in his *Paradoxe sur le comédien.*

70. Nicolas Racot de Grandval, quoted in Bourguinat, *Le siècle du persiflage,* 27.

71. *Epidramatique* is a neologism made from *épique* and *dramatique,* which Mercier will borrow.

72. Connon and Evans, *Anthologie de pièces du théâtre de la foire,* 19–20.

73. The last two lines read, "CI-GÎT, PIRON, qui ne fut rien, / Pas même Académicien." Quoted in Verèb, *Alexis Piron,* 313.

74. Denis Diderot, *Plan d'un opéra-comique,* probably composed before 1762, in *Oeuvres complètes,* 10:515–41.

75. In August 1760 Camille Veronese, a dancer at the Comédie-Italienne, performed, to great acclaim, the role of the statue in Billioni's ballet *Pygmalion.* Charles-Simon Favart reported: "Nothing equals the refinement of her pantomime, especially when the statue gradually comes alive. She depicts her surprise, her curiosity, her budding love, all the degrees of her emotions, with unparalleled expressiveness. One may say that Camille is able to dance her very thoughts. I believe that the ancient art of Greek pantomime could not surpass her talents in that genre." *Oeuvres de M. et Mme Favart* (Paris: Eugène Didier, 1853), quoted in Campardon, *Les comédiens du roi de la troupe italienne,* 2:199.

76. Vienne was nicknamed Beauvisage because of the ugliness of his face and his freakish capacity to mold it into the strangest shapes and expressions. He had started his career as an *aboyeur.* When he founded the Théâtre des Associés, at the Foire Saint-Laurent, in 1774, he played tragedies and *drames*—Mercier's *Jenneval* and *La boutique du vinaigrier,* among others—altering them through his comic talents and his "bovine mooing." On Vienne and the Associés see Campardon, *Les spectacles de la foire,* 1:26–28 and 2:457–59.

77. Root-Bernstein, *Boulevard Theatre and Revolution,* chap. 7.

Epilogue. The Costume of Modernity

Epigraph: Denis Diderot, *The Salon of 1767,* vol. 2 of *Diderot on Art,* trans. John Goodman (New Haven, CT: Yale University Press, 1995), 208.

1. See Katie Scott, *The Rococo Interior* (New Haven, CT: Yale University Press, 1995).

2. See Marie-Jean-Antoine-Nicolas de Caritat, marquis de Condorcet, "Des avantages et des progrès des sciences," inaugural speech to the French Academy, 21 February 1782, www.academie-francaise.fr/immortels/index.html.

3. Roland Barthes, "Le dernier des écrivains heureux" (1958), in *Essais critiques* (Paris: Seuil, 1964), 94–100.

4. Diderot, *Salon of 1767,* 110–20.

5. Ibid., 66–67.

6. "Why does a beautiful sketch accord greater pleasure than a beautiful painting? Because it has more life and fewer forms. The more forms one introduces, the more life disappears. . . . Such sketches thrive on enthusiasm and genius, while paintings demand work, patience, prolonged study and extensive technical experience." Ibid., 212 (on Hubert Robert's sketches).

7. Thomas Crow, *Painters and Public Life in Eighteenth-Century Paris* (New Haven, CT: Yale University Press, 1985), 186.

8. See Thomas Crow, *Emulation: Making Artists for Revolutionary France* (New Haven, CT: Yale University Press, 1995).

9. Longinus *Traité du sublime* 9.1–3.

10. Diderot, *Salon of 1767,* 188.

11. Ibid., 187.

12. Diderot has inherited Boileau's horror for *Caton galant* and *Brutus dameret,* as Boileau puts it in his satirical *Dialogue des héros de roman* (1665), in which he upbraids Mlle de Scudéry for having dressed up those heroes *à la mode* in her novels.

13. Diderot, *Salon of 1767,* 188. For a similar position see William Hogarth, *The Analysis of Beauty* (1753; reprint, Oxford: Clarendon, 1955), 48.

14. Diderot, *Salon of 1767,* 25, 189. Another acerbic critique of modern costume, inspired by Rousseau, may be found in Louis Carrogis de Carmontelle's commentary on Ménageot's painting *La mort de Léonard de Vinci* (1781), in his anonymously published Salon pamphlet *La patte de velours,* of the same year, quoted in Régis Michel, "Diderot et la modernité," in *Diderot et l'art, de Boucher à David,* ed. Marie-Catherine Sahut and Nathalie Volle (Paris: Editions de la Réunion des Musées Nationaux, 1984), 110–21; on Carmontelle see 121.

15. Literally so, if we think of the Fountain of Regeneration featured at the Festival of Unity and Indivisibility, held on 10 August 1793, in which representatives drank the water squirting from the breasts of a gigantic statue of Isis, in truth not a republican icon but an Egyptian deity, the emblem of Nature's mythical origins and of the golden age. I thank Daniel Edelstein for this reference.

16. Diderot, *Salon of 1767,* 208, translation modified, emphasis added. "Laus

temporum, non hominis," Cicero's *De officiis* 3.31: "Glory of the times and not of the man."

17. Denis Diderot, *Notes on Painting* (1765), in *Diderot on Art,* trans. John Goodman, vol. 1, *The Salon of 1765 and Notes on Painting* (New Haven, CT: Yale University Press, 1995), 191.

18. Ibid., 231.

19. Charles Baudelaire, "Modernité," in *Le peintre de la vie moderne* (1863), trans. Jonathan Mayne as *The Painter of Modern Life and Other Essays* (London: Phaidon, 1964), 13–14.

20. The first known use of the word *modernity* may be ascribed to Honoré de Balzac (*La dernière fée,* 1823), but it became acceptable in aesthetic discourse only about the time of the Second Empire. See Claude Pichois's notes to Charles Baudelaire, *Critique d'art* (Paris: Gallimard Folio Essais, 1992), 647–48.

21. Baudelaire, "Modernité," 13–14.

22. "It is doubtless a taxing effort [for painters] to invent fortunate physiognomies in the midst of people who display none; proud or generous features when one views only slaves and masters; true expression in a country of dissimulation; strong and vigorous postures among models whom either poverty or debauchery have rendered hideous, and who, in order to provoke less disgust, carefully cover themselves in cloth of gold or in rags." Louis de Carmontelle [Louis Carrogis], *La patte de velours* (1781), 36, translated in Crow, *Painters and Public Life,* 186. Carrogis, commonly called Carmontelle, was a shoemaker's son and a self-taught artist. In 1763 he was appointed reader to the son of the duc d'Orléans. He wrote *parades* and designed and supervised their production. He also helped to organize a literary salon at the Palais Royal. At court gatherings he entertained by projecting painted panoramas through a magic lantern, and he drew portraits on the spot, *aux trois crayons* and in pencil, with watercolor and gouache.

23. Keith Michael Baker, "Transformations of Classical Republicanism in Eighteenth-Century France," *Journal of Modern History* 73, no. 1 (2001), 36.

24. Antoine Compagnon, *Les antimodernes, de Joseph de Maistre à Roland Barthes* (Paris: Gallimard, 2005).

25. Charles de Secondat, baron de Montesquieu, *The Spirit of the Laws,* trans. Anne M. Cohler, Basia Carolyn Miller, and Harold Samuel Stone (Cambridge: Cambridge University Press, 1989), bk. 28, chap. 41, p. 595, translation modified.

26. Louis-François Delisle de la Drevetière (1682–1756) was the author of the very popular *Arlequin sauvage,* performed at the Théâtre-Italien in 1721. Arlequin—whom Lelio, who has been shipwrecked on a distant land, has brought back with him to Marseilles—has never been exposed to modern French customs; he reacts to them in the manner that is to be expected from a character who owes a great deal to Montaigne and Lahontan.

27. Diderot, *Salon of 1767,* 106.

28. Lionel Gossman, "*Ce beau génie qui n'a point compris sa sublime mission:* An Essay on Voltaire," *French Review* 56, no. 1 (1982): 41.

Index